EXPLAINING REVELATION

Copyright © 2024 Matthew Falsetti

All rights reserved.

No part of this publication may be reproduced in any form, stored in any retrieval system, or transmitted in any form or by any means electronic, mechanical, photocopying, recording, or otherwise, without the prior written permission of the author and publisher, except as permitted by U.S. copyright law.

ISBN 979-8-218-58782-6 (hardback)
ISBN 979-8-218-45552-1 (paperback)
ISBN 979-8-218-47339-6 (eBook)

Book cover design copyright © 2024 by Matthew Falsetti.
Illustrations copyright © 2024 by Matthew Falsetti.
Design copyright © 2024 by Matthew Falsetti.

West Park Press | Hamilton, NJ, United States of America

First edition published August 2024.
This edition published August 2024.

Manufactured in the United States of America.

*To those in my life who passed
before I could see the truth*

CONTENTS

I

DANIEL AND THE APOSTASY

3   Interpretations
13 Daniel's Dreams
31 Daniel's Seventy Weeks
59 The Apostasy

II

BABYLON AND THE ANTICHRIST

69   Mystery Babylon
77   Mystery Solved
119 The Antichrist in Prophecy
127 The Antichrist Revealed

III

THE TRIBULATION AND THE CHURCH

153 The Great Tribulation
159 The Second Beast
181 The Seven Churches

IV

HISTORICAL FULFILLMENT

203 The Seven Seals
225 The Seven Trumpets
267 The Interlude
283 God's Wrath Is Poured Out

V

TODAY

297 The Sixth and Seventh Vials
317 The Second Coming
331 The End

VI

APPENDIX

345 Time Frames and Fulfillments
348 The Path to Salvation
349 Notes

I

DANIEL AND THE APOSTASY

1

INTERPRETATIONS

We have all been deceived.

The religious leaders whom we trust to guide us in our faith have taught inaccurate interpretations of the Bible's end-times prophecies for more than a century. It is not their fault. Few modern theologians have attempted the ambitious task of conquering the complex concepts in Revelation. Instead, most rely on what they were taught in seminary school. The problem, as you will soon see, is that what the seminaries teach is verifiably wrong.

There are interested parties inside the Christian sphere with the incentive to deceive us by misinterpreting the Bible in a way that deflects any negative attention away from them. Others mistake these fraudsters for friends and teach their misinterpretations as scriptural facts. Throughout the history of Christianity, this heartbreaking and disastrous deception has cost the lives of many—both on earth and in eternity.

You will soon be introduced to the main themes of the Biblical end-times prophecies found within the books of Daniel and Revelation. From Mystery Babylon to the Antichrist, the Great Tribulation to the second coming of Jesus Christ, this book will gradually peel away the layers of confusion that obscure the Bible's descriptions of these topics until all that remains is the true meaning of God's message.

However, interpreting the book of Revelation does not mean trying to predict "the day, nor the hour" of Christ's return. After all, Jesus told us that even he did not know the timing of his second coming.[a] God gave us these prophecies so we could understand their meanings and avoid the deception of false religion, not so we would know exactly when Jesus will return.

Eschatology

Eschatology—from the Greek words *éskhatos*, meaning "end or last,"[1] and *logos*, meaning "a word, discourse, tale, or reason"[2]—is defined as studies or opinions of the end of the world. In essence, eschatology is the study of the "end tale" of the world based on an interpretation of Biblical prophecy. Christian theology has three main eschatological interpretations—Preterism, Historicism, and Futurism. The simplest way to explain the many differences between the three views is that Preterists believe Revelation has already been fulfilled, Historicists believe it is continuously being fulfilled over time, and Futurists believe the book has yet to be fulfilled.

Futurism

Whether you are Protestant or Catholic, you have probably been taught the Futurist interpretation of the end times. Under Futurism, one Antichrist figure will rule the world for seven years. The first three and a half years will be peaceful and prosperous. After this period of relative calm, the Antichrist will enter a rebuilt Temple in Jerusalem, declare himself God, and begin a severe period of persecution known as the Great Tribulation. He will impose the "mark of the beast" on the entire world, prohibiting anyone without the mark from participating in commerce. Many Futurists believe the Christians alive at that time would be raptured—or brought to Heaven—just before the Great Tribulation begins, though some believe the church will be forced to endure this persecution.

According to Futurism, all signs in Revelation 4-20 occur in this window of only seven years. However, there are numerous conceptual problems with Futurism. Most Bible commentators throughout Christian history believed the church would remain on earth during these chapters. If the rapture occurs

---

[a] **Mark 13:32** But of that day and that hour knoweth no man, no, not the angels which are in heaven, neither the Son, but the Father.

before the Tribulation, which Christians would the Antichrist persecute? If an Antichrist-like world leader declares himself God inside a rebuilt Jewish Temple in Jerusalem, the entire world would know Christ would return in three and a half years. Why would God provide such precise advance notice of Jesus' second coming? Futurism would suggest anyone alive before the arrival of the Antichrist would not need to stay vigilant and watch for Jesus' return as he directed us to.[b] Also, once the non-Christians left on earth after the rapture notice all the Christian churches are empty, why would they not immediately convert?

Catholic Futurists believe the apostasy Paul predicted in II Thessalonians will be a falling away from the Catholic Church rather than a falling away from God.[c] This view elevates the importance of the Catholic Church above that of God and presumes God cared more about which denomination his believers belong to than if they were faithful followers of Jesus Christ. Some Protestants of the Futurist school comparably believe Paul's apostasy will be fulfilled by falling away from churches, although they usually do not specify a denomination. The Futurist school manipulates scripture, particularly the books of Daniel and Revelation, and applies Biblical prophetic symbolism inconsistently. Futurism also contradicts the view of the early church leaders, who believed Revelation would begin to be fulfilled shortly after John wrote his visions down.

For Futurism to be correct, we must assume God had nothing to tell us about the world from the destruction of the Temple in the first century until the re-establishment of the state of Israel in 1948. This hypothesis would mean he provided no roadmap for the church to survive the temptations and dangers that awaited it after the Apostolic Age. Futurism robs Christians of God's guidance over the critical period of church history after those with first-hand accounts of Jesus' life and ministry had died.

---

[b] **Matthew 24:42-44** 42 Watch therefore: for ye know not what hour your Lord doth come. 43 But know this, that if the goodman of the house had known in what watch the thief would come, he would have watched, and would not have suffered his house to be broken up. 44 Therefore be ye also ready: for in such an hour as ye think not the Son of man cometh.

[c] **II Thessalonians 2:2-3** 2 That ye be not soon shaken in mind, or be troubled, neither by spirit, nor by word, nor by letter as from us, as that the day of Christ is at hand. 3 Let no man deceive you by any means: for that day shall not come, except there come a falling away first, and that man of sin be revealed, the son of perdition;

The cleverness behind Futurism's lengthy delay between the life of Jesus and the appearance of the Antichrist is that its theories cannot be proven or disproven. Futurism persuades Christians to ignore both the past and present fulfillment of Revelation's prophecies and constantly search for future signs that will never arrive. Christianity has had a long-term persecutor over the centuries; however, most Christians today ignore this evil antagonist as they are too busy looking for an Antichrist who has not yet come. Sadly, nearly all Christian denominations now teach a future fulfillment of Revelation.

Preterism

The term "Preterism" originates from the Latin word *praeter*, meaning "past." The Preterist view attempts to assign the fulfillment of the book of Revelation to events that occurred during the apostles' generation. Those who belong to the Preterist school look to validate their theories through the events of the first century, within forty years of Jesus Christ's crucifixion and resurrection. Generally, the Preterists assign the identity of the Antichrist to Emperor Nero and the Great Tribulation to the First Jewish-Roman War in 66-73 AD. They believe the purpose of Revelation was nothing more than anti-Nero propaganda.

Many in the Preterist school even believe Jesus returned to earth during the 70 AD fall of Jerusalem. Conveniently, these Preterists assert that he only returned in the spirit—so no one alive could witness his second coming. The Preterists' assessment of Revelation directly contradicts the writings of Paul, who stated with certainty that Jesus would return loudly—with shouts, the voice of the archangel, and trumpets.[d] The apostle John also refuted the idea of an invisible second coming, writing that "every eye shall see him" when he ultimately returns.[e] Jesus and his apostles told Christians to watch for his reappearance several times in the New Testament, meaning we will be able to witness the second coming when it occurs. John also prophesied that this

---

[d] **I Thessalonians 4:16** For the Lord himself shall descend from heaven with a shout, with the voice of the archangel, and with the trump of God: and the dead in Christ shall rise first:

[e] **Revelation 1:7** Behold, he cometh with clouds; and every eye shall see him, and they also which pierced him: and all kindreds of the earth shall wail because of him. Even so, Amen.

event would prompt the resurrection of martyred Christians who had already died, which unquestionably has not happened.

Jesus proclaimed his followers would "be hated of all nations" before his second coming.[f] Did widespread hatred of Christians exist by 70 AD? The Jews and Romans persecuted early Christians, but they were not extensively hated outside of the Roman Empire. Christianity was little known beyond the Mediterranean region in the four decades following Christ's resurrection, meaning Jesus' prophecy directly contradicts Preterism.

In addition, Nero cannot be the Antichrist for several reasons. First, the emperor died by suicide in 68 AD, well before the destruction of Jerusalem's Temple two years later. For the destruction of the Temple to fulfill the Great Tribulation prophecy, as most Preterists believe, a Neronian Antichrist would have died before the peak of his own persecution.

Second, Nero's persecution was alleged to have begun shortly after the Great Fire of Rome on July 18, 64 AD. The Romans suspected their emperor was the arsonist behind the fire, and he needed a scapegoat. Pagan historian Tacitus was the primary source for the narrative that Nero passed the blame onto Rome's Christians. "Therefore, to scotch the rumor," he wrote, "Nero substituted as culprits, and punished with the utmost refinements of cruelty, a class of men, loathed for their vices, whom the crowd styled Christians. Christus, the founder of the name, had undergone the death penalty in the reign of Tiberius, by sentence of the procurator Pontius Pilatus."[3] If Nero's persecution began in July 64 AD, whether it continued until his death in June 68 AD or through the razing of the Temple in Jerusalem in 70 AD, it would represent a four or six-year Great Tribulation rather than the three and a half years written in prophecy. Each of these Preterist Tribulation theories runs contrary to the scriptural evidence.

Third, Nero ruled during the golden age of the Roman Empire, centuries before its eventual decline. This timing contradicts the prophetic timeline in Daniel 7, which stipulates that the Antichrist would only emerge following Rome's collapse and the subsequent overthrow of three of the ten successor kingdoms that rose from Rome's ruins. Neither Nero nor any other Roman emperor could fulfill the prophecy of the Antichrist.

---

[f] **Matthew 24:9** Then shall they deliver you up to be afflicted, and shall kill you: and ye shall be hated of all nations for my name's sake.

Perhaps the clearest evidence that Nero is not the Antichrist is found in Revelation 19:20. The scripture leaves no room for ambiguity: when Christ returns, the Antichrist and False Prophet will be captured and thrown into Hell alive.[g] Because Nero's death is a matter of clear historical record, he fails to meet this crucial requirement of the Biblical Antichrist narrative.[4]

Lastly, Nero and the sack of Jerusalem during the First Jewish-Roman War predated the book of Revelation by about three decades. The prophetic basis of Revelation would be invalidated if John was writing about events that already occurred. The Preterists bypass this inconvenience by simply moving the date of Revelation's authorship forward without empirical evidence from 95 to 65 AD. While a 65 AD date contradicts established Christian tradition and the accounts of the earliest church writers, Preterists are forced to adopt an earlier date so that scripture accommodates their predetermined opinions. However, if Revelation was composed in 65 AD to prophesy the destruction of Jerusalem only five years later, why did John address the book to churches in Anatolia instead of the congregations threatened by the events in Judea?

Another issue with a 65 AD date is that Revelation 2:13 refers to the martyrdom of a Christian named Antipas.[h] According to tradition, he was not killed until 92 AD—long after the Preterists claim Revelation was written.

The Preterists also ignore the difference between the Christian church and Jewish history, choosing to apply prophecies indisputably written for the church to the first-century Jews of Judea. The Great Tribulation is a prophecy that predicts the persecution of Christians, not the suffering of the Jews at the hands of the Romans. Preterism also explains away many of Revelation's prophecies by assigning them spiritual fulfillments rather than visible ones. If the Preterists cannot find the fulfillment for a prophetic sign within the first-century historical record, it is easier to claim these events happened in the spiritual world than to admit their entire interpretation is wrong.

---

[g] **Revelation 19:20** And the beast was taken, and with him the false prophet that wrought miracles before him, with which he deceived them that had received the mark of the beast, and them that worshipped his image. These both were cast alive into a lake of fire burning with brimstone.

[h] **Revelation 2:13** I know thy works, and where thou dwellest, even where Satan's seat is: and thou holdest fast my name, and hast not denied my faith, even in those days wherein Antipas was my faithful martyr, who was slain among you, where Satan dwelleth.

Few serious theologians preach Preterism today. It requires scripture to be so thoroughly distorted and misrepresented that its claims cannot be taken seriously. Somehow, these concepts still permeate in the most obscure and radical corners of Christianity. Preterism is such an impossible interpretation that its advocates lose any credibility the moment they support it. Its absurd claims should have been abandoned centuries ago, yet it persists due to the strength of the forces supporting it as an alternative to Historicism.

Historicism

Historicism maintains the view that Revelation has been in the process of being fulfilled gradually over the centuries since John's miraculous visions occurred in 95 AD. The Historicist school views Revelation as a roadmap to help guide Christians during the years between the lives of the apostles and Jesus' return. It is the only eschatological interpretation that preserves the chronological order of Revelation. Historicism has real-world explanations for all signs in the Bible's end-times prophecies. It does not need to excuse absent fulfillments by claiming they occurred or will occur in the spiritual world, as both Preterism and Futurism do.

Historicism focuses on what the Bible says, basing its interpretation on the scriptural text. Futurists and Preterists first form an opinion, such as "the Antichrist will arrive at some point in the future" or "Nero is the Antichrist," which they then attempt to validate with scripture. In contrast, Historicists stay within the language of the Biblical text and use it to guide their opinions. Historicists look for fulfillments that fit the Biblical text, while Preterists and Futurists look for text that they can force to fit their desired fulfillments.

Idealism

There is a fourth eschatological interpretation of Biblical prophecy, albeit an uncommon one. The theory of Idealism suggests the entirety of end-times prophecy is allegorical. Under Idealism, all the prophecies in Revelation have fulfillments that human eyes cannot observe, as all these events occur in the spiritual realm. It is a lazy reading by some theologians who do not wish to expend any effort to attempt to understand what God told us in Revelation's end-times prophecies.

There are several problems with this interpretation. First, why would God bother to deliver these prophecies if we could not see their fulfillments? There was no logical reason to provide John with this series of warning signs if there would be no real-world evidence for them. The book contains several indicators of time that must be ignored if the events do not happen in the physical world. The first verse of Revelation declares the events described in the book "must shortly come to pass,"[i] and verse three reaffirms that "the time is at hand."[j] There is no reason for us to be the intended recipients of the prophecies, as Revelation says we are, if we cannot see their fulfillment.

Another reason Idealism is incorrect can be found in Revelation 10. John wrote of a vision during which seven thunders spoke to him. In the vision, Jesus specifically told John not to write down what these thunders said. This indicates that, while he did not want us to know the details of these seven signs, God *did* want us to receive the rest of the book. If the seven thunders addressed events that would only occur in the spiritual realm and cannot be seen, why would it be so essential to withhold their messages?[k]

Lastly, Revelation is a meticulous and complex book. If its fulfillments take place solely in the spiritual realm, it would not have required such minute details to deliver its prophetic contents. While events are certainly happening in the spiritual world that align with the earthly fulfillments of the prophecies of Revelation, Idealism disregards all earthly events in human history in favor of fulfillments that cannot be proven or disproven.

Separating Fact from Fiction

This book aims to discover the Biblical end-times prophecies exactly as presented in the scriptural text. Once an impenetrable scriptural foundation has been laid, we will examine the messages found in every prophecy and

---

[i] **Revelation 1:1** The Revelation of Jesus Christ, which God gave unto him, to shew unto his servants things which must shortly come to pass; and he sent and signified it by his angel unto his servant John:

[j] **Revelation 1:3** Blessed is he that readeth, and they that hear the words of this prophecy, and keep those things which are written therein: for the time is at hand.

[k] **Revelation 10:4** And when the seven thunders had uttered their voices, I was about to write: and I heard a voice from heaven saying unto me, Seal up those things which the seven thunders uttered, and write them not.

decipher how they have been fulfilled over time. After identifying the correct fulfillments for the Bible's end-times prophecies, we will locate where we are in the timeline of Revelation—and how little of the book remains unfulfilled.

While realizing that we are close to the end of Revelation may make some readers apprehensive, it is crucial to focus on the positive. After God's earthly judgments on humanity are finished, Jesus will return to collect his followers and bring us to Heaven for eternity. The more you see how many of the Bible's end-times prophecies have been proven true, the more faith you will have that the best parts of the Bible are also true. Identifying the historical fulfillment of Revelation will boost your faith and confidence in the second coming of Jesus Christ, his millennium reign, and eternal life.

Be prepared to open your mind to God's Word and it will change your thinking about the end times. While this commentary may be uncomfortable at times as it becomes clear how we have been misled by the religious leaders we trust most, the information you will soon discover will strengthen your faith in God and help you grow in your walk with Jesus as you learn how his promises have come true.

Chapter Synopsis

Preterism
- Revelation has already been fulfilled
- Emperor Nero was the Antichrist
- Either the 70 AD destruction of the Temple or the First Jewish-Roman War was the Great Tribulation
- The other signs in Revelation were spiritual and unobservable
- Jesus' second coming occurred in 70 AD, but only in the spirit
- Nero cannot be the Antichrist because he died before Revelation was written, his reign preceded the fall of Rome (contradicting Daniel 7), and he was not thrown into Hell alive (contradicting Revelation 19:20)
- Cannot explain why Revelation was written to seven churches in modern Turkey instead of the churches in Judea where the war would occur

Futurism
- Revelation has not yet been fulfilled
- The Antichrist is a future world leader who will reign for seven years
  - The first three and a half years will be peaceful
  - After reigning for three and a half years, the Antichrist will enter a rebuilt Temple in Jerusalem and declare himself God
  - The Great Tribulation will occur during the last three and a half years
- The Antichrist will force everyone alive to take the "mark of the beast" to participate in commerce
- Most Christian denominations teach Futurism today
- Would require a nearly 2,000-year gap in fulfilled prophecy between the first century and the seven years before Jesus returns

Historicism
- Revelation is being fulfilled gradually over time
- Does not claim any allegorical spiritual fulfillments
- The only interpretation where Revelation is in chronological order
- Historicists look for a fulfillment that fits the text, while Preterists and Futurists look for text to fit their desired fulfillment

Idealism
- All events in Revelation occur in the spiritual world and are unobservable

2

DANIEL'S DREAMS

Most Christians and non-Christians know something about the book of Revelation. That confusing, frightening, often overlooked book buried deep in the back of the New Testament was Jesus' final scriptural message to us through his apostle John. In the book, he dispenses valuable information to help his followers avoid the risks of false Christian doctrines. Revelation is Christ's warning of the trials, deceptions, and persecutions that awaited his followers during the end times and his promise of the eternal rewards that await those who remain faithful to him.

End-times prophecies are scattered throughout the Bible in the books of Revelation, Isaiah, Jeremiah, Daniel, Matthew, II Thessalonians, and more. Some are more difficult to decipher than others, and many are shrouded in symbolism, but all tell the same story. Cross-referencing the interpretations of prophecies in one book against those in another will help us comprehend the complete picture of the end times.

Apart from Revelation, the book of Daniel contains the most important descriptions of the end times. In chapter seven, the prophet's dream of four beasts provides the Bible's clearest account of the Antichrist outside of John's Revelation, including his location of origin, the timing of his arrival, and clues about the length of his Great Tribulation. Later, within a separate prophecy predicting the timing of the ministry and death of Jesus Christ, Daniel's ninth chapter reaffirms the location of the Antichrist's origin.

Daniel and Nebuchadnezzar

Nebuchadnezzar II was king of the Neo-Babylonian Empire from 605 until 562 BC. His father, King Nabopolassar, was credited with freeing the Babylonians from the Assyrians' control.[1] Nabopolassar's revolt ended when the Babylonians, in concert with the Medes, Persians, and Scythians, defeated the Assyrians and Egyptians in the 605 BC Battle of Carchemish to achieve their independence.

Before his ascension to the throne, Nebuchadnezzar made a name for himself through military conquests. He was the victorious commander of the Babylonian army at Carchemish, where, after the battle ended, he received word of his father's death and was proclaimed the new king of Babylon.[2]

Before returning home to Babylon, Nebuchadnezzar and his army laid siege to Jerusalem. Jehoiakim, the king of Judea, ended the siege by pledging to pay tribute to Babylon, though these payments would only last three years. Later, Nebuchadnezzar's forces suffered heavy casualties when he attempted to conquer Egypt in 601 BC. Believing he could take advantage of the weak condition of Babylon's army, Jehoiakim canceled his tribute and switched Judea's allegiance from Babylon to Egypt. Nebuchadnezzar responded by laying siege to Jerusalem again. However, this time, the king would not settle for a restoration of Judea's payments.[3]

Jerusalem eventually fell to the Babylonians in 597 BC.[4] Daniel, the man who would become one of the most important prophets in both Judaism and Christianity, was likely a teen or adolescent from a noble family in the early sixth century BC. He was described in Daniel 1:3-4 as one of the children of Israel who had "no blemish, but well favoured, and skilful in all wisdom, and cunning in knowledge, and understanding science"[a] and was among the 3,023 Jewish youths transported to Babylon by Nebuchadnezzar in the first of a series of Jewish exiles.[5]

---

[a] **Daniel 1:3-4** 3 And the king spake unto Ashpenaz the master of his eunuchs, that he should bring certain of the children of Israel, and of the king's seed, and of the princes; 4 Children in whom was no blemish, but well favoured, and skilful in all wisdom, and cunning in knowledge, and understanding science, and such as had ability in them to stand in the king's palace, and whom they might teach the learning and the tongue of the Chaldeans.

Nebuchadnezzar's Nightmare

Once in Babylon, Daniel served in the court of Nebuchadnezzar where he learned the Chaldean language. While much of the first six chapters of the book of Daniel focus on stories from the prophet's life, the most important sections to help understand the end times are Nebuchadnezzar's dream in chapter two and Daniel's prophetic visions in chapters seven, eight, and nine.

Shortly after the first Jewish exile, Nebuchadnezzar had a frightening nightmare that awoke him in the middle of the night. In a panic, the king summoned all his astrologers, magicians, and sorcerers to interpret the dream for him. But there was a problem—Nebuchadnezzar could not remember the content of his dream.[6]

After a heated back and forth, the king threatened to execute all his so-called wise men if they could not tell him the dream and interpret it. The advisors rightfully responded, "It is a rare thing that the king requireth, and there is none other that can shew it before the king, except the gods, whose dwelling is not with flesh." But Nebuchadnezzar was so unnerved that he furiously condemned them all to death—even Daniel, who was not present.[7]

Arioch, the captain of the king's guard, found Daniel and arrested him. When Daniel asked why the king ordered his advisors' deaths, Arioch told him about Nebuchadnezzar's nightmare and the inability of the wise men to decipher it. Daniel then asked for the opportunity to recall the king's dream and interpret its meaning. Later that night, God revealed both the contents and meaning of Nebuchadnezzar's nightmare to Daniel in a vision.[8]

> **Daniel 2:31-35**
> 31 Thou, O king, sawest, and behold a great image. This great image, whose brightness was excellent, stood before thee; and the form thereof was terrible.
> 32 This image's head was of fine gold, his breast and his arms of silver, his belly and his thighs of brass,
> 33 His legs of iron, his feet part of iron and part of clay.
> 34 Thou sawest till that a stone was cut out without hands, which smote the image upon his feet that were of iron and clay, and brake them to pieces.
> 35 Then was the iron, the clay, the brass, the silver, and the gold, broken to pieces together, and became like the chaff of the summer threshingfloors; and the wind carried them away, that no place was found for them: and the stone that smote the image became a great mountain, and filled the whole earth.

Nebuchadnezzar had dreamed of a statue with four distinct sections. In his interpretation, the prophet told the king that each segment represented a different empire that would rule the land of Babylon. He then proceeded to interpret the symbolism of each section of the statue for Nebuchadnezzar. These same four empires would later reappear in chapter seven when Daniel himself had a comparable but more detailed prophetic dream. First, Daniel explained that the head of gold represented King Nebuchadnezzar and the Neo-Babylonian Empire.

> **Daniel 2:36-38**
> 36 This is the dream; and we will tell the interpretation thereof before the king.
> 37 Thou, O king, art a king of kings: for the God of heaven hath given thee a kingdom, power, and strength, and glory.
> 38 And wheresoever the children of men dwell, the beasts of the field and the fowls of the heaven hath he given into thine hand, and hath made thee ruler over them all. Thou art this head of gold.

Daniel did not name the other three kingdoms but described the next empire, the silver breast and arms, as inferior to Babylon. Biblical scholars recognize this kingdom as the Medo-Persian Empire.[9] Commonly called the Achaemenid Empire today, the Medo-Persians would later conquer Babylon on the night of Belshazzar's famous feast in Daniel 5, when the hand of God wrote a message on the palace wall foretelling of Babylon's collapse and the king's untimely death.

Next, Daniel told Nebuchadnezzar that the Achaemenid Empire would be followed by a brass empire that would "rule over all the earth." This brass empire was a reference to the conquerors of the Achaemenids—the Greek Empire under the Macedonian king Alexander the Great.

> **Daniel 2:39**
> 39 And after thee shall arise another kingdom inferior to thee, and another third kingdom of brass, which shall bear rule over all the earth.

At its peak, the Greek Empire controlled land once held by many of the other great empires that pre-dated Alexander's reign—the Assyrians, Hittites, Babylonians, Achaemenids, and Egyptians. To the Jews and Babylonians of Daniel's time, this was much of the known world.

Daniel 2:40
40 And the fourth kingdom shall be strong as iron: forasmuch as iron breaketh in pieces and subdueth all things: and as iron that breaketh all these, shall it break in pieces and bruise.

After the brass empire, Daniel 2:40 describes an empire as strong as iron. The Roman Empire followed Greece on the world stage, breaking into pieces and subduing lesser tribes and kingdoms of Europe, North Africa, and the Near East. While the strength of iron is a metaphor for Rome's power and fierceness, Daniel explains that the iron feet and toes were flawed.

Daniel 2:41-43
41 And whereas thou sawest the feet and toes, part of potters' clay, and part of iron, the kingdom shall be divided; but there shall be in it of the strength of the iron, forasmuch as thou sawest the iron mixed with miry clay.
42 And as the toes of the feet were part of iron, and part of clay, so the kingdom shall be partly strong, and partly broken.
43 And whereas thou sawest iron mixed with miry clay, they shall mingle themselves with the seed of men: but they shall not cleave one to another, even as iron is not mixed with clay.

The authors of *The Pulpit Commentary* believed the iron mixed with clay represented Rome's strong, civilized society integrating barbarian kingdoms in Gaul, Africa, Eastern Europe, and the Middle East. "We admit certainly that the LXX [Septuagint] translates in a way that suggests the marriage of a superior with an inferior race," they explained. "But there is no reference in reality to marriage, but to the mingling of two distinct culture-elements, the infusion of barbarous races into the midst of a civilized; and the barbarians taking on some of the outward forms of civilization would represent better the thing indicated."[10] The conquered barbarians were assimilated into the empire and its army, but their inferiority caused unsustainable weakness in the empire.

After revealing the four empires in Nebuchadnezzar's nightmare, Daniel predicted God would establish a fifth kingdom during the Roman Empire. Daniel explained this meant God would institute an eternal kingdom that would destroy the earthly kingdoms of man. In the dream, a stone kingdom was carved from a mountain "without hands," implying that humans were not involved in its creation. This stone kingdom was stronger than the gold, silver, brass, and iron of the four empires in Nebuchadnezzar's dream. It smashed all four metals into pieces, symbolizing God overcoming all earthly kingdoms through the death and resurrection of Jesus Christ.

> **Daniel 2:44-45**
> **44** And in the days of these kings shall the God of heaven set up a kingdom, which shall never be destroyed: and the kingdom shall not be left to other people, but it shall break in pieces and consume all these kingdoms, and it shall stand for ever.
> **45** Forasmuch as thou sawest that the stone was cut out of the mountain without hands, and that it brake in pieces the iron, the brass, the clay, the silver, and the gold; the great God hath made known to the king what shall come to pass hereafter: and the dream is certain, and the interpretation thereof sure.

Jesus was born about three decades after Rome became an empire. His crucifixion likely occurred in the year 30 AD—only eighty-seven years before the Roman Empire reached its greatest territorial extent under Trajan.[11] Jesus' entire life and ministry occurred while the Roman Empire was growing under the first two Roman emperors, Augustus and Tiberius, fulfilling the prophecy that God would establish his spiritual kingdom "in the days of these kings."

Daniel's Dream of Four Beasts

The theme of four empires in Nebuchadnezzar's nightmare would repeat later in Daniel's life. In chapter seven, Daniel describes a prophetic dream of his own. In it, he watches as four terrifying and unusual beasts rise out of the sea. Each beast represents one of the same four empires foreshadowed by Nebuchadnezzar's dream in Daniel 2.

> **Daniel 7:1-3**
> **1** In the first year of Belshazzar king of Babylon Daniel had a dream and visions of his head upon his bed: then he wrote the dream, and told the sum of the matters.
> **2** Daniel spake and said, I saw in my vision by night, and, behold, the four winds of the heaven strove upon the great sea.
> **3** And four great beasts came up from the sea, diverse one from another.

In Biblical prophecies, water usually represents masses of people. The imagery of beasts coming out of the sea in Daniel's dream signifies the human composition of these empires and their armies.[b] Near the end of the vision, Daniel asked someone standing next to him to explain the meaning of the four beasts. This individual interpreted the beasts as four kings who will arise.

> **Daniel 7:16-17**
> **16** I came near unto one of them that stood by, and asked him the truth of all this. So he told me, and made me know the interpretation of the things.
> **17** These great beasts, which are four, are four kings, which shall arise out of the earth.

Many of the Bible's end-times prophecies are intertwined. It is essential to understand Daniel's four-empire prophecies before attempting to interpret the shared themes found in later prophecies. Babylon, beasts, horns, the sea, the Tribulation, and the Antichrist's battle against Christians are common threads between Daniel, Revelation, and many other end-times prophecies. The symbolic elements of these themes have the same or similar meanings across different end-times prophecies as if they were written by the same author throughout the centuries, which Christians believe supports the divine inspiration of scripture.

As a reference point for the year of Daniel's prophecy, Babylon's crown prince, Belshazzar, ruled as a regent in his father's absence from 553 until 543 or 542 BC.[12] He was likely killed when Persia's king Cyrus II—now called Cyrus the Great—captured Babylon on October 12, 539 BC.[13]

Belshazzar's father, King Nabonidus, had entered a self-imposed exile at Tayma in Arabia beginning in May 553 BC.[14] May corresponds with Iyar and Sivan, the second and third months in the Hebrew calendar. In Babylon, the reigns of kings were counted from the first month of the year, Nisan, which aligns with March and April. Since Nabonidus was the sole king of Babylon on the first day of Nisan in 553 BC, that year would have been counted as a part of his reign, even though Belshazzar's regency would have begun no more than two months later. This implies Daniel's dream in chapter seven occurred between March 552 BC and April 551 BC.

---

[b] **Revelation 17:15** And he saith unto me, The waters which thou sawest, where the whore sitteth, are peoples, and multitudes, and nations, and tongues.

The Lion with Eagle's Wings: The Neo-Babylonian Empire

> **Daniel 7:4**
> 4 The first was like a lion, and had eagle's wings: I beheld till the wings thereof were plucked, and it was lifted up from the earth, and made stand upon the feet as a man, and a man's heart was given to it.

Daniel began by describing the first beast he encountered in his dream. Like the golden head in King Nebuchadnezzar's nightmare, this winged lion symbolizes the Neo-Babylonian Empire, where Daniel and the Jews were held captive at the time of the prophecy. Babylon was approaching its end as a world empire, and God showed Daniel the great powers that would follow it on the regional stage.

The Babylonian Empire expanded at the expense of smaller neighboring kingdoms. As it conquered, it exemplified a fierce lion, its wings symbolizing the empire's ability to ascend above other regional powers. In Daniel's dream, the lion's wings were plucked, representing a halt to its growth.

As the formerly winged lion was pacified, it became more peaceable and humane, foreshadowed by the fact that it stood on its hind legs like a civilized man with a human heart. At this point in its history, Babylon would no longer rapidly overcome other kingdoms. The imagery of the next beast in Daniel's dream predicted the fall of the Babylonian Empire thirteen years later.

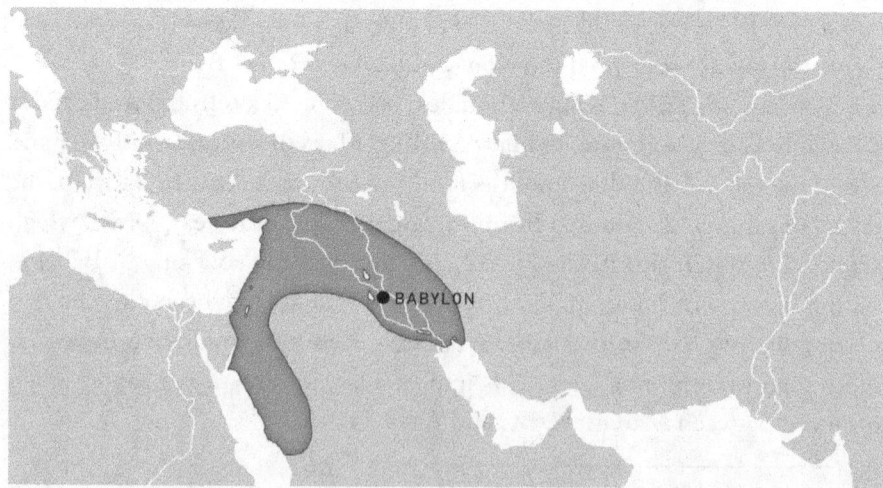

Figure 1: The first beast of Daniel 7; the Neo-Babylonian Empire, 539 BC.

The Unbalanced Bear: The Achaemenid (Medo-Persian) Empire

> **Daniel 7:5**
> 5 And behold another beast, a second, like to a bear, and it raised up itself on one side, and it had three ribs in the mouth of it between the teeth of it: and they said thus unto it, Arise, devour much flesh.

The fall of Babylon was also predicted by the earlier prophets Isaiah[c] and Jeremiah,[d] both of whom even mentioned the Medes by name as the empire's conquerors. The Medes built a vast empire in the Middle East in the seventh century BC. They continued to expand their reach, ultimately defeating the Neo-Assyrian Empire in 609 BC. Although this victory made Media one of the leading powers of the ancient Near East, its empire was short-lived. The Persian king Cyrus the Great revolted against the Medes in 553 BC. In 550, Media was conquered when its king, Astyages, was captured by his soldiers and handed over to the Persian conquerors.[15]

After the rebellion, the Medes were subjects of the Persians but remained well-respected within the new Achaemenid Empire. The Persians adopted many Median traditions and rituals, and their nobles were even assimilated into the Persian political class and military hierarchy.[16] For this reason, the Achaemenid Empire is sometimes referred to as the Medo-Persian Empire. Daniel's unbalanced bear was higher on one side than the other—just as the Persians had more power than the Medes in their shared empire. The empire was Persian, but the Mede nobility retained significant influence.

The 552 or 551 BC date of Daniel's dream, as recorded by the prophet, indicates his prophecy would have occurred in the middle of the war between Media and Persia, before the Achaemenid Empire existed. Babylon's 539 BC defeat occurred thirteen years after Daniel's prophecy predicted it. The three ribs in the mouth of the bear likely symbolized the three empires that would comprise the Achaemenid Empire: Persia, Media, and Babylon. At its height, the empire was the most expansive the world had seen.

---

[c] **Isaiah 13:17** Behold, I will stir up the Medes against them, which shall not regard silver; and as for gold, they shall not delight in it.

[d] **Jeremiah 51:11** Make bright the arrows; gather the shields: the Lord hath raised up the spirit of the kings of the Medes: for his device is against Babylon, to destroy it; because it is the vengeance of the Lord, the vengeance of his temple.

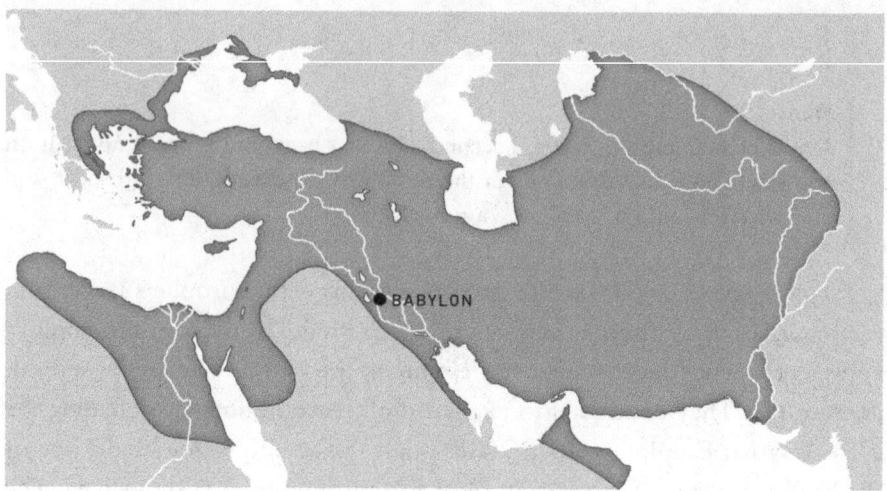
Figure 2: The second beast of Daniel 7; the Achaemenid Empire, 479 BC.

The Leopard with Four Wings and Heads: The Greek Empire

> **Daniel 7:6**
> **6** After this I beheld, and lo another, like a leopard, which had upon the back of it four wings of a fowl; the beast had also four heads; and dominion was given to it.

While the Persians still held the territory of Anatolia in modern Turkey, another kingdom began to rise. After the assassination of King Philip II of Macedon at Aegae in 336 BC, the king was succeeded by his twenty-year-old son, Alexander. The Greek states of Thessaly, Thebes, Athens, and Thrace—vassals subjugated to Macedonian rule—attempted to take advantage of the transfer of power and revolted. The young king mobilized his cavalry and marched south to subdue the uprising. After quelling the revolts in southern Greece, Alexander was named Hegemon, or Supreme Commander, of the unified Greek city-states.

With stability restored at home, Alexander could shift his focus to the Achaemenid Persians stationed across the Bosporus in the east.[17] In 334 BC, Alexander crossed the strait and invaded Anatolia. Over the next four years, he rapidly conquered Syria, Egypt, Babylon, and Persia. By 330 BC, the entire Achaemenid Empire lay conquered at Alexander's feet.[18]

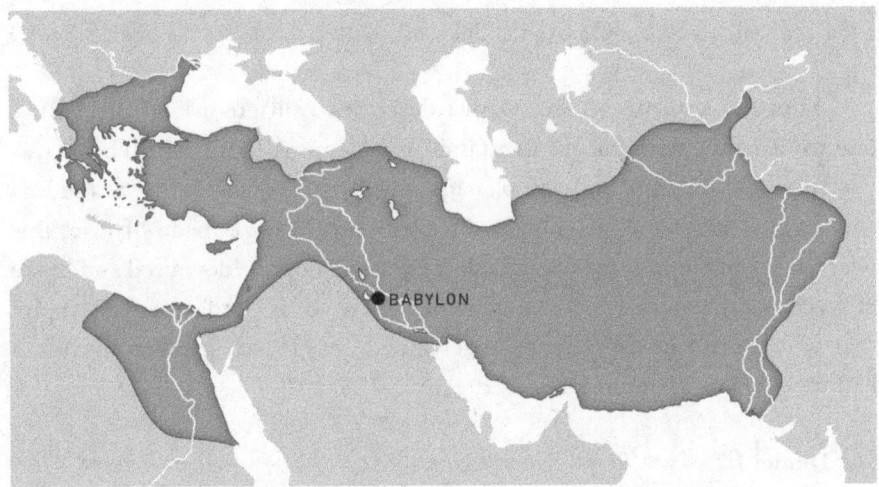

Figure 3: The third beast of Daniel 7; the Macedonian Empire, 323 BC.

Alexander the Great swept through much of the known world, running through kingdoms and empires with the speed of a leopard without losing a single battle. When he died at the age of thirty-two without an heir, his empire was divided among several successors, known today as the Diadochi. These men fought against each other for more than two decades during four wars historians call the Wars of the Diadochi. Only four Diadochi remained after the 301 BC Battle of Ipsus: Cassander, Ptolemy, Lysimachus, and Seleucus—the four heads and wings of Daniel's leopard beast.

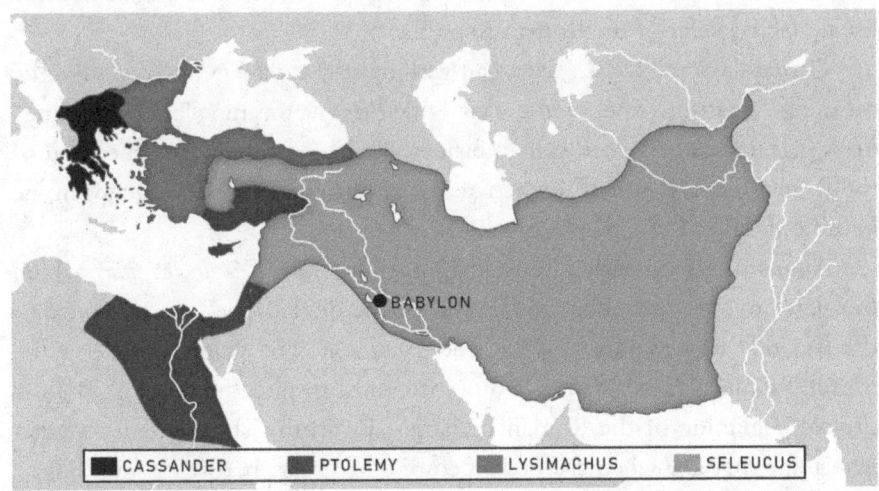

Figure 4: The divided Macedonian Empire after the Fourth War of the Diadochi, 301 BC.

The Dreadful, Terrible, and Exceedingly Strong Beast: The Roman Empire

After the leopard empire, Daniel describes a different kind of beast—one without any resemblance to a familiar wild animal. This fourth beast was described as "dreadful and terrible, and strong exceedingly." Just as the legs and feet of the statue in Nebuchadnezzar's dream were made of iron, this beast had iron teeth. Daniel watched as the fourth beast "devoured and brake in pieces, and stamped the residue with the feet of it," indicating an empire that would effortlessly conquer lesser kingdoms. It also had ten horns—a feature explained later in Daniel's dream.

> **Daniel 7:7**
>
> **7** After this I saw in the night visions, and behold a fourth beast, dreadful and terrible, and strong exceedingly; and it had great iron teeth: it devoured and brake in pieces, and stamped the residue with the feet of it: and it was diverse from all the beasts that were before it; and it had ten horns.

In around 509 BC, the Roman Kingdom was replaced by a republic. Not long after the division of Alexander's Macedonian Empire, the Roman army conquered—or devoured—much of the known world. Rome's republican system survived for nearly five centuries until Julius Caesar's assassination and the subsequent civil war between rivals Octavian and Mark Antony. When Octavian defeated Antony at the Battle of Actium in 31 BC, he became the de facto leader of the Roman Republic.

On January 16, 27 BC, Octavian was granted the religious title *Augustus*, meaning "illustrious one," and the civil title *Princeps*, meaning "increased one" or "venerated one."[19] *Princeps* had historically been presented to the head of the Roman Senate. When the Senate bestowed this title upon Octavian, he became the first Roman emperor, Caesar Augustus.[20]

Augustus also awarded himself the title *Imperator Caesar divi filius*, which translates to "Commander Caesar, son of the deified one"—a reference to the fact that he was Julius Caesar's adopted son. The word *Imperator* is the source for the English words "emperor" and "empire," making 27 BC the official beginning of the Roman Empire.[21] From this starting date, we can determine that Daniel envisioned an empire 525 years before its founding.

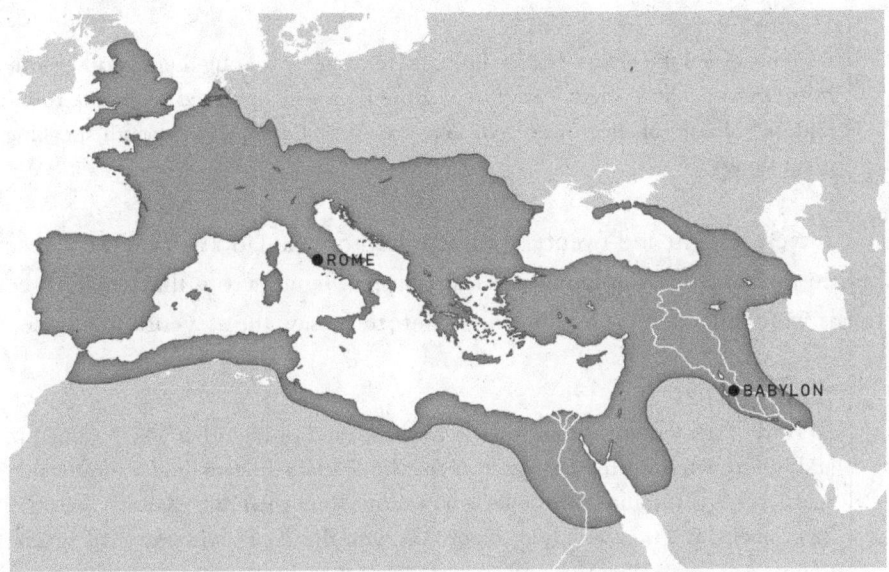

Figure 5: The fourth beast of Daniel 7; the Roman Empire, 117 AD.

The Ten Horns of the Roman Beast

In Daniel's dream, the Roman beast was seen with ten horns. Daniel 7:24 unambiguously states that the ten horns represent ten kingdoms that will arise out of Rome following the collapse of its empire.

> **Daniel 7:24**
> 24 And the ten horns out of this kingdom are ten kings that shall arise: and another shall rise after them; and he shall be diverse from the first, and he shall subdue three kings.

By now, you may be wondering what these four ancient empires have to do with the end times. While describing the Roman beast in chapter seven, Daniel 7 goes one step further, providing valuable insight into the identity of the Antichrist that Nebuchadnezzar's dream in chapter two did not.

Although Daniel initially saw ten horns on the Roman beast, an eleventh horn was revealed in verse eight. This horn was "diverse" from the others, representing a different type of power than the first ten kings. The eleventh horn represents not a *political* leader but a *religious* one—the Antichrist.

> **Daniel 7:8**
> 8 I considered the horns, and, behold, there came up among them another little horn, before whom there were three of the first horns plucked up by the roots: and, behold, in this horn were eyes like the eyes of man, and a mouth speaking great things.

In verses eight and twenty, we learn that three kingdoms would collapse before the Antichrist assumes his full power. Daniel wrote that these three horns were "plucked up by the roots" before he saw the eleventh horn rise.

> **Daniel 7:20-21**
> 20 And of the ten horns that were in his head, and of the other which came up, and before whom three fell; even of that horn that had eyes, and a mouth that spake very great things, whose look was more stout than his fellows.
> 21 I beheld, and the same horn made war with the saints, and prevailed against them;

Later in his dream, Daniel watched as the Antichrist horn "spake very great things" and "made war with the saints, and prevailed against them." This imagery aligns with descriptions of the Antichrist found elsewhere in the Bible. From these two verses, we know the Antichrist—while speaking grandiloquently and emulating a Christian—would persecute the followers of Jesus Christ.

The Ten Kingdoms

To date, the most extensive eschatological study on the Biblical end times is Edward Bishop Elliott's masterwork, *Horae Apocalypticae*, first published in 1837. Elliott identified two potential timeframes for the ten kingdoms, the first being 486 AD. He argued for this date because it took a decade following the collapse of Rome for the Roman general Syagrius' stronghold in Gaul to be subjugated. Those kingdoms were the Alemanni, Anglo-Saxons, Baiuvarii, Burgundians, Franks, Heruli, Ostrogoths, Suevi, Vandals, and Visigoths.[22]

However, the Rugii are a more accurate choice than the Baiuvarii, as their kingdom was active in 486 while the Baiuvarii Kingdom had yet to emerge. Of these kingdoms, the first three to fall were the Rugii, the Alemanni, and the Heruli. The Rugian Kingdom fell in 487 when it was defeated by Odoacer shortly after he conquered the Western Roman Empire.[23] Next, the Alemanni lost their kingdom sometime around the year 496.[24] The Heruli were third, with their final monarch, King Rodulf, suffering a decisive defeat at the hands of the Lombards in about 508 AD.[25] The eradication of the Heruli Kingdom signaled the third horn kingdom had been "plucked up."

The year 508 is the earliest point that a candidate for the Antichrist could come to power. Daniel specifically said that exactly three kingdoms would fall before the Antichrist's arrival, so the date the fourth kingdom collapsed is equally as important as the date the third was conquered. Identifying the fourth kingdom to collapse will give us the latest possible date the Antichrist could have come to power, just as the third kingdom gave us the earliest date. The Vandal Kingdom became the fourth to lose its sovereignty when it was defeated by the famed Byzantine general Belisarius in March of 534.[26] This means that any candidates for the role of the Antichrist must have appeared in the twenty-six years between 508 and March 534.

The dates of the ultimate collapses of the Heruli and Vandal kingdoms are essential clues to determine the identity of the Antichrist. The end dates of Daniel 7's kingdoms indicate that the Antichrist will not be a future world figure. While the collapse of the Western Roman Empire was a future event when Revelation was written, all ten kingdoms that arose from the empire have been lost to history. If an Antichrist were to emerge in the future, his appearance would occur centuries after the respective collapses of the third and fourth kingdoms, invalidating Daniel's prophecy.

Elliott's second option for the ten horns was decades later, in 533. The Anglo-Saxons, Baiuvarii, Ostrogoths, Suevi, Vandals, and Visigoths remained from his 486 list, but the Franks had split into three kingdoms—the Franks of Central France, the Burgundian-Franks, and the Alemanni-Franks—and the Lombards were added to the list.[27] Elliott believed that these kingdoms were those meant by Daniel's prophecy. However, this is likely incorrect, as the Baiuvarii Kingdom did not ascend immediately after the fall of Rome and the Lombards did not become a kingdom until 568 AD. In fact, the Rugii, Alemanni, Heruli, Burgundians, Vandals, and Ostrogoths from our 486 list had all lost kingdom status before the founding of the Lombard Kingdom. Their delayed arrival makes it unlikely that the Baiuvarii and Lombards could have been two of the ten kingdoms of Daniel 7.

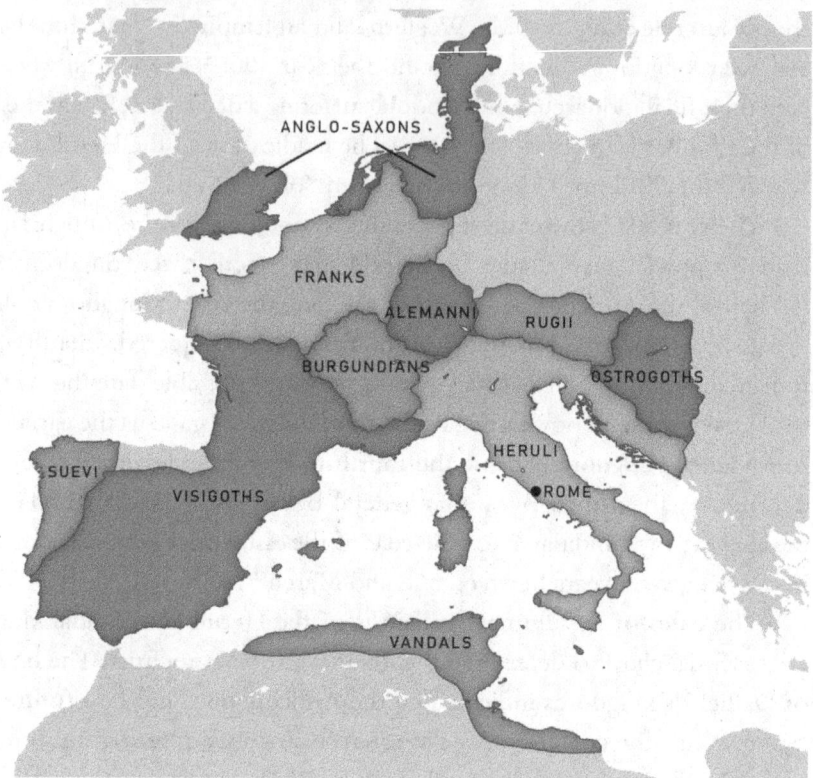

Figure 6: 486 AD borders of the ten kingdoms that arose from the collapsed Western Roman Empire.

> **Daniel 7:25**
> 25 And he shall speak great words against the most High, and shall wear out the saints of the most High, and think to change times and laws: and they shall be given into his hand until a time and times and the dividing of time.

Later in Daniel 7, an angel explains the prophet's dream to him. Within this interpretation, we receive additional insight into the Antichrist when the angel predicts he will speak blasphemously against God and persecute his followers. The phrase "a time and times and the dividing of time" in verse twenty-five refers to the length of the severe persecution of Christians known as the Great Tribulation. Bible scholars almost universally accept it to mean "a year, two years, and a half year"—or three and a half *prophetic years*. In the next chapter, we will define the difference between *prophetic* and *calendar* years.

Chapter Synopsis

The Four Empires and God's Kingdom
- Both Nebuchadnezzar's nightmare in Daniel 2 and Daniel's own dream in Daniel 7 were prophecies describing four major ancient empires—the Neo-Babylonians, Medo-Persians (Achaemenids), Greeks, and Romans
- In Nebuchadnezzar's dream, a stone is cut "without hands," representing God's kingdom
  - The stone strikes the statue on the feet—the Roman segment
  - This predicted that Jesus would arrive during the Roman Empire
  - Daniel prophesied that God's kingdom would be established during the time of these empires and would destroy earthly kingdoms
  - The stone becomes a "great mountain" that covers the whole earth, representing the spread of Christianity
- In Daniel's dream, the Roman Empire beast has ten horns representing the ten kingdoms that would arise from the empire's collapse

The Antichrist
- The eleventh horn on the head of the fourth beast in Daniel 7 represents the Antichrist, who therefore must come from Rome
- The Antichrist could only come to power after the defeat of exactly three of the ten kingdoms that arose from the fallen Roman Empire
  - The third kingdom to fall was the Heruli, who were defeated no later than 508 AD
  - The fourth kingdom to be conquered was the Vandals, who fell in 534 AD
  - Candidates for the role of the Antichrist must have appeared in the twenty-six years between 508 and 534 AD
  - If the Antichrist were to come at a future date, he would appear long after the defeats of all ten kingdoms
- Daniel 7 tells us the Antichrist will also speak great words against God, wear out the saints, and change the times and laws
- The saints shall be given into the Antichrist's hand for "a time and times and the dividing of time"—three and a half prophetic years

3

DANIEL'S SEVENTY WEEKS

The Seventy Weeks Prophecy

Sometime after his dream of the four beasts, Daniel studied the writings of Jeremiah, an earlier prophet who prophesied of Jerusalem's destruction. Jeremiah prophesied that the exiled children of Israel would be held captive in Babylon for seventy years as punishment for worshipping the pagan god Ba'al.[1] Daniel was overcome with emotion as he studied Jeremiah's prophecy. He began fasting and praying for God's forgiveness for his sins and the sins of the Israelites who had neglected their faith. While praying, Daniel received a visit from the angel Gabriel, who told him that God greatly loved him. The angel explained that he had come with a message that he would give Daniel the ability to understand.[2]

Daniel wrote the angel's message in Daniel 9:22-27. Gabriel prophesied seventy weeks would elapse between the decree to rebuild Jerusalem and the arrival of the Messiah, who would "finish the transgression, and to make an end of sins, and to make reconciliation for iniquity, and to bring in everlasting righteousness, and to seal up the vision and prophecy, and to anoint the most Holy." The angel said this would "seal up the vision and prophecy," implying the promise of God's covenant with David would be fulfilled.[a]

---

[a] **II Samuel 7:12-16** 12 And when thy days be fulfilled, and thou shalt sleep with thy fathers, I will set up thy seed after thee, which shall proceed out of thy bowels,

> **Daniel 9:24-25**
> **24** Seventy weeks are determined upon thy people and upon thy holy city, to finish the transgression, and to make an end of sins, and to make reconciliation for iniquity, and to bring in everlasting righteousness, and to seal up the vision and prophecy, and to anoint the most Holy.
> **25** Know therefore and understand, that from the going forth of the commandment to restore and to build Jerusalem unto the Messiah the Prince shall be seven weeks, and threescore and two weeks: the street shall be built again, and the wall, even in troublous times.

In Daniel 9:25, Gabriel advises the prophet that the first sixty-nine of the seventy weeks would pass between the commandment to rebuild Jerusalem and the start of the Messiah's ministry. Following his annexation of Babylon, Cyrus the Great issued a proclamation to rebuild the Temple in 539 BC, but this decree did not order the rebuilding of the rest of the city.[3] Artaxerxes I Longimanus most likely issued the decree to rebuild the entire city in 458 BC, his seventh year as the king of the Achaemenid Empire.[4]

The month of the decree is not listed in the Bible, but we do know Ezra left for Jerusalem on the first day of the Hebrew month of Nisan in 457 BC.[5] The decree would have been given several months before that point, likely near the end of 458 BC, to allow enough time for Ezra to recruit volunteers and procure supplies to prepare for a departure in late March or early April.

According to the writings of Luke, the ministry of John the Baptist began during "the fifteenth year of the reign of Tiberius Caesar."[6] Before becoming emperor, Tiberius started a military campaign in Illyricum in 10 AD, which lasted two years.[7] According to the historian Suetonius, "After two years he returned to the city from Germany and celebrated the triumph which he had postponed, accompanied also by his generals, for whom he had obtained the triumphal regalia. And before turning to enter the Capitol, he dismounted from his chariot and fell at the knees of his father, who was presiding over the ceremonies…the consuls caused a law to be passed soon after this that

---

and I will establish his kingdom. 13 He shall build an house for my name, and I will stablish the throne of his kingdom for ever. 14 I will be his father, and he shall be my son. If he commit iniquity, I will chasten him with the rod of men, and with the stripes of the children of men: 15 But my mercy shall not depart away from him, as I took it from Saul, whom I put away before thee. 16 And thine house and thy kingdom shall be established for ever before thee: thy throne shall be established for ever.

he should govern the provinces jointly with Augustus."[8] Tiberius most likely became co-regent in 12 AD, which would be considered the first year of his reign. Therefore, the best estimate for the start of John the Baptist's ministry and Jesus' baptism is 26 AD, or year fifteen of Tiberius' rule. Since Jesus' baptism is considered the official start of his ministry, this event would mark the arrival of the Messiah and the end of the sixty-ninth week of the Seventy Weeks Prophecy.[9]

Many Christian traditions regarding the timing of Jesus Christ's death are incorrect. Certain contradictions in the Biblical text cannot be resolved with a single Sabbath during Christ's crucifixion week. For example, according to Mark 16:1, Mary, the mother of James, Mary Magdalene, and Salome bought and prepared spices to anoint Jesus' body after the Sabbath day.[b] However, Luke 23:56 says this took place *before* the Sabbath.[c]

In ancient Judaism, the week of the Passover usually had two Sabbaths. The traditional weekly Sabbath would have occurred on Saturday, while the Passover was considered a High Sabbath. Recognizing this fact gives a much clearer picture of the date of Jesus' crucifixion.

The Passover would have been observed on the night before the first full moon of the Hebrew year. Three and a half years after Jesus' 26 AD baptism, this full moon occurred on April 6, 30 AD.[10] That year, the Passover would have been celebrated from Wednesday at twilight until Thursday at sunset, as days began and ended at sunset in the Hebrew calendar. Since the start of Passover and the Last Supper were most likely observed on Wednesday night, Tuesday night into Wednesday would be the Day of Preparation, when the Jews did all the necessary work before the Sabbath to prepare for a day of rest. The Olivet Discourse would have occurred before sunset on Tuesday, as the Bible says it happened two days before Passover.[d]

---

[b] **Mark 16:1** And when the Sabbath was past, Mary Magdalene, and Mary the mother of James, and Salome, had bought sweet spices, that they might come and anoint him.

[c] **Luke 23:56** And they returned, and prepared spices and ointments; and rested the Sabbath day according to the commandment.

[d] **Matthew 26:2** Ye know that after two days is the feast of the passover, and the Son of man is betrayed to be crucified.

Mark 14:1 After two days was the feast of the passover, and of unleavened bread: and the chief priests and the scribes sought how they might take him by craft, and put him to death.

Jesus' arrival in Bethany occurred six days before the Passover, which would have been on Friday before sunset. According to John's account, that evening—considered the next day in the Hebrew calendar—Mary, the sister of Lazarus, anointed Jesus' feet with oil and cleaned them with her hair. Jesus' triumphal entry into Jerusalem occurred the next day, on Palm Sunday.[e] The Cleansing of the Temple, when Jesus overturned the moneychangers' tables, would have occurred on Monday.

With this understanding, events after the 30 AD Passover also become clearer. Matthew 27:1 places Jesus' trial and crucifixion on the morning after the Last Supper. Therefore, he would have been crucified on Thursday late morning and afternoon.[f] Joseph of Arimathaea obtained Christ's body from Pontius Pilate on Thursday afternoon and buried him after sunset,[g] because Luke wrote that Jesus was buried on the Day of Preparation.[h] On Friday, the women from Galilee bought and prepared their anointing spices. This event occurred on the day between the Passover Sabbath and the weekly Sabbath, which reconciles the perceived conflict between Mark and Luke. The next day was the weekly Sabbath,[i] when the chief priests and the Pharisees asked Pilate to place guards outside of Jesus' tomb out of fear that his body would be stolen so that his followers could claim he rose from the dead.[j] Finally, the morning after the Sabbath, when the women brought their spices to the tomb to anoint Jesus' body, they found he had risen from the dead—on Sunday, April 9, 30 AD.[k]

---

[e] **John 12:1** Then Jesus six days before the passover came to Bethany, where Lazarus was, which had been dead, whom he raised from the dead.

[f] **Matthew 27:1** When the morning was come, all the chief priests and elders of the people took counsel against Jesus to put him to death:

[g] **Matthew 27:57-58** 57 When the even was come, there came a rich man of Arimathaea, named Joseph, who also himself was Jesus' disciple: 58 He went to Pilate, and begged the body of Jesus. Then Pilate commanded the body to be delivered.

[h] **Luke 23:54** And that day was the preparation, and the sabbath drew on.

[i] **Luke 23:56** And they returned, and prepared spices and ointments; and rested the Sabbath day according to the commandment.

[j] **Matthew 27:62-63** 62 Now the next day, that followed the day of the preparation, the chief priests and Pharisees came together unto Pilate, 63 Saying, Sir, we remember that that deceiver said, while he was yet alive, After three days I will rise again.

[k] **Matthew 28:1** In the end of the Sabbath, as it began to dawn toward the first day of the week, came Mary Magdalene and the other Mary to see the sepulchre.

EVENTS AROUND JESUS' 30 AD CRUCIFIXION IN HEBREW DAYS

Hebrew Days	Dates	Events
DAY OF PREPARATION	☾ Thursday, March 30	
	☀ Friday, March 31	Jesus arrives in Bethany
WEEKLY SABBATH	☾ Friday, March 31	Lazarus' sister Mary anoints Jesus' feet
	☀ Saturday, April 1	
NISAN 11	☾ Saturday, April 1	
	☀ Sunday, April 2	Triumphal Entry
NISAN 12	☾ Sunday, April 2	
	☀ Monday, April 3	Cleansing of the Temple
NISAN 13	☾ Monday, April 3	
	☀ Tuesday, April 4	Jesus teaches in Temple, Olivet Discourse
DAY OF PREPARATION	☾ Tuesday, April 4	Woman anoints Jesus' head with oil
	☀ Wednesday, April 5	Disciples prepare the upper room
PASSOVER SABBATH	☾ Wednesday, April 5	Last Supper
	☀ Thursday, April 6	Jesus' arrest and crucifixion
DAY OF PREPARATION	☾ Thursday, April 6	Joseph of Arimathaea buries Jesus
	☀ Friday, April 7	Women prepare spices for Jesus' body
WEEKLY SABBATH	☾ Friday, April 7	
	☀ Saturday, April 8	Pharisees request soldiers to guard tomb
NISAN 18	☾ Saturday, April 8	
	☀ Sunday, April 9	Resurrection, women bring spices to tomb

Figure 7: Likely timeline of events around the death and resurrection of Jesus shown in Hebrew days, which began and ended at sunset. Sabbath days are displayed in white. Note that in 30 AD, the day Mary, the mother of James, Mary Magdalene, and Salome bought and prepared spices for Jesus' body was in between the Passover and weekly Sabbaths, which resolves the timing conflict between Mark 16:1 and Luke 23:56.

TIMELINE OF JESUS' CRUCIFIXION AND RESURRECTION

Day	Events	Biblical Text	Verse
Friday afternoon	Jesus arrives in Bethany outside of Jerusalem	"Six days before the Passover"	John 12:1
Friday night	Lazarus' sister Mary anoints Jesus' feet	"There they made him a supper"	John 12:2
Sunday	Triumphal Entry	"On the next day"	John 12:12
Monday	Cleansing of the Temple	"And on the morrow"	Mark 11:12
Tuesday	Teaching in the Temple	"Now in the morning"	Matt. 21:18
Tuesday	Olivet Discourse	"After two days is the feast of the Passover"	Matt. 26:2
Tuesday night	Day of Preparation begins, Woman anoints Jesus' head with oil	"As he sat at meat"	Matt. 26:7 Mark 14:3
Wednesday	Disciples prepare the upper room	"And the first day of unleavened bread"	Mark 14:12 Luke 22:7
Wednesday night	Passover (High Sabbath), Last Supper, Jesus' arrest	"Now when the even was come"	Matt. 26:20
Thursday	Jesus' crucifixion	"When the morning was come"	Matt. 27:1
Thursday night	Day of Preparation begins, Joseph of Arimathaea obtains Jesus' body from Pontius Pilate, Jesus' burial	"When the even was come, because it was the preparation, that is, the day before the sabbath,"	Matt. 27:57 Mark 15:42
		"And that day was the Preparation"	Luke 23:54
Friday	Mary Magdalene, James' mother Mary, and Salome buy and prepare spices for Jesus' body	"When the (Passover) Sabbath was past"	Mark 16:1
		Before the women "rested the (weekly) Sabbath day"	Luke 23:56
Friday night	Weekly Sabbath begins	"Rested the Sabbath day"	Luke 23:56
Saturday	Pharisees request soldiers to guard Jesus' tomb	"Now the next day, that followed the Day of the Preparation"	Matt. 27:62
Sunday	Jesus' resurrection, Mary, Mary, and Salome bring spices to the tomb	"Now upon the first day of the week, very early in the morning"	Luke 24:1

Table 1: Timeline of the Passion of Jesus Christ, most likely March 31-April 9, 30 AD.

Reconciling the evidence in the gospels proves a 30 AD crucifixion date, meaning we now have established 458 BC as the start of the Seventy Weeks Prophecy and 26 AD as the end of the prophecy's sixty-ninth week. As you can tell, this is far longer than the time frame predicted by Daniel. Because there was no year zero, 458 BC to 26 AD is 483 years. But this is where the prophecy becomes fascinating; sixty-nine weeks equals *483 days*.

The first sixty-nine weeks of the prophecy predicted the exact year of the beginning of Jesus' public ministry. To avoid confusion, we will refer to time within the context of a prophecy as *prophetic* days, months, or years. When discussing days or years in the fulfillment of a prophecy, we will refer to them as *calendar* days or years. For example, Daniel predicted that 483 *prophetic days* would elapse between the order to rebuild Jerusalem and the coming of the Messiah. In real time, those 483 prophetic days were fulfilled by 483 *calendar years*. This formula, which theologians have termed the "day-year principle," consistently applies to all end-times prophecies in Daniel and Revelation.

However, this only covers the first sixty-nine weeks of the prophecy. The last two verses of Daniel 9 explain what would occur in the final prophetic week. The Futurist and Preterist theologians have distorted these verses to discredit the Historicist interpretation of the end times. For this reason, it is essential to fully comprehend the rest of the Seventy Weeks Prophecy exactly as it was written.

> **Daniel 9:26-27**
> 26 And after threescore and two weeks shall Messiah be cut off, but not for himself: and the people of the prince that shall come shall destroy the city and the sanctuary; and the end thereof shall be with a flood, and unto the end of the war desolations are determined.
> 27 And he shall confirm the covenant with many for one week: and in the midst of the week he shall cause the sacrifice and the oblation to cease, and for the overspreading of abominations he shall make it desolate, even until the consummation, and that determined shall be poured upon the desolate.

Gabriel explains that once sixty-nine weeks pass, the Messiah will be "cut off," meaning Jesus would be killed. Daniel 9:27 provides precise timing for his death, stating, "In the midst of the week he shall cause the sacrifice and the oblation to cease." In the Old Testament, God made several covenants with the Israelites, including a promise to David in II Samuel 7. God told the prophet Nathan to visit David and deliver a message—if David would build a Temple to God, the Messiah would come from his lineage.[1]

In Daniel 9:26-27, Gabriel prophesies that the Messiah would confirm the Davidic Covenant "in the midst of" the seventieth week. This implies that Jesus' crucifixion, the event that fulfilled this covenant, would occur in the middle of the final seven calendar years, three and a half years into his ministry. These last two verses cover the seven years from 26 through 33 AD, when Jesus ministered to the Jews for the first three and a half years and his disciples followed his example until they fled Judea in 33 AD.

Jesus' crucifixion in April of 30 AD—three and a half years after his fall of 26 AD baptism—marked the end of the Old Covenant, under which God required animal sacrifice to atone for sins. With the New Covenant, Jesus—the Lamb of God—was sacrificed on the cross as one final offering for the atonement of sins. After his death, animal sacrifice was no longer necessary.[11]

The People of the Prince Who Shall Come

The most misunderstood part of this prophecy is the phrase, "and the people of the prince that shall come shall destroy the city and the sanctuary." The "prince who shall come" is the Antichrist, who we know from Daniel 7 would eventually come from Rome—making the Romans his people. The commonly misinterpreted aspect is that this verse discusses *"the people* of the prince that shall come," not the prince himself.

When the Roman general Pompey invaded Palestine in 63 BC, a wealthy and influential Edomite named Antipater supported Rome. After Pompey conquered Palestine and seized Jerusalem, Julius Caesar rewarded Antipater with the position of procurator of Judaea in 47 BC. Antipater then appointed his son Herod as governor of Galilee in the same year.[12] The Roman Senate elevated Herod, who would eventually be known as Herod the Great, as their puppet king of Judea in 40 BC.[13] Herod was uniquely positioned to be king—he was a Jew, a loyal ally of Rome through his lifelong friend Mark Antony,

---

[1] **II Samuel 7:5, 12-13** 5 Go and tell my servant David, Thus saith the Lord, Shalt thou build me an house for me to dwell in?...12 And when thy days be fulfilled, and thou shalt sleep with thy fathers, I will set up thy seed after thee, which shall proceed out of thy bowels, and I will establish his kingdom. 13 He shall build an house for my name, and I will stablish the throne of his kingdom for ever.

and his mother was the daughter of a nobleman from the Nabatean kingdom to the east.[14]

After more than a century, the Jews had grown weary of Roman rule. Their list of grievances was long, and the tension would not require much instigation to explode. The Jewish historian Flavius Josephus tells us in *The Jewish War* that the violence began with a seemingly benign event in Caesarea during the twelfth year of Emperor Nero's reign, in 66 AD.

According to Josephus, the Greeks had obtained the right to govern Caesarea from Nero despite its location in Judea. The Jews had attempted to purchase a building near their Caesarean synagogue from its Greek owner, going so far as to offer to pay several times its value, which the owner refused. Instead, he built several other shops on the land until the Jews only had a narrow path to their synagogue.

The Jews protested to Gessius Florus, the Roman procurator of Judea. Florus was a Greek himself and had a history of discriminating against the Jews. He refused to allow the Jews to use force, so they offered to give him eight talents to stop the new construction. After getting his payment, Florus left Caesarea and traveled to Sebaste. In Josephus' opinion, this was his way of turning a blind eye and allowing the Jews to use force after all.[15]

The next day, as the Jews were crowding into their synagogue, a Greek man "of a seditious temper" upturned a large terracotta jar at the entrance to the synagogue and used it to sacrifice birds. To the enraged Jews, this was an appalling insult. In Jewish religious law and customs, sacrificing animals to pagan gods was a desecration of their synagogue. The Jews did not know that the Greeks nominated this man to incite the Jews to fight, but it would not have mattered. Their anger only needed a minor spark to ignite.[16]

In response, Eleazar ben Hanania, the governor of the Jewish Temple in Jerusalem, convinced the officiants of "divine service" to decline any gifts or sacrifices on behalf of any foreigner. As a result, all offerings on behalf of the Roman emperor Nero ceased. According to Josephus, this was the moment when the skirmish between the Jews and Greeks of Judea evolved into a war between the Jews and the Roman Empire.[17]

Rather than returning to Caesarea to quell the Jews' anger, Florus instead dispatched soldiers to Jerusalem with an order to steal seventeen talents from the Temple's treasury. The soldiers' act of entering the Holy of Holies—the most sacred part of the Temple and off-limits to anyone but the Jewish high priest—was the abomination of desolation predicted in Daniel 9:26-27. This was the event that Jesus indicated would be the warning to flee Judea and take refuge in the mountains during his Olivet Discourse.^m

After learning of the theft, the local Jews ran to the Temple in disbelief. Enraged, they mockingly passed around a basket, collecting money for Florus as if he were a beggar. Once word reached Florus, he prepared his army to march on Jerusalem to suppress the revolt and steal from the Temple again.[18]

When he arrived in Jerusalem, Florus unleashed his soldiers with orders to plunder the Temple's Upper Marketplace and kill anyone who gave them resistance. But the Romans not only looted the Upper Marketplace; they forced their way into every house, killing the Jewish residents and stealing anything of value.

Once the Jews witnessed the unfolding chaos, they attempted to flee the city. Many could not escape the soldiers, who captured everyone they could. Josephus wrote that many of the detained "quiet people"—those uninvolved with the revolt—were brought before Florus, who ordered them flogged and crucified. Josephus estimated that around 3,600 men, women, and children were massacred that day by the Romans.[19]

As a result of the violence, the final Roman client-king of the Herodian dynasty, Herod Agrippa II, fled Jerusalem for Galilee with his sister Berenice. When Nero learned of the rebellion, he dispatched his general Titus Flavius Vespasianus, who would later become the emperor Vespasian, to quell the violence. By 68 AD, Vespasian and his son Titus, who would succeed him as emperor, had recovered most of the territory lost to the Jewish Zealots.[20]

However, in June of 68, Nero committed suicide in Rome. Nero's lack of an heir apparent caused turmoil throughout the empire, leading to the "Year of the Four Emperors" in 69 AD. This power vacuum encouraged Vespasian's army and the Roman legions stationed in Egypt and Syria to take an oath of loyalty naming him the new emperor.[21] Vespasian then returned

---

^m **Matthew 24:15-19** 15 When ye therefore shall see the abomination of desolation, spoken of by Daniel the prophet, stand in the holy place, (whoso readeth, let him understand:) 16 Then let them which be in Judaea flee into the mountains: 17 Let him which is on the housetop not come down to take any thing out of his house: 18 Neither let him which is in the field return back to take his clothes. 19 And woe unto them that are with child, and to them that give suck in those days!

to Rome to assert his claim to the throne, leaving his son Titus in charge of the army to march on Jerusalem and finish the war.

The Romans were initially unable to breach the city walls. As a result, they set up camp, dug a trench around Jerusalem, and laid siege to the city. Jews who attempted to flee Jerusalem were caught in the trench and captured by the Romans. Josephus wrote, "They caught every day five hundred Jews; nay, some days they caught more." Titus, who did not want to dedicate the manpower necessary to guard such high numbers of Jewish deserters, instead chose to have them tortured and crucified, an event predicted by Jesus.[22, n]

After seven months, the Roman army successfully penetrated the walls of Jerusalem. The Jewish soldiers inside the city quickly lost ground to the invading army and were forced to take refuge in Jerusalem's last fortified stronghold, the Temple. Titus recognized the battle was essentially over and ordered the Temple to be spared from destruction.

This attempt to protect the Temple infuriated Titus' men to the point where he began to fear for his safety. When he believed his soldiers might turn their anger onto him if he did not reverse his position, Titus gave the order to light the building's gates on fire.[23]

The fire swiftly escalated and engulfed the rooms around the Temple. Titus hurried to the complex to command his incensed soldiers to extinguish the flames. However, once he entered the building and found its riches were far more than he had imagined, Titus' focus promptly shifted to plunder. The Roman army enthusiastically looted the complex, leaving the fire burning to consume the sanctuary.[24]

Rome's demolition of the Second Temple marked a critical moment in Jewish history. It was a demarcation between two distinct religious periods—the Temple era and the post-Temple era. Imagine being a Jew in the first century. The Temple had stood in Jerusalem for your entire life—585 years, in fact. Then, in one day, it was gone.

By the end of the sack of Jerusalem, the city was destroyed, and ninety percent of the population lay slaughtered. Fighting would continue outside

---

[n] **Luke 19:43-44** 43 For the days shall come upon thee, that thine enemies shall cast a trench about thee, and compass thee round, and keep thee in on every side, 44 And shall lay thee even with the ground, and thy children within thee; and they shall not leave in thee one stone upon another; because thou knewest not the time of thy visitation.

of the city until as late as 73 AD. By its conclusion, the war had claimed the lives of approximately one-third of the Jews in all of Judea and left the region desolate, just as Gabriel warned it would in Daniel 9:26-27.[25]

Gospel Preached in All the World

Daniel 9:27 tells us the Messiah "shall confirm the covenant with many for one week." We have seen how the prophecy's seventieth and final week began with Jesus' baptism in 26 AD. Jesus ministered to the Jews of Judea for three and a half years—the first half of the week. His crucifixion occurred in the middle of the concluding week, exactly as Gabriel predicted. So, what happened in the second half of week seventy?

The purpose of Jesus' ministry was always to save God's chosen people, the Jews. Matthew 15 contains a story of a Canaanite mother whose daughter was "grievously vexed with a devil." The woman pleaded with Jesus for help, but he ignored her until his disciples asked him to send her away. In response, Jesus told her, "I am not sent but unto the lost sheep of the house of Israel."[26]

Eventually, Jesus exorcised the demon, but this story illustrates how he viewed the Jews as the focus of his ministry. After his death and resurrection, the disciples followed Christ's example and continued to minister to the Jews vigorously. When Christianity began to spread, the same Jewish leaders who killed Jesus became increasingly envious and hostile toward his disciples.

One example of the persecution of the earliest Christians is found in Acts 4:1-22. After Peter and John healed a crippled man, they were arrested and threatened by the Sadducees. Acts 5:17-42 details a separate event in which Peter and several other apostles healed the sick and cast out demons. Again, the apostles were arrested by the high priest and the Sadducees, incarcerated, interrogated by the Jewish Sanhedrin, and lashed.

Over time, the Jewish assault on Christianity intensified. After preaching in Jerusalem, Stephen, a Jew of Greek descent, performed "great wonders and miracles."[27] When the other Greek Jews in the synagogue tested Stephen on his teachings, he methodically refuted every one of their challenges. This embarrassed the synagogue's members, who dragged him to the Jewish court and falsely claimed he had been preaching against both God and Moses.[28]

When the high priest of the Sanhedrin asked Stephen if the accusations were true, he denied them and delivered a long dissertation on the history of

Israel's relationship with God. From Abraham to Moses and eventually to Jesus, he utilized the history of Judaism to prove Jesus was not undermining Mosaic law but fulfilling it. Stephen then asked the Jewish leaders, "Which of the prophets have not your fathers persecuted?"º

Stephen's question sent the Sanhedrin into a frenzy. The committee was insulted by Stephen's mastery of the history of the Jewish people and how he had used it against them so effortlessly, accusing them of murdering the very Messiah whom God had promised. Not helping his case, he ended his lecture by stating, "Behold, I see the heavens opened, and the Son of man standing on the right hand of God."

This claim provoked the Sanhedrin into a murderous rage. They dragged Stephen outside of Jerusalem and furiously stoned him to death, making him the first known Christian martyr. Fearing for their lives, many of the disciples fled Judea and "went everywhere preaching the word."

> **Acts 7:59-8:4**
> **59** And they stoned Stephen, calling upon God, and saying, Lord Jesus, receive my spirit.
> **60** And he kneeled down, and cried with a loud voice, Lord, lay not this sin to their charge. And when he had said this, he fell asleep.
> **8:1** And Saul was consenting unto his death. And at that time there was a great persecution against the church which was at Jerusalem; and they were all scattered abroad throughout the regions of Judaea and Samaria, except the apostles.
> **2** And devout men carried Stephen to his burial, and made great lamentation over him.
> **3** As for Saul, he made havock of the church, entering into every house, and haling men and women committed them to prison.
> **4** Therefore they that were scattered abroad went every where preaching the word.

From the start of Jesus' ministry until the stoning of Stephen, the Jews were the sole target of Christian evangelism, while the Gentiles were mainly ignored. Stephen's death marked a fundamental change in Christian history; the moment God stopped attempting to gain acceptance from the Jews and

---

º **Acts 7:52** Which of the prophets have not your fathers persecuted? and they have slain them which shewed before of the coming of the Just One; of whom ye have been now the betrayers and murderers:

instead turned to the Gentiles. This was the shift Jesus predicted in the Olivet Discourse when he told his disciples, "This gospel of the kingdom shall be preached in all the world for a witness unto all nations" before the Second Temple would be destroyed.p

Stephen's stoning also marked the end of the Seventy Weeks Prophecy, which lasted not 490 *days* but 490 *years*. The prophecy correctly predicted the year of Jesus' baptism and the start of his ministry in 26 AD, 483 years after Artaxerxes I Longimanus' 458 BC decree to rebuild Jerusalem. It foretold his crucifixion three and a half years later, in the middle of the seventieth week. Importantly, it provided the necessary knowledge to decipher the day-year principle and determine the length of all other end-times prophecies.

The Bible never declares that the end times will be a short, seven-year period leading up to Christ's second coming, as the Futurists claim. Acts 2:17 indicates the end times had already begun by the first Pentecost.q On that day, the 120 closest followers of Jesus received the Holy Spirit, empowering them to begin ministering in foreign languages they did not previously know. The beginning of the end times period likely aligns with the New Covenant— the time following Jesus' crucifixion as an atonement for our sins, after which animal sacrifice was no longer required.

Figure 8: Timeline of the Seventy Weeks Prophecy.

---

p **Matthew 24:14** And this gospel of the kingdom shall be preached in all the world for a witness unto all nations; and then shall the end come.

q **Acts 2:17** And it shall come to pass in the last days, saith God, I will pour out of my Spirit upon all flesh: and your sons and your daughters shall prophesy, and your young men shall see visions, and your old men shall dream dreams:

Christians as God's Chosen People

The conclusion of Daniel's Seventy Weeks Prophecy marked the end of the Jews' time as God's people and the beginning of Christian evangelism to the Gentiles. Evidence of this reversal can be found shortly after Stephen's martyrdom. In Acts 13, Paul and Barnabas were preaching in Pisidia, a town near Antioch in Anatolia. When the local Jews noticed that most of the town had gathered to hear the apostles' sermon, they became envious and began "contradicting and blaspheming" against them. The apostles replied that they had come to the Jews first, but when the Jews rejected the gospel, they turned to the Gentiles.

> **Acts 13:45-46**
> **45** But when the Jews saw the multitudes, they were filled with envy, and spake against those things which were spoken by Paul, contradicting and blaspheming. **46** Then Paul and Barnabas waxed bold, and said, It was necessary that the word of God should first have been spoken to you: but seeing ye put it from you, and judge yourselves unworthy of everlasting life, lo, we turn to the Gentiles.

Nascent Christianity dealt with several questions on what was required of Gentiles who joined the faith. Since Jesus spent his entire ministry striving to reach the Jews, he provided no precedent or advice for the assimilation of non-Jews into the faith. Acts 15 describes a scene featuring a debate amongst some of the earliest followers of Christ. The issue in question was whether Gentiles who found salvation should be compelled to follow Jewish law and be circumcised. Paul and Barnabas headed to Jerusalem to speak to Jesus' original apostles and listen to their opinions.

After some debate, Peter stood and gave his input, "Men and brethren, ye know how that a good while ago God made choice among us, that the Gentiles by my mouth should hear the word of the gospel, and believe," he said. "And God, which knoweth the hearts, bare them witness, giving them the Holy Ghost, even as he did unto us; And put no difference between us and them, purifying their hearts by faith."[29] Peter felt a person's background as a Jew or a Gentile was irrelevant once they accepted Jesus as their savior.

When Peter finished speaking, James addressed the conference. In his monologue, the apostle referenced a passage from the Old Testament book of Amos, written around 750 BC. In chapter nine, Amos revealed a prophecy that, on its surface, predicted the destruction of the Temple in Jerusalem by the Babylonians and its eventual reconstruction. However, this prophecy—like many others in the Bible—had a double meaning.

The Tabernacle was a temporary, tent-like structure built by King David for the Israelites to worship God and offer sacrifices. It preceded the First Temple, which was completed by David's son and successor, Solomon.[30] The word "tabernacle" was also used later in reference to the Temple.

In his speech, James focused on the symbolism behind the "Tabernacle of David." Scripture repeatedly states that Jesus was a descendant of David.[31] In Amos 9:11, the prophet used the pronoun "his" to describe the Temple's ruins. This word selection indicates Amos' focus was on the metaphorical meaning of the original passage, as "*his* ruins" would mean the crucified body of Jesus Christ would be "raised up" and resurrected. When James said the "Tabernacle of David" had "fallen down" and would be "built again" in Acts 15, he was referring to Christ's crucifixion and resurrection.

When you read the words of Amos 9 and Acts 15 in parallel, you can see the similarities between the passages. Rather than "possessing the remnant of Edom," as Amos wrote, James declares the purpose of Jesus' crucifixion was to allow men to "seek after the Lord." He also cleverly replaces Amos' word "heathen" with "Gentiles" in his oration to show that non-Jews were now the people chosen by God.

Amos 9:11-12	**Acts 15:16-17**
11 In that day will I raise up the tabernacle of David that is fallen,	**16** After this I will return, and will build again the tabernacle of David, which is fallen down;
and close up the breaches thereof; and I will raise up his ruins,	and I will build again the ruins thereof,
and I will build it as in the days of old:	and I will set it up:
12 That they may possess the remnant of Edom,	**17** That the residue of men might seek after the Lord,
and of all the heathen,	and all the Gentiles,
which are called by my name,	upon whom my name is called,
saith the Lord that doeth this.	saith the Lord, who doeth all these things.

Questions About Daniel's Authenticity

The promoters of the Futurist and Preterist eschatological views realize there are several flaws in their interpretations. Rather than attempting to use the Bible to prove their points, some attempt to delegitimize the entire book of Daniel. Many of Daniel's detractors point to the book being written in two different languages: Hebrew and Aramaic. They claim there were two writing styles, as the first six chapters were written in the third person while the last six were in the first person. The chapters about a mid-second century Greek Seleucid king named Antiochus IV Epiphanes are incredibly detailed, which critics of Daniel contend are too specific to be prophecies. They also claim there are no ancient Jewish sources with references to Daniel before the end of the reign of Antiochus in 164 BC, so it could not have been written earlier. However, all these assertions have significant flaws.

Biblical scholars have contested Daniel's dating for years. The questions some scholars raise in their attempt to discredit Daniel lead to two potential date ranges. The time frame favored by Daniel's critics is the end of the reign of Antiochus, around 167-164 BC. The second range is the dates found in the text—the sixth century BC.

Multiple Languages

Daniel's first chapter covers the events directly impacting the Jews in the aftermath of Nebuchadnezzar's 605 BC siege of Jerusalem and the exile of young Jewish nobles to Babylon. The author begins in Hebrew, as the Jews were the chapter's primary focus and the book's target audience. In the first three and a half verses of chapter two, Daniel introduces Nebuchadnezzar's dream in Hebrew. Then, in verse four, the prophet quotes Nebuchadnezzar's advisors in Aramaic. Aramaic was a primary language of the Babylonians, and the one that Daniel reports the Chaldeans were using.[r] Chapters two through six contain narratives from Daniel's life in Babylon, so the local Aramaic was used. The prophet continued writing in Aramaic through chapter seven, which illustrates Daniel's dream of four beasts. Like Daniel 2, this chapter

---

[r] **Daniel 2:4** Then spake the Chaldeans to the king in Syriack, O king, live for ever: tell thy servants the dream, and we will shew the interpretation.

contains a prophecy of the four great empires that would control Babylon. Much of the content of this chapter is also specific to Babylon, so Aramaic was again the language of choice. For the final five chapters—the part of the book that contains prophecies around cataclysmic future events impacting the Jewish people—the prophet returned to Hebrew.[32]

The original authors did not create the chapter and verse divisions found in the Bible. They were later additions, believed to be the work of Archbishop Stephen Langton in the thirteenth century.[33] For this reason, the chapter and verse divisions can occasionally be a distraction. It is more important to focus on the book's content than its partition into chapters and verses.

At this point, the prophet likely spoke and wrote primarily in Aramaic, especially in the palace, where he would have spent most of his time. We cannot disregard the fact that Daniel would have communicated primarily in Aramaic while living in Babylon, and his dialogues with the kings of Babylon and Persia would have been easier to record in their original language without translating them into Hebrew.

The dialect of Aramaic in Daniel 2:4b-7:28 is Imperial. Imperial Aramaic was spoken in Mesopotamia and Persia before Alexander the Great, from around 700 until 330 BC. Researchers have analyzed the language in the book of Daniel and determined that an earlier, pre-330 BC authorship was more likely, as the Aramaic matched this Imperial form of the language rather than the Middle Aramaic spoken after the Macedonian conquest of the region.[34]

Following the discovery of the Elephantine Papyri in the early twentieth century, Franz Rosenthal spent four decades studying the similarities between the Aramaic in the fifth-century BC papyri and the book of Daniel. Rosenthal concluded the "old linguistic evidence" for a later, second-century-BC dating of Daniel had to be "shelved." His examination determined that the Aramaic used in Daniel was, in fact, Imperial.[35]

There are also nineteen Persian loan words used in Daniel. These are older Persian words, dating to 300 BC at the latest, a fact which also argues against a later date. Four of these words do not translate well into the version of Daniel included in the Septuagint—the Greek translation of the Hebrew scriptures from the mid-second century BC. Had Daniel been written in or around 164 BC, it would be impossible for their meanings to have been lost by the time the Septuagint was completed only a few years later.[36]

Topic	Daniel	Language	Viewpoint
Introduction	1:1-1:21	Hebrew	Third Person
Introduction of Nebuchadnezzar's Dream	2:1-2:4a		
Nebuchadnezzar's Dream of Four Empires	2:4b-2:49	Aramaic	
The Fiery Furnace	3:1-3:30		
Nebuchadnezzar's Tree Dream	4:1-4:37		
Belshazzar's Feast	5:1-5:31		
Daniel in the Lion's Den	6:1-6:28		
Daniel's Dream of Four Beast Empires	7:1-7:28		First Person
Vision of a Ram and a Goat	8:1-8:27	Hebrew	
Daniel's Prayer	9:1-9:20		
Seventy Weeks Prophecy	9:21-9:27		
Kings of the North and South	10:1-12:13		

Table 2: The book of Daniel by topic, original language, and author's point of view.

Daniel's dream of four beast empires in chapter seven foretold the future of Babylon. Just as Nebuchadnezzar's similar dream of a statue representing the same four empires was written in Aramaic, Daniel's dream was as well. The content of this chapter is an extension of Nebuchadnezzar's dream and employs the same language. The topics covered in chapters one and eight through twelve affected the Israelites, not the Babylonians, so the prophet wrote in Hebrew.

Author's Point of View

Daniel's first six chapters are written from the third-person point of view, while the remaining chapters are written in the first-person. This aligns with the book's split between the historical stories in the court of the kings of Babylon and Persia in chapters one through six and the apocalyptic visions of chapters seven through twelve.

The historical narratives in the first half of the book are autobiographical. Ancient authors often wrote accounts of their lives in the third person. The prophet's use of this point of view in the first six chapters may be unusual to readers today, but it aligns with the writing style of other autobiographical works of the time.[37]

Antiochus IV Epiphanes

The return to Hebrew for the final five chapters aligns with the change in the content of the book. Chapter eight covers the rise of Alexander the Great and the fall of the Achaemenids before moving on to the rise of Rome and the Antichrist. Chapter nine predicts the timing of Jesus' ministry and crucifixion, which would "put an end to sin" and "cause the sacrifice and the oblation to cease." It also predicted the ruin of a yet-to-be-built Temple. The prophecies in chapters ten through twelve are believed to refer to the second-century-BC tyrant Antiochus IV Epiphanes, who ruled the Seleucid Empire from 175 BC until his death in 164 BC. During his reign, Antiochus harshly persecuted the Jews and desecrated their religion. He restricted many Jewish practices and sacrificed a swine—considered an unclean animal in Judaism—at the image of Moses on the Altar of Burnt Offering in the Temple. After the sacrifice, he sprinkled the pig's blood on the Jews, poured the broth made from the sacrifice on the Jewish religious books, and forced the Jews and their high priest to eat its meat. He even put out the Temple menorah, which was considered an immortal flame that burned uninterruptedly. Antiochus' actions directly led to the Maccabean revolt.[38] Although the Aramaic chapters of Daniel deal with events in Babylon, each of the last five chapters impacts the Jewish religion and was rendered in the Hebrew tongue.

The prophetic references to Antiochus IV Epiphanes in Daniel 10-12 are the most vivid and specific in all of Daniel. Biblical scholars who advocate for a later date of the book of Daniel use the level of detail in these chapters to declare the book a mid-second-century forgery intended as anti-Antiochus propaganda and defamation. They argue that these chapters are too accurate to be a prophecy, so in their view, the entire book must be discarded.

The theory that Daniel was written around the time of Antiochus was first proposed by Greek historian Porphyry, who lived in 233-304 AD, eight hundred years after Daniel's lifetime. Porphyry was a Neoplatonist—a later follower of Plato's teaching—and an ardent critic of the Bible. *Encyclopedia Britannica* says, "Porphyry is well known as a violent opponent of Christianity and defender of paganism."[39]

Around a century later, the early Christian writer Jerome methodically dismantled Porphyry's claims. After Jerome published his writings, historical scholars dismissed Porphyry as a mere pagan detractor whose opinions were fashioned by a naturalist bias. In the eighteenth century, the atheists of the Enlightenment—who were themselves naturalists—criticized and rejected all supernatural elements of the Christian faith. These atheists found a kindred spirit in Porphyry, and his writings were revived.[40]

It is not a coincidence that the only end-times prophecies in Daniel and Revelation where one prophetic day does not equal one calendar year are the 1,290-day and 1,335-day prophecies located in Daniel's Antiochus chapters. The glaring inconsistency between these chapters and end-times prophecies elsewhere in Daniel and Revelation where the day-year principle is uniformly applied is an indication that Daniel 10-12 may have been later additions to an authentic book written by the prophet centuries earlier. However, the more likely explanation is that the day-year principle only applies to prophecies that were at least partially fulfilled during the end times, while the prophecies in these chapters were fulfilled before the death and resurrection of Jesus Christ prompted the start of the end-times age.

Daniel 8 and Antiochus

There is no scholarly consensus on the interpretation of Daniel 8. Many apply the little horn of this chapter to the Romans, while some identify it as Muhammad, the founder of Islam. The critics of both the book of Daniel and the Historicist view attempt to interpret chapter eight as a reference to Antiochus. The reason for making this claim is that if chapter eight was added in 164 BC along with chapters ten, eleven, and twelve, chapter nine would be in the middle of the later additions to Daniel. It would then be easy to declare the Seventy Weeks Prophecy a forgery. This would help critics invalidate the day-year principle and Historicism and define the "people of the prince that shall come" as the Greeks rather than the Romans.

A reading of Jesus' Olivet Discourse in Matthew 24 shows he believed the prophecy of the abomination of desolation found in Daniel 9:26-27 had not been fulfilled before his crucifixion. This fact would not only add support for the authenticity of the book of Daniel from the mouth of Jesus himself, it would also invalidate the flawed opinions that Antiochus was the Antichrist prince in verse twenty-six and that the Greeks destroyed Jerusalem and the Temple. Jesus prophesied, "When ye therefore shall see the abomination of desolation, spoken of by Daniel the prophet, stand in the holy place, Then let them which be in Judaea flee into the mountains."[s] Jesus believed that the "people of the prince that shall come" had not destroyed the Temple before 30 AD, undermining the belief that Daniel 9:26 referred to the Greeks. Many dishonest interpretations of Daniel 9:26 also disregard the word "destroy." Antiochus undeniably desecrated the Temple, but he never destroyed the building or the city of Jerusalem.

Daniel 8 could not have been a prophecy about Antiochus for several reasons. First, the Second Temple was not destroyed until 233 years after his death, which means that Antiochus did not "cast down" the place of the sanctuary as predicted in Daniel 8:11.[t]

Second, Antiochus' life does not align with the time frame of Daniel's prophecies. If Daniel's dream in chapter nine occurred in 539 BC—the first year of the Achaemenid Empire—an immediate decree to rebuild Jerusalem would mean a 490-year fulfillment of the Seventy Weeks Prophecy would have ended in 49 BC. Even if the decree were issued immediately after Daniel was taken captive in 597 BC, contrary to Daniel's writings, the last week of the prophecy would have ended in 107 BC.

In this hypothesis, even if the seventieth week of the prophecy predicted the coming of the Antichrist as the Preterists and Futurists falsely claim, the Antichrist could not have appeared before the beginning of the seventieth week in 114 BC, long after Antiochus' death. This places Antiochus' reign sometime in the middle of the Seventy Weeks Prophecy and means he cannot align in any way with its final week. The Biblical scholars who see Antiochus as the little horn of chapters seven and eight and the prince that shall come of chapter nine delegitimize their claims with embarrassingly poor math.

Third, Daniel 8:8-9 describes the little horn in grander terms than the goat's horn, which represents Alexander the Great.[u] Antiochus was a minor

---

[s] **Matthew 24:15-16** 15 When ye therefore shall see the abomination of desolation, spoken of by Daniel the prophet, stand in the holy place, (whoso readeth, let him understand:) 16 Then let them which be in Judaea flee into the mountains:

[t] **Daniel 8:11** Yea, he magnified himself even to the prince of the host, and by him the daily sacrifice was taken away, and the place of the sanctuary was cast down.

[u] **Daniel 8:8-9** 8 Therefore the he goat waxed very great: and when he was strong, the great horn was broken; and for it came up four notable ones toward the four winds of heaven. 9 And out of one of them came forth a little horn, which waxed exceeding great, toward the south, and toward the east, and toward the pleasant land.

king of the Seleucid Empire, which was only a fraction of Alexander's Greek Empire. The little horn is portrayed more powerfully than the goat's horn, but Antiochus was far less formidable than Alexander. He was not even the strongest leader amongst his contemporaries, as Alexander was.

Fourth, Historicism is the cleanest of all eschatological interpretations of Daniel and the only one that fulfills all elements of its prophecies. Under Historicism, the little horn of Daniel 8 is the same figure as the little horn of Daniel 7—the Antichrist.

After the "great horn" representing Alexander is broken in verse twenty-two, four kingdoms arise from his empire. Like the four wings and heads of the leopard beast in Daniel 7:6, these horns represent the four Diadochi.[v]

The fifth reason Antiochus was not the little horn of Daniel 8 is that he did not rise to power in the latter part of the four Diadochi kingdoms. Verse twenty-three predicts another "king of fierce countenance" will arrive on the scene "in the latter time of their kingdom." Antiochus' reign occurred close to the Seleucid Empire's midpoint, not its end.

> **Daniel 8:21-23**
> 21 And the rough goat is the king of Grecia: and the great horn that is between his eyes is the first king.
> 22 Now that being broken, whereas four stood up for it, four kingdoms shall stand up out of the nation, but not in his power.
> 23 And in the latter time of their kingdom, when the transgressors are come to the full, a king of fierce countenance, and understanding dark sentences, shall stand up.

Rome eventually conquered or absorbed each of the Diadochi kingdoms. Cassander's Macedonian Kingdom became a Roman province in 148 BC.[41] Lysimachus' territory included Thrace and the Kingdom of Pergamon, which was bequeathed to Rome in 133 BC.[42] Next to fall was what little remained of the Seleucid Empire, which was annexed by Pompey the Great in 63 BC.[43] Finally, Ptolemy's Egyptian Kingdom fell to Rome under Octavian following the suicide of Cleopatra in 30 BC.[44]

---

[v] **Daniel 7:6** After this I beheld, and lo another, like a leopard, which had upon the back of it four wings of a fowl; the beast had also four heads; and dominion was given to it.

Rome overtook all four Diadochi kingdoms as it matured at the expense of what remained of Alexander's once-great empire. This Roman expansion is described in Daniel 8:23 as the king of fierce countenance "standing up" near the end of the four Diadochi kingdoms.

> **Daniel 8:24-25**
> 24 And his power shall be mighty, but not by his own power: and he shall destroy wonderfully, and shall prosper, and practise, and shall destroy the mighty and the holy people.
> 25 And through his policy also he shall cause craft to prosper in his hand; and he shall magnify himself in his heart, and by peace shall destroy many: he shall also stand up against the Prince of princes; but he shall be broken without hand.

This prophecy of a Roman king appears to have a double meaning. Its fulfillment is found in both the Roman emperors and the Antichrist, whom Daniel predicted would also be of Roman origin. For example, the phrase "shall destroy the mighty and the holy people" is a reference to both the Romans' destruction of Judea during the First Jewish-Roman War and the Antichrist's persecution of Christians. Daniel 8 proclaimed that the little horn would cause "craft to prosper," predicting that the pagan religions of both the Roman emperors and Antichrist would be steeped in witchcraft and false doctrine. The meaning of the phrase "by peace shall destroy many" suggests a nonviolent and deceptive destruction that is spiritual rather than physical. The prophecy predicts that the pagan religions of the Roman Empire and the Antichrist would deceive many people, inhibiting them from embracing true Christianity. Lastly, the Roman emperors and the Antichrist would be revered as deities. The ancient Romans worshipped many emperors as gods through the imperial cult. Likewise, the Antichrist would eventually "stand up against the Prince of princes," positioning himself as an equal to Christ. In 164 BC, Jesus had not been born, so Antiochus would have been unable to magnify himself and claim equivalency with him. An educated reading of Daniel 8-9 makes it clear that the little horn cannot possibly be Antiochus.

Importantly, for the eschatological arguments made within this book, the Antiochus chapters of Daniel 10-12 have been ignored when analyzing the prophet's end-times prophecies. These three chapters, whether authentic or forged, have nothing to do with the end times, as their fulfillment occurred more than 160 years before the birth of Jesus Christ.

No Jewish Historical References to Daniel

Another point some scholars use to discredit Daniel is that other ancient Jewish sources do not include Daniel in their canon before the mid-second century BC, when Daniel first appeared in the Greek Septuagint.[45] However, if Daniel were a contemporary book, or one only recently completed in the second century BC, it almost certainly would have been excluded from such a significant religious text. In fact, ancient writers around Antiochus' time viewed Daniel in high esteem. The book was quoted in the first-century-BC Florilegium 4Q174 of the Dead Sea Scrolls, which explicitly states that two of its verses are written in "the book of Daniel, the Prophet."[46]

Although no Jewish sources that reference Daniel predate Antiochus, the first-century Jewish historian Josephus described an event when Alexander the Great reached Jerusalem in 332 BC. He wrote, "And when the Book of Daniel was showed him wherein Daniel declared that one of the Greeks should destroy the empire of the Persians, he supposed that himself was the person intended: and as he was then glad, he dismissed the multitude for the present."[47] After this event, Alexander spared Jerusalem from destruction.

Even though Josephus lived two centuries after Antiochus, the event he documented took place 157 years before Antiochus' reign. If Daniel 8 was shown to Alexander at Jerusalem in 332 BC, this chapter could not have been a later addition intended to defame Antiochus.

Authenticity of Daniel 9

You may be wondering, "Why are only chapters ten, eleven, and twelve potentially forged? The ninth chapter was also written in Hebrew—is it not convenient to leave the chapter containing the Seventy Weeks Prophecy off the list of potentially forged chapters?" Applying critical thinking to how a forger would have written this chapter gives us our answer.

The ancient Jews knew Ezra left Babylon to rebuild Jerusalem in March or April of 457 BC, on the first day of the first month in the Hebrew calendar. According to the Talmud, he delayed his trip to Jerusalem to stay in Babylon and care for his ailing mentor, the renowned disciple of Jeremiah, Baruch ben Neriah.[48] This suggests Artaxerxes I Longimanus issued his decree to rebuild Jerusalem sometime in late 458 BC.[w] The Jews alive in Antiochus' day could not possibly have understood the day-year principle, as its ending date could not be calculated until the first year of Christ's ministry was known. Second-century Jews would have believed the Messiah should have arrived in May of 456 BC at the latest for the prophecy to have been accurately fulfilled, as they would have read "seventy weeks" literally. If chapter nine were a forgery, the forger would not have written a false prophecy with a time frame that had previously expired unfulfilled since the Messiah had not arrived that year. A forger would have chosen a much longer time frame which would have taken the prophecy well beyond 164 BC, as the seventy-week period would have appeared inaccurate to the pre-Christ readers of Daniel. For this reason, chapter nine could not have been a later addition to Daniel.

The fact is, even if Daniel chapters ten, eleven, and twelve were added—or, for argument's sake, even if it was entirely written—in 164 BC, the book as the Jews knew it at the time of Antiochus predates the Roman Empire, the destruction of the Second Temple, and the life of Jesus. The book vividly predicted the rise and fall of Rome, as well as the years of the start of Christ's ministry and his crucifixion, further legitimizing its prophetic basis.

No matter which arguments are made against Daniel's sixth-century-BC dating, Daniel 9 is not invalidated by the existence of references to Antiochus in later chapters. Daniel was included in the Septuagint two centuries before the life of Christ fulfilled the Seventy Weeks Prophecy. This fact points to the authenticity and divine inspiration of the first nine chapters, even if you exclude the potentially pseudepigraphical later additions related to Antiochus in chapters ten through twelve.

---

[w] **Ezra 7:8-9** 8 And he came to Jerusalem in the fifth month, which was in the seventh year of the king. 9 For upon the first day of the first month began he to go up from Babylon, and on the first day of the fifth month came he to Jerusalem, according to the good hand of his God upon him.

Chapter Synopsis

Seventy Weeks Prophecy
- Predicted the years of the beginning of Jesus' ministry and crucifixion
- This prophecy established the day-year principle, where one prophetic day in end-times prophecy represents a fulfillment of one calendar year
- Began near the end of 458 BC when Artaxerxes I Longimanus issued his decree to rebuild Jerusalem
- The first sixty-nine weeks—or 483 calendar years—ended in late 26 AD with the baptism of Christ and the beginning of his ministry
- In the middle of the seventieth week, the Messiah would put an end to sin and "cause the sacrifice and the oblation to cease," representing Jesus' fulfillment of the Davidic Covenant
- The prophecy ended in 33 AD with the stoning of Stephen, which caused the disciples to flee Jerusalem
  - This event marked the end of the Jews' time as God's people
  - According to Acts 8:4, the disciples "that were scattered abroad went every where preaching the word" to the Gentiles

The Authenticity of Daniel
- There is a debate over when Daniel was written, but the latest possible proposed date is around 164 BC
  - This would not invalidate the prophecies predicting the rise of Rome or the Seventy Weeks Prophecy predicting the start of Jesus' ministry and crucifixion, as these were fulfilled after 164 BC
  - This would also not invalidate the day-year principle
- If any part of Daniel is a forgery, the most likely scenario is that chapters ten through twelve were added to the end of the book around 164 BC
  - These chapters refer to Antiochus IV Epiphanes in vivid detail, and the 1,290-day and 1,335-day prophecies of chapter twelve are the only prophecies in Daniel or Revelation that do not adhere to the day-year principle

4

THE APOSTASY

In II Thessalonians 2, Paul provides important pieces of evidence for when Christ's second coming will occur. Writing to the church in the town of Thessalonica, the apostle prophesied that two events would happen before Christ's return: first, he predicted a "falling away" from God, and second, the Antichrist would be revealed.

> **II Thessalonians 2:1-4**
> **1** Now we beseech you, brethren, by the coming of our Lord Jesus Christ, and by our gathering together unto him,
> **2** That ye be not soon shaken in mind, or be troubled, neither by spirit, nor by word, nor by letter as from us, as that the day of Christ is at hand.
> **3** Let no man deceive you by any means: for that day shall not come, except there come a falling away first, and that man of sin be revealed, the son of perdition;
> **4** Who opposeth and exalteth himself above all that is called God, or that is worshipped; so that he as God sitteth in the temple of God, shewing himself that he is God.

The "falling away" in II Thessalonians 2:3 is colloquially referred to as "the apostasy." An apostasy is the abandoning of a faith or a religion by an individual or group. When you first read that definition of an apostasy, did it immediately remind you of today?

Yes, Paul wrote to the Thessalonians that future Christians would turn away from God, but resist the urge to find a connection to our world today. One of the problems preventing Christians from accurately interpreting the Bible's end times is the tendency to apply these prophecies to their era. No one would disagree that people are turning away from God as fast as ever, but do not fall victim to recency bias. The apostasy described by Paul was not a gradual falling away that occurred over several decades or centuries—it was a single event in world history.

An earlier historical episode must be discussed to properly set the stage for this apostasy. Once we have done so, it will be easier to recognize the correct fulfillment of Paul's apostasy in II Thessalonians 2.

When Was the Apostasy?

The ancient empire of Babylon is a common theme in the Bible. Many scriptural references to the city are meant to be interpreted literally. However, when employed in the context of a prophecy, Babylon is typically used as a metaphor for Satan's evil in contrast with God's righteousness.

The Neo-Babylonian Empire practiced the same religion as most of the Mesopotamian region, one which was centered around a pagan sun god by the name of Shamash. After Babylon fell to the Achaemenids, its priests were allowed to continue practicing their religion, although many religious rituals were incomplete. Most of their ceremonies required the presence of a king, and the Persian kings rarely performed these religious duties. Babylon was no longer the imperial capital, so the Persian kings lived elsewhere. These kings also stopped building new temples and seldom offered gifts to Babylonian gods, which angered the people. The disregard for basic religious tasks would have been received as a failure in their duties to the gods, which meant that the Persians lacked divine recognition as the rightful kings of Babylon.[1]

After fifty-five years of Achaemenid rule, the city's residents had grown tired of their Persian masters. In July of 484 BC, a series of religious revolts occurred in Babylon against the king of the Achaemenids, Xerxes I. The Daiva inscription, written on stone tablets dating to Xerxes' reign, records the suppression of a rebellion which historians generally believe to be the Babylon revolts of 484. When the Persian army restored order in October,

Xerxes severely punished Babylon's aristocracy and religious leaders.[2] As a result of Xerxes' brutality against the Babylonians and their religion, the city's priests fled to Pergamon in modern Turkey.[3] In the Bible, Revelation 2:13 even says Satan's seat was in this city, as the successors of the pagan priests of the Mesopotamian sun cult who had escaped Babylon were still practicing there when Revelation was written.[a]

When the final king of Pergamon, Attalus III, died without an heir in 133 BC, he bequeathed his kingdom to Rome.[4] This incorporation into the Roman Republic helped to facilitate the migration of the Babylonian religion from Pergamon to Rome. The ancient sun cult quickly became almost as widely practiced as Roman paganism. In fact, Babylonian sun worship was so popular in Rome that the city was at times called "New Babylon."

Babylon's sun cult was still practiced in Rome during the fourth-century reign of Constantine. Before the 312 AD Battle of the Milvian Bridge, he and his army saw a light in the sky with an interlocked Chi-Rho symbol and the words "by this conquer." According to the contemporary Greek historian Eusebius of Caesarea, "About the time of the midday sun, when the day was just turning, he said he saw with his own eyes up in the sky and resting over the sun, a cross-shaped trophy formed from light, and a text attached to it which said, 'By this conquer.' Amazement at the spectacle seized both him and the whole company of soldiers which was then accompanying him on a campaign he was conducting somewhere, and witnessed the miracle."[5]

After the vision, Constantine debated what the sign could mean. The writings of Eusebius tell us that night, as the emperor slept, "the Christ of God appeared to him with the same sign which he had seen in the heavens, and commanded him to procure a standard made in the likeness of that sign, and to use it as a safeguard in all engagements with his enemies."[6] Emperor Constantine made a replica of the crossed Chi-Rho from his vision, ordered it to be carried at the front of his army, and won the battle over Maxentius, his rival and co-emperor.[7] The following year, Constantine issued the *Edict of Milan*, which legalized Christianity throughout the empire.

---

[a] **Revelation 2:12-13** 12 And to the angel of the church in Pergamos write; These things saith he which hath the sharp sword with two edges; 13 I know thy works, and where thou dwellest, even where Satan's seat is: and thou holdest fast my name, and hast not denied my faith, even in those days wherein Antipas was my faithful martyr, who was slain among you, where Satan dwelleth.

After his conversion, Constantine worked to convert the entire Roman Empire to Christianity. He knew this would be difficult, as the Romans were zealous pagans who were deathly afraid of upsetting their gods. Constantine determined it would be easier to merge Rome's existing pagan religion with the Christian faith rather than instantaneously attempting an abrupt, empire-wide conversion. The issue with this approach is that instead of converting the empire to Christianity, Constantine merely created a new pagan-Christian hybrid religion.

The pagan origin of this new religion poisoned the pure Christian faith and dragged unwitting believers away from God. Copies of scripture in the fourth century were difficult to come by, and aspiring Christians had limited access to them. Literacy rates in the empire were low, so most of the Romans interested in Christian ideas would have struggled to read scriptural excerpts. While these individuals believed Jesus Christ was the Son of God, they had limited knowledge of God's commandments and expectations for them in their daily lives.

Constantine's merger of Christianity with paganism fulfilled the apostasy Paul prophesied in II Thessalonians. This new religion corrupted Catholicism in God's eyes, making it no better than pure paganism. Countless believers were deceived into following meaningless tradition instead of scripture. This false version of Christianity was no longer based on God's commandments and distorted fundamental topics like salvation, repentance, and idolatry.

The distinction between faith and religion is vital to comprehend. If you are a Christian, *faith* is your firm belief that Jesus Christ is the Son of God and that he died for the forgiveness of sin based on your assessment of God's Word. *Religion* is a man-made social construct—an institutionalized system of rituals, practices, and observances built around a faith. With that difference in mind, which do you believe is more likely: that God sent his son to die for our sins to create a new *religion* or to inspire and ignite our pure, natural *faith*?

John Wesley described Paul's apostasy in a discussion on the Holy Spirit. "It does not appear that these extraordinary gifts of the Holy Ghost were common in the church for more than two or three centuries," he wrote. "We seldom hear of them after that fatal period when the Emperor Constantine called himself a Christian…the Christians had no more of the Spirit of Christ than the heathens."[8]

On February 27, 1821, Thomas Jefferson wrote to former Massachusetts senator Timothy Pickering. In the letter, he observed, "The religion-builders have so distorted and deformed the doctrines of Jesus, so muffled them in mysticisms, fancies, and falsehoods, have caricatured them into forms so monstrous and inconceivable, as to shock reasonable thinkers, to revolt them against the whole, and drive them rashly to pronounce its founder an impostor."[9] The following year, in a letter to Dr. Benjamin Waterhouse on July 19, 1822, Jefferson wrote, "Happy in the prospect of a restoration of primitive Christianity, I must leave to younger athletes to encounter and lop off the false branches which have been engrafted into it by the mythologists of the middle and modern ages."[10]

While Jefferson was certainly not a Christian, his analysis is nevertheless correct. These statements describe the apostasy of II Thessalonians 2:3—one that is not a modern or future apostasy relative to our place in history, but a falling away from the pure, organic form of the Christian *faith* observed by the early church in favor of a pagan-Christian hybrid *religion*.

The Antichrist and the Temple of God

> **II Thessalonians 2:4**
> 4 Who opposeth and exalteth himself above all that is called God, or that is worshipped; so that he as God sitteth in the temple of God, shewing himself that he is God.

According to Paul, the Antichrist would sit "as God" in "the temple of God." Two of the most important words to study in verse four are "sitteth" and "temple," both of which will provide invaluable context to understand the Antichrist's identity.

In Catholicism and some Protestant denominations, a "seat" refers to a bishop's home church and the area over which he has authority. For example, one Catholic name for Vatican City is the "Holy See." In this context, "see" originates from the Latin *sedes*, meaning "seat."[11] If the Antichrist "sitteth" in the temple of God, he will have authority over this temple.

In Koine Greek, there were two words for "temple:" ἱερόν, or *hieron*, and ναός, or *naos*. Whenever Paul used *naos*, as in II Thessalonians 2:4, he used it as a metaphor for the body of Christian believers—a spiritual temple rather than a physical building.[12] According to *The Pulpit Commentary*, this use of *naos* "is a favourite metaphor of Paul to compare believers in particular, or the Church in general, to the temple of God."[13]

When we examine the meanings of these two Greek words, we can piece together the original intent of Paul's prophecy. Paul was writing that the seat of the Antichrist—the area he would have authority and power over—would be those who believed in Jesus Christ.[14]

But the Antichrist would go even further—he would sit "as God" and "show himself that he is God." Not only would the Antichrist have religious authority over those who believe in Jesus Christ, but he would be elevated to a god-like position and present himself as if he were God on earth.

The Restrainer

In Paul's time, the Antichrist had not been revealed because a powerful force was holding him back. The King James Version calls this figure the "withholder." Several other English translations, such as the New King James Version and the New American Standard Bible, use the more modernized designation "the restrainer."[15] Paul tells us that this restrainer must be "taken out of the way" before the Antichrist can ascend to power.

> **II Thessalonians 2:6-10**
> **6** And now ye know what withholdeth that he might be revealed in his time.
> **7** For the mystery of iniquity doth already work: only he who now letteth will let, until he be taken out of the way.
> **8** And then shall that Wicked be revealed, whom the Lord shall consume with the spirit of his mouth, and shall destroy with the brightness of his coming:
> **9** Even him, whose coming is after the working of Satan with all power and signs and lying wonders,
> **10** And with all deceivableness of unrighteousness in them that perish; because they received not the love of the truth, that they might be saved.

Paul wrote that the "mystery of iniquity" was already secretly at work in the background during his time, but the restrainer was far too powerful for the Antichrist to come out of the shadows. Once the restrainer is removed, he will no longer inhibit the Antichrist's power. In the chapter *The Antichrist Revealed*, we will identify who this restrainer was.

Chapter Synopsis

- Paul wrote that two things would occur before Jesus' second coming: a falling away from God and the revealing of the Antichrist
- The apostasy occurred in 312 AD when Constantine merged the pagan sun cult practiced in Rome with Christianity to make it easier to convert the Romans
    - This turned pure Christianity into an impure pagan-Christian hybrid
- The Antichrist would have authority over the believers in Jesus Christ
- The Antichrist would "as God sitteth in the temple of God, shewing himself that he is God"
    - He would elevate himself to a god-like position and present himself as if he were God on earth
    - Each time Paul used the Greek word *naos* for "temple," he intended it as a metaphor for the body of believers, not a physical building
    - This means the Antichrist would falsely claim to be a Christian
- When II Thessalonians 2 was written, the power of the Antichrist was inhibited by an even stronger leader called the "restrainer" who had yet to be removed

II

BABYLON AND THE ANTICHRIST

5

MYSTERY BABYLON

John's Vision

Revelation 17 contains one of the most curious and intriguing prophecies in the entire Bible. In this vision, an angel carries John to the wilderness and shows him a strange woman named Mystery Babylon. The first six verses of the chapter illustrate John's account in remarkable detail. After describing what he saw, John admits the experience left him perplexed. Fortunately, the rest of the chapter contains the angel's interpretation of the prophecy.

Be sure to keep an open mind and allow the facts to shape your opinion about the message God is attempting to convey to us through Revelation 17. The prophecy of Mystery Babylon may be uncomfortable for those who have never studied it honestly. Still, it must be understood if we are to avoid the religious deceptions added over the centuries to disguise her identity. Only then can we know the truth of what God is showing us through John's vision of Mystery Babylon.

> **Revelation 17:1-2**
> 1 And there came one of the seven angels which had the seven vials, and talked with me, saying unto me, Come hither; I will shew unto thee the judgment of the great whore that sitteth upon many waters:
> 2 With whom the kings of the earth have committed fornication, and the inhabitants of the earth have been made drunk with the wine of her fornication.

An allegory of a woman is common in Biblical symbolism and is regularly used in prophecy as a metaphor for the church. If the woman is a virgin or has no defined sexual history—including in II Corinthians 11, Ephesians 5, and Revelation 12—she represents the true church. But in the prophecy in Revelation 17, the woman is a prostitute. Since a virgin represents God's true church, in contrast, a prostitute must be a false church. And Mystery Babylon is not just any prostitute—she is a "*great* whore."

When inviting John to go see Mystery Babylon, the angel tells him this woman "sitteth upon many waters." According to the angel's explanation in verse fifteen, the water represents people, multitudes, nations, and languages. The sensible inference is that Mystery Babylon signifies a false church with an international reach, comprised of people from around the world.

> **Revelation 17:15**
> **15** And he saith unto me, The waters which thou sawest, where the whore sitteth, are peoples, and multitudes, and nations, and tongues.

The angel also informs John that "the kings of the earth have committed fornication" with Mystery Babylon and that "the inhabitants of the earth have been made drunk with the wine of her fornication." Here, the angel provides background information about Mystery Babylon before John sees her. This evidence is enormously important to interpret the prophecy accurately and provides insight that cannot be gleaned from the visual cues within the vision itself. The angel informed John that world leaders would collaborate with this false church and contribute to her innumerable sins, suggesting that Mystery Babylon significantly influences geopolitical issues.

> **Revelation 17:3-5**
> **3** So he carried me away in the spirit into the wilderness: and I saw a woman sit upon a scarlet-colored beast, full of names of blasphemy, having seven heads and ten horns.
> **4** And the woman was arrayed in purple and scarlet color, and decked with gold and precious stones and pearls, having a golden cup in her hand full of abominations and filthiness of her fornication:
> **5** And upon her forehead was a name written, MYSTERY BABYLON THE GREAT, THE MOTHER OF HARLOTS AND ABOMINATIONS OF THE EARTH.

Once John finds himself in the wilderness, he sees the prostitute sitting on top of a seven-headed, ten-horned, scarlet beast. The woman is dressed in purple and scarlet clothing, adorned with gold, precious stones, and pearls, and holding a gold cup. The colors of her clothing, description of her jewelry, and her gold cup are all important clues that will help determine what she represents, so keep verse four in mind as you form your opinions.

The beast Mystery Babylon sat upon is described similarly to the seven-headed dragon in Revelation 12, which John explicitly identifies as Satan.[1] The parallels in the imagery between the two visions strongly imply that the two beasts are closely related. This correlation indicates the false church of Mystery Babylon is erected upon the back of Satan and his false religion of pagan idolatry.

> **Revelation 17:6**
> 6 And I saw the woman drunken with the blood of the saints, and with the blood of the martyrs of Jesus: and when I saw her, I wondered with great admiration.

Mystery Babylon's malicious character becomes even more troubling in verse six, which warns that the woman would be "drunken with the blood of the saints, and with the blood of the martyrs of Jesus." The implication is that this prostitute represents not only a Satanic false church, but one that would violently murder Christians. Mystery Babylon even enjoys slaughtering Christians to the point of drunkenness as if murder were a festivity.

Descriptive imagery like this makes it clear that Mystery Babylon is not a friend of Christianity. As a false church, she disguises herself as Christian—attempting to deceive believers through false teaching—while simultaneously using violence against true Christians for their beliefs.

> **Revelation 17:7-8**
> 7 And the angel said unto me, Wherefore didst thou marvel? I will tell thee the mystery of the woman, and of the beast that carrieth her, which hath the seven heads and ten horns.
> 8 The beast that thou sawest was, and is not; and shall ascend out of the bottomless pit, and go into perdition: and they that dwell on the earth shall wonder, whose names were not written in the book of life from the foundation of the world, when they behold the beast that was, and is not, and yet is.

After the angel sees John staring at the prostitute and the beast on which she sat, he asks John, "Wherefore didst thou marvel?" He then proceeds to tell John the meaning of the vision in detail. First, he describes three stages of the beast: "was," "is not," and "yet is." Initially, the angel only lists the first two stages—"was" in the past tense and "is not" in the present tense. This implies the beast was in the "is not" stage when John experienced this vision in the first century. Later in verse eight, the angel looks to the future and adds the "yet is" stage.

Next, we learn the beast would arise out of Hell at some point but will eventually go into perdition—the final state of God's judgment and eternal damnation. The angel also tells John that anyone whose name was not written in the Book of Life—the list of all those who will receive eternal life—will admire the beast.

> **Revelation 17:9-10**
> 9 And here is the mind which hath wisdom. The seven heads are seven mountains, on which the woman sitteth.
> 10 And there are seven kings: five are fallen, and one is, and the other is not yet come; and when he cometh, he must continue a short space.

Verse nine provides the angel's explanation for the meaning behind the beast's seven heads and ten horns. The phrase, "here is the mind which hath wisdom," at the start of verse nine means that anyone relatively perceptive can understand where this false church is located. The Contemporary English Version is even more direct in its translation, plainly declaring, "Anyone with wisdom can figure this out."

The seven heads are a clue to the location of the false church of Mystery Babylon. The angel tells John that the church is sitting on seven mountains. Although the King James translators chose "mountains" for the Greek word ορη, the Good News Translation, New Living Translation, Amplified Bible, Weymouth New Testament, New American Bible, and the New International Version all chose to translate it as "hills." The identity of the seven-hilled city would have been evident to anyone alive when John wrote Revelation in the late first century. At the time, as is still the case today, the "city of seven hills" was a common epithet for Rome.[2]

The angel then reveals a second meaning behind the beast's seven heads. He tells John they also represent seven kings, of which five had fallen, one was in power in John's time, and the seventh had yet to arrive. He also reveals that this future king would only hold his power for a "short space" of time. Since the seven heads indicate the location of Mystery Babylon, it would be logical to expect these seven kings to do so as well. Because the false church sits in the seven-hilled city of Rome, the kings should also be Roman.

As was the case in Daniel 7:24, "kings" does not mean individual rulers but the leadership positions of kingdoms over time. These seven leaders are directly tied to Rome, but exactly which roles they signify is not as apparent. Many Bible commentators agree that the five fallen kings represent the first types of Roman leaders—kings, consuls, tribunes, decemvirs, and dictators—but there is some debate among scholars on which forms of government the sixth and seventh kings represent. Some commentators, including Matthew Poole, believed the sixth king—the king who "is" during John's time—was the pagan emperors, while the seventh king was the Christian emperors.[3] The problem with this interpretation is that it ignores the fact that both the pagan and Christian emperors were all emperors.

The emperors ruling Rome in the first century when John's Revelation was written were pagans. They held power for 338 years—from Augustus' ascension as the first Roman emperor in 27 BC until Constantine's 312 AD conversion to Christianity. The Christian emperors ruled for 164 years until the fall of Rome in 476 AD. For Rome's Christian emperors to be the seventh king, 164 years would need to be interpreted as a "short space." A more likely assertion is that the sixth king represented all Roman emperors, both pagan and Christian. So, which leadership position followed the emperors and only ruled in Rome for a short time?

The reign of the emperors ended with the fall of the Roman Empire in 476 AD. The conquering general, Odoacer, took the title *Rex Italiae*, or "King of Italy," until his assassination seventeen years later, in 493. Including the Ostrogothic leaders who took the same title from 493 until the end of their occupation of Rome in 538 would only constitute a sixty-two-year reign. Compared to the emperors' five centuries of power, sixty-two years would easily be labeled a "short space." This would also be significantly shorter than the 164-year reign of Christian emperors in Matthew Poole's interpretation.

After interpreting the beast's seven heads as seven kings, the angel makes an astonishing proclamation about what this creature represents.

> **Revelation 17:11-13**
> 11 And the beast that was, and is not, even he is the eighth, and is of the seven, and goeth into perdition.
> 12 And the ten horns which thou sawest are ten kings, which have received no kingdom as yet; but receive power as kings one hour with the beast.
> 13 These have one mind, and shall give their power and strength unto the beast.

The angel tells John that the beast "is the eighth, and is of the seven." If the seven heads represent the hills and kings of Rome, the beast will also. This means the Antichrist who leads this false church would be the eighth type of king of Rome, becoming the city's leader after the Kings of Italy.

The beast is a reference to the idolatrous religion of the Antichrist. If the beast is a false religion and Mystery Babylon is this religion's false church, the reason the prostitute is sitting on the beast again becomes clear. While the seven heads indicate Rome as the site of Mystery Babylon, the Antichrist's idolatry would support the false church. Mystery Babylon sat on the beast, just as the church she represents was built upon Satan's religious doctrine.

The ten horns mentioned in verse twelve refer to the same ten horns of the fourth beast in Daniel 7. In Revelation 17:3, the ten horns are on the beast's seven heads, so their corresponding kings should come from Rome, just as Daniel's ten kings did. The angel also told John that these kings had not yet come to power by 95 AD. Like Daniel's ten kings, they received their dominions after the Roman Empire collapsed into ten smaller kingdoms.

John also learns that the Antichrist would receive his power from these kingdoms, which would "share one mind" with him. This indicates that the Antichrist would think similarly to the kingdoms, including sharing the same religion. After the fall of Rome, these ten kingdoms covered most of the geographical region of early organized Christendom, so the Antichrist should have similar beliefs. In verse fourteen, we learn that the ten kingdoms would also "make war with"—or persecute—Christ and his faithful followers. If these kingdoms must persecute Christians and share the same mind with the pseudo-Christian Antichrist, they must also mistakenly believe themselves to be Christians.

> **Revelation 17:14**
> **14** These shall make war with the Lamb, and the Lamb shall overcome them: for he is Lord of lords, and King of kings: and they that are with him are called, and chosen, and faithful.

The chapter's final verse offers one of the last clues to Mystery Babylon's identity. The angel concludes his interpretation of the vision by telling John that the false church is also a city that "reigneth over the kings of the earth," which suggests that she would have some level of control over the world's political leaders.

> **Revelation 17:18**
> **18** And the woman which thou sawest is that great city, which reigneth over the kings of the earth.

Chapter Synopsis

Mystery Babylon
- Mystery Babylon is described in Revelation 17 as a "great whore," which in prophecy means a significant false church (Revelation 17:1)
- It is comprised of many different types of people, languages, and nations from around the world (Revelation 17:15)
- It holds influence over world leaders, committing sins, or "fornication," with the "kings of the earth" (Revelation 17:2, 17:18)
- It is located on seven hills—the city of Rome (Revelation 17:9)
- Her beast would be the eighth king of Rome (Revelation 17:10)
- The eighth hill and eighth king are "of the seven" (Revelation 17:11)
  - This means Mystery Babylon would be associated with an eighth hill of Rome, and the Antichrist would reign as the eighth king of Rome after the Kings of Italy left the city in 538 AD
- It would receive its power from the ten kingdoms that arose from the fallen Roman Empire (Revelation 17:12-13, 17:17)
- It would be "drunken with the blood of the saints, and with the blood of the martyrs of Jesus" (Revelation 17:6)
- "Arrayed in purple and scarlet color and decked with gold and precious stones and pearls, having a golden cup in her hand" (Revelation 17:4)
- Written on her forehead was "Mystery Babylon the Great, the Mother of Harlots and Abominations of the Earth" (Revelation 17:5)
- Anyone whose names are not written in the Book of Life and will not receive eternal life shall look upon her with wonder (Revelation 17:8)
- The beast that Mystery Babylon sat upon "was, and is not, and yet is" (Revelation 17:8)
- Mystery Babylon is also a city that "reigneth over the kings of the earth" (Revelation 17:18)

6

MYSTERY SOLVED

Today's religious scholars assign various identities to Mystery Babylon—including the United States of America, the United Nations, a future global governmental system, and more. However, none of these identities satisfy all, or even most, of the descriptive elements provided in the Bible.

Mystery Babylon represents the Roman Catholic Church. Catholicism did not exist at the time of John's exile on the isle of Patmos, so its identity would not have been clear to him. Still, God provided this prophecy so that later Christians could recognize the Catholic Church for what it was. If you are not convinced, this chapter will scrutinize each element of the description of Mystery Babylon individually to help you see how John's vision points to the Roman Catholic Church.

Why Mystery Babylon Is the Roman Catholic Church

Mystery Babylon Is a Prostitute

According to the angel, Mystery Babylon is a prostitute. From the name etched across her forehead, we also know that she is the mother of all other prostitutes. Because a prostitute represents a false church in prophecy, this woman characterizes not only a pseudo-Christian church herself but also the mother of all other false churches.

Astonishingly, in 1564 AD, after the Council of Trent, Pius IV published an oath that he claimed must be observed to qualify for eternal life. The oath read, in part, "I recognize the Holy Catholic and Apostolic Roman Church as *the mother and mistress of all churches*; and I promise and swear true obedience to the Roman pontiff, successor of St. Peter, prince of the apostles, and vicar of Jesus Christ."[1] The pope himself published an oath describing the Catholic Church in the same way the Bible describes Mystery Babylon—as the mother of all other churches and a mistress, which implies sexual promiscuity—and he did so *after* the Protestant Reformers identified the Catholic Church as Mystery Babylon.

The significance of the name "Mystery Babylon" is also impossible to disregard. The word "mystery" is a synonym for deception or secrecy—an obfuscated religion that is not clearly understood. Babylon is repeatedly used throughout the Bible as a representation of Satan's evil forces in contrast with the goodness of God. We know the priests of the Babylonian sun cult fled to Pergamon after the religious revolts of 484 BC and migrated to Rome once Pergamon joined the Roman Republic. Centuries later, when Constantine converted to what he believed was Christianity, he merged the early faith with Roman paganism to appease the Roman aristocracy and military leadership, most of whom remained pagan. It was through this merger that Constantine created the false church of Mystery Babylon. In his apostasy prophecy, Paul described this pagan form of Christianity as "the *mystery* of iniquity," and the symmetry of his word choice with Revelation 17 does not seem accidental.[a]

God intentionally showed John the name "Mystery Babylon the Great" on the prostitute's forehead. The name alludes to both the Babylonian origin of Catholicism and the secretive way this pagan religion has disguised itself as a Christian church—the final iteration of Babylonian paganism.

It Is Comprised of People from Around the World

The angel told John precisely what the waters in his vision signified. "The waters which thou sawest, where the whore sitteth," the angel declared, "are peoples, and multitudes, and nations, and tongues." Today, over 1.3 billion

---

[a] **II Thessalonians 2:7** For the mystery of iniquity doth already work: only he who now letteth will let, until he be taken out of the way.

people identify as Catholic. The religion is conducted in numerous languages, with a foothold in most countries.[2] The Roman Catholic Church's fulfillment of the waters in Revelation 17 is as obvious and straightforward as the angel's explanation of what the water represents.

Non-Christians Will Be Deceived

The hidden pagan identity of Mystery Babylon has conned billions into believing Catholicism is a Christian religion. Revelation 17:8 predicted this deception, saying those whose names are not found written in the Book of Life would look upon Mystery Babylon with wonder and admiration. There is a clear distinction between those who view the Catholic Church as pagan and those who do not. If your name is written in the Book of Life, you may be able to see through the deceptive *mystery* of Catholic doctrine. If it is not, you would likely be unable to see through her false Christian disguise, and you are destined for Hell.

Arrayed in Purple and Scarlet, Decked with Jewelry, Gold Cup in Her Hand

In Revelation 17:4, John describes seeing Mystery Babylon dressed in purple and scarlet. These are the same colors as the attire of the higher ranks of the Catholic clergy, where cardinals wear scarlet and non-cardinal bishops and archbishops wear purple.[3] But the illustration of Babylon's appearance goes further, describing her as "decked with gold and precious stones and pearls, having a golden cup in her hand."

Since the eighth century, popes have worn extravagant tiaras for formal ceremonies. In the fourteenth century, these ornate tiaras took on a triple-crowned form called the triregnum. Papal tiaras are always adorned with gold and precious stones and usually include pearls. The mitre is a less formal, pointed hat embroidered with gold thread, often containing precious stones and pearls. In fact, most pieces of papal regalia—including the falda, fanon, mantum, and chasuble—at least contain gold embroidery.

John could see these signs of Mystery Babylon's material riches in his vision. But the golden cup in her hand was not about wealth—it was a direct reference to Catholicism's use of gold chalices when its priests perform the Eucharist ritual during masses.

Figure 9: Popes wearing the triregnum and other vestments with gold, precious stones, and pearls.
(Top, from left) Pope Gregory IX, various popes from the Ghent Altarpiece, Sixtus IV.
(Bottom, from left) Pope Gregory XII, Pius VI, Leo XIII.

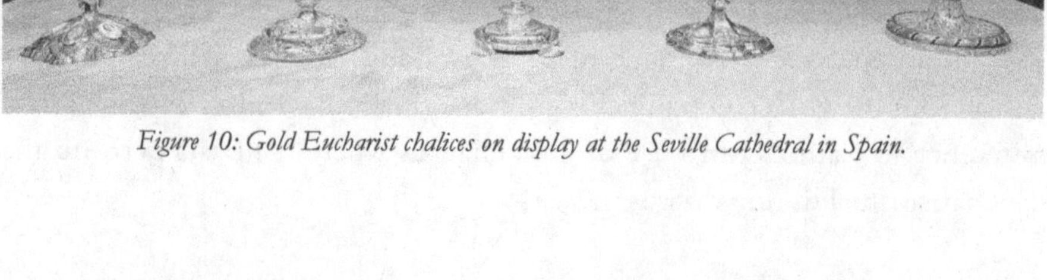

Figure 10: Gold Eucharist chalices on display at the Seville Cathedral in Spain.

It Is Located on Seven Hills

The Servian Walls were the only defensive walls encircling Rome from their construction in 378 BC until the late third century AD. For most of its history, the size of the empire was the city's primary defense. By the time any foreign incursions reached Rome, reinforcements stationed elsewhere in the empire could come to the city's aid.

As the empire weakened, the city began to be threatened militarily more regularly. The centuries-old Servian Walls had become obsolete and would not have withstood a siege from more advanced militaries. In 275 AD, the emperor Aurelian built new walls around the city to defend it more effectively against outside threats. These colossal walls still stand today as a testament to ancient Rome's former strength.

During antiquity, Rome was widely known as the "city of seven hills," based on the number of hills within the limits of the original Servian Walls.[4] When John wrote Revelation in the first century, the city had expanded far beyond the Servian Walls, but the moniker persisted. This nickname is still so famous today that dozens of modern cities have adopted it to associate with the legacy of ancient Rome.[5] Anyone in the first century who read a letter that mentioned a seven-hilled location would have interpreted it as Rome. The apostle Peter, believed to have written the epistle of I Peter in Rome, even referred to the city as "Babylon" in I Peter 5:13. This suggests that he knew of the link between the city of seven hills and Babylon.[b]

The Eighth Hill and Eighth King Are "Of the Seven"

The Catholic identity of Mystery Babylon gives us the answer to how the beast represents an eighth hill of Rome. Another hill lies outside of the city's original walls, just west of the Tiber. Tradition holds that the apostle Peter was crucified and buried on this hill, as were many other early Christians. By the fourth century, the tombs of the apostles and early Christians martyred there were still visible. In 322 AD, Emperor Constantine built the first Saint Peter's Basilica over their graves—on Vatican Hill.

---

[b] **I Peter 5:13** The church that is at Babylon, elected together with you, saluteth you; and so doth Marcus my son.

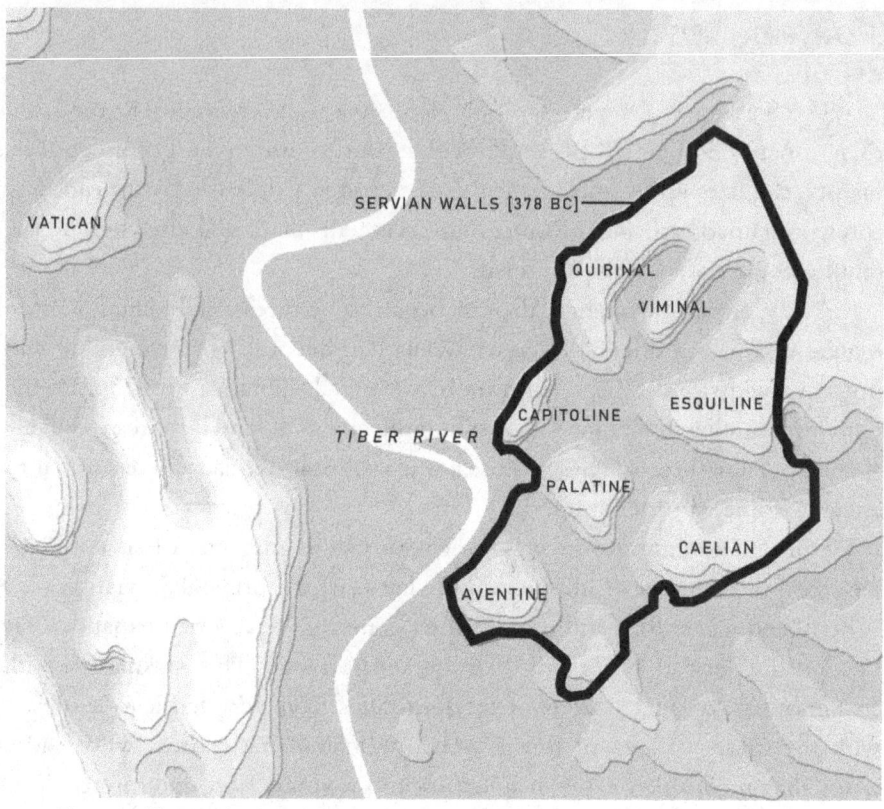

Figure 11: Topographical map of the seven hills of Rome within the city's ancient Servian Walls.

It Was, and Is Not, and Yet Is

Revelation 17:8 says the scarlet beast would have three distinct phases: "was," "is not," and "yet is." These stages help bring the identity of the scarlet beast into focus. In his *A Commentary on the Holy Bible*, Matthew Henry wrote, "The beast on which the woman sat was, and is not, and yet is. It was a seat of idolatry and persecution, and is not; not in the ancient form, which was pagan: yet it is; it is truly the seat of idolatry and tyranny, though of another sort and form. It would deceive into stupid and blind submission all the inhabitants of the earth within its influence, except the remnant of the elect."[6] Similarly to its seven heads, the beast itself has two fulfillments. The angel reveals it represents the eighth king of Rome, but it also represents an anti-Christian, idolatrous religion on an eighth hill—an evil, Satanic religious force in opposition to true faith in God—which was, is not, and would be again.

Its representation as the seat of idolatry and persecution becomes more evident when you consider when Revelation was written. The idolatrous sun cult had a seat in Babylon until the revolts of 484 BC and was resurrected after the creation of Roman Catholicism. Revelation was written between these two periods, which explains why the angel conveyed to John that this pagan religion "is not" during his lifetime.

It Would Receive Its Power from Ten Future Kingdoms

Nebuchadnezzar and Daniel experienced their dreams of four empires more than a millennium before the 476 AD fall of Rome. Their dreams both contained predictions that the last empire would fragment into ten kingdoms. Nebuchadnezzar's dream alluded to the ten kingdoms, as the statue's iron legs and feet divided into ten toes, though this interpretation is not explicitly mentioned in the prophecy.[7] Daniel's account of his dream contained a direct declaration on the fate of the Roman beast, as the angel unequivocally said, "The ten horns out of this kingdom are ten kings that shall arise."[8]

Like Daniel, John saw ten horns on the heads of the scarlet beast Mystery Babylon sat upon. The angel in John's vision explained that these ten horns also represented ten kings who had yet to come to power at the time of his vision. John received this vision at the height of Rome's dominance, nearly four centuries before the empire's fall brought the ten kingdoms to power.[9]

It Will Have "Made War with the Saints, and Prevailed Against Them"

During the Middle Ages and Counter-Reformation, the Catholic Church was responsible for the deaths of an incredible number of Christian martyrs. While the exact number is impossible to calculate accurately, many experts have attempted to come close. Modern Catholic sources range in the tens of thousands, as they underestimate the staggering numbers to hide their history of genocides and atrocities. On the contrary, Protestants frequently cite death totals in the tens of millions, occasionally as high as fifty million or more.

While both the lower and higher estimates are likely biased exaggerations, the number of Christians slaughtered by the Catholic Church is easily in the millions. If the deaths that resulted from the European Wars of Religion are included, the estimates in the tens of millions could certainly be realized over more than twelve hundred years.[10]

Ultimately, the actual number of Christians murdered by the Vatican is inconsequential. What is important is that the Catholic Church—a church that is supposed to be Christian—spent centuries slaughtering Christians by the thousands, fulfilling the prophecies that anticipated Mystery Babylon's maniacal bloodlust against true Christians.

It Holds Great Influence Over World Leaders

Revelation 17:2 prophesied that "the kings of the earth have committed fornication" with Mystery Babylon. The Catholic Church undoubtedly holds great influence over leaders in politics, international banking, entertainment, business, and other fields. Heads of state, legislators, and political candidates often meet with the pope. It is common for popes to issue calls to action to world leaders on a variety of issues, including those unrelated to religion.

Mystery Babylon Is a City That "Reigneth Over the Kings of the Earth"

While capital cities reign over countries, only one city can be described as reigning over all the kings of the earth—Vatican City. Throughout history, the papacy has exerted immeasurable control over politics. While heads of state are sovereign leaders, the papacy's power comes from claims of religious and moral authority. Medieval kings and political leaders craved the pope's endorsement and feared angering him. Popes claimed to have the power to excommunicate anyone who crossed them, supposedly banishing them to Hell. A dispute with the pope could take away political legitimacy, forcing subjects to choose between obeying their king or their pope.

The pope's political control only grew after the Protestant Reformation began. During the period that historians call the Counter-Reformation, the Catholic Church created a plan to respond to the Protestants. This response included the foundation of the Jesuits, who would eventually become known as the "shock troops of the Counter-Reformation." The Jesuit Order secretly infiltrated governments and institutions around the world, including various Protestant denominations, to influence and control politics and religion in their struggle against true Christianity.[11]

Figure 12: Illustration in Martin Luther's translation of the New Testament showing Mystery Babylon wearing a papal tiara. Woodcut by Lucas Cranach the Elder, 1522.

God's Warning About Mystery Babylon

> **Revelation 18:4-5**
> 4 And I heard another voice from heaven, saying, Come out of her, my people, that ye be not partakers of her sins, and that ye receive not of her plagues.
> 5 For her sins have reached unto heaven, and God hath remembered her iniquities.

When reading these verses, you can sense the agony and urgency in the mysterious voice's words as it desperately pleads with believers to abandon Catholicism. It warns us that if we remain in the Catholic Church, we will be "partakers of her sins" and will share in her punishments.

Catholic apologists will have you believe Mystery Babylon is not a false church. They claim it is anything from the United States to a future one-world government. The United States was not founded on seven hills, nor is it a false church, a "great city," or made up of many nations, so it clearly cannot fulfill the prophecy of Mystery Babylon. The warning to "come out of her" means we would be free to leave it, which is impossible under a one-world government. Preterists identify her as the Roman Empire, which was also not a false church, nor was it "many nations." The Roman Empire did not receive its power from the ten kingdoms since they did not exist until after the empire collapsed. Also, the empire fell in 476 AD, more than four centuries after the Preterists' supposed 70 AD second coming of Christ.

It is essential to allow the Biblical text to speak for itself. The evidence provided in Revelation 17 is straightforward and makes Mystery Babylon easy to identify. It should be clear from their false interpretations that the Futurists and Preterists are uninterested in discovering the accurate fulfillments for Mystery Babylon and the rest of Revelation. The motive behind their deceit is clear—to help the Roman Catholic Church preserve its pseudo-Christian illusions and prevent it from being exposed as a pagan false church.

The warning for believers to leave Catholicism should also help to clarify Jesus' unnerving prediction in Matthew 7:21-23. Out of context, these verses may be terrifying to Christians. Is Jesus telling us that there will be Christians who believe they did everything God expects of them in life, but were still not good enough to enter Heaven?

> **Matthew 7:21-23**
> **21** Not every one that saith unto me, Lord, Lord, shall enter into the kingdom of heaven; but he that doeth the will of my Father which is in heaven.
> **22** Many will say to me in that day, Lord, Lord, have we not prophesied in thy name? and in thy name have cast out devils? and in thy name done many wonderful works?
> **23** And then will I profess unto them, I never knew you: depart from me, ye that work iniquity.

Three critical elements in these verses could identify the poor souls who will fall into this category. First, these people do believe Jesus is the Messiah, as evidenced by the fact that they call him "Lord." Second, the phrase, "but he that doeth the will of my Father which is in heaven," informs us that only those who follow God's commandments and act in accordance with his will while on earth will receive eternal life. The last phrase to scrutinize is "ye that work iniquity." Jesus is warning that those people who believe in him but continue to sin will be denied admittance into Heaven.

Faith Without Works Is Dead

Jesus' words in Matthew 7 reverberate through James 2, which proclaims four times that "faith without works is dead." So, if the Bible makes it clear that works are an essential and necessary part of the equation, why do so many Protestants alive today believe that faith in Jesus Christ is all that is needed for salvation?

The Protestant Reformers and their pre-Reformation predecessors were not infallible. One example of theological error was the belief that many held in the concept of *sola fide*, meaning "faith alone." Sola fide holds that faith in Jesus Christ is sufficient for salvation—if you believe in him, you will receive eternal life—nothing else is required. The theory is heavily reliant on Paul's words in Ephesians 2:8-9.

> **Ephesians 2:8-9**
> **8** For by grace are ye saved through faith; and that not of yourselves: it is the gift of God:
> **9** Not of works, lest any man should boast.

However, Ephesians 2:8-9 sets faith in Jesus as the *minimum* standard for salvation; it does not eliminate works as a contributing factor. These verses explain that God's grace allows those of us who have faith in Jesus to receive eternal life. Without the combination of his grace and our faith, we cannot be saved, no matter how good of a person we are. Paul was not saying faith alone will get us into Heaven—he was saying works alone will not.

Sola fide contradicts the Bible in several ways. In I Corinthians 6:9-10 and Galatians 5:19-21, Paul wrote that many actions could disqualify us from Heaven. If works were not a part of the criteria to get into Heaven, why would they keep us out? Paul gave us these two lists of works Christians must avoid so we could "inherit the kingdom of God." Those who fall into these categories of sinners may believe in Jesus Christ, but according to Paul, their sins will prohibit them from reaching Heaven.

> **I Corinthians 6:9-10**
> **9** Know ye not that the unrighteous shall not inherit the kingdom of God? Be not deceived: neither fornicators, nor idolaters, nor adulterers, nor effeminate, nor abusers of themselves with mankind,
> **10** Nor thieves, nor covetous, nor drunkards, nor revilers, nor extortioners, shall inherit the kingdom of God.

> **Galatians 5:19-21**
> **19** Now the works of the flesh are manifest, which are these; Adultery, fornication, uncleanness, lasciviousness,
> **20** Idolatry, witchcraft, hatred, variance, emulations, wrath, strife, seditions, heresies,
> **21** Envyings, murders, drunkenness, revellings, and such like: of the which I tell you before, as I have also told you in time past, that they which do such things shall not inherit the kingdom of God.

If doctrinally correct, sola fide would be a free pass to sin. People could commit any sin they want and still reach Heaven if they believe Jesus Christ is the Son of God who died for our sins. This is not how God wants his followers to behave. The epistle of James plainly declares that "faith without works is dead." This means those who believe in Jesus must also act in a way that glorifies God to receive eternal life.

MYSTERY SOLVED

> **James 2:14-26**
> **14** What doth it profit, my brethren, though a man say he hath faith, and have not works? can faith save him?
> **15** If a brother or sister be naked, and destitute of daily food,
> **16** And one of you say unto them, Depart in peace, be ye warmed and filled; notwithstanding ye give them not those things which are needful to the body; what doth it profit?
> **17** Even so faith, if it hath not works, is dead, being alone.
> **18** Yea, a man may say, Thou hast faith, and I have works: shew me thy faith without thy works, and I will shew thee my faith by my works.
> **19** Thou believest that there is one God; thou doest well: the devils also believe, and tremble.
> **20** But wilt thou know, O vain man, that faith without works is dead?
> **21** Was not Abraham our father justified by works, when he had offered Isaac his son upon the altar?
> **22** Seest thou how faith wrought with his works, and by works was faith made perfect?
> **23** And the scripture was fulfilled which saith, Abraham believed God, and it was imputed unto him for righteousness: and he was called the Friend of God.
> **24** Ye see then how that by works a man is justified, and not by faith only.
> **25** Likewise also was not Rahab the harlot justified by works, when she had received the messengers, and had sent them out another way?
> **26** For as the body without the spirit is dead, so faith without works is dead also.

Also, what is the purpose of judgment day if works are not considered? If all God needs to determine is whether we believe in Jesus Christ, what is he judging? Many examples are found throughout the New Testament of works being judged by God,[c] and when John saw his vision of three angels in Revelation 14, the third angel explained that the works of those who died

---

[c] **Matthew 16:27** For the Son of man shall come in the glory of his Father with his angels; and then he shall reward every man according to his works.
 John 5:27-29 27 And hath given him authority to execute judgment also, because he is the Son of man. 28 Marvel not at this: for the hour is coming, in the which all that are in the graves shall hear his voice, 29 And shall come forth; they that have done good, unto the resurrection of life; and they that have done evil, unto the resurrection of damnation.
 Revelation 20:12 And I saw the dead, small and great, stand before God; and the books were opened: and another book was opened, which is the book of life: and the dead were judged out of those things which were written in the books, according to their works.

in Christ would follow them.ᵈ The things we do during our time on earth—both good and bad—will be judged by God. If sola fide is correct, murderers and thieves who believe Jesus Christ is the Son of God would still be granted eternal life despite their immorality. For this reason, faith in Christ does not provide believers the freedom to sin.

In Matthew 19, a rich man asks Jesus how he could receive eternal life. In response, Jesus says he needs to follow God's commands. When the man presses for specifics, Jesus lists four sins and two good works as examples.

> **Matthew 19:16-19**
> **16** And, behold, one came and said unto him, Good Master, what good thing shall I do, that I may have eternal life?
> **17** And he said unto him, Why callest thou me good? there is none good but one, that is, God: but if thou wilt enter into life, keep the commandments.
> **18** He saith unto him, Which? Jesus said, Thou shalt do no murder, Thou shalt not commit adultery, Thou shalt not steal, Thou shalt not bear false witness,
> **19** Honour thy father and thy mother: and, Thou shalt love thy neighbour as thyself.

These are some of the commandments against which our lives will be measured by God. After Jesus provided his advice, the man claimed he had followed God's directives since childhood. He then asked, "What lack I yet?"

> **Matthew 19:21-24**
> **21** Jesus said unto him, If thou wilt be perfect, go and sell that thou hast, and give to the poor, and thou shalt have treasure in heaven: and come and follow me.
> **22** But when the young man heard that saying, he went away sorrowful: for he had great possessions.
> **23** Then said Jesus unto his disciples, Verily I say unto you, That a rich man shall hardly enter into the kingdom of heaven.
> **24** And again I say unto you, It is easier for a camel to go through the eye of a needle, than for a rich man to enter into the kingdom of God.

ᵈ **Revelation 14:12-13** 12 Here is the patience of the saints: here are they that keep the commandments of God, and the faith of Jesus. 13 And I heard a voice from heaven saying unto me, Write, Blessed are the dead which die in the Lord from henceforth: Yea, saith the Spirit, that they may rest from their labours; and their works do follow them.

Here was a wealthy young man who believed in Jesus and had kept God's commandments since childhood. Despite his faith and adherence to God's instructions, he was used as an example of how difficult it is for the wealthy to enter Heaven. For all the sins he avoided, he was not fully committed to Jesus, as his wealth prevented him from helping the poor. As James wrote, "If a brother or sister be naked, and destitute of daily food, And one of you say unto them, Depart in peace, be ye warmed and filled; notwithstanding ye give them not those things which are needful to the body; what doth it profit? Even so faith, if it hath not works, is dead, being alone." It was his inability to accumulate treasures in Heaven by giving to those who needed help that prevented this rich man from being worthy of salvation. The story reaffirms Jesus' eloquent guidance found in Matthew 6, when he said, "For where your treasure is, there will your heart be also."[e]

God does not expect us to sell all our possessions. The concept of tithing originated in the Old Testament books of Genesis and Leviticus. A tithe was generally measured as one-tenth of a person's agricultural output, though it could be applied to other assets.[f] Melchizedek, the priest and king of Salem, blessed Abraham in Genesis 14. As a thanks for his blessing, Abraham gave him a tithe of all his spoils from battle.[g] Separately, after receiving a blessing from God in Genesis 28, Jacob promised him one-tenth of his possessions.[h]

In Mosaic law, tithes went to the priests of the Temple. However, the New Testament does not clarify whether tithes must go to churches under the New Covenant or can be given to other good causes that advance God's will, such as helping the poor, the widowed, and orphans.[i]

---

[e] **Matthew 6:19-21** 19 Lay not up for yourselves treasures upon earth, where moth and rust doth corrupt, and where thieves break through and steal: 20 But lay up for yourselves treasures in heaven, where neither moth nor rust doth corrupt, and where thieves do not break through nor steal: 21 For where your treasure is, there will your heart be also.

[f] **Leviticus 27:30** And all the tithe of the land, whether of the seed of the land, or of the fruit of the tree, is the Lord's: it is holy unto the Lord.

[g] **Genesis 14:20** And blessed be the most high God, which hath delivered thine enemies into thy hand. And he gave him tithes of all.

[h] **Genesis 28:22** And this stone, which I have set for a pillar, shall be God's house: and of all that thou shalt give me I will surely give the tenth unto thee.

[i] **James 1:27** Pure religion and undefiled before God and the Father is this, To visit the fatherless and widows in their affliction, and to keep himself unspotted from the world.

Whether God intended for tithes to be given to the modern church or used for any works that glorify him, there is no limitation on giving above the ten percent threshold of tithes, just like the advice Jesus gave to the rich man. In II Corinthians 9:7, Paul said we should not give "grudgingly, or of necessity: for God loveth a cheerful giver."[j] While tithing is important, Jesus advised us to focus on more significant matters such as faith, showing mercy, and exercising good judgment.[k] Financial support is only one way we can do good works to help those in need. On judgment day, God will evaluate our faith in Christ alongside our actions, including our giving, as salvation cannot be attained through *faith alone*.

God's Judgment on Mystery Babylon

John's vision of Mystery Babylon continues into Revelation 18, which describes the fate of the Roman false church and those who do not leave her. Revelation 18:10, 18:17, and 18:19 prophesy that God's ultimate judgment on the Vatican will occur swiftly—in only one prophetic hour.

> **Revelation 18:8-10**
> **8** Therefore shall her plagues come in one day, death, and mourning, and famine; and she shall be utterly burned with fire: for strong is the Lord God who judgeth her.
> **9** And the kings of the earth, who have committed fornication and lived deliciously with her, shall bewail her, and lament for her, when they shall see the smoke of her burning,
> **10** Standing afar off for the fear of her torment, saying, Alas, alas that great city Babylon, that mighty city! for in one hour is thy judgment come.

From previous examples, we know one prophetic hour would amount to fifteen days. While the phrase "one hour" could be intended to figuratively show the swiftness of God's vengeance, the more likely interpretation is that

---

[j] **II Corinthians 9:7** Every man according as he purposeth in his heart, so let him give; not grudgingly, or of necessity: for God loveth a cheerful giver.

[k] **Matthew 23:23** Woe unto you, scribes and Pharisees, hypocrites! for ye pay tithe of mint and anise and cummin, and have omitted the weightier matters of the law, judgment, mercy, and faith: these ought ye to have done, and not to leave the other undone.

the time interval follows the day-year principle, like all the other prophecies in Revelation that contain specific time frames do.

> **Revelation 18:17-19**
> 17 For in one hour so great riches is come to nought. And every shipmaster, and all the company in ships, and sailors, and as many as trade by sea, stood afar off,
> 18 And cried when they saw the smoke of her burning, saying, What city is like unto this great city!
> 19 And they cast dust on their heads, and cried, weeping and wailing, saying, Alas, alas that great city, wherein were made rich all that had ships in the sea by reason of her costliness! for in one hour is she made desolate.

Heaven Celebrates the Destruction of Mystery Babylon

Verse twenty declares Heaven will celebrate as God avenges the deaths of the Christian martyrs slain by Mystery Babylon over the centuries. The next several verses describe the finality of the Catholic Church's destruction. Read these five verses carefully and scrutinize the text to see how well this part of the description of Mystery Babylon fits the Roman Catholic Church. If Revelation 17 was not clear enough for you to acknowledge the Catholic fulfillment of Mystery Babylon, Revelation 18:20-24 will remove all doubts.

> **Revelation 18:20-24**
> 20 Rejoice over her, thou heaven, and ye holy apostles and prophets; for God hath avenged you on her.
> 21 And a mighty angel took up a stone like a great millstone, and cast it into the sea, saying, Thus with violence shall that great city Babylon be thrown down, and shall be found no more at all.
> 22 And the voice of harpers, and musicians, and of pipers, and trumpeters, shall be heard no more at all in thee; and no craftsman, of whatsoever craft he be, shall be found any more in thee; and the sound of a millstone shall be heard no more at all in thee;
> 23 And the light of a candle shall shine no more at all in thee; and the voice of the bridegroom and of the bride shall be heard no more at all in thee: for thy merchants were the great men of the earth; for by thy sorceries were all nations deceived.
> 24 And in her was found the blood of prophets, and of saints, and of all that were slain upon the earth.

Verse twenty-two predicts, "The voice of harpers, and musicians, and of pipers, and trumpeters, shall be heard no more at all in thee." Catholic masses and rituals regularly have music performed by instrumentalists and choruses. It continues, "No craftsman, of whatsoever craft he be, shall be found any more in thee." The Roman Catholic Church commissioned many of history's greatest artists. Architects, engineers, masons, carpenters, painters, sculptors, glassworkers, jewelers, and metallurgists built and decorated its extravagant churches and cathedrals. The Renaissance would have been much different without the patronage of the church.

"The sound of a millstone shall be heard no more at all in thee" is a figurative prophecy. This phrase is remarkably similar to Mark 9:42, which contains the Bible's most recognizable reference to a millstone. In Mark 9, Jesus said it would be better for a person to drown in the sea with a millstone around his neck than be allowed to harm children.[1] In Revelation 18:21-22, a millstone is again thrown into the sea, alluding to the destruction of Mystery Babylon. In these verses, a parallel is drawn between the deceivers of children in Mark 9:42 and the Roman Catholic Church, which indoctrinates children through false dogma.

The prophecy, "The light of a candle shall shine no more at all in thee," does not require much interpretation. Advent candles, votive candles, paschal candles, baptismal candles, and more are found in every Catholic Church.

"The voice of the bridegroom and of the bride shall be heard no more at all in thee" is a straightforward reference to the weddings held in Catholic churches, a popular venue for brides and grooms.

Verse twenty-three declares, "By thy sorceries were all nations deceived." This is a reference to the way the Catholic Church has led people astray from true Christianity with false doctrine and fabricated miracles.

The Catholic Church slaughtered countless Christian martyrs during the Middle Ages and Counter-Reformation. The phrase, "In her was found the blood of prophets, and of saints, and of all that were slain upon the earth," predicts a type of evaluation where God will judge the Catholic Church for her violence against Christians.

---

[1] **Mark 9:42** And whosoever shall offend one of these little ones that believe in me, it is better for him that a millstone were hanged about his neck, and he were cast into the sea.

The Catholic Church and the Bible

Reconsider the Futurist interpretation of Mystery Babylon. The initial description of the prostitute in Revelation 17 clearly represents the Catholic Church and does not support the Futurist view. When the evidence found in Revelation 18 is also considered, is there any possible way the United States fulfills the prophecy? Could the United Nations? What about a future one-world government? Revelation's evidence can only convict one suspect—the Roman Catholic Church.

The damning evidence proving Catholicism is an anti-Christian religion is found within the pages of the Bible itself. The Vatican knew this, and it drove their actions concerning Bible ownership for centuries. Church leaders understood it was critical to conceal the identity of Mystery Babylon, and the easiest way to do so was to restrict access to the Bible itself.

While most of medieval Europe's population was illiterate, many were educated. Bibles in circulation before the fifteenth-century invention of the printing press were handwritten manuscripts, making them both expensive and scarce. Despite the high illiteracy rates, the Catholic Church still did what it could to limit Bible access for those who could read them. From the early Middle Ages until the end of the eighteenth century, any Christian found with even the smallest excerpts of scripture risked being beaten or even executed.

In a January 2, 1080 letter to King Vratislav II of Bohemia, Pope Gregory VII expressed the Catholic Church's view on Bible censorship, writing, "Not without reason has it pleased Almighty God that Holy Scripture should be a secret in certain places, lost, if it were plainly apparent to all men, perchance it would be little esteemed and be subject to disrespect; or it might be falsely understood by those of mediocre learning, and lead to error."[12]

In his 1199 *Cum ex Injuncto*, Pope Innocent III declared that any layman caught reading the Bible and ministering to others would be stoned to death. Innocent III wrote, "The mysteries of the sacraments of faith should not be explained everywhere to everyone, since they cannot be understood everywhere by everyone, but only to those who can conceive of them by their faithful intellect...Such is the profundity of divine Scripture, that not only simple and illiterate men, but even prudent and learned men do not fully suffice to investigate its wisdom. Because of this Scripture says: 'They have failed in their search.' From this it was rightly once established in divine law that the beast which touches the mountain should be stoned; that is, so that no simple and unlearned man presumes to concern himself with the sublimity of sacred Scripture, or to preach it to others."[13] The letter was later reinforced when it was codified into canon law by the Catholic Church.

In 1215, Pope Innocent III criminalized translating scripture or meeting in private gatherings outside of a church, ordering, "They shall be seized for trial and penalties, who engage in the translation of the sacred volumes, or who hold secret conventicles, or who assume the office of preaching without the authority of their superiors; against whom process shall be commenced, without any permission of appeal."[14]

If any uncertainty remained around the Roman Catholic Church's stance on Bible ownership, the Council of Toulouse removed all doubt with its 1229 decree, stating, "We prohibit also that the laity should be permitted to have the books of the Old and New Testaments; unless anyone from the motives of devotion should wish to have the Psalter or the Breviary for divine offices or the hours of the blessed Virgin; but we most strictly forbid their having any translation of these books."[15] Five years later, the Council of Tarragona was called to ratify the decrees of Toulouse. The bishops ruled that anyone who owned copies of the Bible or excerpts of its books had eight days to turn them over to a local bishop to be burned.[16] By the 1300s, possession of a Bible by a layman was a criminal offense punishable by flogging, confiscation of personal property, or burning at the stake.

Theologian John Wycliffe was the first to translate the New Testament into English. As punishment, he was declared a heretic by the Council of Constance in 1415, thirty-one years after his death. However, the Catholic leaders at the council did not stop there, ordering, "That his body and bones are to be exhumed, if they can be identified among the corpses of the faithful, and to be scattered far from a burial place of the church, in accordance with canonical and lawful sanctions."[17] In 1428, Wycliffe's bones were unearthed and burned before the townspeople. After the flames had waned, his ashes were thrown into the Swift River.[18]

Like Wycliffe, William Tyndale translated most of the Bible into English. Before he could complete his work, he was branded a heretic by the Catholic Church and executed by strangulation in Vilvoorde in 1536. Here was a man killed by a supposedly Christian church for the scandalous act of making the Christian scriptures more accessible to English readers. To the Vatican, his execution was not punishment enough for translating the Bible, so his corpse was then ordered burned at the stake.[19]

In December 1563, ten rules on prohibited books were adopted at the twenty-fifth session of the Council of Trent. Rule III states, "Versions also of ecclesiastical writings, which have hitherto been set forth by condemned authors, provided they contain nothing against sound doctrine, are permitted. But versions of the books of the Old Testament may be allowed only to learned and pious men at the discretion of the bishop, provided they use such versions as elucidations of the Vulgate to understand the sacred scripture, but not as the sound text. But let versions of the New Testament, made by authors of the first class of this index, be allowed to no one, because but little utility, but very much danger is to flow from their perusal."[20] The books of the New Testament—including the gospels and the book of Revelation—were not allowed to be read by the laity due to the risk posed to Catholicism.

Rule IV went even further. In one of the most heretical abuses of power in its history, the Catholic Church claimed unauthorized readers of banned books were not allowed to be forgiven of their sins. The local bishop would fine the bookseller an amount equal to the book's price and subject them to any additional penalties that the bishop deemed appropriate. Rule IV read, "But whosoever shall presume to read them without such power, let him not be able to obtain absolution of his sins, unless he has first given back the books to the ordinary. But the booksellers, who shall sell the Bible written in the vulgar tongue, to a person not having the aforesaid power, or shall in any other way grant it, is to lose the price of the books, which shall be converted by the bishop to pious purposes, and they shall be subject to other penalties, according to the quality of the offence, at the discretion of the same bishop. But regulars are not to have the power of reading or buying them, unless they have power to do so from their prelates."[21]

These perverse rules from the Council of Trent were considered noble by Catholic leaders at the time. French bishop Richard Du Mans, who spoke prominently at the Council, said, "That the Scriptures had become useless, since the schoolmen had established the truth of all doctrines; and though they were formerly read in the church, for the instruction of the people, and still read in the service, yet they ought not to be made a study, because the Lutherans only gained those who read them."[22] This quote is an incredible window into the environment of the day. The people who were finally able to read the Bible quickly realized Catholicism was a pseudo-Christian religion. These people were leaving Catholicism for Protestantism by the thousands—and the Vatican knew it.

Trent's rules were designed for two purposes. First, they restricted the availability of the Bible or any other books damaging to the Vatican. Second, they provided the Catholic Church with the means to threaten and punish the laity into submission. Those who failed to comply with Trent's dictates knew they risked being either tortured or killed for their faith.

The Church's original application of Rules III and IV permitted bishops to grant exceptions to allow some laypeople to read specific passages of the Bible. However, Clement VIII, whose pontificate lasted from 1592 to 1605, prohibited bishops and their superiors from granting these licenses—a ban enforced by the Inquisition.[23]

Like his predecessors, Benedict XIV confirmed the rules of the Council of Trent after becoming pope in 1740. He also mandated that any versions of the Bible in circulation—including those possessed by clergymen—were versions authorized by the Catholic Church.[24]

The Catholic suppression of scripture continued through the end of the eighteenth century. When Pope Pius VI was deposed in February 1798, the papacy's temporal power over all Christendom was revoked. The weakened Catholic Church no longer held enough civil authority to discipline Bible owners, which opened the door for the Bible Society movement.

The British and Foreign Bible Society was founded in 1804 to address the lack of affordable Bibles for Welsh speakers. Emboldened by the Catholic Church's new lack of persecutory power, the desire of the citizenry to have access to affordable Bibles rapidly spread to the other nations of the British Isles, Germany, the United States, and Canada by 1809. Two years later, the Bible Societies of India and Hungary were founded. New organizations in Finland, Russia, the Netherlands, Iceland, Sweden, Switzerland, Prussia, and Denmark joined the effort by 1815. The following year, a Bible Society was founded in Norway. By 1825, Bible Societies had spread as far as Poland, Malta, Greece, Australia, South Africa, and Colombia.[25]

Pius VII, successor to the deposed Pius VI, wrote about the danger Bible Societies posed to the Catholic Church in a June 29, 1816, letter to Ignatius, Archbishop of Gniezno. "We have been truly shocked by this most crafty device by which the very foundations of religion are undermined," he wrote. "We have, with the utmost care and attention, deliberated upon the measures proper to be adopted by our pontifical authority, in order to remedy and abolish this pestilence as far as possible." Pius then congratulated Ignatius "upon the singular zeal you have displayed under circumstances so dangerous to Christianity, in having denounced to the apostolic see this defilement of the faith, so eminently dangerous to souls," and for his actions to "expose the wickedness of this nefarious scheme."[26]

In his letter calling Bible Societies a "defilement of the faith, so eminently dangerous to souls" and a "nefarious scheme," Pope Pius VII was referring to *the desire of Christians to read the Bible*—the fundamental religious text of their faith. Believers wanted access to scripture, and the Roman Catholic Church felt so threatened by its portrayal in Revelation 17-18 that it fought to prevent them from reading it.

The Bible Societies did not stop the Catholic Church's efforts to suppress scripture. The movement was such a risk to Catholicism that less than eight months after becoming pope in 1823, Leo XII issued his *Ubi Primum*, which states, "If the sacred Scriptures be every where indiscriminately published, more evil than advantage will arise thence, on account of the rashness of men."[27] On March 26, 1825, Leo XII republished the list of prohibited books from the Council of Trent to remind everyone how dangerous God's Word was to Catholicism.[28]

In his *Inter Praecipuas*, an 1844 encyclical letter which was subtitled "On Biblical Societies," Pope Gregory XVI declared, "We confirm and renew by Our apostolic authority the prescriptions listed and published long ago concerning the publication, dissemination, reading, and possession of vernacular translations of sacred Scriptures…In particular, watch more carefully over those who are assigned to give public readings of holy scripture, so that they function diligently in their office within the comprehension of the audience; under no pretext whatsoever should they dare to explain and interpret the divine writings contrary to the tradition of the Fathers or the interpretation of the Catholic Church."[29]

As a matter of policy, Catholics were officially discouraged from reading scripture until 1943. Realizing the Vatican's full-scale war against the spread of the Bible had been lost, Pius XII issued the encyclical *Divino Afflante Spiritu*. This letter finally encouraged Catholics to read the Bible, saying it should "be read daily with piety and devotion."[30] After failing to stop Bible ownership, the Vatican now publishes its own translations. However, it still issues a list of which versions of the Bible are authorized for Catholic readers.[31]

There are two methods for translating the Bible—literal and dynamic. A literal translation attempts to preserve the accuracy of the original Hebrew, Aramaic, and Koine Greek languages. Literal translations are prized for their precision, even if modern readers may not find the language smooth or easy to comprehend. Dynamic translations are less precise but more easily read in today's vernacular.

By the time James I became King of England in 1603, King Henry VIII had separated the country from the Roman Catholic Church. Ritualistically, the nascent Church of England was nearly identical to Catholicism. However, it was fundamentally free of the Vatican's influence and control. When King James convened the Hampton Court Conference with the intent to create a new translation of the Bible in 1604, he instructed the translators to use the literal translation method.[32] For these reasons, the King James Version was used for all verses quoted in this book. It is a literal translation, close to the original language and free from the influence and coercion of the Vatican. The King James Version's linguists were at liberty to go anywhere the original language took them, to translate the text accurately without parsing words to conceal the Bible's warnings about the Roman Catholic Church.

Other Ways the Catholic Church Keeps Catholics from God

Whether or not you believe this interpretation of Mystery Babylon, the Catholic Church certainly does. Over the years, the Vatican has proven that it knew that its church fulfilled the prophecy of Mystery Babylon through its actions. Is there another reason the Catholic Church would conceal the Bible from its parishioners? If the overtly anti-Christian act of preventing people from reading the core text of their faith is not eye-opening enough, there are several other ways the Roman Catholic Church has kept people from God.

The Roman Catholic Church Is the Gatekeeper of Salvation

In 1964, the Second Vatican Council published a decree on ecumenism entitled *Unitatis Redintegratio*. This document, which calls for the reunification of all denominations in Christendom, openly proclaims that God passed the "blessings of the New Covenant" to the apostolic college—the apostles Jesus commissioned to spread the gospel after his ascension. The Vatican contends that Peter was the leader of the apostles and that he established "one Body of Christ"—a singular church.

Unitatis Redintegratio continues, "Nevertheless, our separated brethren, whether considered as individuals or as Communities and Churches, are not blessed with that unity which Jesus Christ wished to bestow on all those who through Him were born again into one body, and with Him quickened to newness of life—that unity which the Holy Scriptures and the ancient Tradition of the Church proclaim."

Then, in a remarkable display of heresy and unmerited self-importance, the decree claims, "For it is only through Christ's Catholic Church, which is 'the all-embracing means of salvation,' that they can benefit fully from the means of salvation. We believe that Our Lord entrusted all the blessings of the New Covenant to the apostolic college alone, of which Peter is the head, in order to establish the one Body of Christ on earth to which all should be fully incorporated who belong in any way to the people of God."[33] Such a sacrilegious claim would mean the Catholic Church determines who receives salvation, not God.

Vatican tradition contends the papacy traces its lineage back to Peter. The suggestion that it was Peter's duty to establish "the one Body of Christ" implies that the Catholic Church is the only church that qualifies as part of the body of Christ. However, the Catholic priest and editor of the *Encyclopedia of Catholicism*, Richard McBrien, acknowledged, "Although Catholic tradition regards St. Peter as the first bishop of Rome and therefore as the first pope, there is no evidence that Peter was involved in the initial establishment of the Christian community in Rome…or that he served as Rome's first bishop. Not until the pontificate of St. Pius I in the middle of the second century (142-155) did the Roman church have one bishop as pastoral leader."[34]

In 1967, the Vatican reiterated this claim with its *Indulgentiarum Doctrina*. The document describes it this way; "For the only-begotten son of God...has won a treasure for the militant Church and has entrusted it to blessed Peter, the keybearer of heaven, and to his successors, Christ's vicars on earth, that they may distribute it to the faithful for their salvation, applying it mercifully for reasonable causes to all who are repentant and have confessed their sins, at times remitting completely and at times partially the temporal punishment due sin in a general as well as in special ways insofar as they judge it to be fitting in the eyes of the Lord. It is known that the merits of the Blessed Mother of God and of all the elect...add further to this treasure."[35]

Indulgentiarum Doctrina reinforced the view that Peter was the "keybearer" of Heaven, meaning he—not God—decided who could enter. The popes, who claim to be Peter's successors, use a fabricated line of succession called the "Primacy of Peter" to maintain that they are responsible for distributing salvation to Christians—a wholly heretical and sacrilegious belief.

Salvation Through the Seven Sacraments

The Catholic Church also teaches parishioners that to get to Heaven, one needs to receive salvation through a combination of faith and ritualistic acts called the seven sacraments: baptism, confirmation, the Eucharist, penance, anointing the sick, holy orders, and matrimony.[36] While the sacraments are good and honorable ways to display one's faith publicly, the Bible disagrees on the path to Heaven. John 3:16 and 14:6, Acts 4:12 and 16:31, Ephesians 2:8-9, and Titus 3:5 all proclaim that salvation comes from faith in Jesus.[m]

---

[m] **John 3:16** For God so loved the world, that he gave his only begotten Son, that whosoever believeth in him should not perish, but have everlasting life.

John 14:6 Jesus saith unto him, I am the way, the truth, and the life: no man cometh unto the Father, but by me.

Acts 4:12 Neither is there salvation in any other: for there is none other name under heaven given among men, whereby we must be saved.

Acts 16:31 And they said, Believe on the Lord Jesus Christ, and thou shalt be saved, and thy house.

Ephesians 2:8-9 8 For by grace are ye saved through faith; and that not of yourselves: it is the gift of God: 9 Not of works, lest any man should boast.

Titus 3:5 Not by works of righteousness which we have done, but according to his mercy he saved us, by the washing of regeneration, and renewing of the Holy Ghost;

While faith without works is dead,[37] the Bible contains no checklist of works that must be completed to receive salvation.

The Catholic Church contends that performing the sacraments directly generates a precise supernatural response: salvation. This belief is identical to the recitation of spells in the practice of sorcery and witchcraft. For example, the *Catechism of the Catholic Church*, number 1128 says, "From the moment that a sacrament is celebrated in accordance with the intention of the Church, the power of Christ and his Spirit acts in and through it."[38] As Daniel prophesied of the Antichrist, "Through his policy also he shall cause craft to prosper."[39]

The Pope Is the Head of the Church and Has the Authority of Christ

Ephesians 1:22, 5:23, and Colossians 1:18 all name Jesus as the head of the church.[n] Hebrews 7:22-28 explains that there have been countless priests over the years, but Jesus' priesthood is everlasting. His death and resurrection gave us a "better testament"—a pure, continuous priesthood.[o] Jesus did tell Peter, "Upon this rock I will build my church,"[p] but the phrase was never intended to declare that he was being chosen to lead a new organized religion. Christ's statement was more likely a reference to the apostle's strength and determination to spread the gospel than a transfer of authority.

---

[n] **Ephesians 1:22** And hath put all things under his feet, and gave him to be the head over all things to the church,

Ephesians 5:23 For the husband is the head of the wife, even as Christ is the head of the church: and he is the saviour of the body.

Colossians 1:18 And he is the head of the body, the church: who is the beginning, the firstborn from the dead; that in all things he might have the preeminence.

[o] **Hebrews 7:22-28** 22 By so much was Jesus made a surety of a better testament. 23 And they truly were many priests, because they were not suffered to continue by reason of death: 24 But this man, because he continueth ever, hath an unchangeable priesthood. 25 Wherefore he is able also to save them to the uttermost that come unto God by him, seeing he ever liveth to make intercession for them. 26 For such an high priest became us, who is holy, harmless, undefiled, separate from sinners, and made higher than the heavens; 27 Who needeth not daily, as those high priests, to offer up sacrifice, first for his own sins, and then for the people's: for this he did once, when he offered up himself. 28 For the law maketh men high priests which have infirmity; but the word of the oath, which was since the law, maketh the Son, who is consecrated for evermore.

[p] **Matthew 16:18** And I say also unto thee, That thou art Peter, and upon this rock I will build my church; and the gates of hell shall not prevail against it.

Pius I is believed to have become the bishop of Rome around 142 AD. The Catholic Church, desperate to legitimize itself as the singular Christian church, contends there were eight other "popes" between Peter and Pius I,[40] but history does not support their claims.[41] The Vatican has distorted and misrepresented Jesus' statement to create a lineage of church leaders linking Peter to the first bishop of Rome so that the papacy could falsely claim to possess Christ's divine authorization and empowerment.

The unsubstantiated Catholic contention that the pope is the head of the earthly church directly contradicts the Bible, which assigns the same position to Christ alone. Papal supremacy was contrived to legitimize a church with no more spiritual authority than any other religious organization. It is another deception by Mystery Babylon, as Catholics and other non-Christians believe the pope is God's representative and the head of Christianity. As Revelation 17:8 predicted, these people look upon the pope "with wonder."

Only the Catholic Church Can Interpret Scripture

The *Catechism of the Catholic Church* claims, "Sacred Scripture must be read and interpreted with the help of the Holy Spirit and under the guidance of the Magisterium of the Church according to three criteria: 1) it must be read with attention to the content and unity of the whole of Scripture; 2) it must be read within the living Tradition of the Church; 3) it must be read with attention to the analogy of faith, that is, the inner harmony which exists among the truths of the faith themselves."[42]

For this statement to be spiritually accurate, one must assume that God intended for his believers to require a third party to tell them what to think, what to believe, and how to act. During Jesus' ministry, he typically reached people in small numbers—one by one, handfuls here and there. The earliest converts to Christianity—the first-century Jews of Judea—determined that Jesus was the Messiah they had been waiting for by thinking for themselves. They considered the earliest Hebrew scriptures and the writings of prophets and concluded Jesus was the Son of God whom they had been promised.

King David penned his opinion on individual contemplation of scripture in Psalm 119, writing, "Thy word have I hid in mine heart, that I might not sin against thee. Blessed art thou, O Lord: teach me thy statutes." David did not ask God to help the high priest give him good advice on avoiding sin—

he asked God to guide him through the scriptures he had memorized. He continued, "Thy word is a lamp unto my feet, and a light unto my path." Clearly, David did not believe interpreting God's Word was a task reserved for the clergy.

Jesus instructed his followers to "continue in his word," indicating we should live by his instructions as preserved in scripture.q Paul advised both his disciple Timothy and the Christian community in Rome to read scripture.r God has empowered today's Christians to do the same thing. He made us in his image, as individuals equipped with the ability to think critically and make our own decisions. We can read the Bible, ask ourselves the right questions, and find God's answers without requiring guidance or interpretation from any priest, church, or religious institution.

Interpretation of the Bible by individual Catholics is what frightened the Vatican the most. Once you realize that the motive for banning the Bible was to censor God's warnings about their deceptive pagan practices, it is simple to see the intent behind their stance that the Catholic Church must handle all interpretation of scripture. The Vatican's primary concern is the preservation of the ruse that Catholicism is a Christian religion. If medieval Christians had been allowed to read Revelation, there was a considerable risk that the Roman Catholic Church would have been identified as Mystery Babylon—which is exactly what happened in the sixteenth century.

After the invention of the printing press facilitated the wider distribution of the Bible, individual Christians started to interpret scripture outside the Catholic Church's reach. When these observant theologians published their views, the world's opinion of Roman Catholicism quickly changed. Mystery Babylon was identified, and the Protestant Reformation began.

---

q **John 8:31-32** 31 Then said Jesus to those Jews which believed on him, If ye continue in my word, then are ye my disciples indeed; 32 And ye shall know the truth, and the truth shall make you free.

r **II Timothy 3:15-17** 15 And that from a child thou hast known the holy scriptures, which are able to make thee wise unto salvation through faith which is in Christ Jesus. 16 All scripture is given by inspiration of God, and is profitable for doctrine, for reproof, for correction, for instruction in righteousness: 17 That the man of God may be perfect, thoroughly furnished unto all good works.

Romans 15:4 For whatsoever things were written aforetime were written for our learning, that we through patience and comfort of the scriptures might have hope.

Mary as Mediator, Venerating and Praying to Mary and Saints

The Bible irrefutably declares Jesus Christ is the only mediator between God and man in I Timothy 2:5.

> **I Timothy 2:5**
> 5 For there is one God, and one mediator between God and men, the man Christ Jesus;

Awfully conclusive, is it not? So, why would the Vatican tell us that Mary is actively interceding on our behalf in Heaven? According to the *Catechism of the Catholic Church,* number 969, "This motherhood of Mary in the order of grace continues uninterruptedly from the consent which she loyally gave at the Annunciation and which she sustained without wavering beneath the cross, until the eternal fulfilment of all the elect. Taken up to heaven she did not lay aside this saving office but by her manifold intercession continues to bring us the gifts of eternal salvation…Therefore the Blessed Virgin is invoked in the Church under the titles of Advocate, Helper, Benefactress, and Mediatrix."[43] A "mediatrix" is a female mediator. In Catholicism, the term is almost exclusively used in reference to Mary. The *Catechism of the Catholic Church* gave Mary's fictional role as a mediatrix credit for "bring[ing] us the gifts of eternal salvation."

The Bible does not contain the slightest indication of Mary's intercession on our behalf. The theory is a complete fabrication by the Catholic Church and a corrupt effort to use Mary as a barrier between God and man. After all, if we direct our prayers through Mary or another saint, we are not delivering them to God through our true intercessor, Jesus. As he said in John 14:6, "No man cometh unto the Father, but by me."[s]

The book of Hebrews even states that Jesus lived so that he could "make intercession" for us.[t] We cannot pray to God in the name of Mary or other mortal saints. While they were devout, virtuous people called by God to serve him, they were only human beings.

---

[s] **John 14:6** Jesus saith unto him, I am the way, the truth, and the life: no man cometh unto the Father, but by me.
[t] **Hebrews 7:25** Wherefore he is able also to save them to the uttermost that come unto God by him, seeing he ever liveth to make intercession for them.

In the book of Acts, a man named Cornelius began worshipping Peter, who ordered him to stop because he was only a man.[u] Four chapters later, in Acts 14:11-15, a similar event occurred in Lystra. Paul and Barnabas healed a crippled man, and as a result, the pagan priests of Lystra began to sacrifice oxen to them. When Paul and Barnabas heard what the priests were doing, they made it clear they were only men and should not be worshipped.[v]

For their part, Paul and Timothy directed the church in Philippi to "make their requests known unto God" when praying.[w] Their instructions were not to tell your favorite saint to take your requests before God or to pray to Saint Anthony of Padua to ask the "patron saint of lost things" to help you find your missing keys. Paul and Timothy told us we are to pray directly to God.

The Christian figures who have been canonized as saints by the Catholic Church should not be prayed to or worshipped as if they were supernatural beings. While these saints should be respected for their piety and godliness, Catholic veneration is based on pagan polytheism. Ancient Romans believed there were many different gods in the spiritual pantheon, but Roman priests also posthumously deified exceptional humans who were then venerated as divine by the people. These new deities—typically deceased emperors—were also prayed to and worshipped as gods.

The Bible even tells us some supernatural figures, such as angels, cannot be praised. John worshipped angels in Revelation 19:10 and 22:8-9, but they asked him to stop each time. The angels explained that they were servants of God, just as John was.

---

[u] **Acts 10:25-26** 25 And as Peter was coming in, Cornelius met him, and fell down at his feet, and worshipped him. 26 But Peter took him up, saying, Stand up; I myself also am a man.

[v] **Acts 14:11-15** 11 And when the people saw what Paul had done, they lifted up their voices, saying in the speech of Lycaonia, The gods are come down to us in the likeness of men. 12 And they called Barnabas, Jupiter; and Paul, Mercurius, because he was the chief speaker. 13 Then the priest of Jupiter, which was before their city, brought oxen and garlands unto the gates, and would have done sacrifice with the people. 14 Which when the apostles, Barnabas and Paul, heard of, they rent their clothes, and ran in among the people, crying out, 15 And saying, Sirs, why do ye these things? We also are men of like passions with you, and preach unto you that ye should turn from these vanities unto the living God, which made heaven, and earth, and the sea, and all things that are therein:

[w] **Philippians 4:6** Be careful for nothing; but in every thing by prayer and supplication with thanksgiving let your requests be made known unto God.

Religious Iconography

The Catholic Church prohibits *worshipping* images, such as those of Jesus, Mary, and other saints. However, the Vatican allows for—and encourages—*venerating* them and has successfully convinced Catholics that there is some distinction between these two near-synonyms. Many Catholic churches even position benches and votive candles in front of statues to promote prayer through these graven images to the saints they represent.

God's mandate against religious iconography originated with the Ten Commandments. Exodus' version of the Commandments begins this way:

> **Exodus 20:2-6**
> **2** I am the Lord thy God, which have brought thee out of the land of Egypt, out of the house of bondage.
> **3** Thou shalt have no other gods before me.
> **4** Thou shalt not make unto thee any graven image, or any likeness of any thing that is in heaven above, or that is in the earth beneath, or that is in the water under the earth.
> **5** Thou shalt not bow down thyself to them, nor serve them: for I the Lord thy God am a jealous God, visiting the iniquity of the fathers upon the children unto the third and fourth generation of them that hate me;
> **6** And shewing mercy unto thousands of them that love me, and keep my commandments.

Most Protestant churches render the first commandment as "Thou shalt have no other gods before me," and the next as "Thou shalt not make unto thee any graven image." However, the *Catechism of the Catholic Church* combines those two commandments into one.[44] This devious change creates a two-part test that Catholics must fail to believe they have violated this commandment. Catholic editions of the Bible also use the more specific "idols" in place of the broader term "graven images." The Catholic edition of the New Revised Standard Version reads the first commandment as "You shall have no other gods before me. You shall not make for yourself an idol."[45] This alteration allows Catholics to argue that their graven images must be considered *both* an idol and a god to break this commandment. This scheme also provides a way to claim that the veneration of graven images—including *praying* to them—is not idolatry unless Catholics worship the likeness *and* consider it a god.

The *Catechism of the Catholic Church*, number 2132, dishonestly states, "The Christian veneration of images is not contrary to the first commandment which proscribes idols. Indeed, 'the honor rendered to an image passes to its prototype,' and 'whoever venerates an image venerates the person portrayed in it.' The honor paid to sacred images is a 'respectful veneration,' not the adoration due to God alone."[46]

In other words, the Catholic Church would have you believe kneeling in front of a statue or painting and praying to the saint it represents is not idol worship. Sadly, many Catholics bend over backward in defense of veneration of religious icons using this counter-scriptural interpretation of the Bible's Ten Commandments. Nevertheless, Exodus 20:4-5 forbids not only praying to sculptures, but also to "any likeness of any thing that is in heaven above, or that is in the earth beneath, or that is in the water under the earth." Do Catholics not bow their heads in prayer in front of artistic depictions of Jesus, Mary, and saints, as Exodus 20:5 explicitly prohibits?

In most pagan religions, the participants knew the idols they made were only representations of their gods, yet they prayed to and worshipped their gods through those images. How are these pagan practices different from Catholic veneration of images of Jesus, Mary, and other saints? Do Catholics today not pray to saints through their statues and images?

In the King James Bible, Deuteronomy 5 lists the beginning of the Ten Commandments this way:

> **Deuteronomy 5:6-11**
> **6** I am the Lord thy God, which brought thee out of the land of Egypt, from the house of bondage.
> **7** Thou shalt have none other gods before me.
> **8** Thou shalt not make thee any graven image, or any likeness of any thing that is in heaven above, or that is in the earth beneath, or that is in the waters beneath the earth:
> **9** Thou shalt not bow down thyself unto them, nor serve them: for I the Lord thy God am a jealous God, visiting the iniquity of the fathers upon the children unto the third and fourth generation of them that hate me,
> **10** And shewing mercy unto thousands of them that love me and keep my commandments.
> **11** Thou shalt not take the name of the Lord thy God in vain: for the Lord will not hold him guiltless that taketh his name in vain.

The Catholic Church has tried so hard to normalize the practice of idol worship that the widely-used *Butler Catechism*'s list of the Commandments even leaves out all of Deuteronomy 5:8-10—entirely ignoring God's ban on graven images and likenesses—stating, "1. I am the Lord thy God; thou shalt not have strange gods before me. 2. Thou shalt not take the name of the Lord thy God in vain."

Combining the first two commandments into one creates a new problem for the Catholic Church. The Ten Commandments would be reduced to only nine, so the Vatican needed to find a tenth commandment. To resolve this issue, the Catholic Church split the final commandment into two. The *Butler Catechism* concludes the Commandments like this: "9. Thou shalt not covet thy neighbor's wife. 10. Thou shalt not covet thy neighbor's goods."[47]

However, the wording of the passages in both Exodus and Deuteronomy clearly lists one singular commandment against covetous behavior.

> **Exodus 20:17**
> 17 Thou shalt not covet thy neighbour's house, thou shalt not covet thy neighbour's wife, nor his manservant, nor his maidservant, nor his ox, nor his ass, nor any thing that is thy neighbour's.

> **Deuteronomy 5:21**
> 21 Neither shalt thou desire thy neighbour's wife, neither shalt thou covet thy neighbour's house, his field, or his manservant, or his maidservant, his ox, or his ass, or any thing that is thy neighbour's.

The Vatican knows praying to or venerating saints through their images and likenesses is in direct defiance of the Ten Commandments. If Satan was using Catholicism to deceive many who would otherwise be Christian, would persuading them it was acceptable to worship and pray to the idols of mortal men and women not be an effective way to do so?

The Council of Trent addressed the veneration of relics, saints, and other "sacred images." In its final session, the council overtly supported idolatry with these words; "Moreover, that the images of Christ, of the Virgin Mother of God, and of the other saints, are to be had and retained particularly in temples, and that due honour and veneration are to be given them; not that any divinity, or virtue, is believed to be in them, on account of which they are to be worshipped; or that anything is to be asked of them; or, that trust is to be reposed in images, as was of old done by the Gentiles who placed their hope in idols; but because the honour which is shown them is referred to the prototypes which those images represent; in such wise that by the images which we kiss, and before which we uncover the head, and prostrate ourselves, we adore Christ; and we venerate the saints, whose similitude they bear: as, by the decrees of Councils, and especially of the second Synod of Nicaea, has been defined against the opponents of images."[48]

The council's careful wording reveals the Catholic Church was aware that veneration and idol worship were the same. Trent attempted to distinguish between veneration and idolatry because the Reformers began pointing out Catholicism's hypocrisy on the subject. The Vatican had to try to legitimize veneration to hide its heretical practices. Sadly, the Vatican's distortion of the Ten Commandments and the prohibition of graven images and likenesses has inspired idolatry within Catholicism.

> **Leviticus 26:1**
> **1** Ye shall make you no idols nor graven image, neither rear you up a standing image, neither shall ye set up any image of stone in your land, to bow down unto it: for I am the Lord your God.

Figure 13: Graven images of Mary in Spain: The Virgin of the Snows, *Santa Maria la Blanca, Seville, Spain (left);* The Virgin of the Incarnation, *Cathedral of Granada, Spain.*

Figure 14: Graven images in the collection of the Cathedral of Milan, Italy: God the Father, *Beltramino de Zutti, 1416-1425 (left);* Christ Crucified, *Master of Guadalcanal, late seventeenth century.*

Figure 15: Graven images: The Pietà, *Michelangelo, Saint Peter's Basilica, Vatican City, 1499 (left);* The Immaculate Heart of Mary, *Vicenç Vilarrúbies, Cathedral of Barcelona, Spain, 1942.*

Confession of Sin to a Priest Instead of God

Under the Old Covenant, the Jews had to repent of their sins, and if it were significant enough, they would bring the appropriate sacrifice to a priest who would then offer it to God on their behalf. When Jesus was crucified, his death marked the end of the Old Covenant and the beginning of the New Covenant. He became the final sacrifice for our sins, as Gabriel prophesied in Daniel 9. From that point onward, the New Covenant no longer required a priest to act as an intercessor between God and man. Not only is confession and repentance through a priest no longer necessary, but the Bible frequently affirms that all believers are "the new priesthood."[x]

The Catholic Church will often cite James 5:16 as the basis for requiring confession to priests. The problem is that James never advises us to confess to priests or clergy—he simply says to confess our sins "to one another."[y] If James thought we needed to confess to church leaders, he would have said so. Instead, he said we should confess to our brothers and sisters in Christ. James 5:16 is more evidence that Jesus did not intend to start a new formal religion. James wanted us to confess our sins to other Christians so we could act as a support system and hold each other accountable.

The Vatican will also point to John 20:22-23 to defend confession to priests.[z] There are several problems with their interpretation of those verses. First, the apostles were not priests. Although they were the leaders of the new Christian community, they did not hold an official administrative position in a religion. Second, the apostles were only able to remit sins because they had

---

[x] **I Peter 2:9** But ye are a chosen generation, a royal priesthood, an holy nation, a peculiar people; that ye should shew forth the praises of him who hath called you out of darkness into his marvellous light;
Revelation 1:6 And hath made us kings and priests unto God and his Father; to him be glory and dominion for ever and ever. Amen.
Revelation 5:10 And hast made us unto our God kings and priests: and we shall reign on the earth.
[y] **James 5:16** Confess your faults one to another, and pray one for another, that ye may be healed. The effectual fervent prayer of a righteous man availeth much.
[z] **John 20:22-23** 22 And when he had said this, he breathed on them, and saith unto them, Receive ye the Holy Ghost: 23 Whose soever sins ye remit, they are remitted unto them; and whose soever sins ye retain, they are retained.

received the Holy Spirit. Those who do not receive the Holy Spirit, such as the priests of a false church, cannot remit sins.

Third, the Catholic Church claims to have religious authority through the supremacy of Peter, but Jesus gave the Holy Spirit to all his apostles equally—without any indication Peter was elevated above the others.

Lastly, Jesus was only speaking to the apostles in his presence. The verses do not suggest that the ability to forgive sins would be passed to successive priests—especially not to Mystery Babylon's clergy. Remember, Paul wrote in I Timothy 2:5 that there is no mediator between God and man other than Jesus Christ—not Mary, not saints, and not earthly priests.

The Catholic Church is so dedicated to this belief that the twenty-first constitution of the 1215 AD Fourth Lateran Council stated, "All the faithful of either sex, after they have reached the age of discernment, should individually confess all their sins in a faithful manner to their own priest at least once a year, and let them take care to do what they can to perform the penance imposed on them…Otherwise they shall be barred from entering a church during their lifetime and they shall be denied a Christian burial at death."[49]

Oftentimes in confession, Catholics are told to pray the Rosary or repeat a certain number of "Apostles' Creed," "Our Father," or "Hail Mary" prayers to be absolved of their sins. The same parallel between Catholic doctrine and sorcery observed in performing the sacraments is evident here, as Catholics believe reciting these prayers will directly result in the forgiveness of sin. Jesus explicitly forbids this mindless, "vain repetition" of prayers in Matthew 6:7, which reads as if he were speaking directly to Catholics.

> **Matthew 6:7**
> 7 But when ye pray, use not vain repetitions, as the heathen do: for they think that they shall be heard for their much speaking.

Infant Baptism

The Catholic Church only practices baptism when the individual being baptized is an infant. The Bible contains several examples of baptism being the personal choice of a newly converted Christian. In Mark 16:15-16, Jesus told his disciples to go into all the world preaching the gospel, saying, "He that believeth and is baptized shall be saved."aa How does an infant make the critical and deeply personal decision to believe in Jesus Christ?

The book of Acts contains two examples of some of these conversions occurring. In Acts 2, the Jews of Jerusalem ask Peter how to receive the Holy Spirit. "Repent," he answers, "and be baptized every one of you in the name of Jesus Christ for the remission of sins, and ye shall receive the gift of the Holy Ghost." Not all the Jews followed his instructions, but many did. About three thousand people decided to be baptized into the Christian faith that day.bb Later, following a sermon by Philip in Acts 8, new Christian converts were baptized "when they believed."cc Also, Peter wrote baptism was "the answer of a good conscience toward God," implying it confirms a willingness to serve God.dd Since faith in Jesus Christ and repentance are prerequisites for baptism, and baptism is a confirmation of one's belief, infant baptism is futile—a frightening thought considering Jesus' words in John 3:5.

> **John 3:5**
> 5 Jesus answered, Verily, verily, I say unto thee, Except a man be born of water and of the Spirit, he cannot enter into the kingdom of God.

In April 413, Catholic Roman co-emperors Honorius and Theodosius II enacted a decree against the Donatists, a Christian sect that believed adult baptism was necessary for salvation. Anyone convicted of being baptized a second time was sentenced to death under their law, along with the individual who baptized them.[50] Centuries later, during the Counter-Reformation, the Catholic Church used this ancient law to execute many former Catholics who converted to Protestantism and were baptized the way Jesus had instructed.

---

aa **Mark 16:15-16** 15 And he said unto them, Go ye into all the world, and preach the gospel to every creature. 16 He that believeth and is baptized shall be saved; but he that believeth not shall be damned.

bb **Acts 2:41** Then they that gladly received his word were baptized: and the same day there were added unto them about three thousand souls.

cc **Acts 8:12** But when they believed Philip preaching the things concerning the kingdom of God, and the name of Jesus Christ, they were baptized, both men and women.

dd **I Peter 3:21** The like figure whereunto even baptism doth also now save us (not the putting away of the filth of the flesh, but the answer of a good conscience toward God,) by the resurrection of Jesus Christ:

Masses Held in Latin Until the Mid-1960s

If the Catholic Church wanted to teach parishioners about Jesus Christ and ensure they lived their lives in a way that was pleasing to God, why would they require mass to be held in Latin from the time of the Roman Empire until the mid-1960s?[51] Does it not seem counterintuitive to conduct masses in a defunct language that parishioners cannot understand?

Contrarily, if the Vatican wanted to misrepresent the Bible's teachings and obscure its warning about a false Roman church, would this motive not lead the church to hold mass in a language virtually no one spoke for fifteen centuries and to declare only Catholic priests can interpret scripture?[52]

When you carefully analyze the many contradictions between the Biblical text and Catholic dogma, Satan's efforts to deceive Catholics through a false church become clear. In II Timothy 4:3-4, Paul warned that a time would come when people who believed they were Christians would no longer follow "sound doctrine." These people would prefer to follow comfortable teachers who tell them what they want to hear rather than what God's Word says.

> **II Timothy 4:3-4**
> **3** For the time will come when they will not endure sound doctrine; but after their own lusts shall they heap to themselves teachers, having itching ears;
> **4** And they shall turn away their ears from the truth, and shall be turned unto fables.

For those few who may still be skeptical, think critically; if the Roman Catholic Church *was* a false church being used by Satan to keep us from God, *would they do anything differently*?

Chapter Synopsis

The Catholic Church Fulfills the Full Description of Mystery Babylon
- Mystery Babylon is a prostitute—a false church (Revelation 17:1)
- It is comprised of people from around the world (Revelation 17:15)
- It has deceived Catholics and many Christians through its false doctrine (Revelation 17:2, 17:8)
- Catholic cardinals wear red and bishops wear purple (Revelation 17:4)
- Papal vestments and tiaras are decked in gold, precious stones, and pearls (Revelation 17:4)
- Priests hold gold cups in their hands when celebrating the Eucharist
- It is in the city of seven hills—Rome (Revelation 17:9)
- It is on the eighth Roman hill—Vatican Hill (Revelation 17:11)
- It received its power from the ten kingdoms of the fallen Roman Empire (Revelation 17:12-13, 17:17)
- It martyred countless Christians (Revelation 17:6)
- It holds influence over world leaders (Revelation 17:2, 17:18)
- It is also a city—Vatican City (Revelation 17:18)

Ways the Catholic Church Deceives Would-Be Christians:
- Preventing people from owning or reading the Bible for centuries
- The Roman Catholic Church is the gatekeeper of salvation
- Preaching salvation comes through performing the "seven sacraments"
- The pope claims to be the head of the church and have the authority of Jesus Christ
- Claiming only the Catholic Church can interpret scripture
- The false claim that Mary is a mediator between God and man
- Veneration of Mary and saints
- It encourages prayer to saints rather than God
- The idolatry of religious iconography
- Confession of sin to a priest rather than God
- Forgiveness of sin through penance instead of repentance to God
- Infant baptism, which occurs before a person is old enough to decide to believe in Jesus for themselves
- Masses were conducted in Latin until the 1960s

7

THE ANTICHRIST IN PROPHECY

How Did Daniel and Paul Describe the Antichrist?

The Bible's most detailed descriptions of the Antichrist are found in the books of Daniel and Revelation. In Daniel 7, we learned the Antichrist would come from Rome when an eleventh horn arose from the head of the Roman beast. In chapter nine, an angel reiterated the Roman origin of the Antichrist when he told Daniel the Second Temple would be destroyed by "the people of the prince that shall come." When the Romans leveled the Temple during the First Jewish-Roman War in 70 AD, the angel's prophecy confirmed the Roman origin of the Antichrist.

The ten horns on the beasts in both Daniel 7 and Revelation 17 represent ten smaller kingdoms that would arise after the Roman Empire's eventual collapse. In Daniel 7, we also learned that three of these ten kingdoms would be defeated before the Antichrist realized his full power.

In his description of the apostasy in II Thessalonians 2:4, Paul wrote that the Antichrist would "opposeth and exalteth himself above all that is called God...so that he as God sitteth in the temple of God, shewing himself that he is God." Paul utilized the phrase "temple of God" in four other verses— I Corinthians 3:16-17, II Corinthians 6:16, and Ephesians 2:21—each time the phrase referenced the church body.[1] In II Thessalonians 2:4, Paul predicts that the Antichrist would sit amongst the followers of Jesus Christ, falsely presenting himself as a Christian.

Daniel 7:20 also provides further insight into the Antichrist's character. Daniel predicted he would speak "great things," indicating he would be brash and boastful. This depiction of the Antichrist as one who would speak great things against God is repeated by Paul in II Thessalonians 2:4 and John in Revelation 13:5-6.

> **Daniel 7:20-21**
> **20** And of the ten horns that were in his head, and of the other which came up, and before whom three fell; even of that horn that had eyes, and a mouth that spake very great things, whose look was more stout than his fellows.
> **21** I beheld, and the same horn made war with the saints, and prevailed against them;

Daniel also wrote that the Antichrist's appearance would be more stout, or arrogant, than that of his contemporaries. After the first three horns have fallen, Daniel 7:21 predicts he would make "war with the saints" and prevail against them—a reference to the Great Tribulation. Clearly, the Antichrist would be a persecutor of true Christians.

> **II Thessalonians 2:9-12**
> **9** Even him, whose coming is after the working of Satan with all power and signs and lying wonders,
> **10** And with all deceivableness of unrighteousness in them that perish; because they received not the love of the truth, that they might be saved.
> **11** And for this cause God shall send them strong delusion, that they should believe a lie:
> **12** That they all might be damned who believed not the truth, but had pleasure in unrighteousness.

Doctrinally, the Antichrist's ministry would contradict God. However, for him to speak against God while giving the appearance of being Christian, the Antichrist's false teachings would need to be devious. Just as Revelation 17:8 indicates non-Christians would admire the Antichrist, II Thessalonians 2:9-12 says his followers would be deceived. This means the followers of the Antichrist are not occultists who intentionally worship Satan. Instead, they have the most honest intentions and even believe they are Christians, but this dishonest teacher within the Christian community dupes them into thinking he provides sound spiritual advice. In following his false teaching, they are fooled into a pagan religion and are condemned to Hell because of it.

> **Daniel 7:25**
> 25 And he shall speak great words against the most High, and shall wear out the saints of the most High, and think to change times and laws: and they shall be given into his hand until a time and times and the dividing of time.

Daniel 7:25 predicts he will also "change the times and laws." This verse then concludes by providing insight into the length of the Great Tribulation. Biblical scholars almost universally interpret the phrase "a time and times and the dividing of time" as three and a half prophetic years. The word "time" is believed to be a substitute for the word "year," "times" is interpreted as two years, and a "dividing of time" as a half year. This opinion reinforces the other descriptions of the length of the Great Tribulation found elsewhere in the Bible, where it is written in an equivalent number of months or days.

After reading Daniel and II Thessalonians, we already know much about the Antichrist. He would originate from the Roman Empire and would not receive his full power until three of the ten kingdoms that developed after the fall of Rome were conquered. He would persecute true Christians and prevail against them for three and a half prophetic years. Also, the Antichrist would misrepresent himself as a Christian and cause many to believe that he is the leader of God's earthly church, but those who follow his false teachings will be condemned to Hell. He will come from the body of Christian believers and will portray himself as God despite speaking against him. Lastly, this man will also "change the times and laws."

The First Beast of Revelation 13

Revelation adds more details that will help us uncover the Antichrist's identity. In Revelation 13, Satan empowers two different beasts. The first, which symbolizes the Antichrist, is illustrated in the chapter's first ten verses and is seen rising "out of the sea." In John's Mystery Babylon vision, an angel told him waters represented a group of people. Linking that interpretation with Revelation 13:1 and Paul's word choice for "temple" in II Thessalonians supports the notion that this blasphemous Antichrist would impersonate a member of the Christian community.

> **Revelation 13:1-2**
> 1 And I stood upon the sand of the sea, and saw a beast rise up out of the sea, having seven heads and ten horns, and upon his horns ten crowns, and upon his heads the name of blasphemy.
> 2 And the beast which I saw was like unto a leopard, and his feet were as the feet of a bear, and his mouth as the mouth of a lion: and the dragon gave him his power, and his seat, and great authority.

This Antichrist beast parallels other prophetic beasts in Revelation and Daniel. This sea beast has seven heads and ten horns, just as the dragon in Revelation 12 and the beast in Revelation 17 do. Similarly, the Roman Empire beast in Daniel 7 also had ten horns, though the number of its heads is not included in Daniel's description.

The angel in Daniel's dream told him that the fourth beast's ten horns represented kings who would benefit from the fall of Rome. Revelation 17 also tells us these ten kingdoms would give their power to the Antichrist. In Revelation 13, the ten horns on the Antichrist's beast wore crowns, hinting at an identical fulfillment.

These beasts are all related in many ways and represent the various levels of Satan's pagan Roman power structure. John is explicitly told the dragon represents Satan himself when an angel names him in Revelation 12:9. The fourth beast of Daniel 7 symbolizes the Roman Empire. The scarlet-colored beast of Revelation 17 represents pagan idolatry, while the beast of the sea in Revelation 13 represents the earthly leader of that religion—the Antichrist.

The description of the beast in verses one and two combines elements of each of the four beast empires in Daniel 7. The likely reason for this is that the Antichrist's religious empire would have the combined strength of the four empires from Daniel's vision and succeed them as the next great pagan power after the fall of ancient Rome.

Revelation 13:2 also tells us Satan—the red dragon from Revelation 12—would give the Antichrist his seat and "great authority." If it were not clear from his name, the Antichrist is unquestionably a tool of Satan.

In Revelation 13, John saw the Antichrist beast with a fatal wound on one of its seven heads. At some time after John's life, this wound would be healed, causing the entire world to look upon him with wonder, a prophecy reiterated later in Revelation 17:8. When people practice the beast's pseudo-Christian religion, they are worshipping Satan through him.

> **Revelation 13:3-4**
> 3 And I saw one of his heads as it were wounded to death; and his deadly wound was healed: and all the world wondered after the beast.
> 4 And they worshipped the dragon which gave power unto the beast: and they worshipped the beast, saying, Who is like unto the beast? Who is able to make war with him?

The Antichrist's miraculous recovery from a fatal wound is reminiscent of the three phases of Mystery Babylon's scarlet beast that "was, and is not, and yet is." The sea beast's head was alive, then wounded to death, only to be resurrected later.

The audacity of the Antichrist reverberates through Revelation 13 just as it did in Daniel 7 and II Thessalonians 2. John confirms seeing him "speaking great things and blasphemies," echoing the earlier prophecies by Daniel and Paul.[2] Similarly, the theme of a war between the Antichrist and Christianity continues in Revelation 13:7, which parallels Daniel 7:21's prophecy that the Antichrist would "make war with the saints."

> **Revelation 13:5-7**
> 5 And there was given unto him a mouth speaking great things and blasphemies; and power was given unto him to continue forty and two months.
> 6 And he opened his mouth in blasphemy against God, to blaspheme his name, and his tabernacle, and them that dwell in heaven.
> 7 And it was given unto him to make war with the saints, and to overcome them: and power was given him over all kindreds, and tongues, and nations.

The expansive power of the Antichrist would reach "all kindreds, and tongues, and nations." This language reinforces the relationship between the Antichrist and Mystery Babylon, which would also have a global impact. In Revelation 17, the many "peoples, and multitudes, and nations, and tongues" deceived by Mystery Babylon will find that their names are not written in the

Book of Life. Revelation 17:8 predicts these same people would look upon the Antichrist beast with wonder, and Revelation 13:8 confirms they would also worship him.

> **Revelation 13:8**
> 8 And all that dwell upon the earth shall worship him, whose names are not written in the book of life of the Lamb slain from the foundation of the world.

The wording of verse eight is vitally important. The true Christians who eventually make it to Heaven will not worship the Antichrist, as they will see through his deception. Everyone else—the people who will not make it to Heaven—will admire the Antichrist, seeing him as a righteous man of God instead of the instrument of Satan that he is.

However, the Bible also declares that the Antichrist eventually gets what he deserves. For much of his history, he would kill with the sword—through persecution, violence, and war. The Antichrist is destined to be punished for his violent treatment of Christians—it would just take time. Revelation 13:10 cautioned Christians that they would need patience and strong, unwavering faith to endure the many hardships of the Great Tribulation and avoid falling victim to the Antichrist's religious deception.

> **Revelation 13:9-10**
> 9 If any man have an ear, let him hear.
> 10 He that leadeth into captivity shall go into captivity: he that killeth with the sword must be killed with the sword. Here is the patience and the faith of the saints.

Chapter Synopsis

The Antichrist
- Comes from Rome
  - He would come from the fourth beast: Rome (Daniel 7:7-8)
  - He would come from the people who would both crucify Jesus and destroy the Temple in Jerusalem (Daniel 9:26)
  - He would come from the city of seven hills (Revelation 17:9)
- Diverse from the other ten kings who arose after Rome (Daniel 7:24)
- Three of the ten kingdoms would collapse before he receives his power (Daniel 7:8, 7:20)
- The Antichrist would "subdue three kings" (Daniel 7:24)
- Satan would give him his "seat," "great authority," and power over "all kindreds, and tongues, and nations" (Revelation 13:2, 13:4-5, 13:7)
- Would "speak great things" (Daniel 7:8, 7:11, 7:25, II Thessalonians 2:4, Revelation 13:5)
- Would exalt himself in opposition to God (II Thessalonians 2:4)
- "He as God sitteth in the temple of God, shewing himself that he is God"—he would sit among the body of believers (II Thessalonians 2:4)
- Would change the times and laws (Daniel 7:25)
- Would use Satan's power, signs, and lying wonders to deceive "them that perish"—the people who end up going to Hell (II Thessalonians 2:9-12)
- Would have three stages:
  - One of the beast's heads would be alive, then wounded to death, and then resurrected (Revelation 13:3, 13:12, 13:14)
  - There would be three stages of the Antichrist beast: "was," "is not," and "yet is" (Revelation 17:8-9)
- Would use violence against Christians
  - Would "make war with the saints" (Daniel 7:21, Revelation 13:7)
  - Would be "drunken with the blood of the saints" (Revelation 17:6)
  - Has power during the Tribulation (Daniel 7:25, Revelation 13:5)

8

THE ANTICHRIST REVEALED

In our investigation into the ten horns of Daniel 7, we identified the ten kingdoms that benefited from the collapse of the Western Roman Empire. Daniel told us that three of these kingdoms would fall before the arrival of the Antichrist. We also learned from Revelation 17 that the Antichrist would be Rome's eighth type of leader. The seventh king was the King of Italy, who only reigned in the city for a "short space," from 476 to 538. For a candidate to qualify as the Antichrist, they would have to ascend to power after exactly three of the ten kingdoms had fallen—between 508 and 534—and become the leader of the city immediately following the Kings of Italy.

Remember, in Daniel's prophecy of a beast with ten horns, the eleventh horn—which represents the Antichrist—was described by an angel as being "diverse" from the others. The Antichrist would be a world leader unlike the other ten kings—a religious leader, not a political one. By now, you may have drawn your own conclusions on the Antichrist's identity while reading the prior chapters. If so, you have likely determined that the only leader who fits this description is the Roman Catholic papacy.

The theory that the papacy is the Antichrist is not new. One of the first people to draw this conclusion was Martin Luther, who wrote about the topic in his *On the Babylonian Captivity of the Church*, first published in October 1520. To see how flawlessly the papacy fulfills all the Antichrist's criteria, we will examine each of the Bible's clues individually—just as we did with Mystery

Babylon. In doing so, we will unravel the many layers of deception placed on the Bible's end-times prophecies by those whom the prophecies implicate.

The Catholic Church and the papacy have a vested interest in ensuring the Christian world misinterprets these prophecies to hide their role in God's warnings. The Vatican wants you to assume Catholicism is a scripture-based, Christian religion, while the Bible clearly warns us it is not. You can believe the Catholic Church or you can believe God's Word. The choice is yours.

Why the Papacy Is the Antichrist

The Antichrist Would Come from Rome

Little discussion is required to acknowledge the Roman foundation of the papacy. The original administrative position of the papacy was the bishop of Rome, a title still bestowed upon the pope today. Emperor Constantine informally elevated the bishop of Rome over other bishops through their collaborative relationship. After the collapse of the Western Roman Empire, the Byzantine emperors held considerable influence over the affairs of the Catholic Church from Constantinople. Early in his reign, Justinian I realized the Roman legal system was in disrepair. His solution was to order a formal codification of Roman law called the *Codex Justinianus*, or the *Code of Justinian*.

Before the sixth century, there was no papacy, and there was no single leader of the Catholic Church. In 533, Justinian exchanged letters with the bishop of Rome, John II. In one, the emperor told the bishop, "You are the head of all holy churches. For in all ways, as stated, we strive to increase the honor and authority of Your See."[1] This pronouncement gave the bishop of Rome executive control over all other bishops and made Rome the official headquarters of Catholicism for the first time.[2] Once the letter was codified as law in the *Code of Justinian*, the successors of Pope John II used it to expand their grasp on power.

Daniel 7 predicted the Antichrist would come from the Roman Empire. Daniel 9 established the connection between the Antichrist and the people who would destroy the Second Temple. When the Temple was razed by the Roman army in 70 AD, this directly connected them to the Antichrist as his "people." As the saying goes, all roads lead to Rome.

He "Speaks Great Things," "Opposeth and Exalteth Himself Above All that Is Called God," and "As God Sitteth in the Temple of God, Shewing Himself that He Is God"

In a move of spectacular self-aggrandizement during the early days of the Catholic Church, Pope Gelasius I bestowed upon himself the title "Vicar of Christ" in the late fifth century. This phrase was based on the Latin word *vicarious*, which means "substitute." By assuming this title, Gelasius and all later popes declared themselves *substitute Christs*.

While the title currently refers to the pope, its origins were very different. The first recorded use of the term vicar of Christ was by Tertullian, a prolific early Christian writer in the late second and early third centuries. Tertullian used the term in reference to the Holy Spirit, a use that was suitably aligned with scripture.[3] In the gospel of John, Jesus promised his disciples that God would send a "Comforter" as his substitute.[a] Jesus was clear; his only vicar is the Holy Spirit, not a religious leader like the pope. By heretically declaring themselves Christ's earthly replacement, the popes are undoubtedly *speaking great things* and *exalting themselves*.

Pope Innocent III, the Roman pontiff from 1198 to 1216, was quoted in the *Decretals of Gregory IX* discussing the papal authority to transfer bishops between dioceses. He said, "For it is not man, but God, who separates whom the Roman Pontiff, who takes the place not of a pure man, but of the true God in the lands, dissolves the churches, not by human, but rather by divine authority, weighing the needs or interests of the churches."[4]

When confronted with this quote, Catholic apologists ignore the central issue and make a strawman argument. Their defense of Innocent III's heresy is to claim that the pope was not claiming to be God. They state he was only talking about the ecclesiastical authority of the pope to transfer bishops as the administrator of the church. In reality, both are true. While discussing his authority to transfer bishops, Innocent III clearly stated the Roman pontiff

---

[a] **John 14:16-18, 26** 16 And I will pray the Father, and he shall give you another Comforter, that he may abide with you for ever; 17 Even the Spirit of truth; whom the world cannot receive, because it seeth him not, neither knoweth him: but ye know him; for he dwelleth with you, and shall be in you. 18 I will not leave you comfortless: I will come to you…26 But the Comforter, which is the Holy Ghost, whom the Father will send in my name, he shall teach you all things, and bring all things to your remembrance, whatsoever I have said unto you.

"takes the place not of a pure man, but of the true God in the lands." No matter which topic he was discussing at the time, Innocent declared that the pope takes the place of God.

Innocent III does not stand alone in his haughtiness and self-importance. Factually, many popes have said bizarre and outlandish things that contradict scripture. Another example is Boniface VIII, who wrote in his 1302 papal bull *Unam Sanctam*, "Furthermore, we declare, we proclaim, we define that it is absolutely necessary for salvation that every human creature be subject to the Roman Pontiff."[5] Boniface would also state, "The pope is of so great dignity and excellence, that he is not merely man, but as if God, and the vicar of God...The pope is of so great dignity and power, that he constitutes one and the same tribunal with Christ...so that whatsoever the pope does seems to proceed from the mouth of God...The pope is as God on earth."[6]

Similarly, Pope Pius V, whose pontificate lasted from 1566 to 1572, once claimed, "Christ entrusted his office to the chief Pontiff;...but all power in heaven and in earth had been given to Christ;...therefore the chief Pontiff, who is his vicar, will have this power."[7]

In 1894, Pope Leo XIII's *Praeclara Gratulationis Publicae: The Reunion of Christendom* went further. In addressing all "venerable brethren, all Patriarchs, Primates, Archbishops and Bishops of the Catholic world," Leo XIII said, "We hold upon this earth the place of God Almighty." This was not only a reference to the pope, but to all Catholic leaders.[8]

Cardinal Joseph Sarto, who would later become Pope Pius X, was quoted in the January 1, 1895, issue of *Evangelical Christendom* as having said the pope "is Jesus Christ Himself, under the veil of the flesh."[9] As you can imagine, the publication of a significant cardinal saying something so unambiguously sacrilegious caused a firestorm in the Christian and Catholic communities.

Catholic apologists are quick to discredit this quote by saying *Evangelical Christendom* is a Protestant source. While true, there is a flaw in this argument. The Catholic periodical *Le Catholique National* also printed an excerpt of the cardinal's speech in an issue published on July 13, 1895. *Le Catholique National* quoted Cardinal Sarto this way: "The pope is not only the representative of J.-C. [Jesus Christ], but he is J.-C. himself, hidden under the veil of the flesh. Does the pope speak? It is J.-C. who speaks. Does the pope grant a pardon or pronounce an anathema? It is J.-C. who pronounces the anathema or grants grace. So that, when the pope speaks, there is not to examine, but to obey; one should not criticize its decisions or discuss its precepts. Therefore, everyone, even wearing the crown, must be subject to it by divine right. Here we are! Everything, to end in the absolute domination of the pope!'"[10]

Later that year, a Venetian priest named Don Marino Tommates wrote to Cardinal Sarto to get his side of the story. The Cardinal replied, "I have read all the homilies I have made since my coming here in Venice, and only in the sermon for the anniversary of the election of the Holy Father, I said these exact words: 'The pope represents Jesus Christ Himself, and therefore is a loving Father. The life of the pope is a holocaust of love for the human family. His word is love. Love, his weapons; love, the answer he gives to all those who hate him; love, his flag—i.e., the Cross, which signed the greatest triumph on earth and in heaven.'" Don Marino then wrote to the Catholic Truth Society on January 10, 1896, to provide Cardinal Sarto's response.[11]

The main problem with this defense is that the speech Sarto is quoting is not the same homily. The homily initially called into question by *Evangelical Christendom* was delivered in Saint Mark's Basilica the day after Cardinal Sarto entered Venice, on November 25, 1894.[12] His letter to Don Marino, written sometime before January 10, 1896, referenced a homily from the anniversary of the election of Pope Leo XIII on February 20, 1895—nearly two months after the January 1, 1895, issue of *Evangelical Christendom* published his original sacrilegious quote.

Both Don Marino's letter to the Catholic Truth Society and the homily Sarto referenced in his own defense were dated well after the accusations of heresy were published in *Evangelical Christendom*. When these conflictions in Cardinal Sarto's defense are cited, Catholic apologists desperately resort to discrediting the Protestant periodical as prejudiced and claiming the Catholic source *Le Catholique National* was not a real newspaper. If the publication were fictitious, it would have been a simple task to discredit it in Cardinal Sarto's time. The Swiss publication is not only real, but it is still stored in the library at the University of Bern today.[13]

Another problem for Sarto's defenders is the Catholic Truth Society—the same organization Don Marino wrote his letter to—cited the same quote from *Le Catholique National* in one of its own publications in 1896.[14]

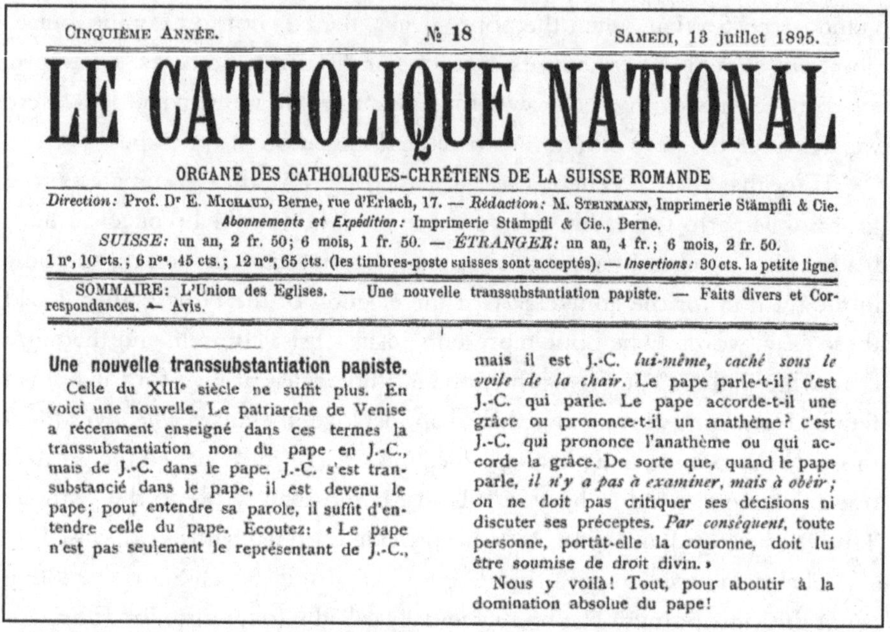

> **CINQUIÈME ANNÉE.   № 18   SAMEDI, 13 juillet 1895.**
>
> # LE CATHOLIQUE NATIONAL
>
> ORGANE DES CATHOLIQUES-CHRÉTIENS DE LA SUISSE ROMANDE
>
> *Direction:* Prof. Dr E. MICHAUD, Berne, rue d'Erlach, 17. — *Rédaction:* M. STEINMANN, Imprimerie Stämpfli & Cie.
> *Abonnements et Expédition:* Imprimerie Stämpfli & Cie., Berne.
> SUISSE: un an, 2 fr. 50; 6 mois, 1 fr. 50. — ÉTRANGER: un an, 4 fr.; 6 mois, 2 fr. 50.
> 1 n°, 10 cts.; 6 n°°, 45 cts.; 12 n°°, 65 cts. (les timbres-poste suisses sont acceptés). — *Insertions:* 30 cts. la petite ligne.
>
> SOMMAIRE: L'Union des Eglises. — Une nouvelle transsubstantiation papiste. — Faits divers et Correspondances. — Avis.
>
> **Une nouvelle transsubstantiation papiste.**
>
> Celle du XIII° siècle ne suffit plus. En voici une nouvelle. Le patriarche de Venise a récemment enseigné dans ces termes la transsubstantiation non du pape en J.-C., mais de J.-C. dans le pape. J.-C. s'est transsubstancié dans le pape, il est devenu le pape; pour entendre sa parole, il suffit d'entendre celle du pape. Ecoutez: « Le pape n'est pas seulement le représentant de J.-C., mais il est J.-C. *lui-même, caché sous le voile de la chair*. Le pape parle-t-il? c'est J.-C. qui parle. Le pape accorde-t-il une grâce ou prononce-t-il un anathème? c'est J.-C. qui prononce l'anathème ou qui accorde la grâce. De sorte que, quand le pape parle, *il n'y a pas à examiner, mais à obéir;* on ne doit pas critiquer ses décisions ni discuter ses préceptes. *Par conséquent,* toute personne, portât-elle la couronne, doit lui être soumise de droit divin. »
> Nous y voilà! Tout, pour aboutir à la domination absolue du pape!

Figure 16: "A New Papist Transsubstantiation," July 13, 1895 issue of Le Catholique National.[15]

More recent popes have also made sacrilegious statements. John Paul II dismissed the ability of Christians to obtain forgiveness of sins "directly from God."[16] His original heretical quote was found in the apostolic exhortation entitled *Reconciliation and Penance*, where he wrote that the Catholic sacrament of confession "is being undermined by the sometimes widespread idea that one can obtain forgiveness directly from God, even in a habitual way, without approaching the sacrament of reconciliation."[17] When attempting to inspire Catholics to go to confession more frequently, he instead ridiculously claimed that God cannot forgive sins unless he hears of them from a Catholic priest.

These quotes placing the pope on an equal or higher level than God and Jesus are exactly what John warned against in I John 2:22-23.

> **I John 2:22-23**
>
> **22** Who is a liar but he that denieth that Jesus is the Christ? He is antichrist, that denieth the Father and the Son.
> **23** Whosoever denieth the Son, the same hath not the Father: he that acknowledgeth the Son hath the Father also.

Before Whom Three of the Ten Kingdoms Will Be "Plucked Up by the Roots"

Daniel was definite—before he saw the Antichrist's eleventh horn on the head of the Roman beast in his dream, he watched as three of the other ten horn kingdoms were defeated. In Daniel 7:8, the prophet wrote, "There came up among them another little horn, before whom there were three of the first horns plucked up by the roots." Later, in verse twenty, Daniel used the phrase "before whom three fell." It is evident from Daniel 7 that three—and only three—of the ten horn kingdoms would be eradicated before the Antichrist reached his full power.

The First Horn: The Rugii [487 AD]

The Rugian Kingdom, established by the Germanic Rugii tribe in the former Roman province of Noricum, met its end in 487 AD after a decisive confrontation with Odoacer. After the collapse of Attila's Hunnic Empire, the Rugii had carved out a powerful sovereign enclave on the north bank of the Danube, frequently involving themselves in the politics of post-Roman Italy.[18] Tensions escalated when the Rugian king Feletheus—influenced by his wife Giso and encouraged by the Byzantine Emperor Zeno—began to threaten Odoacer's northern border.[19] Recognizing the strategic threat posed by a hostile kingdom so close to the Italian heartland, Odoacer preemptively launched a massive campaign into Noricum.[20]

The fall of the kingdom was swift and absolute. Odoacer's army defeated the Rugian forces in battle, capturing King Feletheus and Giso, who were subsequently taken to Ravenna and executed.[21] When the king's son, Frideric, attempted to rally the Rugii survivors and maintain a resistance, Odoacer launched a second expedition in 488 AD that devastated the remaining Rugii settlements.[22] To guarantee the tribe could not rise again, Odoacer forcibly exiled the Rugii population of Noricum to the Italian peninsula, leaving the territory deserted until it was occupied by the migrating Lombards.[23] This collapse effectively ended the Rugii as a sovereign political kingdom, with the fugitives ultimately assimilating into the ascending Ostrogothic confederation under Theodoric the Great.[24]

The Second Horn: The Alemanni [c.496 AD]

History tells us that the second of the ten horn kingdoms to collapse was the Alemanni. The Alemanni were a confederation of Germanic tribes ruled by a king. Their lands bordered the territory of the Ripuarian Franks, whom they frequently raided. Late in the fifth century, the Franks suffered heavy losses during a full-scale invasion by the Alemanni. Sigebert the Lame, king of the Ripuarian Franks, sent a message appealing for help to his ally, Clovis, the king of the Salian Franks. Clovis quickly raised an army and marched to Sigebert's aid.

There are few details in the historical record about the Battle of Tolbiac, which is believed to have occurred in 496 AD. According to the writings of Gregory of Tours, Clovis felt his army was on the verge of losing the battle. Distraught, he cried out in prayer to the God of his Catholic wife, Clotilde. Upon the conclusion of the prayer, the king of the Alemanni was killed by an ax, causing the German soldiers to flee. As a result of the battle, the Alemanni kingdom was lost, and Clovis converted to Catholicism.[25]

The Third Horn: The Heruli [c.508 AD]

The third of the ten kingdoms to fall was the Heruli. The Heruli tribe allied with the Huns during the legendary Hunnic warrior Attila's conquest of Roman Gaul in 451 AD. However, they did not establish a kingdom until the collapse of the Hunnic alliance following Attila's sudden death in 454.

Their kingdom, located in modern Austria, was short-lived. After Attila's death, the Heruli chose a new ally, Odoacer, who had created his own alliance from many of the same tribes and clans that had allied with the Huns. With his military power increased, Odoacer marched on Ravenna and conquered what remained of the Western Roman Empire in 476 AD. The Heruli were such a considerable part of Odoacer's alliance that historians often consider his kingdom Herulian.

In 489, Theoderic, the king of the neighboring Ostrogoths, invaded Italy and began a series of battles against Odoacer and his men. After several years of fighting, Theoderic arranged a banquet with Odoacer to supposedly forge a peace treaty between the two men in March of 493. During the banquet, Theoderic betrayed Odoacer and assassinated him with his own sword.

Odoacer's alliance, much like Attila's, disintegrated upon his death. The Heruli suffered heavy losses on the Italian peninsula as Theoderic executed many of Odoacer's supporters.[26] Eventually, the Heruli allied with Theoderic and retreated to their original territory, residing there until their kingdom was conquered by the Lombards around 508.[27] With the loss of their kingdom, the third horn was "plucked up."

He Would Subdue Three Kings

In Daniel 7:24, the prophet notes that the Antichrist will "subdue three kings." This group of three are distinct from the three horns "plucked up by the roots." Rather than being the same entities, the kingdoms subdued in this verse were those conquered with the papacy's direct influence rather than the earlier powers removed before the Antichrist's ascent.

> **Daniel 7:24**
> 24 And the ten horns out of this kingdom are ten kings that shall arise: and another shall rise after them; and he shall be diverse from the first, and he shall subdue three kings.

The First Horn Subdued by the Papal Antichrist: The Vandals [534 AD]

The fourth kingdom to fall, and the first subdued by the papacy, was the Vandals, who ruled North Africa, Corsica, and Sardinia from 435 until 534. This kingdom's growth coincided with the decline of the Roman Empire. After expanding their realm in North Africa through land battles, the Vandals conducted naval raids across the Mediterranean Sea, enriching themselves at Rome's expense. The Vandals even sacked Rome for fourteen days in 455.[28]

When Justinian became Byzantine emperor in 527 AD, the Vandals were still the most significant threat to Rome. In 530 AD, a man named Gelimer led a revolt that deposed the penultimate Vandal king, Hilderic. Hilderic was a childhood friend of Justinian, who immediately demanded that the king be released from captivity. Gelimer, an Arian Christian, disregarded the Catholic Justinian's ultimatum and began persecuting the Nicene Catholics in Vandal territory, further angering the emperor.

One of the primary objectives of Justinian's reign was his *Renovatio Imperii Romanorum*, or "Renewal of the Roman Empire," campaign, which sought to reconstitute a united Roman Empire. The bishop of Rome, John II, provided the essential ideological support for the Byzantine invasion of North Africa by framing the conflict as a crusade against "heresy."[29] The Vandal Kingdom was an Arian Christian state that frequently persecuted the Nicene Catholic majority. John II used this situation to lobby for imperial intervention. By the time Byzantine Emperor Justinian I prepared his fleet in June of 533, he had secured a formal alliance with the bishop.[30] In a landmark exchange of letters, Justinian addressed John II as the "head of all the Holy Churches," effectively granting the Bishop of Rome supreme moral authority over Catholicism in exchange for his public blessing of the war.[31]

When the famed Byzantine general Belisarius landed, the newly-created papacy's influence ensured that the local Roman-African population viewed the invaders not as foreign conquerors, but as the military representatives of the Church.[32] This internal support was critical, as it allowed the Byzantine forces to move through Vandal territory with minimal resistance from the local populace, who provided supplies and intelligence to the imperial army at the Church's urging. After only nine months, the Vandal Kingdom was annihilated, and the papacy had subdued its first kingdom.[33]

The Second Horn Subdued by the Papal Antichrist: The Ostrogoths [554 AD]

From 493 until 538 AD, the bishop of Rome was heavily influenced by another of Daniel 7's ten kingdoms, the Ostrogoths. During the Ostrogothic papacy, as this era is called, the Ostrogothic kings selected and controlled the bishop of Rome.[34] Throughout his reign, Theoderic had control over much of the territory of the former Western Roman Empire. He ruled as the king of the Ostrogoths in Italy, regent of the Visigoths, and hegemon over both the Vandals and Burgundians before their kingdoms collapsed.[35]

In 526 AD, Theoderic died. His death triggered a series of leadership disputes amongst various claimants to the Ostrogothic throne until a regent queen named Amalasuntha was deposed by her cousin, Theodahad. Justinian supported the dethroned and exiled queen, who was later assassinated in 535.

The queen's murder was the excuse Justinian needed to divert Belisarius and his army into Italy to confront Theodahad. Fresh off his victory against the Vandals, Belisarius landed in Sicily and fought northward through the Italian peninsula. The residents of Rome were hostile to their Ostrogothic occupiers. Realizing their chances of defeating Belisarius and his Byzantine army were weakened by this untenable relationship with their subjects, the Ostrogoths—now ruled by Vitiges—fled Rome through the Flaminian Gate in the north while Belisarius marched into the city unopposed through the Asinarian Gate in the south.

Originally a Gothic appointee, Pope Silverius recognized that the Goths intended to abandon the city to avoid a massacre. To prevent a violent sack, Silverius and the Roman Senate pragmatically welcomed Belisarius.[36] While this allowed the Byzantines to occupy Rome without a battle, it effectively ended the period of Gothic-Papal cooperation and turned the city into the primary target for Gothic counter-attacks.[37] Following an Ostrogothic siege which began in 537, Rome was ultimately captured by the Byzantine forces in March of 538.[38]

By 554, the Italian peninsula was exhausted after nearly twenty years of warfare. Pope Vigilius, who had been held in Constantinople by Justinian, was pressured into acting as the formal voice of the Roman people.[39] He and the Roman aristocracy petitioned the emperor to finalize the "restoration" of Italy. This petition provided Justinian with the legal justification to issue the *Pragmatic Sanction*, which officially declared the Ostrogothic Kingdom dead and incorporated Italy as a province of the Byzantine Empire.[40] With this declaration, the papal Antichrist had subdued a second kingdom.[41]

The Third Horn Subdued by the Papal Antichrist: The Anglo-Saxons [1066 AD]

The papacy's involvement in the Norman Conquest of England was the decisive catalyst that transformed William the Conqueror's 1066 AD invasion from a common dynastic dispute into a sanctioned "holy war." By securing the formal endorsement of Pope Alexander II, William was able to frame his campaign not as a mere grab for power, but as a moral crusade against Harold Godwinson, whom the Normans branded a perjurer for allegedly breaking a sacred oath sworn on holy relics.[42] The pope, influenced by the Archdeacon Hildebrand, who would later become Pope Gregory VII, granted William a papal banner and a ring containing a hair of the apostle Peter.[43] This symbolic support signaled to all Christendom that the invasion had the backing of the Catholic Church, which helped William recruit knights from across Europe eager to fight in a cause framed as a religious reform.[44]

Internally, the papacy's support was also driven by the desire to bring the Anglo-Saxon church into closer alignment with the burgeoning "Gregorian

Reforms," a movement aimed at rooting out corruption and asserting papal authority over secular rulers. Rome ironically viewed the English church as insular and corrupt, specifically targeting the Archbishop of Canterbury, Stigand, who was considered a usurper for holding two sees simultaneously and receiving his pallium from the Antipope Benedict X.[45] William promised to reform the English clergy and ensure the regular payment of "Peter's Pence," a tax collected for the papacy.[46] In backing William and the Normans, the pope aimed to replace the Anglo-Saxon ecclesiastical structure with a Rome-aligned hierarchy that would acquiesce to papal supremacy.[47]

After the Norman victory at the Battle of Hastings, the papacy played a crucial role in consolidating Norman authority and eradicating Anglo-Saxon resistance. In 1070, papal legates presided over the Council of Winchester, where Stigand and other high-ranking Anglo-Saxon clergy were deposed and replaced by Norman reformers, most notably Lanfranc, who became the new Archbishop of Canterbury.[48]

Diverse From the First Ten Kings

The papacy also fulfills Daniel 7:24's prediction that the Antichrist "shall be diverse" from the other ten kings. The authority held by the first ten kings was exclusively political. In contrast, the pope was primarily a religious leader, albeit one who gained temporal power and influence over all of Christendom.

The Eighth King of Rome

In Revelation 17:11, we were told the Antichrist would rule Rome as the city's eighth king. Like Daniel's ten kings, each king represents a leadership position, not an individual person. The sixth different type of leader to rule Rome—the king that "is" because it reigned when Revelation was written in 95 AD—was the emperors. The seventh king was the position of "King of Italy." This title was held by both Odoacer and the Ostrogothic kings, who lost control of the city of Rome in 538. When Justinian wrote his 533 letter to John II declaring the bishop of Rome "the head of all the Holy Churches," this elevated his bishopric to the administrative head over all Catholicism.[49] Once the Byzantines forced the Ostrogothic army away from the city in 538, the new bishop of Rome, Pope Vigilius, used this novel religious significance to fill the political power vacuum created by the eviction of the King of Italy, Vitiges, and his Ostrogothic army.[50] When Pope Vigilius became the political leader of Rome in 538, the papacy's temporal power was realized, making the papacy the eighth "king" of Rome after the seventh king had fled.

A Deadly Wound That Would Be Healed and Three Stages of the Beast

Both the Antichrist beast of Revelation 13 and the scarlet beast Mystery Babylon sat upon in Revelation 17 contain similar allusions to the timeline of idolatrous religion beginning in the time of Daniel. Revelation 13 mentions a deadly wound on one of the seven heads of the Antichrist beast, which was later healed. This head of the beast had three stages—before being wounded, a period where it was dead, and after the wound was healed and the head was revived. Similarly, the scarlet beast of John's Mystery Babylon vision also had three stages: "was," "is not," and "yet is." The beast's head "was" before it was fatally wounded, after which it "was not." When the deadly wound was healed, the beast reached the "yet is" stage.

The Antichrist beast had seven heads, likely a metaphor for the many idolatrous pagan religions. Only one—the head representing the sun cult of Babylon—was wounded to death. It was not Mystery Babylon herself who "was, and is not, and yet is," it was the beast she sat on—Babylonian idolatry.

After Xerxes' religious suppression in response to the Babylonian revolts of 484 BC forced the city's priests to flee, the Babylonian sun cult became a religion without an official home. It migrated westward, first to the Anatolian city of Pergamon, then to Rome. In neither city was it the primary religion the way it had been in Babylon. Although the religion was popular under the pagan emperors, it was never the main religion of Rome. The beast "was" before the revolts in 484 BC wounded it to death. When Revelation 17 was written, the angel said the beast "is not," as its wound had not been healed.

After Constantine's 312 AD conversion, his 313 *Edict of Milan* legalized all religions, including Christianity. Constantine proceeded to infuse Christian ideas into the Babylonian sun cult being practiced in Rome and created a new pagan religion masked as Christianity. During his reign, Catholicism became the most popular religion practiced in Rome. Through the creation of this new religion Babylonian idolatry was revitalized—an event which fulfilled the "yet is" stage of the beast and the healing of its headwound.

Figure 17: Comparison between the Antichrist beast's deadly wound in Revelation 13 and the three phases of the Mystery Babylon scarlet-colored beast, "was," "is not," "and yet is" in Revelation 17.

He Gets His "Seat and Great Authority" from Satan

This prophecy has a straightforward fulfillment. The Bible explains that the Antichrist would be the leader of Satan's false church of Mystery Babylon. Since Mystery Babylon represents the Catholic Church, and the pope is the head of Catholicism, he receives his seat and authority from Satan. Based on this Biblical evidence, it is simple to see how the pope—who certainly has great authority and a seat in Rome—qualifies as the Antichrist.

"Power was Given Him Over All Kindreds, and Tongues, and Nations"

In John's Mystery Babylon vision, an angel explained the waters signified many "peoples, and multitudes, and nations, and tongues." The Antichrist sea beast in Revelation 13 is described similarly. In that vision, John learned this beast would have power "over all kindreds, and tongues, and nations."

The Roman Catholic Church has locations nearly worldwide. Its papacy has ecclesiastical authority over these parishioners, no matter which nation they live in or what language they speak. The correlation between the papacy and the Bible's Antichrist is incontrovertible.

He Will Use Satan's Power, Signs, and Lying Wonders to Deceive "Them that Perish"

Christians and Catholics alike believe the forces at work in the spiritual universe have incredible power to work miracles—either for good or evil.

The Catholic Church has classified many miracles—some of which can be reasonably convincing—including centuries-old bodies of saints that never decay, the healing water of Lourdes, Marian apparitions, stigmata, miracles of levitation, the regular liquefication of the fourth-century blood of Saint Januarius, and many more.

The Catholic Church credits God for these miracles and tells us they are evidence of his power. But since the Bible tells us a false church would arise with a description that irrefutably matches the Catholic Church, why should we believe them? After all, God is not the only being with the supernatural power to work miracles—Satan could just as easily use signs and wonders to intentionally convert people *to Catholicism.*

Whoever you believe the Antichrist to be, the Bible is clear that he will be a false Christian leader and an instrument of Satan on earth. As Paul wrote in II Thessalonians 2:9, the Antichrist's arrival would be "after the working of Satan." The Bible explains the Antichrist will have access to Satan's power, signs, and wonders to deceive would-be Christians, effectively blocking their path to Heaven without them ever realizing it.

He Will Change the Times and Laws

There is no mention in the Bible of God changing the Sabbath day from Saturday to Sunday. In fact, evidence of Jesus' apostles observing the Sabbath after Christ's resurrection is found throughout the book of Acts.[51] According to the *Codex Justinianus 3.12.3*, the first law mandating the formal observance of Sunday as a holy day was issued by Constantine. This law was not released with a Christian title, such as *Sabbatum* (Sabbath) or *Dies Domini* (Lord's Day), but instead under the pagan solar title *Dies Solis* (Day of the Sun). Along with his co-Consul, Crispus, he decreed, "On the venerable Day of the Sun let the magistrates and people residing in cities rest, and let all workshops be closed. In the country, however, persons engaged in agriculture may freely and lawfully continue their pursuits; because it often happens that another day is not so suitable for grain-sowing or for vine-planting; lest by neglecting the proper moment for such operations the bounty of heaven should be lost."[52] The ancient Romans had always observed their holy day on Sunday, as evidenced by Constantine's usage of the adjective "venerable." However, the emperor merely legally required every Sunday to be a day of rest. At this point, nothing related to the times had been changed.

Less than three decades after Constantine's death, the 364 AD Council of Laodicea officially changed the weekly Catholic holy day from Saturday to Sunday. The council's twenty-ninth canon proclaimed, "Christians shall not Judaize and be idle on Saturday, but shall work on that day; but the Lord's day they shall especially honour, and, as being Christians, shall, if possible, do no work on that day. If, however, they are found Judaizing, they shall be shut out from Christ."[53]

In his late-nineteenth-century American publication *The Catholic Mirror*, Cardinal James Gibbons confirmed the Roman Catholic Church's role in the substitution. "The Catholic Church for over one thousand years before the existence of a Protestant, by virtue of her Divine mission, changed the day from Saturday to Sunday," he wrote.[54]

Jesus told us he did not arrive on earth to rewrite Jewish religious laws or customs but to fulfill the prophecies made centuries earlier. In fact, he advised us to observe the old laws and commandments.[b] Most of the ancient Jewish laws are found in the Torah, preserved for Christians as the first five books of the Bible. Among those laws are the Ten Commandments, listed in Exodus 20 and Deuteronomy 5. The fourth commandment instructed the Jews to "remember the Sabbath day, to keep it holy."[c]

Jesus said he was not here to destroy the law, which includes the Ten Commandments. In fact, Jesus even said he was "Lord even of the Sabbath day."[d] He never mentioned changing the holy day to Sunday or abolishing the Sabbath in any way. The Roman Catholic Church's role in changing the weekly holy day from Saturday to Sunday is still more evidence that the pope is the Antichrist.

---

[b] **Matthew 5:17-18** 17 Think not that I am come to destroy the law, or the prophets: I am not come to destroy, but to fulfil. 18 For verily I say unto you, Till heaven and earth pass, one jot or one tittle shall in no wise pass from the law, till all be fulfilled.

Matthew 19:17 And he said unto him, Why callest thou me good? there is none good but one, that is, God: but if thou wilt enter into life, keep the commandments.

[c] **Exodus 20:8** Remember the Sabbath day, to keep it holy.

[d] **Matthew 12:8** For the Son of man is Lord even of the Sabbath day.

Some within Christianity advocate for changing the weekly holy day back to Saturday, a concept referred to as "Sabbatarianism." This book does not advocate Sabbatarianism or changing the Christian holy day back to Saturday. The reason for investigating this topic is to demonstrate one of the ways that the papacy "changed the times"—as Daniel 7:25 predicted.

Technically, the Bible does not identify which day should be the Sabbath; it just says that the Sabbath needs to be observed every seventh day. Paul wrote in Colossians 2:16-17 that the Sabbath as practiced by the Jews of the Old Testament was a "shadow of things to come." He told Christians not to allow others to judge them for eating meat, for what they drink, or for how they observe holy days—as if he was speaking against some of the many ways the Vatican would regulate its parishioners.

> **Colossians 2:16-17**
> **16** Let no man therefore judge you in meat, or in drink, or in respect of an holyday, or of the new moon, or of the sabbath days:
> **17** Which are a shadow of things to come; but the body is of Christ.

The popes did not stop at changing the weekly holy day. With the help of Constantine and other political leaders, the Vatican altered many pagan festivals into Catholic holy days. Christmas,[55] Easter,[56] All Saints Day,[57] and even Saint Valentine's Day[58] are just a few of the many Catholic holidays that originated as usurped pagan festivals that were adopted to make converting pagans less arduous.

Pope Gregory I detailed a similar strategy to assimilate pagans in a now-famous letter he sent in 601 AD to the abbot Mellitus, a missionary in Kent, England. The letter explained the pope's decision to repurpose the pagan temples of Britain as Christian shrines to ease the conversion of the Anglo-Saxons. "The temples of the idols in that nation ought not to be destroyed; but let the idols that are in them be destroyed;" he wrote. "Let holy water be made and sprinkled in the said temples, let altars be erected, and relics placed. For if those temples are well built, it is requisite that they be converted from the worship of devils to the service of the true God; that the nation, seeing that their temples are not destroyed, may remove error from their hearts, and knowing and adoring the true God, may the more familiarly resort to the places to which they have been accustomed."[59] Pope Gregory simplified the conversion process in Britain by recycling pagan temples, just as Constantine had previously adopted pagan holidays into the Catholic liturgical calendar.[60]

If this is not enough evidence to support the papacy's fulfillment of the phrase "he will change the times," Pope Gregory XIII changed quite literally all the times in the year when he created the calendar system currently used in most of the world, the Gregorian calendar. A slight inaccuracy in the Julian calendar had overestimated the length of the year by about twelve minutes and 14.75 seconds, which amounted to a difference of sixteen days between the time of Julius Caesar and Gregory XIII. Gregory reset the calendar back to where it was in 325 AD during the Council of Nicaea, based on the vernal equinox being March 25 that year. This date change was implemented by advancing the calendar from October 4 to October 15 in 1582.[61]

Daniel 7:25 predicts the Antichrist will change not only the times but also the laws. This half of the prophecy is simple to comprehend. The pope has power over canon law and changes it with some regularity. The current canon law, enacted in 1983, declares the pope has "supreme, full, immediate, and universal ordinary power" in the Catholic Church, including legislative authority over religious law. Canon 331 of the Vatican's *Code of Canon Law* explains, "The bishop of the Roman Church, in whom continues the office given by the Lord uniquely to Peter, the first of the Apostles, and to be transmitted to his successors, is the head of the college of bishops, the Vicar of Christ, and the pastor of the universal Church on earth. By virtue of his office he possesses supreme, full, immediate, and universal ordinary power in the Church, which he is always able to exercise freely."[62]

Undoubtedly, the pope is most responsible for changing canon law and, with it, the religious practices, ceremonies, customs, rules, and rituals of the Catholic Church. Papal bulls, briefs, motu proprio, edicts, and decrees are all official documents the pope can write whereby he can change religious laws. However, the pontiff can also "change the laws" in other ways. The bishop of Rome significantly influenced the Roman civil laws in the *Code of Justinian* during the latter part of the empire.

He Will "Make War with the Saints"

In its history, the papacy consistently persecuted, punished, and martyred true Christians. The Middle Ages and Counter-Reformation were incredibly difficult times to be a faithful Christian. The Catholic Church persecuted and suppressed pre-Reformation Protestant groups, including the Albigensians, Waldensians, and Hussites; imprisoned and executed Christians through the Inquisitions in Spain, Portugal, and Italy; and fought the European Wars of Religion against Protestant nations. This period of persecution, murder, and war can easily be described as "making war with the saints."

Who Was the Restrainer?

In Paul's second letter to the Thessalonians, he wrote of a restrainer who would keep the Antichrist contained. Only after this restrainer was removed would the Antichrist be revealed. In II Thessalonians 2:7, Paul explained the Antichrist's "mystery of iniquity" was already active during his lifetime. The many counter-scriptural ideas and systematized rituals that would become the prevailing doctrine of Catholicism were already at work within the Christian community, even in the first century.

However, the "restrainer" was also in place at that time, and his power inhibited these heretical ideas. Eventually, the restrainer would "be taken out of the way," indicating his presence would no longer limit the power of the papacy and the Catholic Church.

> **II Thessalonians 2:6-9**
> 6 And now ye know what withholdeth that he might be revealed in his time.
> 7 For the mystery of iniquity doth already work: only he who now letteth will let, until he be taken out of the way.
> 8 And then shall that Wicked be revealed, whom the Lord shall consume with the spirit of his mouth, and shall destroy with the brightness of his coming:
> 9 Even him, whose coming is after the working of Satan with all power and signs and lying wonders,

The evidence Paul provided in II Thessalonians 2 indicates the restrainer represents the pagan Roman emperors. The emperors persecuted Christians until Constantine's *Edict of Milan*. Even through Rome's "Christian" period, the emperors retained full temporal power over all political and social issues. However, in Rome's post-Constantine era, the Catholic Church held its first ecumenical council, developed the Nicene Creed, crafted the doctrine of the

Trinity, and became exceptionally wealthy. With the Church's endorsement, Constantine and subsequent emperors used punitive legal action and force to persecute any Christian sects that refused to adhere to the official Catholic interpretation of the faith.[63]

The Church's power and heresy increased exponentially between the fall of Rome in 476 and the city's 538 Byzantine reconquest. During this period, the bishop of Rome took the self-aggrandizing title of "Vicar of Christ" and was given power over all Catholicism. After 538, with their novel political influence in hand, the popes severely persecuted any individuals or groups who did not conform to their opinions of what Christianity should be, just as you might expect the Antichrist to do.

Chapter Synopsis

The Papacy Fulfills Every Element of Biblical Antichrist Prophecy
- The pope is in Rome (Daniel 7:7-8, 9:26, Revelation 17:9)
- The popes have historically spoken "great things" (Daniel 7:8, 7:11, 7:25, II Thessalonians 2:4, Revelation 13:5)
- The bishop of Rome received administrative power over the Catholic Church in 533 after exactly three kingdoms had fallen (Daniel 7:8, 7:20)
    - The third horn to lose its kingdom was the Heruli in 508 AD
    - The fourth horn to lose its kingdom was the Vandals in 534 AD
    - The bishop of Rome received power as the "head of all the Holy Churches" in 533 AD between the collapses of the third and fourth kingdoms (Daniel 7:8, 7:20)
    - All ten kingdoms no longer exist, proving the Futurist interpretation of a single, future Antichrist cannot be true
- Catholic allies of the papacy also conquered three kingdoms: the Vandals, Ostrogoths, and Anglo-Saxons (Daniel 7:24)
- The pope was the eighth king of Rome, receiving temporal power after the seventh king, the King of Italy, in 538 AD (Revelation 17:11)
- The pope is a religious leader, not only a political leader, which makes him "diverse" from the other ten kings who arose from the fall of the Western Roman Empire (Daniel 7:24)
- The popes claim to be substitutes for Christ by assuming the title "Vicar of Christ" (Daniel 7:8, 7:11, 7:25, II Thessalonians 2:4, Revelation 13:5)
- The pope has power over many different "kindreds, and tongues, and nations" (Revelation 13:7, 17:15)
- The popes have changed the times and laws (Daniel 7:25)
- The popes "made war with the saints" when they martyred countless Christians for their faith (Daniel 7:21, 7:25, Revelation 13:7, 17:6)

The Restrainer
- Represents the pagan Roman emperors, who kept the Catholic papacy under control until they were taken out of the way with Constantine's conversion in 312 AD

Notable Theologians Who Believed the Papacy Was the Antichrist

Arnulf, Bishop of Orleans (died 1003)
Joachim of Fiore (c.1135-1202)
Peter Waldo (c.1140-c.1205)
Archbishop Eberhard II (1170-1246)
Robert Grosseteste (c.1175-1253)
John Wycliffe (c.1320s-1384)
John Oldcastle (c.1360-1417)
Jan Hus (c.1369-1415)
Jerome of Prague (c.1379-1416)
John Bourchier (1467-1533)
Johannes Oecolampadius (1482-1531)
Martin Luther (1483-1546)
Nicolaus Von Amsdorf (1483-1565)
Ulrich Zwingli (1484-1531)
Hugh Latimer (c.1487-1555)
Miles Coverdale (1488-1569)
Thomas Cranmer (1489-1556)
Martin Bucer (1491-1551)
William Tyndale (c.1494-1536)
George Joye (c.1495-1553)
John Hooper (c.1495-1555)
Robert Barnes (1495-1540)
John Bale (1495-1563)
Philipp Melanchthon (1497-1560)
Nicholas Ridley (c.1500-1555)
Heinrich Bullinger (1504-1575)
John Calvin (1509-1564)
John Bradford (1510-1555)
John Knox (c.1514-1572)
Petrus Ramus (1515-1572)
Girolamo Zanchi (1516-1590)
John Foxe (1516-1587)
Robert Crowley (c.1517-1588)
Theodore Beza (1519-1605)
Matthias Flacius (1520-1575)
John Jewel (1522-1571)
John Whitgift (1530-1604)
Georg Nigrinus (1530-1602)
Thomas Cartwright (1535-1603)
William Fulke (1538-1589)
William Whitaker (1548-1595)
David Pareus (1548-1622)
John Napier (1550-1617)
William Perkins (1558-1602)
Thomas Brightman (1562-1607)
Andrew Willet (1562-1621)
George Downame (1566-1634)
James I of England (1566-1625)
William Gouge (1575-1653)
Thomas Taylor (1576-1632)
William Ames (1576-1633)
Richard Sibbes (1577-1635)
James Ussher (1581-1656)
John Cotton (1585-1652)
Joseph Mede (1586-1639)
Thomas Goodwin (1600-1679)
John Lightfoot (1602-1675)
Roger Williams (c.1603-1683)
Richard Baxter (1615-1691)
John Owen (1616-1683)
Thomas Manton (1620-1677)
James Durham (1622-1658)
Francis Turretin (1623-1687)
Matthew Poole (1624-1679)
Samuel Lee (1625-1691)
John Flavel (c.1627-1691)

Stephen Charnock (1628-1680)
John Bunyan (1628-1688)
Pierre Jurieu (1637-1713)
Increase Mather (1639-1723)
Benjamin Keach (1640-1704)
Samuel Willard (1640-1707)
Isaac Newton (1643-1727)
Robert Fleming (1660-1716)
Alexander Shields (1661-1700)
Matthew Henry (1662-1714)
Cotton Mather (1663-1728)
Isaac Watts (1674-1748)
Samuel Clarke (1675-1729)
John Gill (1697-1771)
John Wesley (1703-1791)
Jonathan Edwards (1703-1758)
Thomas Newton (1704-1782)
Charles Wesley (1707–1788)
George Whitefield (1714-1770)
Jonathan Mayhew (1720-1766)
Samuel Hopkins (1721-1803)
John Brown, Haddington (1722-1787)
Thomas Scott (1747-1821)
Joseph Benson (1749-1821)
Timothy Dwight (1752-1817)
Adam Clarke (c. 1762-1832)
Charles Buck (1771-1815)
William Miller (1782-1849)
Louis Gaussen (1790-1863)
Edward Bishop Elliott (1793-1875)
Charles Hodge (1797-1878)
Albert Barnes (1798-1870)
David Brown (1803-1897)
William Cunningham (1805-1861)
Alexander Hislop (1807-1865)

James Aitken Wylie (1808-1890)
John Cumming (1810-1881)
J.C. Ryle (1816-1900)
A.R. Fausset (1821-1910)
Uriah Smith (1832-1903)
Charles Spurgeon (1834-1892)
H. Grattan Guinness (1835-1910)
August Pieper (1857-1946)
G. Campbell Morgan (1863-1945)
Louis Berkhof (1873-1957)
Oswald T. Allis (1880-1973)
Francis Davidson (1883-1958)
Le Roy Froom (1890-1974)
Cornelius Van Til (1895-1987)
Martyn Lloyd-Jones (1899-1981)
Loraine Boettner (1901-1990)
W.J. Grier (1902-1994)
C. Gregg Singer (1910-1999)
Hendricus Berkhof (1914-1995)
Ian Paisley (1926-2014)
Dave Hunt (1926-2013)
Hans LaRondelle (1929-2011)
Herman Hanko (1930-2024)
Robert Reymond (1932-2013)
Francis Nigel Lee (1934-2011)
David J. Engelsma (born 1939)
George R. Knight (born 1941)
W. Robert Godfrey (born 1945)
Mark Finley (born 1945)
Walter Veith (born 1949)
David W. Cloud (born 1949)
Ted N.C. Wilson (born 1950)
Stephen Bohr (born 1952)
Joel Beeke (born 1952)
Clifford Goldstein (born 1955)

III

THE TRIBULATION AND THE CHURCH

9

THE GREAT TRIBULATION

Now that we have identified both the Antichrist and Mystery Babylon, we can utilize this contextual understanding to inform our interpretations of the warning signs God has provided to us about the harsh period of Christian persecution known as the Great Tribulation.

The Length of the Great Tribulation

The Bible describes the length of the Great Tribulation in three different ways: "a time, times, and a half time," "forty-two months," and "1,260 days." We are told the duration of the Great Tribulation would be "a time, times, and half time" in Daniel 7:25, 12:7, and Revelation 12:14. A "time" is almost universally interpreted by Biblical scholars to mean a year, so "a time, times, and half time" would mean "a year, two years, and half year."

The Old Testament Hebrew administrative calendar had a 360-day year, so three and a half years equals 1,260 days.[1] This calendar also had thirty-day months, so by doing the math, forty-two months would also equal 1,260 days. Whether the length of the Great Tribulation was written as three and a half years, forty-two months, or 1,260 days, the length of time described is the same under the Hebrew administrative calendar used in antiquity.

The key to understanding the Biblical day-year principle was revealed when Jesus Christ's arrival fulfilled the Seventy Weeks Prophecy. Since the

Antichrist would have the power to persecute Christians for 1,260 prophetic days, applying the day-year principle to the Tribulation shows that this time of persecution would last 1,260 calendar years.

The Jews regularly adjusted their lunar calendar to align with the solar year to avoid seasonal creep caused by an annual difference of about 11.24 days. On Passover, Shavuot, and Sukkot, agricultural crops were brought to the Temple as tithes to God. If the Jewish calendar were not adjusted, these springtime holidays would quickly occur at a time of year when there would be no crops to offer.[2] The same is true of the administrative calendar, which needed an adjustment of about 5.24 days.

Although forty-two prophetic months equals 1,260 calendar years, the events that fulfill those 1,260 years must include the adjustments made to the Hebrew calendar. This is because, while the Hebrew calendar was based on the moon's phases, the year was regularly adjusted to begin at the same point in the solar year. Whereas the Hebrew administrative calendar's year had 360 days, the average year with these adjustments was still 365.24 days. Although calculations in prophetic time, such as the conversion of three and a half years to 1,260 days, are based on the 360-day administrative calendar, identification of the prophecies' fulfillments cannot ignore these adjustments and must be based on the solar year.

The Timing of the Tribulation

While we have removed some of the misconceptions about the Great Tribulation's length, we did not discuss when it occurred—*occurred*—in the past tense. For anyone terrified about the potential of having to live through an unprecedented period of Christian persecution, the good news is you will not have to. Biblical scholars unanimously agree that the Antichrist would be the driving force behind the Great Tribulation. So, when did the papacy lead a severe persecution of Christians?

The Byzantine emperor Justinian I cooperated with several popes to use Roman law as an instrument of persecution against non-Catholic Christians. His *Novellae Constitutiones* contains several examples of this weaponization of the law. Justinian's legal code defined a heretic as anyone who did not receive the sacraments from a member of the Catholic priesthood, particularly if they professed to be a Christian. *Novellae Constitutiones XXXVII* pronounced, "A heretic shall not confer the rite of baptism, or discharge the duties of a public office, and a catechumen shall not circumcise anyone. No heretic shall, under any circumstances, have a house of worship, or a place of prayer." *Novellae Constitutiones CIX* similarly disqualified heretics from holding public office or working for the government. *Novellae Constitutiones LXVII* prohibited true Christians from holding private gatherings in their homes for worship.

Novellae Constitutiones CXLIV declared Christians could not pass on an inheritance unless given to a Catholic. It also sentenced any Christians who kept the Jewish Sabbath to exile. Justinian declared, "If any Samaritan, after having proved himself worthy to receive baptism, should return to his former error and be detected in observing the Sabbath, or in doing anything else which proves that he was only baptized through simulated conversion, We order that he shall be proscribed, and sentenced to exile for life."[3]

The Start of the Great Tribulation

Justinian's expansion of civil law to encourage the persecution of non-Catholics would also allow for a gradual power shift from the government of the Byzantine Empire to the Catholic Church. After his 533 letter to John II giving the bishop of Rome full temporal authority over Christendom was codified in *Codex Justinianus 1.1.4*, the only limitation on papal power was the Ostrogothic occupation of Rome. Once the Byzantine army drove the Goths from the city in 538, the series of laws that Justinian enacted during his reign wildly expanded papal temporal supremacy to the point of unrestricted power to persecute true Christians.

From 538 onward, papal persecutions magnified rapidly. Popes tortured and killed many Christians whom they considered to be heretics, convened the Inquisition, started wars against Protestant nations primarily on religious grounds, and ordered the executions of many who translated or published the Bible.

Now that we have identified 538 AD as the plausible starting point for the Great Tribulation, an equally significant event must have occurred 1,260 years later for 538 to be the correct start date. So, the question becomes: what event occurred in 1798 that could be considered the end of the Antichrist's Great Tribulation?

1798 and the Deposing of Pope Pius VI

During the War of the First Coalition, Napoleon pushed the Austrians out of northern Italy in 1796. After a siege of Mantua, the Austrian garrison surrendered on February 2, 1797. With France's path to his city no longer blocked, Pius VI was forced to agree to France's peace terms to prevent an invasion of Rome. Under the Treaty of Tolentino, Pius ceded Avignon, the nearby Comtat Venaissin region, and the Italian Romagna region to France. Eight months after the treaty was signed, the war ended in a French victory.

A fragile European peace lasted from the end of the war on October 17, 1797, until the French general Mathurin-Léonard Duphot was killed amid a late-December riot in Rome. Enraged and eager for retribution, Bonaparte ordered the French Army of Italy to march on Rome.

Due to the weakened condition of the papal armies, France's General Louis-Alexandre Berthier entered the city unopposed on February 10, 1798, and occupied the Vatican complex. Five days later, Berthier organized a new Roman Republic and demanded that the pope relinquish his temporal power. When Pius refused to capitulate—claiming he received his authority directly from God—the French general deposed and exiled him on February 20.[4]

This event was tremendously significant in Christian, Catholic, and world history. The removal of temporal power from the papacy in 1798 had a direct impact on the Roman Catholic Church's ability to persecute Christians. While a form of temporal power was restored during the papacy of Pius VII, it was significantly limited. This also "shortened" the Great Tribulation as predicted by Jesus in the Olivet Discourse in Matthew 24:22 and Mark 13:20.[a]

We have already discussed several Bible passages that describe how the Antichrist persecutes Christians. Daniel 7:21 says the prophet watched as the Antichrist "made war with the saints, and prevailed against them." Four verses later, we are told that the Antichrist "shall wear out the saints of the most High." Revelation 13's description of the Antichrist explains, "It was given unto him to make war with the saints, and to overcome them."

---

[a] **Matthew 24:22** And except those days should be shortened, there should no flesh be saved: but for the elect's sake those days shall be shortened.
Mark 13:20 And except that the Lord had shortened those days, no flesh should be saved: but for the elect's sake, whom he hath chosen, he hath shortened the days.

The Bible not only cautions us that the papal Antichrists would persecute Christians, but that Mystery Babylon would as well. John wrote of the false church, "And I saw the woman drunken with the blood of the saints, and with the blood of the martyrs of Jesus," in Revelation 17:6. In Revelation 19:2, John predicts that God will bring his judgment upon her and "avenge the blood of his servants at her hand." The apostle also prophesied that the church would be judged by God for its treatment of Christians following its destruction, which still has not occurred.[b]

A close examination of the Biblical evidence shows the Antichrist and Mystery Babylon would persecute Christians for 1,260 years, not 1,260 days, during the Great Tribulation. A review of the historical record shows these verses conclusively describe the tyrannical actions of the papacy between 538 and 1798 AD in a way that is impossible for Catholic apologists to dispute.

This is the Historicist reading of the Great Tribulation. Historicism views the Tribulation as 1,260 years across history, not just a fabricated three-and-a-half-year period. It interprets Revelation's prophecies, including the seven seals, seven trumpets, seven vials, and the papal persecution of 538-1798, as a single prophetic continuum fulfilled by real-world events.

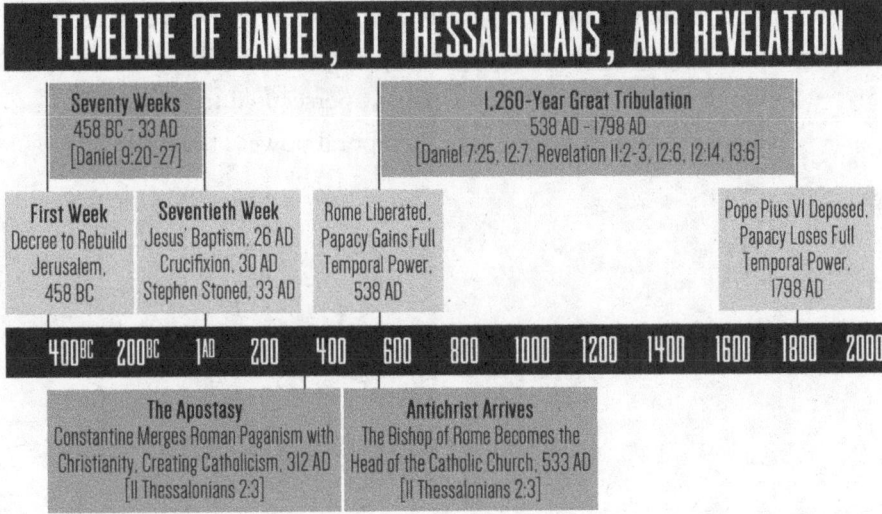

Figure 18: *Timeline of prophecies of Daniel and Revelation, along with their historical fulfillments.*

---

[b] **Revelation 18:24** And in her was found the blood of prophets, and of saints, and of all that were slain upon the earth.

Chapter Synopsis

- The Bible lists the length of the Great Tribulation in three different ways:
  - A time, times, and a half time—or three and a half years (Daniel 7:25, 12:7, Revelation 12:14)
  - Forty-two months (Revelation 11:2, 13:5)
  - 1,260 days (Revelation 11:3, 12:6)
- The Old Testament-era Hebrew administrative calendar had a 360-day year and thirty-day months, which means three and a half years, forty-two months, and 1,260 days are all equivalent lengths of time
- 1,260 prophetic days converts to 1,260 calendar years
- Byzantine emperor Justinian I declared the bishop of Rome "the head of all the Holy Churches" in 533 AD
  - Justinian's letter elevated the bishop of Rome to the administrative head over the entire Catholic Church
  - This letter was codified in Roman law in the *Codex Justinianus*
- The pope used his new authority to obtain temporal power in Rome after the Ostrogoths fled the city in 538 AD
- The pope retained temporal power for 1,260 years—from 538 AD until France's General Berthier deposed Pope Pius VI in 1798
  - During these 1,260 years, the papacy persecuted true Christians
  - The papacy never regained full temporal power after 1798

10

THE SECOND BEAST

Description of the Second Beast of Revelation 13

> **Revelation 13:11**
> 11 And I beheld another beast coming up out of the earth; and he had two horns like a lamb, and he spake as a dragon.

Once John finishes portraying the beast of the sea in Revelation 13, he introduces a second beast that comes "out of the earth." Importantly, this earth beast has the appearance of a lamb but speaks like a dragon, which in the prior chapter was a metaphor for Satan. Colloquially known as the "False Prophet," this earth beast uses his lamb-like disguise to trick Christians into seeing him as a friend, while his motivation is Satanic.

While water usually represents people in Bible prophecy, in this vision, the sea appears to draw a contrast between the beginnings of the beasts. The Antichrist beast originated early in the history of the church. The bishop of Rome became the head of Catholicism in 533, a tumultuous time in history.[1] Europe remained unsettled from the collapse of the Western Roman Empire six decades earlier, the Catholic Church was experiencing major changes of its own, and life, like the sea, was dangerous and turbulent.

In contrast, the False Prophet beast comes from the earth—a far more stable beginning. A standard Biblical word for earth is "firmament," which indicates a solid foundation. The Catholic Church of the second beast would have a well-defined hierarchical structure in a far more stabilized society.

Interestingly, this beast has two horns. As we have established, a horn in Biblical prophecy represents a position of power. The ten horns on the head of the Roman beast in Daniel 7 each represent one of ten distinct kingdoms. Similarly, the False Prophet's two horns represent a dual power structure.

> **Revelation 13:12-14**
> **12** And he exerciseth all the power of the first beast before him, and causeth the earth and them which dwell therein to worship the first beast, whose deadly wound was healed.
> **13** And he doeth great wonders, so that he maketh fire come down from heaven on the earth in the sight of men,
> **14** And deceiveth them that dwell on the earth by the means of those miracles which he had power to do in the sight of the beast; saying to them that dwell on the earth, that they should make an image to the beast, which had the wound by a sword, and did live.

The first beast would empower the second, and the second beast would reciprocate by making people worship the first. The Greek word chosen for worship, προσκυνέω, or *proskynéo*, means "to kiss the hand to (toward) one, in token of reverence."[2] With over 1.3 billion Catholics globally, many people "worship" the pope as a revered religious leader.

The False Prophet is a swindler and a con man with incredible power to dupe many into believing that the pope is a servant of God. The only example scripture provides is that "he maketh fire come down from heaven on the earth in the sight of men." The description of this astonishing supernatural power is reminiscent of the alleged "Miracle of the Sun," the last in a series of purported apparitions of Mary, the mother of Jesus, near Fátima, Portugal.

Three shepherd children, Lúcia dos Santos and her cousins Francisco and Jacinta Marto, announced that Mary had appeared to them several times. In the penultimate apparition on September 13, 1917, Mary told the children that she would perform a miracle in October so that "everyone may believe." The apparition claims were reported in local newspapers, which caused an incredible amount of excitement in the populace. On October 13, between thirty and one hundred thousand people gathered in Cova da Iria, Portugal, to see what Mary would do.[3]

According to the accounts of many who were present, after a rainstorm ended and the dark clouds lifted, the sun began to behave uncharacteristically. At first, it appeared as a dull, spinning disc high in the sky. It then began to shine rainbow-colored light rays like a prism onto the spectators. Suddenly, the sun appeared to speed toward Earth before zig-zagging back into place.[4] Many observers claimed their rain-soaked clothes which "had been drenched and soggy with the pelting, unremitting rain, were suddenly and completely dry"[5]

Of the three children, only Lúcia dos Santos survived to adulthood. In 1941, then-Sister Lúcia recounted the second apparition, which had occurred on June 13, 1917. According to her, she asked the woman she identified as Mary if the children would go to Heaven when they died. Mary said, "Yes, I shall take Francisco and Jacinta soon, but you will remain a little longer, since Jesus wishes you to make me known and loved on earth. He wishes also for you to establish devotion in the world to my Immaculate Heart."[6]

By February 1920, both Francisco and Jacinta had died in the Spanish flu pandemic. Francisco and Jacinta's mother, Olímpia Marto, even said the two children repeatedly predicted their deaths in the short time after the second Marian apparition.[7]

There is not enough evidence in Revelation 13:13 to infer that the power of the False Prophet beast to "maketh fire come down from heaven on the earth in the sight of men" could be directly attributed to the 1917 Miracle of the Sun. However, the spectators' accounts of the sun's behavior could easily be described in that way.

Whether or not the alleged Miracle of the Sun was the future event that Revelation 13:13 prophesied, the Bible clearly states that the False Prophet would have tremendous supernatural power. Many of the astonishing signs and wonders recognized by the Vatican bring new converts into the Catholic faith, just as the events in Fátima certainly did.

It would be impossible to find any conclusive evidence that these kinds of miracles are works of Satan, but can you think of a reason God might push people closer to a false church? We have established that the veneration of Mary is a Catholic ruse. If this were a sign from God, why would *Mary* be the one whom he wanted the three young Portuguese shepherd children to make "known and loved on earth?"

> **Revelation 13:15**
> 15 And he had power to give life unto the image of the beast, that the image of the beast should both speak, and cause that as many as would not worship the image of the beast should be killed.

The False Prophet would "give life unto the image of the beast." This suggests that, before the arrival of the False Prophet, the Antichrist will have begun losing his vigor. He would not have become entirely lifeless, but his power would be diminished. In this verse, we learn that the False Prophet, whom the Antichrist originally empowered, would reinvigorate its creator.

But the second beast would go further than simply breathing life back into the Antichrist. Verse fifteen concludes with a warning that the second beast would "cause that as many as would not worship the image of the beast should be killed." The prophecy implies there would be a separation from Catholicism—an intolerable development for Satan and the Antichrist. The False Prophet would then be authorized to use torture, violence, and murder to subdue those who would not worship or revere the Antichrist.

666 and the Mark of the Beast

> **Revelation 13:16-18**
> 16 And he causeth all, both small and great, rich and poor, free and bond, to receive a mark in their right hand, or in their foreheads:
> 17 And that no man might buy or sell, save he that had the mark, or the name of the beast, or the number of his name.
> 18 Here is wisdom. Let him that hath understanding count the number of the beast: for it is the number of a man; and his number is Six hundred threescore and six.

There is some debate over the number 666 itself. Papyrus 115, a third-century copy of Revelation, and the fifth-century *Codex Ephraemi Rescriptus* each render the number as χις, or 616. However, nearly all other manuscripts and translations of Revelation use χξς, which translates to 666. Papyrus 115, which is just a tiny fragment missing much of the passage, has a hole in the page followed by η χις, which translates to "or 616." This leaves room for a hypothesis that the scribe who copied the verse, who may have been unsure of the correct number himself, could have written "666 or 616."[8]

Second-century Christian writer Irenaeus believed 666 was the correct number, attributing 616 to a transcriber's error. As a disciple of one of John's disciples, his opinion carries extra significance. "This number being set down in all the good and old copies," he wrote, "and testimony being given by the persons themselves who had seen John with their eyes, and reason teaching us that the number of the name of the Beast, according to the Greeks' reckoning by the letters therein will have 600 and 60 and 6."[9]

The phrase that precedes 666 was translated in the King James Bible as "for it is the number of a man." However, the original Koine Greek requires contextual interpretation, as it could also be translated as "for the number is that of man" or "for that is man's number." These alternate translations mean 666 would signify mankind's number in contrast to God's. In the Bible, seven is the heavenly number of completion and perfection, and six is the number of incompletion and imperfection—the highest number attainable by man before Heaven's perfect number.[10]

In Revelation 7, God sealed his true believers with a figurative mark. The mark of the beast would seem to contrast with God's seal, suggesting it also is a symbolic, spiritual mark rather than a physical one. The obvious question is, if the mark is not physical, how can it be on the right hand or forehead of the Antichrist's followers?

In his commentary on Revelation, Reverend William Boyd Carpenter wrote, "It is utterly unnecessary to take this brand of evil literally, any more than we took the seal of Christ literally. That seal we understood as spiritual, in the faith and in the character; this evil brand we must interpret in like manner. It surely means the acquiescence in character and action to the principles of this tyrannical world-power: the right hand is the symbol of toil and social intercourse: the forehead is the symbol of character, as time is ever writing its awful tale upon men's brows."[11]

The number 666 has been applied to a practically endless list of people, groups, and entities over the last two millennia, making it possibly the most misinterpreted prophecy in the entire Bible. The Preterists misconstrue the number by applying it to the Roman emperor Nero. Futurists misinterpret it by suggesting it is a physical mark that will be applied to the followers of an individual Antichrist in the last seven years before Jesus' second coming. While there is no definitive interpretation of this prophecy like the ones that we have found for Daniel's Seventy Weeks Prophecy, Mystery Babylon, the Antichrist, and the Tribulation, one interpretation is the most plausible.

Because the mark could be either the name or its equivalent number, the numerical value of the beast's name would need to equal 666 in either Greek or Hebrew. Both languages assign numerical values to their letters, a system called *isopsephy* in Greek and *gematria* in Hebrew.

One possible solution was first recognized in the late second century by Irenaeus. The Greek word for the ancient Roman people was *Lateinos*, spelled Λατεινοσ in the original language. "The name Lateinos contains the number of six hundred and sixty-six;" he wrote, "and it is very likely, because the last kingdom is so called, for they are Latins who now reign." The "last kingdom" Irenaeus cited was the fourth kingdom of Daniel 7—the Roman Empire—which held power throughout his entire lifetime. The Hebrew word for the Romans was *Romiinth*, or רומיית. In a remarkable linguistic and numerological synchronism perhaps too improbable to label a coincidence, the letters that form the words for the Romans in both languages add up to 666.[12]

Throughout history, the Catholic Church has embraced and emphasized its connection to the Roman Empire. Participants in papal councils spoke to each other in Latin, and the Council of Trent ordered the Latin Vulgate to be the only version of scripture used. Canons and papal bulls are issued in Latin. Masses, hymns, homilies, and even prayers were said in Latin centuries after the fall of Rome. In short, everything in Catholicism is Latinized.

THE GREEK AND HEBREW NAMES FOR THE ROMANS

GREEK: *LATEINOS*

Λ	A	T	E	I	N	O	Σ	TOTAL
30	1	300	5	10	50	70	200	666

HEBREW: *ROMIINTH*

ת	י	י	מ	ו	ר	TOTAL
400	10	10	40	6	200	666

Figure 19: Comparison of the Greek and Hebrew names for the Romans.

Irenaeus' interpretation is fascinating, but its accuracy is immaterial. The mark is a figurative seal—an invisible identifier of the Catholics' unwitting allegiance to the Antichrist and his false church. If you are waiting for an Antichrist to force people to brand themselves to be allowed to buy and sell as a sign that Jesus' second coming is near, you will be disappointed. God has no interest in telling us exactly when Jesus' return will occur by providing a warning three and a half years in advance.

But what about the prohibition on buying and selling for the unmarked? Has history recorded any examples of the Catholic Church restricting the commerce of Christians? Enter Pope Alexander III.

In 1163, the Albigensians—a group now classified as pre-Reformation Protestants—were spreading rapidly through France. The Council of Tours ordered that "no man should presume to receive or assist them, no, not so much as to hold any communion with them in selling or buying, that, being deprived of the comfort of humanity, they may be compelled to repent of the error of their way."[13]

Alexander III held another council in the year 1179. The Third Council of the Lateran also took aim at the pre-Reformation Protestants. By this time, the Waldensians had begun to spread their ideas, adding a new level of danger for Catholicism. The canon of the council chronicled the Catholic Church's fear of both the Albigensians and Waldensians, stating, "We declare that they and their defenders and those who receive them are under anathema, and we forbid under pain of anathema that anyone should keep or support them in their houses or lands or should trade with them."[14]

In the fifteenth century, a similar sentiment returned in the form of Pope Martin V. On March 1, 1420, he issued the *Omnium Plasmatoris Domini*. This papal bull called all Catholics to unite against pre-Reformation Protestants for the purpose of "the destruction of the Wycliffites, Hussites, and all other heretics in Bohemia." The bull not only called for this new type of crusade, it also demanded that Catholics not trade with these perceived heretics.[15] By this time, the papacy's severe persecutions of Christians—ostracization, exile, the Inquisitions, executions, and now commercial restrictions—had replaced and far exceeded those of the pagan Roman emperors.

Identity of the Second Beast

With the little information we have about the second beast, we can come to a reasonable conclusion about its fulfillment. Because of the presence of the two horns, we can assume that the beasts of the sea and the earth rule together. Within this context, we must identify a candidate who shares his power with the papal Antichrist.

This beast is described as a deceptive fraud who looks like a lamb but speaks like Satan. He uses his lamb-like façade to fool Catholics into believing he is a servant of God while speaking blasphemously. The pope empowered the second beast to do a task he could not do himself: make people worship and revere him.

The False Prophet would also have the spiritual power to work incredible miracles. These unexplainable phenomena would drive many people closer to Catholicism, breathing life back into the Antichrist papacy at a time of weakness. However, the False Prophet's power would not be solely spiritual. If anyone refused to worship the Antichrist, he would have the authority to put them to death.

The early Methodist reverend Joseph Benson saw the second beast as the corrupted clergy. The leaders of the medieval Catholic Church carried out the wicked, anti-Christian dictates of the papacy. Centuries later, during the Reformation, the medieval Catholic clergy evolved into a group of far more sadistic foot soldiers—the Society of Jesus, colloquially known as the Jesuits.

Once the Bible became more accessible to those outside the Catholic power structure, the men who would lead the Protestant Reformation could finally read and analyze God's Word for themselves. The Reformers, many of whom were originally Catholics themselves, realized the Catholic identity of the Antichrist and Mystery Babylon and began to preach what they had discovered. They told people to listen to God's warning in Revelation 18:4 and "come out of her"—and millions left Catholicism to become Christians.

Due to this schism, Ignatius of Loyola founded the Society of Jesus, or Jesuit Order, with the approval of Pope Paul III in 1540. According to the Jesuits, their founding mission was one of reconciliation. Today, the Jesuits claim that the objective of this reconciliation is "so that women and men can be reconciled with God, with themselves, with each other and with God's creation."[16] However, this is what every Catholic priest has always done. Why would Pope Paul III and Ignatius of Loyola need to create the Jesuits to do the same thing?

The Jesuits' mission was not to reconcile men and women with God but to reconcile *Protestants with Catholicism*. Their goal was to combat the rapid spread of Protestantism in the early years of the Reformation using whatever means were necessary.

The Jesuits do not operate like pacifist priests. Instead, they behave like an intelligence agency, using clandestine fifth-column tactics to infiltrate and manipulate organizations from the inside. When an influence operation fails, the Jesuits often resort to violence. As Jesus cautioned during the Sermon on the Mount, "Beware of false prophets, which come to you in sheep's clothing, but inwardly they are ravening wolves."[a]

One example of Jesuit violence occurred after Protestant King James I expelled the Jesuits from England on February 22, 1604. The following year, on November 5, 1605, the Jesuits attempted the Gunpowder Plot, a failed effort to demolish the Parliament building and assassinate the King and his Protestant government. At the time, the Jesuits' role in the conspiracy was so transparent that it was known as the "Jesuit Treason."[17]

The Society of Jesus has either been suspected or proven to be behind the assassinations of numerous heads of state and religious leaders. For their actions, the Jesuits have been expelled from dozens of countries since their inception. Portugal, France, Sicily, Malta, Parma, Spain, Austria, and Hungary expelled the Order in the second half of the eighteenth century.[18] At least thirty-five significant and well-documented occurrences of Jesuit expulsion occurred between 1590 and 1990.[19]

However, the number of Jesuit expulsions may be significantly higher. According to Jesuit priest Thomas J. Campbell, the Jesuits were banned from at least eighty-three countries, city-states, and cities between 1555 and 1931. In fact, the Order has been expelled from every European country at one time or another.[20] Virtually every expulsion was due to infiltration, political intrigue, subversion, or incitement to insurrection.[21]

---

[a] **Matthew 7:15** Beware of false prophets, which come to you in sheep's clothing, but inwardly they are ravening wolves.

PARTIAL LIST OF NOTABLE JESUIT EXPULSIONS

Start	Country	Expeller	Immediate Cause	End
Dec 1594	France	Parliament of Paris	Murder attempts on Henry IV	1603
Nov 1605	England	-	Gunpowder Plot	-
May 1606	Venice	-	Pope puts Venice under interdict	1656
1615	Japan	-	-	-
1639	Malta	-	-	1640
Jun 1705	Holland	-	Revocation of the *Edict of Nantes*	-
Sep 1758	Portugal	Marquês de Pombal	Plot to assassinate the king	1839
Nov 1764	France	Parliament of Paris	La Valette bankruptcy	1850
Apr 1767	Spain	Count of Aranda	Esquilache riot, Lorenzo Ricci letter	1815
Nov 1767	Two Sicilies	Bernardo Tanucci	Plot to assassinate king's fiancée	-
Feb 1768	Parma	Guillaume du Tillot	-	-
Apr 1768	Malta	-	-	-
Jul 1773	World	Pope Clement XIV	Suppression of the Order	1814
1818	Netherlands	William I	-	-
1820	Russia	-	-	-
Jun 1828	France	Comte de Montlosier	Interdiction to teach	1850
Mar 1834	Portugal	-	Suppression of all religious orders	-
Jul 1835	Spain	The Cortez	-	1848
Nov 1847	Switzerland	-	Sonderbund civil war	-
Mar 1848	Austria	Joseph II	Revolution	1848
1850	Colombia	-	Revolution	-
Jul 1872	Germany	Bismarck, Falk	Declaration of Papal Infallibility	1917
1873	Italy	Parliament	Dispute with Pius IX	-
1874	Austria	Count Von Beust	Declaration of Papal infallibility	-
May 1880	France	Jules Ferry	Interdiction to teach	1940
1889	Brazil	-	Coup, Dom Pedro II deposed	-
Oct 1901	France	Waldeck-Rousseau	Dreyfus affair	1940
Oct 1910	Portugal	-	Revolution	-
Dec 1931	Spain	-	New Constitution	1939

Table 3: Partial list of significant expulsions of the Society of Jesus.[22]

You will notice from the list of Jesuit expulsions that one stands out from the others. On July 21, 1773, Pope Clement XIV issued *Dominus ac Redemptor*, a papal brief that entirely dissolved the Jesuit Order. Upon signing the decree, the pope—knowing well the evil methods of the Jesuits—declared, "I have signed my death warrant." Fourteen months later, he was proven correct. Before his death, a suffering Pope Clement said, "I knew that I would pay with my life for what I did; but I never anticipated such a long-drawn-out agony and such refinement of cruelty."[23]

Clement XIV was succeeded by Pius VI, the pope eventually deposed by Napoleon's army in 1798. Pope Pius VI's successor was a pope of the same name—Pius VII. In the first year of his pontificate, Pope Pius VII signed the *Catholicae Fidei*, which allowed the Jesuits to work in Russia. Several years later, in August of 1814, his *Sollicitudo Omnium Ecclesiarum* restored the Jesuit Order in full.[24]

Even Pope John Paul I, who served as pope for only thirty-three days before his sudden death on September 29, 1978, was rumored to be a victim of Jesuit assassination. In his book *The Jesuits: The Society of Jesus and the Betrayal of the Roman Catholic Church*, Irish Catholic priest Malachi Martin detailed the Jesuits' potential motive. John Paul I was scheduled to give a critical speech to the General Congregation of the Jesuits in Rome on September 30, 1978, the day after his premature death. Martin wrote, "One of the striking features of his speech was John Paul I's repeated reference to doctrinal deviations on the part of Jesuits. 'Let it not happen that the teachings and publications of Jesuits contain anything to cause confusion among the faithful.' Doctrinal deviation was for him the most ominous symptom of Jesuit failure. Veiled beneath the polished veneer of its graceful romanità, that speech contained a clear threat: the Society would return to its proper and assigned role, or the pope would be forced to take action."[25]

The leader of the Jesuit Order is the Jesuit superior general, who, like the pope, reigns for life. The superior general is so influential that many believe he is more powerful than the pope, even sharing twin nicknames based on their attire—the "white pope" and the "black pope." These two men—one who operates in the sunlight, the other in the shadows—are the two religious leaders represented by the horns upon the head of the False Prophet beast of the earth.

> **Revelation 13:12, 15**
> 12 And he exerciseth all the power of the first beast before him, and causeth the earth and them which dwell therein to worship the first beast, whose deadly wound was healed.
> 15 And he had power to give life unto the image of the beast, that the image of the beast should both speak, and cause that as many as would not worship the image of the beast should be killed.

Revelation 13:12 and 13:15 seem to describe the actions of the Catholic Church during the Great Tribulation, particularly after the Reformation and the convening of the Council of Trent in 1545. The council's purpose was twofold: first, to find ways to bring the Protestants back to Catholicism and, more importantly, to protect the Roman Catholic Church and its papacy from being exposed as Mystery Babylon and the Antichrist.

The climax of church malice and tyranny occurred between the start of the Protestant Reformation in 1517 and the papacy's loss of temporal power in 1798. The Jesuits pressured Catholic nations into wars against Protestant nations. Christians who would not worship or show reverence to the pope and his church endured humiliation, torture, floggings, and burnings at the stake. During the later part of the Great Tribulation, an extraordinary amount of violence was caused by the laughably-named Society of Jesus.

If the Catholic Church wanted to prove the early Protestant Reformers correct—if it was purposefully trying to demonstrate Catholicism was a false church and the papacy was the Antichrist—it was tremendously successful. The more the church used persecution and intimidation, the less Christian it appeared, and the more parishioners Catholicism lost to Protestantism.

The Vatican's loss of temporal power made its war on Christianity more difficult. Rather than open and transparent persecutions, the Jesuits resorted to clandestine tactics—presenting themselves as benevolent priests focused on ministry, education, science, community service, and social issues while their true mission remained political influence and the defeat of Christianity.

The Jesuits' methods were so effective that Adolf Hitler selected their Order as the model for the infamous Nazi SS squads. After World War II, the former chief of Nazi counter-espionage, Walter Schellenberg, confessed, "The SS organization had been built up by Himmler on the principles of the order of the Jesuits. The service statutes and spiritual exercises prescribed by

Ignatius Loyola formed a pattern which Himmler assiduously tried to copy. Absolute obedience was the supreme rule; each and every order had to be accepted without question. The 'Reichsfuehrer SS'—Himmler's title as the supreme head of the SS—was intended to be the counterpart of the Jesuits' 'General of the Order,' and the whole structure of the leadership was adopted from these studies of the hierarchic order of the Catholic Church."[26] The SS was the Nazi paramilitary organization most responsible for the Holocaust.

The Creation of Futurism and Preterism

The Protestant Reformers were nearly all Historicists. Before Preterism and Futurism existed, these Christian theologians taught Daniel's seventieth week was right where it should be—immediately following the sixty-ninth. They recognized the Antichrist would originate from the same people who destroyed the Second Temple—the Romans. They warned Christians that Mystery Babylon—the worldwide false church headquartered in Rome—was the Catholic Church. They cautioned that the papacy was the Antichrist and the Great Tribulation was the period of papal persecution that began during the early Middle Ages and was still active in the sixteenth century. The Roman Catholic Church and its papacy, facing an existential crisis, needed to react.

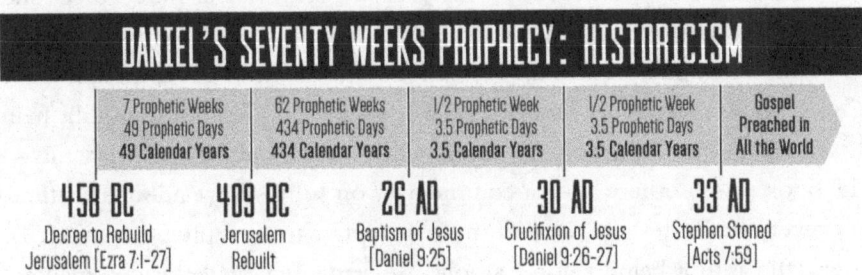

Figure 20: The Historicist view of Daniel's Seventy Weeks contains no gap and is easily interpreted.

Futurism

In 1590, a Jesuit priest named Francisco Ribera released *In Sacrum Beati Ioannis Apostoli, & Evangelistiae Apocalypsin Commentarij* (English: *In the Sacred Book of Blessed John the Apostle and Commentary on the Gospel of the Apocalypse*), a commentary on the Biblical end-times prophecies.[27] This book, written solely to discredit Historicism and deflect attention from the Reformers' criticisms of the Catholic Church, claimed that the prophetic chapters of Revelation would all be fulfilled sometime in the future.

According to Ribera, the apostasy Paul described in II Thessalonians 2 would be a falling away of the Catholic Church from the papacy rather than from God. After this papal apostasy, an Antichrist would confirm a covenant with Israel—a misinterpretation of Daniel 9:27, a verse that predicts Jesus' death would fulfill the Davidic Covenant—and reign peacefully for three and a half years. After this time of calm, the Antichrist would violate his covenant, declare himself God inside a yet-to-be-built Third Temple in Jerusalem, and abolish all other religions. According to Ribera's theories, the Antichrist will then persecute true Christians during a three-and-a-half-year Tribulation, and anyone who does not submit to a physical mark of the beast would be shut out of the global financial system.[28]

The eschatological interpretation Ribera produced is what scholars now call Futurism. Rome quickly adopted this viewpoint as the official position of the Catholic Church. Nevertheless, discerning Christians quickly identified this interpretation as a deliberate distortion of Biblical prophecy. The Vatican needed a new approach to persuade Protestants to abandon Historicism in favor of their Futurist ruse.

The Jesuits were unsuccessful for over two centuries, as the accuracy and simplicity of Historicism made it the only correct interpretation for those not under the manipulative thumb of Catholicism. Then, in 1811, the book *The Coming of Messiah in Glory and Majesty* was published. Written by Rabbi Juan Josafat Ben-Ezra—purportedly a Jew who had converted to Christianity—the book was another Futurist commentary on John's Revelation. This time, however, the Protestants were far more receptive to the Futurist opinion. To them, the author being a non-Catholic Messianic Jew made his commentary more acceptable than one written by a Jesuit priest. But there was a problem. Rabbi Ben-Ezra did not write *The Coming of Messiah in Glory and Majesty*. In fact, he did not exist. Rabbi Juan Josafat Ben-Ezra was a pen name used to disguise the author's identity; Manuel de Lacunza, a Spanish Jesuit priest.[29]

Lacunza's work promptly gained credibility amongst Spanish speakers, particularly in Spain, Mexico, and South America. The Spanish Inquisition purposely banned the book in 1819, and Pope Leo XII placed it on the Index of Prohibited Books in 1824. Both acts were probably intended to enhance Protestants' impression of it as an unapproved exposition that did not align with Roman Catholic teaching.

After the book's publication in London, it was discovered by the Scottish reverend Edward Irving, who had a rudimentary understanding of Spanish. Irving was so enamored with Lacunza's Futurist opinions that he translated the book into English, which he then released as a two-volume set in 1827.[30] Before Irving's translation, the Futurist view of Revelation was unknown to the Protestants of North America.[31] His English translation of *The Coming of the Messiah in Majesty and Glory* was the unfortunate catalyst that eventually led to the adoption of Futurism in most Protestant denominations.

Edward Irving was also the man most responsible for the anti-scriptural theory of a pre-Tribulation rapture—an idea with no basis in scripture.[32] This development also benefited the Catholic Church—if a rapture had to occur before the start of the Tribulation, the Catholic persecution of true Christians between 538 and 1798 could be easily excused as a long series of unfortunate incidents instead of the works of the Antichrist.

The Futurist eschatological interpretation is based on a misinterpretation of the final week of Daniel's Seventy Weeks Prophecy. In Futurism, the first sixty-nine weeks align with the Historicist reading of the prophecy. However, after the sixty-ninth week, the Futurists change the focus of the prophecy from Jesus to the Antichrist. This misinterpretation inserts a two-millennium gap between the sixty-ninth and seventieth weeks, as the subscribers to this view claim the Antichrist has not yet emerged. Futurism also depends on an intentional misinterpretation of the phrase, "and the people of the prince that shall come shall destroy the city and the sanctuary," a reference to the actions of the destroyers of the Temple, not the actions of the Antichrist himself.

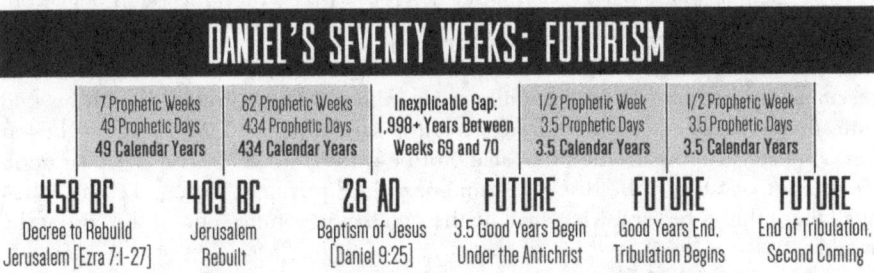

Figure 21: Futurist interpretation of Daniel's Seventy Weeks Prophecy, with a gap of at least 1,998 years.

Preterism

The Jesuits of the Counter-Reformation were not comfortable relying on Futurism alone to confuse the Protestant converts and remaining Catholics. Luis del Alcázar, another Spanish Jesuit priest, wrote his own commentary on Revelation with vastly different views from the Futurists and Historicists. In his 1614 posthumously-published work entitled *Vestigatio Arcani Sensus in Apocalypsi* (English: *A Trace of the Mysterious Meaning in the Apocalypse*), Alcázar proposed that Revelation's prophecies had been completely fulfilled in the first century. According to his theory, Daniel's seventieth week was fulfilled by the First Jewish-Roman War, which lasted from 66 to 73 AD.

Preterism is based on a dual translation of a single word in Jesus' Olivet Discourse, delivered only days before the Last Supper. After teaching in the Temple, Jesus casually predicted the building would be demolished. Stunned, his disciples asked two separate questions. Of the Temple's destruction, they questioned, "Tell us, when shall these things be?" Next, they asked, "And what shall be the sign of thy coming, and of the end of the world?"[b]

Jesus' response simultaneously answered both questions, which makes for a challenging interpretation. Towards the end of his sermon, Jesus said, "This generation shall not pass, till all these things be fulfilled."[c] The Greek word Jesus used for "generation" in Matthew 24:34, Mark 13:30, and Luke 21:32 is γενεά, or *genea*. Preterists latch onto this word to claim the end times should have occurred during the lives of the disciples. Because the Olivet Discourse occurred in 30 AD, the 70 AD destruction of the Second Temple certainly would have transpired during the lives of some of Jesus' disciples and, therefore, within their generation as we define the word today.

However, the word γενεά had other meanings. Joseph Thayer's *A Greek-English Lexicon of the New Testament* defines it as "that which has been begotten,

---

[b] **Matthew 24:1-3** 1 And Jesus went out, and departed from the temple: and his disciples came to him for to shew him the buildings of the temple. 2 And Jesus said unto them, See ye not all these things? verily I say unto you, There shall not be left here one stone upon another, that shall not be thrown down. 3 And as he sat upon the mount of Olives, the disciples came unto him privately, saying, Tell us, when shall these things be? and what shall be the sign of thy coming, and of the end of the world?

[c] **Matthew 24:34** Verily I say unto you, This generation shall not pass, till all these things be fulfilled.

men of the same stock, a family," or "the several ranks in a natural descent, the successive members of a genealogy."³³ These alternate definitions suggest the two meanings of Jesus' prophecy interpreted γενεά differently. First, he predicted the destruction of the Temple would occur during the disciples' generation, which it did. Second, he promised the lineage of Christians would continue through his second coming, never to be extinguished.

Preterism is the easiest eschatological interpretation to refute. It has far more versions and modifications than any other eschatological view. Various elements of the Biblical text must be twisted, distorted, or ignored to give the appearance of alignment with scripture. Similarly to Futurism, Preterism adds a subversive pause between the sixty-ninth and seventieth weeks in Daniel's prophecy. Its sixty-ninth week ends in 26 AD, but its seventieth week does not start until 66 AD. Preterism also has no explanations for the seven seals, trumpets, and vials of Revelation other than to claim these events occurred in the spiritual world. For these reasons, Preterism was also rejected by the Protestants and only found acceptance within a desperate Catholic Church.³⁴

Most Preterists believe that Emperor Nero was the Antichrist and his persecution of Christians was the Great Tribulation. However, there is scant historical evidence of the Neronic persecution. Most of it comes from early church writers a century later, and there is no evidence that it lasted precisely three and a half years as they claim. If Nero did persecute Christians after the Great Fire of Rome in 64 AD, it likely only impacted Christians within the city and not across the empire. Other Preterists contend that the Temple's destruction in 70 AD represents the Great Tribulation, despite it occurring two years after their alleged Antichrist's death.

Like the Futurists, Preterists claim Daniel 9:27 predicted the Antichrist would confirm a covenant with many, but Nero never did. There is also no evidence that he restricted Christians from buying and selling. Nero's 68 AD suicide, before the Preterists' Great Tribulation occurred through either the Temple's destruction or the conclusion of the Jewish-Roman War, invalidates his candidacy for the role of the Antichrist. No event occurred in 61 AD that might represent a starting point for a Neronian Antichrist's final seven-year period of Daniel's prophecy for the Preterists who base the seventieth week on the last seven years of Nero's life. Nero also never "caused the sacrifice and the oblation to cease." Most importantly, Jesus has not returned.

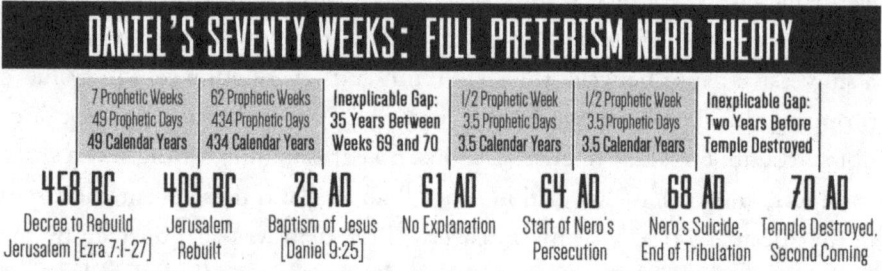

Figure 22: *In one of many Preterist theories, the seventieth week occurs during the First Jewish-Roman War.*

Figure 23: *Another Preterist theory, which shows Nero's persecution as the Tribulation.*

This interpretation has so many flaws that the Preterists cannot agree on what to believe. Some believe Nero was the Antichrist, but the Tribulation was fulfilled by the First Jewish-Roman War. The war lasted seven years, but five of the seven years occurred after the death of their supposed Antichrist. Full Preterists believe the entirety of Revelation has been fulfilled, including the second coming of Jesus Christ. In their belief, Jesus returned in the spirit during the First Jewish-Roman War. If Christ returned in the first century, his living followers, including the gospel authors Luke and John, would have written about the event.

Other issues with a Nero Antichrist exist. Nero died before the fall of the Roman Empire, which contradicts Daniel 7. Nero was also dead before the apostasy in II Thessalonians 2 occurred, which Paul stated would precede the arrival of the Antichrist. Preterists argue that "Nero Caesar" equals 666, but this requires a circuitous approach: taking Nero's *Greek* name *and title*, transliterating into *Hebrew*, and then applying gematria. This hermeneutical complexity suggests a forced premise, discrediting the entire interpretation.

Many Preterists claim judgment day was a prophecy fulfilled by the fall of Jerusalem in 70 AD rather than God's judgment against the entire world.

Some claim judgment day is ongoing even today, and others double down on their misinformed views and declare that we are currently living in the era of the new Heaven and new Earth described at the end of Revelation.[d]

A major problem with the Preterists' interpretation is that their theories apply all end-times prophecies to the Jews of Judea. However, John's first sentence in Revelation, "The Revelation of Jesus Christ, which God gave unto him, to shew unto *his servants* things which must shortly come to pass," proves the book was intended to warn Christians, not Jews.

When it was written, Revelation was a prophetic book, not a historical recollection of past events. For Preterism to be correct, Revelation had to be written *before* the start of the First Jewish-Roman War in 66 AD. However, nearly all non-Preterists agree that the book was written around 95 AD. Most of the earliest church writers believed John wrote his Apocalypse in the latter part of Domitian's reign. At the end of the second century, Irenaeus wrote, "For at no long time ago was it seen, but almost in our generation, in the end of Domitian's reign."[35] Irenaeus was a disciple of Polycarp, one of John's disciples. In his book *Salvation for the Rich,* written around 203 AD, Clement of Alexandria wrote, "when after the death of the tyrant he removed from the island of Patmos to Ephesus."[36] Clement's reference to "the tyrant" dates John's return from exile to just after the death of Domitian.

Victorinus of Pettau wrote his analysis of Revelation, *Commentary on the Apocalypse of the Blessed John,* shortly after 260 AD. "When John said these things he was in the island of Patmos, condemned to the labour of the mines by Caesar Domitian," he asserted. "There, therefore, he saw the Apocalypse; and when grown old, he thought that he should at length receive his quittance by suffering, Domitian being killed, all his judgments were discharged. And John being dismissed from the mines, thus subsequently delivered the same Apocalypse which he had received from God."[37] Other early church writers, including Jerome and Eusebius, supported the later 90-96 AD date for the book of Revelation.

---

[d] **Revelation 20:12** And I saw the dead, small and great, stand before God; and the books were opened: and another book was opened, which is the book of life: and the dead were judged out of those things which were written in the books, according to their works.
Revelation 21:1 And I saw a new heaven and a new earth: for the first heaven and the first earth were passed away; and there was no more sea.

DANIEL'S SEVENTY WEEKS: PARTIAL PRETERISM JEWISH WAR THEORY

7 Prophetic Weeks 49 Prophetic Days 49 Calendar Years	62 Prophetic Weeks 434 Prophetic Days 434 Calendar Years	Inexplicable Gap: 40 Years Between Weeks 69 and 70	1/2 Prophetic Week 3.5 Prophetic Days 3.5 Calendar Years	1/2 Prophetic Week 3.5 Prophetic Days 3.5 Calendar Years	Inexplicable Gap: 1,951+ Years Before Rev. 19:11
458 BC	**409 BC**	**26 AD**	**66 AD**	**70 AD**	**73 AD**	**FUTURE**
Decree to Rebuild Jerusalem [Ezra 7:1-27]	Jerusalem Rebuilt	Baptism of Jesus [Daniel 9:25]	First Jewish-Roman War Begins	Great Tribulation. Temple Destroyed	First Jewish-Roman War Ends	Second Coming of Jesus Christ

Figure 24: Partial Preterist interpretation of Daniel's Seventy Weeks, with a future second coming.

Importantly, if Revelation was written after the beginning of the First Jewish-Roman War, the Preterists' views are invalidated. To circumvent this substantial inconvenience, Preterists claim John wrote Revelation in 65 AD without any supporting evidence. Unfortunately for Preterism, the emperor at that time was Nero, who did not exile Christians.

Preterism is so inconsistent that yet another version of the interpretation exists. "Partial Preterism" takes most of the same positions as Full Preterism, but stops short of alleging Jesus has already returned. These Preterists believe the prophecies of Revelation 4-18 were fulfilled in the first century, but Jesus will return sometime in the future. This view still suffers from most of the same errors plaguing Full Preterism, including the distortion of the Seventy Weeks Prophecy. The only issue Partial Preterism attempts to resolve is Jesus' missing second coming.

The seventeenth-century Dutch humanist and amateur theologian Hugo Grotius was the first prominent Protestant to adopt Preterism. Shortly after he told the Jesuit Denis Pétau he believed the Reformation was unwarranted, Grotius anonymously published a Preterist work called *Commentary on Certain Texts Which Deal with Antichrist* in 1640. However, Grotius also had to make his own changes to Preterism because of the interpretation's many errors. He applied the seven seals to the time between Jesus' life and the Jewish-Roman War, which predated John's Revelation. He hypothesized that the 1,260-day prophecy of two witnesses in Revelation 11 was fulfilled when the Temple of Jupiter was built in Jerusalem, despite the relative unimportance of this event in Christian history. Curiously, he assigned the mark of the beast to the Roman emperor Trajan but attributed the Great Tribulation to Domitian's Christian persecution—both of whom ruled after the Romans destroyed the Second Temple in Jerusalem.

After the true authorship of Grotius' absurd commentary was exposed, he dropped all pretenses and enthusiastically worked to reunify Protestantism with Catholicism—a goal that aligned his objectives with Rome's. Grotius was so eager to reunite Christianity and Catholicism that his concessions to Rome caused many to accuse him of converting to Catholicism. Eventually, the man who once authored his Preterist commentary anonymously openly advised Protestants to return to Roman Catholicism.[38]

Nineteenth-century Biblical scholar Moses Stuart noted that the Preterist view espoused by Luis del Alcázar was advantageous to Rome as it freed the Catholic Church from the villainous role it plays in Revelation.[39] The same observation can be made not only for Alcázar, but the Jesuit priests Francisco Ribera, Manuel de Lacunza, and Denis Pétau, each of whom helped to create or advance Futurism and Preterism to obscure the Historicist interpretation and shroud the Roman Catholic fulfillment of Mystery Babylon.

The process by which the early Protestants' understanding of Revelation was clouded by the false interpretations of Futurism and Preterism shows all the signs of a Jesuit infiltration manipulating Protestantism from the inside. Once these two false interpretations gained a foothold within Protestantism, the Jesuit superior general and his priests pushed further. Due to centuries of effective covert tactics by the Jesuits, nearly all Christian denominations teach Futurism in their churches and seminaries today.

Figure 25: Solar emblems of the ancient Babylonian sun god Shamash[40] (left) and the Catholic Jesuit Order.

Chapter Synopsis

Description of the Second Beast (Revelation 13:11-18)
- Comes from the earth—a solid foundation and stable church
- The second beast has two horns—a dual power structure
- He has a lamb-like appearance but speaks blasphemously like Satan
  - Lamb-like disguise deceives Christians into viewing him as a friend
  - Speaks like a dragon—his doctrine is Satanic
- The second beast is empowered by the first—the Antichrist pope
- He will "give life unto the image of the beast"
- The second beast then makes everyone on earth respect the pope
- He has tremendous spiritual power to work miracles
- Uses his power to bring new converts to Catholicism
- He will "cause that as many as would not worship the image of the beast should be killed"—the False Prophet would martyr true Christians

Interpretation
- Corrupt clergy, especially the Jesuits and the Jesuit superior general
- Two horns represent the pope and the Jesuit superior general
- The pope created the Jesuits in 1540 when the church structure was more stable and the papacy was threatened by Historicism

Mark of the Beast
- The Antichrist's followers would be sealed on the right hand or forehead
  - This mark is a contrast to God's seal in Revelation 7
  - This mark is symbolic, not physical
- Both the Greek and Hebrew words for "Romans" equal 666
  - The interpretation of 666 is irrelevant to who the Antichrist is

Futurism and Preterism
- The Protestant Reformers studied the end times and were Historicists
- The Jesuits were responsible for creating and popularizing both Futurism and Preterism to distract from the Reformers' Historicist interpretation
- Most Protestant churches teach Futurism today due to the influence and infiltration of the Jesuit Order

11

THE SEVEN CHURCHES

The book of Revelation can be summarized as a sequence of apocalyptic visions that the apostle John experienced around 95 AD while in exile on the Greek island of Patmos in the Aegean Sea.[1] The visions, while confusing and unusual on their surface, were given to John by God to warn Christians about the persecutions they would face over the centuries, help them to identify the deceptions of Catholicism, and encourage them to remain faithful.

The earliest church writers tell us that John, the apostle and one of Jesus' twelve disciples, wrote Revelation. One of John's disciples, Polycarp, told his disciple Irenaeus that John had written the book, and Irenaeus preserved this knowledge in his *Against Heresies*. Before Irenaeus, another early Christian writer, Justin Martyr, also confirmed that John was the author of the book of Revelation in 155 AD.[2]

Jesus had a special relationship with his twelve disciples, whom the Bible says he personally called to follow him. Jesus also had this unique connection with Paul, whom he chose as an apostle in a vision on the road to Damascus.[3] The authorship of Revelation by an apostle lends additional credence to the divine inspiration of the book and the power of its prophecies.

Domitian, the emperor of Rome from 81 AD until his assassination in 96 AD, was fond of exiling those whom he believed were "atheists." He used this charge against one of his own cousins, a consul of Rome named Titus Flavius Clemens, and Clemens' wife, Domitilla. As punishment, he executed

Clemens and banished Domitilla to the island of Pandeteria. According to the Roman historian Cassius Dio, "The charge brought against them both was that of atheism, a charge on which many others who drifted into Jewish ways were condemned."[4] Dio's reference to "Jewish ways" suggests Clemens and Domitilla were punished for converting to Christianity.

After Domitian's assassination in 96 AD, the same ancient writer tells us his successor, Nerva, "restored the exiles."[5] Irenaeus likewise wrote that John was released from his exile in Patmos and moved to western Anatolia, the region of modern Turkey where Revelation's seven churches were located. He evangelized there until his death early in the reign of Trajan, which began in 98 AD.[6]

Revelation is a highly structured book. The first chapter is essentially an introduction. It begins with a three-verse prologue followed by a greeting to the seven early churches in Anatolia and concludes with a depiction of John's first vision of Jesus. In the second and third chapters, Jesus provides several sentences for John to deliver to each of these seven churches. He applauds them for what they are doing well, rebukes them for their failures, offers advice on how to improve, and promises a reward if they succeed.

Jesus' evaluation of the seven churches had two purposes. The first and more obvious objective was to guide the first-century Christians in each city. The second, less obvious intent has implications for us today. Theologians often apply these churches' lessons to seven distinct ages throughout church history. The order in which Jesus lists the seven churches in Revelation aligns chronologically with these eras.

This second interpretation adds even more credibility to the Historicist view of Revelation. If Jesus provided messages for each era in Church history, why would he ignore these eras in the rest of the book and only give warning signs for the seven years that precede his second coming? While the Futurists generally support the view that the messages for the seven churches are also intended for each church era throughout history, they believe Revelation's other chapters only apply to the final seven years before Jesus' return. These two contradictory opinions further weaken the justification for Futurism. On the other hand, Preterists generally believe that there is no second meaning behind these messages. In their view, they were only meant to guide the seven churches in John's time.

Ephesus: The Apostolic Age [30-100 AD]

> **Revelation 2:1-7**
> 1 Unto the angel of the church of Ephesus write; These things saith he that holdeth the seven stars in his right hand, who walketh in the midst of the seven golden candlesticks;
> 2 I know thy works, and thy labour, and thy patience, and how thou canst not bear them which are evil: and thou hast tried them which say they are apostles, and are not, and hast found them liars:
> 3 And hast borne, and hast patience, and for my name's sake hast laboured, and hast not fainted.
> 4 Nevertheless I have somewhat against thee, because thou hast left thy first love.
> 5 Remember therefore from whence thou art fallen, and repent, and do the first works; or else I will come unto thee quickly, and will remove thy candlestick out of his place, except thou repent.
> 6 But this thou hast, that thou hatest the deeds of the Nicolaitanes, which I also hate.
> 7 He that hath an ear, let him hear what the Spirit saith unto the churches; To him that overcometh will I give to eat of the tree of life, which is in the midst of the paradise of God.

The first message Jesus gives John is directed to the church in Ephesus. In church history, Ephesus represents the apostolic age, which began with Jesus' ascension and lasted through the deaths of the original twelve apostles. This period would have ended shortly after John received Revelation on the Isle of Patmos in 95 AD.

John wrote that Jesus knew the church's works and labors—their good deeds and struggles as a new, persecuted faith—and their patience. Jesus also told John that the Ephesians had "tried them which say they are apostles, and are not." This suggests that there were many false apostles near Ephesus in the first century whom the church recognized as imposters.

However, Jesus also offered constructive criticism to the Ephesian age. Though the soft wording of Jesus' criticism foreshadows the far more severe admonishments he would have for the other churches, he does critique them by saying, "Thou hast left thy first love." The Greek word used for "thou hast left" is ἀφίημι, or *aphiemi*, which means "to give up, keep no longer."[7]

This passage describes how the Ephesians were still believers suffering for Jesus' name's sake. However, when the church's first generation died off and was replaced by younger members, their love for him had lost some of its original zeal and passion. Jesus tells the Ephesians to repent and return to the type of Christians they were earlier in the first century, when they were more enthusiastic about him.

During this period, Christians were harshly persecuted—first by the local Jewish leaders in Judea, then by the Romans. The persecutions of believers by the emperors Nero and Domitian occurred in the first century AD. The hardships faced by these early church converts were beginning to cause them to drift in their faith. Jesus advised that if they returned to him, they would eat of the Tree of Life in Heaven with him for eternity.

Smyrna: The Church Under Roman Persecution [100-313 AD]

> **Revelation 2:8-11**
> 8 And unto the angel of the church in Smyrna write; These things saith the first and the last, which was dead, and is alive;
> 9 I know thy works, and tribulation, and poverty, (but thou art rich) and I know the blasphemy of them which say they are Jews, and are not, but are the synagogue of Satan.
> 10 Fear none of those things which thou shalt suffer: behold, the devil shall cast some of you into prison, that ye may be tried; and ye shall have tribulation ten days: be thou faithful unto death, and I will give thee a crown of life.
> 11 He that hath an ear, let him hear what the Spirit saith unto the churches; He that overcometh shall not be hurt of the second death.

As Christianity grew, the Roman authorities paid more attention to its converts. The localized first-century persecutions became more widespread during the second and third centuries, eventually becoming a matter of public policy throughout the empire.

No historical evidence demonstrates that Marcus Aurelius was personally responsible for the widespread Christian persecution that occurred while he was emperor in the mid-second century.[8] However, the persecution which coincided with his reign was particularly intense.[9] John Fox, in his *Fox's Book of Martyrs*, wrote, "Marcus Aurelius Antoninus Verus, who began the fourth persecution, in which many Christians were martyred, particularly in several parts of Asia, and in France. Such were the cruelties used in this persecution, that many of the spectators shuddered with horror at the sight, and were astonished at the intrepidity of the sufferers. Some of the martyrs were obliged to pass, with their already wounded feet, over thorns, nails, sharp shells, etc. others were scourged till their sinews and veins lay bare; and after suffering the most excruciating tortures, they were destroyed by the most terrible deaths."[10]

Although this period of suffering ultimately subsided, persecution soon returned with more severe violence. In the third century, emperors became the driving force behind the oppression of Christians. In 249 AD, Emperor Decius, who reigned for only two years, required all inhabitants of the Roman Empire to make a sacrifice to the god Jupiter. At this point, the persecution of Christians evolved from localized to empire-wide. Many Christians across the empire refused to sacrifice to a pagan god and were tortured or executed. Others went into hiding to avoid choosing between angering God or Rome. The effect of the edict on the Christian community was deeply felt, and many recanted their faith out of fear.[11] Emperor Trebonianus Gallus, who reigned from 251 to 253 AD, would also persecute Christians, although on a smaller scale. The persecution during Gallus' reign was possibly limited to exiling the community's religious leaders.

Like Decius, Emperor Valerian required Christians to sacrifice to Roman gods and ordered the deaths of Christian leaders. This posture of persecution would persist until Valerian was captured in battle and his son and successor, Gallienus, repealed his edicts.[12]

At the start of the fourth century, Diocletian began another persecution of Christians, which lasted from February 303 until February 313 AD. Due to its ruthlessness, the decade-long Diocletianic Persecution, also called the Great Persecution, is generally considered the worst Christian persecution in the history of the Roman Empire.[13]

The verses dedicated to the Smyrna church and its corresponding church age are directly connected to these persecutory events. Jesus tells Smyrna he knows their works, *tribulation*, and poverty. While the Christians in Smyrna exhibited good works as Christians, they faced considerable hardships. They were rich in Christ, but financially poor due to the oppression they faced.

John then mentions the tribulation the Smyrnaeans would face a second time, telling this church it would "have tribulation ten days." Since this is a prophecy, ten days means ten calendar years—the same length as Diocletian's persecution. Although many Christians suffered horrific earthly deaths, Jesus promised that they would be rewarded with a "crown of life." He advised his followers that if they were faithful to him until the end of their lives, they would not suffer a second, *spiritual* death.

Pergamon: The Church During Early Catholicism [313-533 AD]

> **Revelation 2:12-17**
> **12** And to the angel of the church in Pergamos write; These things saith he which hath the sharp sword with two edges;
> **13** I know thy works, and where thou dwellest, even where Satan's seat is: and thou holdest fast my name, and hast not denied my faith, even in those days wherein Antipas was my faithful martyr, who was slain among you, where Satan dwelleth.
> **14** But I have a few things against thee, because thou hast there them that hold the doctrine of Balaam, who taught Balac to cast a stumblingblock before the children of Israel, to eat things sacrificed unto idols, and to commit fornication.
> **15** So hast thou also them that hold the doctrine of the Nicolaitanes, which thing I hate.
> **16** Repent; or else I will come unto thee quickly, and will fight against them with the sword of my mouth.
> **17** He that hath an ear, let him hear what the Spirit saith unto the churches; To him that overcometh will I give to eat of the hidden manna, and will give him a white stone, and in the stone a new name written, which no man knoweth saving he that receiveth it.

The Pergamon age of church history began in 313 AD when the *Edict of Milan* legalized Christianity throughout the Roman Empire. This event, along with Constantine's efforts to convert the entire empire with him, led to the creation of the Mystery Babylon Catholic Church—a hybrid pagan-Christian false church that has deceived billions of people throughout history.

The alignment of this era with the city of Pergamon is itself significant. Pergamon is the city where the pagan sun cult migrated after the Babylonian revolts of 484 BC. For this reason, Jesus told the Pergamene Christians that their city was "where Satan's seat is." The fusion of the Babylonian sun cult and Christianity during this church age is why Pergamon was the city chosen to represent it.

Jesus' condemnation of the Pergamene church draws upon an anecdote from the Old Testament book of Numbers. In the story, a devious prophet named Balaam was offered a bribe by a Moabite king named Balac to curse his fellow Israelites. God permitted Balaam to meet with Balac under the condition that he only said what God told him to. When the king expected Balaam to issue a curse against the Israelites, he instead blessed them. Balac tried to extract a curse from Balaam six more times, and each time, Balaam blessed Israel. But the greedy Balaam still wanted his bribe to be paid. With God still refusing to allow him to curse his people, the prophet tried a new strategy. Rather than cursing Israel, he betrayed them. Balaam told Balac how to get the Israelites to sin, causing them to bring God's anger on themselves.[14]

The stumblingblock metaphor in Revelation 2:14 alludes to how Balaam and Balac used idol worship to cause the Israelites to sin before God. Balaam caused the Israelites to stumble in their faith, just as Roman Catholicism has caused parishioners to stumble with iconography. While Balaam was greedy and wicked, he did hear from God and was used by him. Balaam was both a prophet of God and evil—a religious hybrid—the perfect metaphor for this period of church history.

Thyatira: Papal Power Increases [533-1517 AD]

> **Revelation 2:18-19**
> **18** And unto the angel of the church in Thyatira write; These things saith the Son of God, who hath his eyes like unto a flame of fire, and his feet are like fine brass;
> **19** I know thy works, and charity, and service, and faith, and thy patience, and thy works; and the last to be more than the first.

The Thyatira church age began in the notable year of 533 AD. Jesus had more to say about this church period than any other. Its fulfillment represents the longest of the seven periods of church history. Once Rome was liberated from the Ostrogoths, the bishop of Rome leveraged his new power as "the head of all the Holy Churches" to seize temporal power over the city. During this period, institutionalized papal power increased. Catholic leadership was organized into a hierarchy with the bishop of Rome at its head.[15] This era saw the Catholic Church organize, crack down on Bible possession, launch crusades and Inquisitions, and execute countless martyrs.

Jesus commended the Thyatira church on the things they were doing well in verse nineteen. John preserved Jesus' message to Thyatira as, "I know thy works, and charity, and service, and faith, and thy patience, and thy works; and the last to be more than the first." In the Thyatira era, Christians still did good, charitable works to serve others. Their belief in Jesus was strong, but they had the misfortune of living in an era when the Roman Catholic Church hijacked Christianity. Rome's control of the faith caused many who believed in Jesus to erroneously presume the Catholic religion was Christian.

The inclusion of patience here is fascinating. Christians had to endure a millennium of papal persecution before the Reformation freed their minds from the Catholic domination of Christendom. The faith was repressed and restrained by papal power during the Thyatira age, and the Catholic Church became the official authority on what it meant to be "Christian." The laity could not read God's Word due to high illiteracy rates and limited access to scripture, making it difficult to remain faithful to God while waiting patiently for this bleak period of church history to end.

After Jesus praised the Christians of Thyatira, he stated, "and the last to be more than the first." This phrase suggests Jesus would be more pleased by the actions and faith of the Christians living at the end of the Thyatira era than those at the beginning. Pre-Reformation leaders—such as Jan Hus, John Wycliffe, and Peter Waldo—and their followers who lived towards the end of this age endured agonizing persecution. Still, their sacrifices set the stage for the wider Protestant movement of the sixteenth century.

> **Revelation 2:20-21**
> 20 Notwithstanding I have a few things against thee, because thou sufferest that woman Jezebel, which calleth herself a prophetess, to teach and to seduce my servants to commit fornication, and to eat things sacrificed unto idols.
> 21 And I gave her space to repent of her fornication; and she repented not.

Jezebel was a queen of Israel and a follower of the pagan god Ba'al during the time of the Old Testament prophet Elijah. She was responsible for both a slaughter of the prophets of God and the institutionalization of pagan idol worship.[16] In Revelation 2, Jesus refers to her as "that woman Jezebel, which calleth herself a prophetess," drawing attention to both her womanhood and her imitation of a prophetess to allude to the metaphor of a false church.

The parallels between Mystery Babylon and the Thyatira church era can be seen in Revelation 2:20-21. Utilizing nearly identical nomenclature to the words found later in Revelation 17, Jesus explained that Jezebel would seduce Christians into sin and said he "gave her space to repent of her fornication," though she did not. Just as it does in Revelation 17, the word "space" in this context refers to an extended period, as this church age was the longest of the seven. Nearly one thousand years after the Thyatira church age began in 533 AD, Jesus' patience ran out—and the Protestant Reformation began.

The parallels between the linguistic choices made by Jesus and the angel of Revelation 17 do not stop there. Jesus used "fornication" again by saying that the false prophetess of Thyatira would use her teachings to "seduce my servants to commit fornication." The wording of Revelation 2:20-21 reflects Revelation 17:2, where the angel said the kings of the earth had "committed fornication" with Mystery Babylon.

Jesus condemns this church age by telling them they "sufferest" the false church represented by Jezebel. In Old English, the word "sufferest" meant "allow." The Christians of medieval Europe had allowed the Roman Catholic Church to gradually seize control of their faith. Consequently, believers were victimized by the church during the Great Tribulation of 538-1798 AD—a period that closely aligned with the Thyatira church age of 533-1517 AD.

Jesus then employs brutal language to describe the actions of Jezebel's coconspirators and the punishment that awaited them.

> **Revelation 2:22-23**
> **22** Behold, I will cast her into a bed, and them that commit adultery with her into great tribulation, except they repent of their deeds.
> **23** And I will kill her children with death; and all the churches shall know that I am he which searcheth the reins and hearts: and I will give unto every one of you according to your works.

Any Christian who committed adultery with Jezebel was effectively being unfaithful to Jesus by participating in the Antichrist's false Christianity. When Jesus warns, "I will kill her children with death," he is threatening to kill the followers of Catholicism, not with a physical death, but a spiritual one. This is the same threat of an eternal death he conveyed to the Smyrnaean church period when he advised, "He that overcometh shall not be hurt of the second death." This correlation was made clear at the end of verse twenty-three when Jesus told Thyatira that these adulterers would be judged, declaring, "all the churches shall know that I am he which searcheth the reins and hearts: and I will give unto every one of you according to your works."

> **Revelation 2:24-25**
> 24 But unto you I say, and unto the rest in Thyatira, as many as have not this doctrine, and which have not known the depths of Satan, as they speak; I will put upon you none other burden.
> 25 But that which ye have already hold fast till I come.

At the conclusion of the passage, the Thyatira church receives a positive message. Jesus acknowledges that there are many people who "have not this doctrine, and which have not known the depths of Satan." These Christians, including the pre-Reformation Protestants, were not deceived by Catholic dogma. They suffered enough pain while on earth, so Jesus promised that he would not add the weight of eternal damnation.

Sardis: The Protestant Reformation Church [1517-1730 AD]

> **Revelation 3:1-6**
> 1 And unto the angel of the church in Sardis write; These things saith he that hath the seven Spirits of God, and the seven stars; I know thy works, that thou hast a name that thou livest, and art dead.
> 2 Be watchful, and strengthen the things which remain, that are ready to die: for I have not found thy works perfect before God.
> 3 Remember therefore how thou hast received and heard, and hold fast, and repent. If therefore thou shalt not watch, I will come on thee as a thief, and thou shalt not know what hour I will come upon thee.
> 4 Thou hast a few names even in Sardis which have not defiled their garments; and they shall walk with me in white: for they are worthy.
> 5 He that overcometh, the same shall be clothed in white raiment; and I will not blot out his name out of the book of life, but I will confess his name before my Father, and before his angels.
> 6 He that hath an ear, let him hear what the Spirit saith unto the churches.

The Sardian church age began with the dawn of the Reformation in 1517 and continued well into the eighteenth century. When looking over the entire Sardis age, Jesus judged the church as "dead." In verse three, he reminds the Sardians to remember what they had "received and heard," as he wanted the Christians living at the end of this church age to recall the messages received at its start. The earliest Protestants identified many of the conflicts between Catholicism and scripture and advocated for a return to a Bible-based faith rather than a ritualistic, idolatrous religion. These Christian thought leaders used the printing press to distribute their religious ideas to the public widely. The start of the Sardis age would have certainly made Jesus optimistic.

However, the hope brought by the Reformation gradually degraded until it simply replaced one faulty religious doctrine with several. New Protestant denominations soon formed around the ideas of the early Reformers. Many of these new religions would become as doctrinally corrupt as the Catholic dogma the Reformers objected to. The vitality that characterized the start of the Reformation gradually disappeared until most Protestant denominations became just as formalized and ritualistic as Catholicism. During this age, the ecclesiastical battle between Catholics and Protestants would intensify into several full-scale conflicts now known as the European Wars of Religion. The Reformation's failure to make meaningful change fulfilled the prophecy of Revelation 3:2, which predicted Christianity was "ready to die."

Jesus did not compliment the Sardis church. He used the phrase "I know thy works" to praise several church ages, but here he followed it by adding, "I have not found thy works perfect before God." Jesus' examination of the works of the Sardis church had resulted in his disapproval. Satan had thrown all he had at the Protestants and nearly killed the promise of the Reformation.

Again, Jesus reprimanded the church and told it how to self-correct. In verse three, he advised, "Remember therefore how thou hast received and heard, and hold fast, and repent." Jesus was pleading with the members of the Sardis church to leave the construct of organized, ritualistic religion and go back to their roots—the organic, foundational Christian faith.

While Jesus chastised the Sardis church era, he recognized that not all Christians in this church age were dead. He described those who desired to return to the basic tenets of Christianity as "clothed in white"—a symbol of purity and virtuousness used throughout Revelation. Jesus explained that the

Christians in Sardis who faithfully followed him would not have their names blotted out of the Book of Life.

Conditions in the Sardian church era would continue to deteriorate until the time of John and Charles Wesley, Jonathan Edwards, George Whitefield, Gilbert Tennent, and other evangelists. These men, the "few names even in Sardis which have not defiled their garments," protested against Catholicism *and Protestantism*, as the movement had fallen so far from the original intents of its founders. This new brand of Protestant leaders would ignite the First Great Awakening revival and the missionary period—the Philadelphian age of the church.

Philadelphia: The Missionary and Revival Church [1730-1930 AD]

> **Revelation 3:7-13**
> 7 And to the angel of the church in Philadelphia write; These things saith he that is holy, he that is true, he that hath the key of David, he that openeth, and no man shutteth; and shutteth, and no man openeth;
> 8 I know thy works: behold, I have set before thee an open door, and no man can shut it: for thou hast a little strength, and hast kept my word, and hast not denied my name.
> 9 Behold, I will make them of the synagogue of Satan, which say they are Jews, and are not, but do lie; behold, I will make them to come and worship before thy feet, and to know that I have loved thee.
> 10 Because thou hast kept the word of my patience, I also will keep thee from the hour of temptation, which shall come upon all the world, to try them that dwell upon the earth.
> 11 Behold, I come quickly: hold that fast which thou hast, that no man take thy crown.
> 12 Him that overcometh will I make a pillar in the temple of my God, and he shall go no more out: and I will write upon him the name of my God, and the name of the city of my God, which is new Jerusalem, which cometh down out of heaven from my God: and I will write upon him my new name.
> 13 He that hath an ear, let him hear what the Spirit saith unto the churches.

Many theologians use the year 1798 to end the Sardis period, as this aligns with the papacy's loss of temporal power. However, Jesus' focus for these church eras is on the history of his church, not the history of Satan's false church. Based on Jesus' descriptions of the Sardis and Philadelphia churches, the more likely start of the Philadelphian church age is 1730—the beginning of the First Great Awakening.

Only two of the seven churches were not rebuked by Jesus—Smyrna and Philadelphia. Smyrna represented the persecuted pre-Constantine church and received considerable sympathy from Jesus for its suffering. The Philadelphia church received profuse praise from him for its enthusiastic evangelism, even though it only had "a little strength."

Jesus knows no one is without faults, so he does not wait for perfection to praise our triumphs and successes. In his eyes, the Philadelphians' hearts were right and their motives were pure. The members of the sixth church age expressed a zeal for Christ, as evidenced by the revivals, evangelism, and rise of Bible Societies in the eighteenth and nineteenth centuries.[17] Because of the efforts to spread the Christian faith throughout the world during this church age, Jesus told the Philadelphians that he "set before thee an open door"—the door to Heaven—which "no man can shut."

In verse nine, Jesus promises to make those who are "of the synagogue of Satan, which say they are Jews, and are not, but do lie" worship at the feet of the Philadelphian church. Since the messages to the seven churches have a dual meaning, the word "Jews" in verse nine could be confusing. In the first century, there was no widely-used name for Christians. Acts 11:26 tells us the term was first used in Antioch, but nascent Christianity was considered an offshoot of Judaism in most places.[18] In the context of the first century, Jesus' use of the word "Jews" in Revelation 3:9 is a reference to those who falsely claim to be what we now call "Christians."

The imposters Jesus described within the Philadelphia age of Christianity were the Catholic members of the Mystery Babylon "synagogue of Satan." General Berthier's French army subdued the papacy by revoking its temporal power during this church era. The Catholic Church was humbled at the feet of the Philadelphian Christians, not because they defeated Catholicism, but because it was suddenly less significant to Christianity in comparison. In verse ten, Jesus promises to keep the Philadelphian Christians safe from "the hour of temptation"—the era of the seventh and final church age, Laodicea.[a]

---

[a] **Revelation 3:10** Because thou hast kept the word of my patience, I also will keep thee from the hour of temptation, which shall come upon all the world, to try them that dwell upon the earth.

Laodicea: The Modern Lukewarm Church [1930 AD-Present]

Jesus' promise to protect the Philadelphian church from the temptations that the Laodiceans would face was interpreted by John Gill in *Exposition of the New Testament* this way: "This hour seems to refer...to some affliction and distress which will befall the reformed churches." Gill believed that Christ would "purge his floor of all his formal professors and hypocrites; and it will be known who are his true churches, and pure members; and these he will keep close to himself, and preserve safe amidst all the distress and confusion the world will be in."[19]

As the last of the seven churches, Laodicea represents the modern era of Christianity. When reading Jesus' message to this final church era, consider today's culture.

> **Revelation 3:14-17**
> **14** And unto the angel of the church of the Laodiceans write; These things saith the Amen, the faithful and true witness, the beginning of the creation of God;
> **15** I know thy works, that thou art neither cold nor hot: I would thou wert cold or hot.
> **16** So then because thou art lukewarm, and neither cold nor hot, I will spue thee out of my mouth.
> **17** Because thou sayest, I am rich, and increased with goods, and have need of nothing; and knowest not that thou art wretched, and miserable, and poor, and blind, and naked:

Immediately after the Philadelphian age—the era most on fire for God—Laodicea is a dire disappointment. Jesus explained that he "knows the works" of Laodicea and found they were not what he expected of Christians. The wealthy and materialistic Laodiceans "say they are rich," yet they are unaware of their spiritual bankruptcy. The same can be said of most Christians today.

The lukewarm analogy used by Jesus has an interesting historical context. Laodicea was about five miles away from two cities with springs: Hierapolis, the site of a hot spring, and Colossae, which had a cold spring. Laodicea had aqueducts running from both springs to supply water to the city.[20] When hot water traveled the five miles from Hierapolis, it would have lost much of its heat. The same would be true of the cold water flowing from Colossae—the air temperature would have warmed it before it could reach its destination.[21] Whether Laodicea's water was initially hot or cold, the external environment quickly caused it to become tepid.

Jesus said he would spit out the lukewarm Laodicean church, not because warm water is an uncomfortable temperature, but because it is useless. Christ did not use water temperature to measure how passionate Christians' faith is. Both hot and cold water have distinct purposes, but lukewarm water does not. For this reason, Jesus said he wanted the Laodiceans to be either "cold *or* hot" in verse fifteen.[22]

The temperature of our Laodicean church era is not uncomfortable. On the contrary, we have become *too comfortable*. Christians today are too focused on accumulating wealth and possessions, unaware of how we fail to live up to God's expectations. This is a time of great prosperity unmatched in world history, but greed has created a consumer culture fixated on self-gratification. Today's society closely matches the warning from Paul in II Timothy 3:1-5.

> **II Timothy 3:1-5**
> **1** This know also, that in the last days perilous times shall come.
> **2** For men shall be lovers of their own selves, covetous, boasters, proud, blasphemers, disobedient to parents, unthankful, unholy,
> **3** Without natural affection, trucebreakers, false accusers, incontinent, fierce, despisers of those that are good,
> **4** Traitors, heady, highminded, lovers of pleasures more than lovers of God;
> **5** Having a form of godliness, but denying the power thereof: from such turn away.

Many people today are "lovers of pleasures more than lovers of God." Paul cautioned us to avoid such people, even those who define themselves as Christians. Although they may go to church and say the right things, they are far from embodying the traits of the Philadelphian church age that Jesus complimented so strongly. Paul describes the lukewarm Christians as "having a form of godliness, but denying the power thereof." We see this in today's church—Christians rarely attempt to convert new believers, as faith is viewed as more of a personal choice than something to share. Laodiceans go through the motions of Christianity, but most do not share their beliefs with others or live according to God's commandments. They are spiritually "wretched, and miserable, and poor, and blind, and naked."

While Philadelphia received no reprimand from Jesus, Laodicea received no compliment. But once again, Jesus offers some advice for the Laodicean Christians of today. In verse eighteen, Jesus delivers a series of three symbolic metaphors to encourage spiritual purification and improvement.

> **Revelation 3:18-19**
> **18** I counsel thee to buy of me gold tried in the fire, that thou mayest be rich; and white raiment, that thou mayest be clothed, and that the shame of thy nakedness do not appear; and anoint thine eyes with eyesalve, that thou mayest see.
> **19** As many as I love, I rebuke and chasten: be zealous therefore, and repent.

He first asks us to "buy of me gold tried in the fire." Interestingly, Jesus is asking the same church he described as spiritually poor to buy him gold. He is not asking us to give to him financially, but instead to make a spiritual investment in ourselves. When gold is placed into a fire, alloys and impurities are burned off, producing a purified metal. Like the purification process for gold, we Christians can become spiritually rich when our secular impurities and sins are burned away.

In the second metaphor, Jesus advises the Laodiceans to buy pure white clothing to resolve our spiritual nakedness because our faith lacks vigor and depth. As he told Sardis, Jesus promises Laodicea that those who overcome their spiritual trials will be clothed in white—a symbol of purity and honor.

Lastly, in verse seventeen, Jesus condemns the Laodiceans as blind. He advises us to heal our eyes by putting an ointment on them, as we cannot see our spiritual failures. If we live as zealous, pure Christians and repent of our sins, we will receive Jesus' love instead of his criticism.

At the close of the chapter, Jesus uses a metaphorical phrase that should be familiar to all Christians to show us that there is still hope.

> **Revelation 3:20-21**
> **20** Behold, I stand at the door, and knock: if any man hear my voice, and open the door, I will come in to him, and will sup with him, and he with me.
> **21** To him that overcometh will I grant to sit with me in my throne, even as I also overcame, and am set down with my Father in his throne.

What to Learn from the Seven Churches

How should we live our lives with Jesus' advice to the Laodicean church in mind? The answer lies in Jesus' messages to the only two churches with no criticism—Smyrna and Philadelphia. The members of the Smyrna church age suffered greatly for their beliefs. Yet, throughout their persecution, they continued serving God and remained "faithful unto death." Because of their devotion, Jesus said he would give them a "crown of life" and promised they would not be "hurt of the second death."

The Philadelphia church represents the era most on fire for Jesus. During this age, the Roman Catholic Church lost its power to persecute Christians and suppress Bible ownership. As a result, Bible Societies spread worldwide, missionaries were dispatched, Protestant church membership grew, and new denominations were founded. Jesus was proud of Philadelphia, as evidenced by his profuse praise of their works, his open declaration of love for them, and his lack of a condemnation.

Each of us can personally benefit from Jesus' advice in these chapters. Mimic the things he says the churches are doing well and avoid their spiritual failures. Read your Bible regularly, especially the New Testament. Emulate the Smyrnaean and Philadelphian Christians. Do not fear bigotry, ridicule, or persecution. Keep God's Word, and do not deny his name. Vigorously share your faith with others, and avoid being the type of person Paul warned us to turn away from in II Timothy 3:1-5.

It is also critical that we do not succumb to the many temptations that Jesus warned would come during the Laodicean period. Recent technological advances have led to new enticements and distractions. Movies, television, music, social media, and the internet are some of the ways we prioritize our entertainment when we should be sharing God with others. Our desire for wealth and luxury has caused us to lose sight of what is important: spreading the gospel and living the Christian life that would make Jesus proud.

Chapter Synopsis

- In Revelation 2-3, Jesus analyzes the seven churches in Anatolia
- Jesus' message to each church contains a compliment, a condemnation, advice, and a potential reward
- Each message also represents a different age of church history
- Christians can learn a lot about Jesus' expectations for their daily lives by studying these messages

Figure 26: The seven church eras and their historical fulfillment, Revelation 2-3.

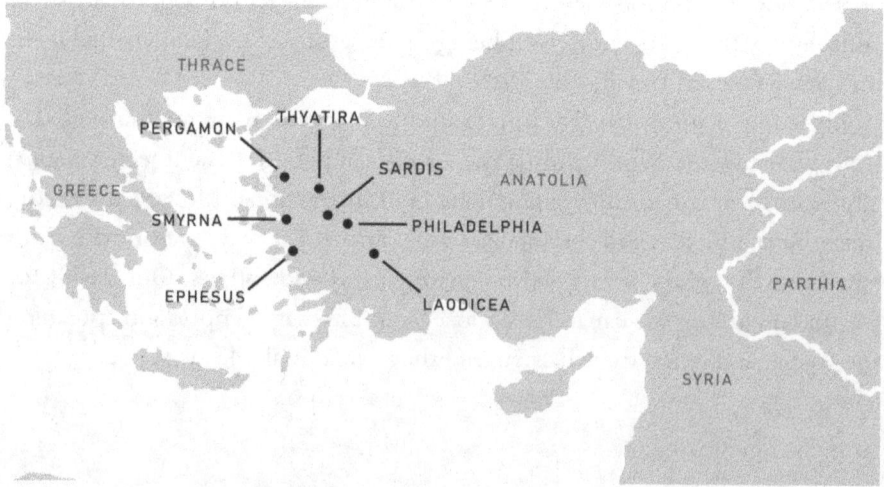

Figure 27: The seven churches of Anatolia in the late first century AD, Revelation 2-3.

Ephesus: The Apostolic Church [30-100 AD]
- Compliment: Works, labour, patience, cannot bear evil, tried false apostles and found them liars, hates Nicolaitanes
- Condemnation: Thou hast left thy first love
- Challenge: Remember where you fell from, repent, and do the first works
- Reward: Eat of the tree of life

Smyrna: The Church Under Roman Persecution [100-313 AD]
- Compliment: Works, tribulation, and poverty (but thou art rich)
- Condemnation: None
- Challenge: Do not fear suffering, tribulation, be faithful unto death
- Reward: I will give you a crown of life, you will not be hurt of the second death

Pergamon: The Church During Early Catholicism [313-533 AD]
- Compliment: Works, thou holdest fast my name, hast not denied my faith
- Condemnation: Hast there them that hold doctrines of Balaam and Nicolaitanes
- Challenge: Repent
- Reward: Eat the hidden manna, give him white stone with a new name written

Thyatira: Papal Power Expands [533-1517 AD]
- Compliment: Works, charity, service, faith, patience, and works
- Condemnation: Thou sufferest the false prophetess Jezebel to teach and seduce my servants to commit fornication, and eat things sacrificed to idols
- Challenge: Have not the doctrine of Jezebel, hold fast till I come
- Reward: No other burden, power over nations, will give him the morning star

Sardis: The Protestant Reformation Church [1517-1730 AD]
- Compliment: Hast a few names which have not defiled their garments
- Condemnation: Works, that thou hast a name that thou livest, and art dead
- Challenge: Be watchful, strengthen things which remain
- Reward: Clothed in white, will not blot out his name from Book of Life

Philadelphia: The Missionary and Revival Church [1730-1930 AD]
- Compliment: Works, a little strength, kept my word, has not denied my name
- Condemnation: None
- Challenge: Hold that fast which thou hast
- Reward: Make a pillar in the temple of God, write upon him the name of God

Laodicea: The Modern Lukewarm Church [1930 AD-Present]
- Compliment: None
- Condemnation: Works, thou art neither cold nor hot
- Challenge: Buy me gold tried in fire and white raiment, anoint thine eyes
- Reward: Sit with me in my throne

IV

HISTORICAL FULFILLMENT

12

THE SEVEN SEALS

When John wrote the book of Revelation, he began by stating that Jesus had given him these prophecies "to shew unto his servants things which must shortly come to pass."[a] The indication is that the visions he communicated in Revelation represent events that would begin to occur, not thousands of years in the future, but almost immediately. This is more evidence against the Futurist interpretation. If the apocalypse is a seven-year period that has not begun, John's prophecies were not fulfilled shortly after 95 AD.

In chapters five and six, the apostle described a haunting vision of a book fastened with seven seals. He observed as Jesus opened each seal individually, releasing a unique catastrophic event with each one. The Historicist school applies these prophecies to the Roman Empire from the time of the apostle John through the late fourth century, with the first seal likely fulfilled during his lifetime.

Familiarizing yourself with the meaning of the seven seals, and the seven trumpets and seven vials that follow them, will provide valuable evidence for where we are in these prophecies today and help you accurately explain the signs of Revelation to others.

---

[a] **Revelation 1:1** The Revelation of Jesus Christ, which God gave unto him, to shew unto his servants things which must shortly come to pass; and he sent and signified it by his angel unto his servant John:

The First Seal

> **Revelation 6:1-2**
> 1 And I saw when the Lamb opened one of the seals, and I heard, as it were the noise of thunder, one of the four beasts saying, Come and see.
> 2 And I saw, and behold a white horse: and he that sat on him had a bow; and a crown was given unto him: and he went forth conquering, and to conquer.

When Jesus opened the first seal, John saw a man riding a white horse armed with a bow and wearing a crown. This rider is the first of the famous "Four Horsemen of the Apocalypse." John wrote that this horseman "went forth conquering, and to conquer."

In 95 AD, the Roman Empire was still on the rise. The first seal applies to the expanding empire as its armies "went forth conquering," an agreeable interpretation based on the imagery of the second verse. The word John used for crown—στέφανος, or *stefanos*—translates as a royal diadem of triumph.[1] White horses were used by conquering generals as they paraded through the streets of Rome in triumphs.[2] The empire did not reach its greatest territorial extent until the end of Trajan's reign, which lasted from 98 to 117 AD and began only about three years after John wrote Revelation.[3] Trajan's military campaigns, which started in 101 AD, represent the fulfillment of the first seal.

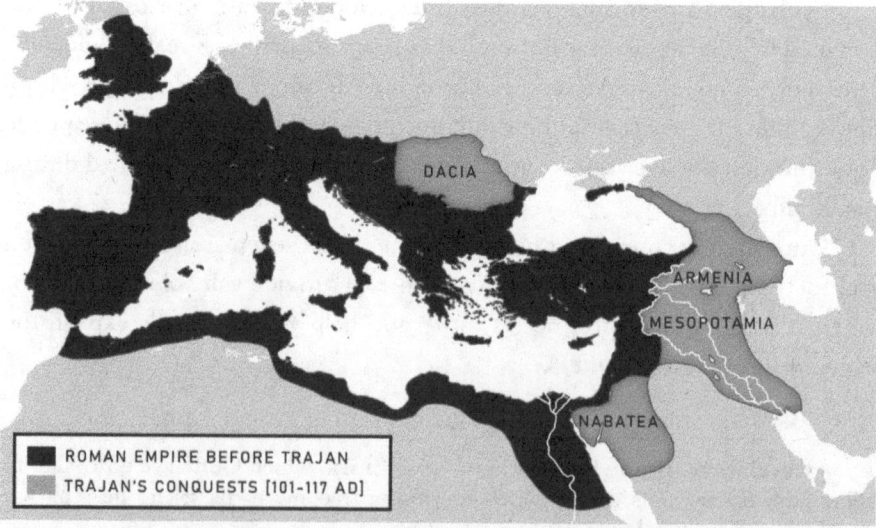

Figure 28: Roman conquests and annexations under Trajan, 101-117 AD.

The Second Seal

> **Revelation 6:3-4**
> 3 And when he had opened the second seal, I heard the second beast say, Come and see.
> 4 And there went out another horse that was red: and power was given to him that sat thereon to take peace from the earth, and that they should kill one another: and there was given unto him a great sword.

The second horseman John saw was riding on a red horse. This rider was empowered to "take peace from the earth." In contrast to the external wars of expansion fought by the conquering horseman of the first seal, the phrase "that they should kill *one another*" implies internal struggle.

Trajan, his predecessor, Nerva, and successors Hadrian, Antoninus Pius, and Marcus Aurelius are known collectively as the "Five Good Emperors," as the empire remained relatively stable during their reigns. After the death of Marcus Aurelius in 180 AD, his debauched son Commodus became the sole emperor. Modern historians consider the chaos of his reign to be the conclusion of the period now known as *Pax Romana*—or "Roman Peace"—a prolonged, 206-year age of imperial stability that began in 27 BC with the ascension of the first emperor, Caesar Augustus.

After the end of Pax Romana, the unrest that followed "took peace from the earth"—precisely as God warned it would in the second seal. Commodus' assassination in 193 AD brought about a power struggle among political and military rivals known as the "Year of the Five Emperors."[4] This environment of bloody civil wars, usurpations, and assassinations lasted nearly a century until the conclusion of the "Crisis of the Third Century" in 284 AD.[5]

While an argument could be made that the first seal is vague enough to apply to any ancient conquering army, the added context John provides in Revelation 1:1 that these signs "must shortly come to pass" made it clear that the rider on the white horse represents Rome. However, the second seal is less ambiguous, with strong allusions to the civil wars, chaos, and instability that characterized the period following the end of Pax Romana.

The Third Seal

> **Revelation 6:5-6**
> **5** And when he had opened the third seal, I heard the third beast say, Come and see. And I beheld, and lo a black horse; and he that sat on him had a pair of balances in his hand.
> **6** And I heard a voice in the midst of the four beasts say, A measure of wheat for a penny, and three measures of barley for a penny; and see thou hurt not the oil and the wine.

The third seal provides more detail than the two preceding it, as there are three principal clues to the event it represents. First, the horseman was seen with a pair of balances in hand. The second clue is the quantities of food that could be purchased for a penny: one measure of wheat or three measures of barley. The King James Version's choice of "penny" was the translators' effort to simplify the term to make it easier for seventeenth-century English readers to comprehend. The original Koine Greek word used was δηναρίου, which means *denarius*—a standard Roman coin equivalent to one day's wage. The last clue comes from a voice John heard in the vision, which instructs, "See thou hurt not the oil and the wine."

The initial interpretation most readers take from these verses is that of a famine. However, as Edward Bishop Elliott explored in *Horae Apocalypticae*, the prices defined in Revelation 6:6 were not high enough to indicate famine.[6] Citing Pliny the Elder's *The Natural History*, he wrote, "Judging by what the elder Pliny reports of prices not very long before, we shall find that though the price of wheat here named might be a scarcity-price, it could hardly be called one of famine."[7] So, what factors could have caused scarcity prices if not a famine?

The first clue we identified for the fulfillment of the third horseman was the "pair of balances in his hand." Elliott noted that even in John's time, the simplest and most common interpretation of balances was as a symbol of law and justice.[8] By the reign of Marcus Aurelius Antoninus—better known as Caracalla—the civil wars were beginning to take a toll on the Roman treasury. Furthermore, the empire's financial situation worsened due to a pay increase Caracalla decreed for Rome's soldiers.[9] As the emperor proclaimed, "Nobody should have any money but I, so that I may bestow it upon the soldiers."[10]

Caracalla needed to quickly identify new revenue sources to fund Rome's military defenses.

In 212 AD, Caracalla introduced an inventive solution to address Rome's dwindling treasury called the *Constitutio Antoniniana*. This eponymous decree granted Roman citizenship to all free men living within the boundaries of the empire. The third-century Roman jurist Ulpian explained, "Everyone living in the Roman world has been made a Roman citizen as a consequence of the enactment of the Emperor Antoninus."[11] This assimilation of barbarians and other foreigners into the citizenry of the Roman Empire is the fulfillment of the "iron mixed with clay" in Nebuchadnezzar's dream in Daniel 2:41-43.

According to the writings of the contemporary Roman historian Cassius Dio, Caracalla's rationale for this proclamation was to increase the Roman tax-paying population. The new citizens were now accountable for taxes on their inheritances and vicesima libertatis taxes for the emancipation of slaves. *Constitutio Antoniniana* also raised inheritance taxes from five to ten percent and abolished tax exemptions. Cassius Dio rationalized, "This was the reason why he made all the people in his empire Roman citizens; nominally he was honouring them, but his real purpose was to increase his revenues by this means, inasmuch as aliens did not have to pay most of these taxes."[12]

While the prices for wheat and barley were high, they did not indicate a famine. This price inflation was not caused by a drought, war, crop failure, or natural disaster but by the higher tax burden charged to Roman citizens, which abruptly became oppressive. Caracalla and his successors robbed the working class to pay significantly higher wages to Rome's soldiers and finance the extravagance of the imperial court.

In *The History of the Decline and Fall of the Roman Empire*, English historian Edward Gibbon explains how the third-century Roman agricultural industry suffered economically under the weight of these taxes. "The animating health and vigour were fled," he wrote. "The industry of the people was discouraged and exhausted by a long series of oppression."[13] This tax burden demoralized the farmers, leading to a production shortage and a depression, as many grew less food and others stopped growing altogether. The strategic abandonment of farmland to evade predatory taxation—a practice known as *agri deserti*—ignited a food crisis. As cultivation plummeted and the value of its currency collapsed, Rome found itself unable to subsidize grain or sustain its military.[14]

This production shortage would explain the trivial amount of food that could be purchased for a full day's wage in Revelation 6:6 and the command, "See thou hurt not the oil and the wine." The voice John heard that issued these directives came from "the midst of the four beasts." The verse makes clear that the third horseman did not utter these instructions. If the directions were instead a command to the horseman, there should be an indication in the passage that he intended to commit the destruction of oil and wine before he was stopped, but there is no suggestion of this. If the voice is not directed at the horseman, who is its order intended for?

Oil and wine were not luxury items in the ancient world—they were daily essentials. These products were important exports and significant sources of revenue for the empire. It would have been critical to the Roman economy to guarantee that all olive growers and viticulturists continued to produce the necessary quantities of oil and wine.[15]

A close examination of the economic environment of Caracalla's Rome and the three clues we initially identified in verses five and six clarifies the interpretation of this passage. If the voice that made the proclamation on wheat and barley prices was the Roman government, wouldn't the simplest explanation of the command to "hurt not the oil and wine" be that it also represents the government?

Caracalla's *Constitutio Antoniniana* levied oppressive taxes on the Roman people. The balances in the hand of the horseman in the context of the verse indicate a strict application of the law. The impulse of many Roman subjects was to damage the production of goods to reduce their tax burden, so much so that the voice fixing prices for wheat and barley also commanded olive and grape growers not to hurt Rome's exports by damaging their trees and vines. Our voice in verse six is aimed at Roman farmers, demanding they not destroy their olive trees and grapevines to avoid paying higher taxes.

Ascending to the throne just a decade after the passage of the *Constitutio Antoniniana*, Emperor Severus Alexander assumed power at the young age of thirteen. Despite his adolescence, he is noted by historians for his effective economic interventions—particularly in stabilizing the prices of grain and other essential commodities—though most of the credit for these reforms is attributed to his mother Julia Avita Mamaea, his grandmother Julia Maesa, and the influential jurist Ulpian.

Severus Alexander built state-sponsored regional grain storehouses and allowed any citizens who lacked private granaries to use them.[16] He increased the volume of imports from overseas territories in North Africa and Egypt by providing significant tax breaks and legal privileges to the navicularii—the Roman shipowners and merchants involved in the grain trade.[17] Alexander's reforms also laid the foundation for the later emperor Aurelian to improve and expand the Cura Annonae, the state-run system of grain distribution, to ensure stable prices. Aurelian also increased the distribution of baked bread rather than raw grain in the empire. This reform lowered the cost of bread to the poor, as they no longer had to pay for milling or baking.[18]

The restraints placed by the government limiting the damage to wheat and barley while sparing oil and wine do not suggest a differentiation between wants and needs, as oil and wine were almost necessities in ancient Rome. It does not indicate a class distinction between the continued prosperity of the rich and the simultaneous suffering of the poor, as some suggest. It also does not indicate a drought or famine, as the grains used to make bread would suffer a similar fate as the olive trees and grape vines used to produce oil and wine under such conditions. Instead, the indication is that the olive growers and winemakers were equally concerned about the weight of the taxes as the Roman farmers, but were commanded not to reduce production by the same government entity that fixed prices for the primary ingredients of bread.[19] This high-tax environment introduced under Caracalla in 212 AD lingered until the reign of Emperor Diocletian at the end of the third century.[20]

The Fourth Seal

> **Revelation 6:7-8**
> 7 And when he had opened the fourth seal, I heard the voice of the fourth beast say, Come and see.
> 8 And I looked, and behold a pale horse: and his name that sat on him was Death, and Hell followed with him. And power was given unto them over the fourth part of the earth, to kill with sword, and with hunger, and with death, and with the beasts of the earth.

There is no debate about what the fourth rider represents, as his name is provided. Death, as the rider of the pale horse is called, rides across the earth using four different methods to kill. Close behind Death follows Hell, ready to ensnare those who are slain for an eternity of suffering.

The phrase "the fourth part of the earth" over which Death was given power appears to have been slightly mistranslated by the King James Bible. The Latin Vulgate Bible, translated between 382 and 405 AD by Jerome,[21] uses a slightly different phrase. The *Codex Amiatinus*, the oldest surviving copy of the Vulgate, uses "super quatuor partes terræ," which translates to "on the four parts of the earth" rather than "the fourth part."[22] This difference is not insignificant. If "the fourth part" is the correct translation, this would imply that only a quarter of the earth would be impacted by this seal. However, "the four parts of the earth" would be comparable to the four corners of the earth or its four cardinal directions, symbolizing a global catastrophe.

To find the correct fulfillment of the fourth seal, we must examine the historical record for a period following Caracalla's *Constitutio Antoniniana* in 212 AD which could easily be defined as a time of widespread death in the Roman world—one with deaths caused by wars, starvation, disease, and even wild animals.

After Pax Romana ended, civil wars and wars of succession raged from 193 AD through the end of the third century. The climax of this violent and turbulent period was the aforementioned Crisis of the Third Century, which lasted from the ascension of Maximinus Thrax following the assassination of Severus Alexander in 235 AD until shortly after the beginning of Diocletian's reign in 284. This chaotic fifty-year period saw twenty legitimate emperors recognized by the Senate and numerous others who claimed the title. Civil wars between ambitious generals and their military factions severely depleted the financial and personnel resources of the empire, which further weakened Rome's ability to defend itself.

This disastrous period was not limited to civil wars within the empire's borders. Rival kingdoms sensed Rome's vulnerability and acted aggressively. Shapur I of the Sassanid Empire invaded Roman territory in Mesopotamia, defeating the imperial forces at the battles of Rhesaina and Misiche in 243 and 244 AD and gaining territory in the process. After an eight-year peace, Shapur earned another victory in 252 AD over the Romans at Barbalissus in Syria before losing at nearby Emesa the following year.

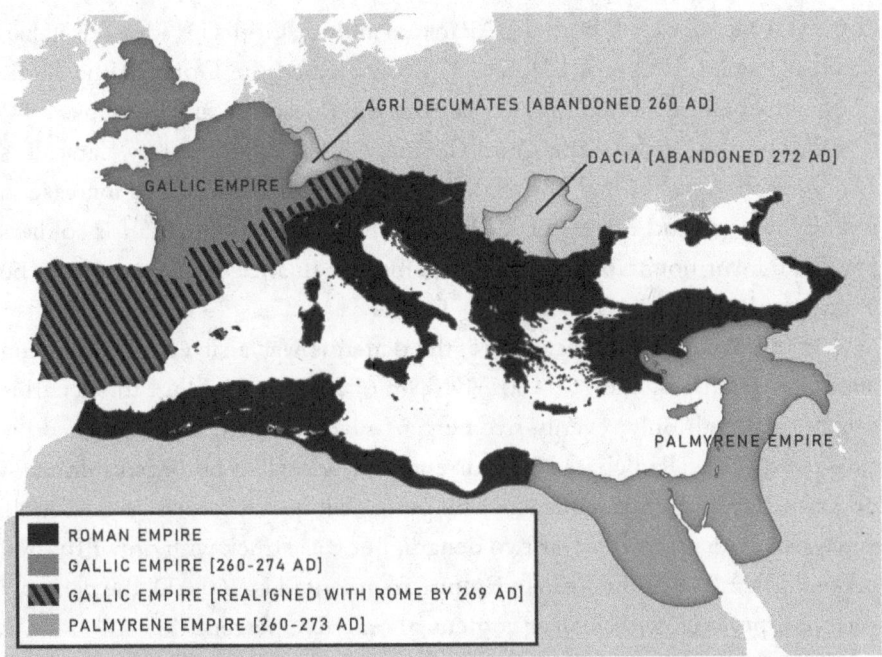

Figure 29: The tripartite division of the Roman Empire during the Crisis of the Third Century.

In 256 AD, Shapur advanced on the Roman fortress of Dura-Europos and razed it to the ground. Emperor Valerian's forces stopped the Sassanid army's progress, but the stalemate was only temporary. Hostilities culminated at Edessa in 260 AD when Shapur captured Valerian—the first time a Roman emperor was taken alive in battle.

The Sassanids were far from the sole opportunists to profit at Rome's expense. The Goths raided the Roman provinces in Anatolia and the Balkans from the northwestern coast of the Black Sea in 238 AD. In 259 AD, another East Germanic tribe, the Alemanni, crossed the Alps and invaded the Italian peninsula from the north.

Rome's situation deteriorated into unprecedented chaos in 260 AD when its territory fractured into three independent regions. The southeasternmost provinces seceded and formed the Palmyrene Empire, which survived until its Roman reconquest in 273. All Roman lands to the north and west of Italy broke away to form the Gallic Empire, which Rome partially reconquered in 260 and completely subjugated after the Battle of Châlons in 274.[23]

Emboldened by the Roman infighting, the Heruli invaded the regions of Greece, Macedonia, and Thrace from the territory around the Sea of Azov in

267 AD. One year later, both the Alemanni and the Goths invaded the Italian peninsula again. Emperor Claudius II first defeated the Goths at the Battle of Naissus before routing the Alemanni at the Battle of Lake Benacus.

During the Crisis of the Third Century, the issues caused by Caracalla's *Constitutio Antoniniana* had not abated. The emperor's substantial increase in military salaries and expansion of both enlistment and benefits for soldiers placed an insurmountable strain on the empire's finances which could not be overcome by simply increasing taxes further.

At the dawn of Rome's empire, the denarius was a silver coin weighing about 4.5 grams. By the 161-180 AD reign of Marcus Aurelius, the denarius was minted with only seventy-five percent silver. Shortly after he issued his *Constitutio*, Caracalla debased the currency further when he began minting a new coin called the antoninianus. This coin, colloquially known as a "double denarius," had a face value of two denarii, but was struck with only fifty-two percent silver. When the Roman Empire fragmented in 260 AD, the denarius was a copper coin with a silver content of only five percent.[24]

This debasement of Roman currency caused hyperinflation throughout the empire, with prices ballooning an estimated one thousand percent. The inflationary environment required more salary increases to retain the soldiers' loyalty as the value of the coins they were paid decreased. This required an increase in the amount of coinage in circulation, deepening the problem.

Currency debasement magnified the food production shortage caused by the high taxes of the *Constitutio Antoniniana*. The cost of empire had increased while Rome was no longer plundering the riches of its enemies and its money had become nearly worthless. Scarcity quickly became pervasive, as farmers kept much of their limited crop yield for their families. The denarius was so severely devalued that many foreigners refused to accept it, which restricted trade and forced many Romans to resort to bartering amongst themselves to avoid starvation.[25]

The third method of death in Revelation 6:8 is the Koine Greek word θανάτῳ, or *thanáto*. While the King James Bible translators' word choice was "death," other versions were more specific, choosing to render the word as either "pestilence,"[26] "plague,"[27] or "disease."[28] *Thayer's Greek Lexicon* defines *thanáto* as "the death of the body."[29] Whichever Bible translation you choose, the meaning of the third type of death is more accurately written as "disease" than merely "death." In fact, *Thayer's* also says that the original Greek word describing the color of the third horse, χλωρός, or *chlorós*, translates to "green" or "yellowish-pale"—colors which imply sickness.[30]

Thirty-seven years after the *Constitutio Antoniniana* was enacted, a plague began to spread in Africa. Ancient sources place the probable beginning of the pandemic in Ethiopia, though the accuracy of this detail is uncertain due to the primitive understanding of contagions in antiquity. What is known is that the disease initially reached the Roman Empire in Egypt in 249 AD and moved northwest. Historians refer to this disease as the Plague of Cyprian, after the North African bishop who documented the contagion in detail.[31]

This outbreak ravaged various parts of the Roman Empire until as late as 270, twenty-one years after the first cases in Egypt. At its peak in 262, the *Historia Augusta* estimated that five thousand people died daily in Rome and the Greek cities in Achaea.[32] The novel disease was catastrophic enough to make many people believe it was an apocalyptic sign from God. Christianity spread widely during the two decades of the Plague of Cyprian, as countless people searched for answers in religion during this period of such pervasive tragedies.[33] The already perilous agricultural shortage caused by oppressive taxation and currency debasement was intensified by a reduction in personnel to work the fields during the Plague of Cyprian, leading to further starvation throughout Europe.

In his comments on the fourth and final cause of death in Revelation 6:8, the Biblical scholar Albert Barnes explained, "This, too, would be one of the consequences of war, famine, and pestilence. Lands would be depopulated, and wild beasts would be multiplied. Nothing more is necessary to make them formidable than a prevalence of these things; and nothing, in the early stages of society, or in countries ravaged by war, famine, and the pestilence, is more formidable. Homer, at the very beginning of his *Iliad*, presents us with a representation similar to this. Compare Ezekiel 14:21; 'I send my four sore judgments upon Jerusalem, the sword, and the famine, and the noisome beast, and the pestilence.'"[34]

Barnes was not alone in his assessment of the relationship between man and wild animals in antiquity. In *Against the Heathen*, written in 296 AD, the early Christian writer Arnobius described the hardships during his era. "Men complain, there are now sent us from the gods pestilence, droughts, wars, scarcities, locusts, hail, and other things noxious to man," Arnobius wrote. "But was it not so in ancient times also? Were there not wars with wild beasts, and battles with lions, and destruction from venomous snakes, before our time?" Arnobius acknowledged that all four causes of death in Revelation 6:8 remained threats to the Roman citizenry in 296 AD, including wild beasts.[35]

In the ancient world, the range of the lion was far broader than it is today. Fourth-century writer Themistius documented his regret that Thessaly could no longer furnish lions for Roman beast shows, suggesting they had not gone extinct in the Balkan peninsula until his lifetime. Barbary lions were prevalent in Roman Africa throughout the life of the empire and survived there until the middle of the twentieth century.[36] In the medieval Middle East, the lion could be found as far as India in the east, Palestine and Turkey in the west, Arabia in the south,[37] and the Caucasus in the north.[38] In addition to lions, other carnivorous animals like wolves and bears inhabited Europe and could have also hunted Roman citizens.

Each disaster that occurred during the third century—civil wars, limited crop yields, invasions, inflation, the Plague of Cyprian, and wild animals—intensified the severity of the others. These crises caused lasting damage to the Roman Empire, from which it would never fully recover.

The Fifth Seal

> **Revelation 6:9-11**
> **9** And when he had opened the fifth seal, I saw under the altar the souls of them that were slain for the word of God, and for the testimony which they held:
> **10** And they cried with a loud voice, saying, How long, O Lord, holy and true, dost thou not judge and avenge our blood on them that dwell on the earth?
> **11** And white robes were given unto every one of them; and it was said unto them, that they should rest yet for a little season, until their fellowservants also and their brethren, that should be killed as they were, should be fulfilled.

When Jesus opened the fifth seal, John saw Christian martyrs under an altar in Heaven. The martyrs cried out to God, "How long, O Lord, holy and true, dost thou not judge and avenge our blood on them that dwell on the earth?" Instead of seeking vengeance on his followers' behalf, God gave the martyrs white robes and comforted them by suggesting they rest a little longer while the remaining believers destined for martyrdom were killed. This seal does not require much effort to understand. It represents a harsh persecution of Christians sometime after the tumultuous Crisis of the Third Century.

The emperor Diocletian stabilized most of the issues facing Rome after his ascension in 284 AD. He more than doubled the number of provinces to reduce the power of generals, as their ambition had been a leading catalyst of the domestic chaos of the prior fifty years. He also increased the number of government officials to lessen their authority and bestowed less power upon soldiers within local provinces. Diocletian also placed limits on commodity prices to reduce the cost of living and minted new gold and silver coins to reduce inflation.[39]

With their problems largely stabilized, the Romans celebrated the festival of Terminalia on February 23, 303 AD. This annual feast honored Terminus, the Roman god of boundaries. At the suggestion of his second-in-command, Caesar Galerius, Diocletian felt it fitting to mark the event by issuing the first in a series of four edicts so ruthless that they would irreversibly *terminate* the Christian faith. The Diocletianic or Great Persecution would be the last and cruelest Christian persecution in the history of the empire.[40]

Diocletian would abdicate his throne in 305 AD, but his policies towards Christians continued. Caesar Galerius, whose severe temper was well-known, was promoted to Augustus and promptly escalated the persecution. Six years into his reign, Galerius realized that a tyrannical monarch's extermination campaign could not eradicate the Christian faith. As Edward Gibbon wrote, "The frequent disappointments of his ambitious views, the experience of six years of persecution, and the salutary reflections which a lingering and painful distemper suggested to the mind of Galerius, at length convinced him that the most violent efforts of despotism are insufficient to extirpate a whole people, or to subdue their religious prejudices." In 311 AD, Galerius recoiled. That year, he issued the *Edict of Serdica*—also called the *Edict of Toleration*—which repealed several of Diocletian's laws. However, the persecution would not officially end until Constantine's *Edict of Milan* in February 313.[41]

The Great Persecution fell at the end of the Smyrnaean church age in Revelation 2:8-11. Jesus told the Christians of Smyrna that they "shall have tribulation ten days," but if their faith did not waiver during the persecution they endured, they would not be "hurt of the second death." The ten-day tribulation of the Smyrnaean church age represents the ten calendar years of the Great Persecution and the fulfillment of the fifth seal, from February 303 to February 313 AD.

The Sixth Seal

> **Revelation 6:12-14**
> **12** And I beheld when he had opened the sixth seal, and, lo, there was a great earthquake; and the sun became black as sackcloth of hair, and the moon became as blood;
> **13** And the stars of heaven fell unto the earth, even as a fig tree casteth her untimely figs, when she is shaken of a mighty wind.
> **14** And the heaven departed as a scroll when it is rolled together; and every mountain and island were moved out of their places.

The sixth seal of Revelation 6:12-17 presents terrifyingly vivid imagery. When Jesus tore open this seal, a great earthquake occurred, the sun turned black, the moon became like blood, and stars fell from the sky. After these calamities, Heaven disappeared like a rolled-up scroll, and every mountain and island was displaced. This seal signifies a historical event so momentous that it was represented by allegories of unnatural celestial phenomena.

Verse twelve contains the first earthquake metaphor in Revelation, all of which represent monumental shifts in both Christian and world history. The earthquake represents a tumultuous religious event on earth. The metaphor is replicated later in both Revelation's sixth trumpet and the final warning of Revelation, the seventh vial. Of these three earthquake prophecies, the sixth seal and the sixth trumpet will be similarly significant, but the earth would recuperate. The seventh vial is the most violent, and is defined in Revelation 16:18 as "a great earthquake, such as was not since men were upon the earth." The fulfillment of the sixth seal prophecy would cause a substantial religious disruption in Rome following the Great Persecution.

In Biblical prophecy, the sun, moon, and stars often represent leadership structures. The Old Testament prophets Isaiah and Ezekiel wrote remarkably similar prophecies foretelling the downfalls of the enemies of Israel. Ezekiel delivered a prophecy to the Egyptian pharaoh in Ezekiel 32:7-8 predicting

Babylon's victory over Egypt at the Battle of Carchemish in 605 BC. In it, the prophet describes a darkening of the sun, moon, and stars.[b]

Isaiah's prophecies often had both short-term and long-term meanings. In Isaiah 13, the short-term fulfillment was a physical battle—a prophecy fulfilled in 539 BC when Cyrus the Great, king of the Medo-Persian Empire, conquered Babylon. God used the Medo-Persians to exact revenge on the Babylonians for their defeat of Israel and the resulting Jewish captivity. The long-term fulfillment will be God's eventual victory over Mystery Babylon.[c]

Isaiah was later shown another prophetic vision, this time representing the fall of Edom, where "all the host of heaven" dissolves. Just as they do in the sixth seal of Revelation 6, the heavens roll up like a scroll, and the host—meaning a large number or multitude—falls from the sky. This represents another prophetic example of celestial objects falling like figs from a tree.[d]

The heavenly bodies, always so structured and orderly, were suddenly disrupted upon Jesus' opening of the sixth seal. The great politico-religious earthquake unleashed with the sixth seal signifies such a significant event that it would send shockwaves throughout the Roman Empire and forever change world history: Constantine's conversion to Christianity following the 312 AD Battle of the Milvian Bridge.

Verse fourteen predicts that every mountain and island would be "moved out of their places." Scholars do not interpret this as a physical movement but as a symbol of the consequential shift in the Roman religious and political landscape caused by Constantine's conversion. Albert Barnes, in his *Notes, Explanatory and Practical, on the Book of Revelation*, explained the sixth seal this way; "This would denote convulsions in the political or moral world, as great

---

[b] **Ezekiel 32:7-8** 7 And when I shall put thee out, I will cover the heaven, and make the stars thereof dark; I will cover the sun with a cloud, and the moon shall not give her light. 8 All the bright lights of heaven will I make dark over thee, and set darkness upon thy land, saith the Lord God.

[c] **Isaiah 13:1, 10** 1 The burden of Babylon, which Isaiah the son of Amoz did see...10 For the stars of heaven and the constellations thereof shall not give their light: the sun shall be darkened in his going forth, and the moon shall not cause her light to shine.

[d] **Isaiah 34:4-5** 4 And all the host of heaven shall be dissolved, and the heavens shall be rolled together as a scroll: and all their host shall fall down, as the leaf falleth off from the vine, and as a falling fig from the fig tree. 5 For my sword shall be bathed in heaven: behold, it shall come down upon Idumea, and upon the people of my curse, to judgment.

as would occur in the physical world if the very mountains were removed, and the islands should change their places. We are not to suppose that this would literally occur; but we should be authorized from this to expect that, in regard to those things which seemed to be permanent and fixed on an immovable basis, like mountains and islands, there would be violent and important changes. If thrones and dynasties long established were overthrown; if institutions that seemed to be fixed and permanent were abolished; if a new order of things should rise in the political world, the meaning of the symbol, so far as the language is concerned, would be fulfilled."[42]

Revelation 6:15-17 predicted people would be so terrified by the event these metaphors represent that both rich and poor, powerful and powerless, would hide from God. Imagine the uncertainty of dueling emperors battling so close to your city that you can see the commotion. A messenger enters Rome and spreads the news that Constantine and his men saw a vision of a Christian Chi-Rho symbol, of which he made a gold replica so that it could be carried into battle at the vanguard of his army as he led them to victory. Suddenly, the pagan persecutors risked becoming the persecuted. Rome's military and political leadership abruptly faced an uncertain future. Would Constantine exact revenge on those who persecuted Christians? It is easy to imagine the Roman nobles hiding in fear upon hearing news of the emperor's religious conversion.

> **Revelation 6:15-17**
> **15** And the kings of the earth, and the great men, and the rich men, and the chief captains, and the mighty men, and every bondman, and every free man, hid themselves in the dens and in the rocks of the mountains;
> **16** And said to the mountains and rocks, Fall on us, and hide us from the face of him that sitteth on the throne, and from the wrath of the Lamb:
> **17** For the great day of his wrath is come; and who shall be able to stand?

The early nineteenth-century English theologian Joseph Benson wrote, "The great lights of the heathen world, the sun, moon, and stars, the powers civil and ecclesiastical, were all eclipsed and obscured, the heathen emperors and Caesars were slain, the heathen priests and augurs were extirpated, the heathen officers and magistrates were removed, the temples demolished, and their revenues appropriated to better uses."[43] The Roman aristocratic class—

the same authorities who were slaughtering Christians only one year prior—now found their emperor had converted to the religion of their victims.

Constantine quickly legalized all religions through the *Edict of Milan*. He then merged Christianity with Roman paganism, which laid the foundation for the Catholic Church and fulfilled Paul's apostasy of II Thessalonians 2:3. The last verse of chapter six says, "For the great day of his wrath is come; and who shall be able to stand?"

Revelation 7: Marking God's Servants

The answer to that question is found almost instantly, at the beginning of chapter seven. In this vision, John saw four angels holding back the four winds of the earth. A fifth angel told the others not to hurt the earth, sea, or trees until he first sealed the servants of God. This seal is not visible—it is a spiritual mark identifying followers of Jesus to protect them from Hell. The people righteous enough to receive God's seal are those who "shall be able to stand" in Revelation 6:17.

> **Revelation 7:1-3**
> **1** And after these things I saw four angels standing on the four corners of the earth, holding the four winds of the earth, that the wind should not blow on the earth, nor on the sea, nor on any tree.
> **2** And I saw another angel ascending from the east, having the seal of the living God: and he cried with a loud voice to the four angels, to whom it was given to hurt the earth and the sea,
> **3** Saying, Hurt not the earth, neither the sea, nor the trees, till we have sealed the servants of our God in their foreheads.

This mark is the contrasting seal to the Antichrist's mark of the beast in Revelation 13. The religious revolution caused by Constantine's conversion created a dichotomy between the Catholics of Satan's false church and the Christians of Jesus' true church. For most, Catholicism was indistinguishable from Christianity, and it developed into the authority on what it meant to be "Christian." At this consequential moment, God cut through the deception of pseudo-Christianity to identify and protect his followers.

God's purpose for labeling true Christians was not to protect them from the physical harm of the upcoming Great Tribulation but to save them from a second, spiritual death. Similarly, these four angels do not allow the earth, seas, and trees to be "hurt" until after this sealing occurs. God had promised the Smyrna church age, "He that overcometh shall not be hurt of the second death." The sixth seal occurred when the Smyrna church age ended with the *Edict of Milan*, and the seal of Revelation 7 was his way of identifying the souls who would not be deceived by Catholicism and would receive eternal life.[44]

However, Revelation 7:4 says the number of sealed believers is limited to only one hundred forty-four thousand "children of Israel," far less than the number you would expect to see if Heaven contained souls from across all human history.

> **Revelation 7:4**
> 4 And I heard the number of them which were sealed: and there were sealed an hundred and forty and four thousand of all the tribes of the children of Israel.

Before agonizing over your eligibility to enter Heaven, verse nine should put you at ease. In it, John saw another group of Christians from all nations, kindreds, people, and tongues praising God. The number of believers in this group was so large that John wrote that they could not be counted.

> **Revelation 7:9-10**
> 9 After this I beheld, and, lo, a great multitude, which no man could number, of all nations, and kindreds, and people, and tongues, stood before the throne, and before the Lamb, clothed with white robes, and palms in their hands;
> 10 And cried with a loud voice, saying, Salvation to our God which sitteth upon the throne, and unto the Lamb.

The Seventh Seal

> **Revelation 8:1**
> 1 And when he had opened the seventh seal, there was silence in heaven about the space of half an hour.

After the sixth seal, the seventh is described simply as "silence in heaven about the space of half an hour." There are several possible explanations for this seal's fulfillment. First, if the half-hour time frame was an insignificant detail merely meant to represent an easing of religious tension, this seal was fulfilled with the *Edict of Milan* and the legalization of Christianity in 313.[45] God's revenge on the Roman pagans for executing so many of his followers was complete—the pagans lost power, and Heaven could finally be at peace. A second possibility is if the half-hour silence was what John experienced himself—a literal half-hour pause in his vision. Both interpretations are likely incorrect, as they would be inconsistent with Revelation's other prophecies containing time frames that all adhere to the day-year principle.

The third interpretation would follow this principle like all the other end-times prophecies, calculating the half-hour in prophetic time. Under the day-year principle, a prophetic half-hour equals 7.5 days. Edward Bishop Elliott preferred this fulfillment in *Horae Apocalypticae*. In his view, the seventh seal was fulfilled by the death of Theodosius I, the final emperor of the unified Roman Empire before it was permanently split between East and West.

Theodosius attempted to rule as a Catholic emperor. He was behind the formal adoption of the Trinity as church doctrine and made Catholicism the official state religion of the Roman Empire in 381 AD. Of the three possible fulfillments, the death of Theodosius is most likely. Because of its proximity to the next sign—Alaric I and the Goths' military campaign against Rome—Theodosius' death more accurately fits the prophecy of a peaceful half-hour silence in Heaven. After his death on January 17, 395, the Goths stationed in Illyricum would have likely received word in only a few days.[46]

In Christian theology, seven is considered the number of completeness. In contrast, six is the number of incompleteness.[47] The seal and trumpet signs in Revelation each contain only six prophecies punishing their targets. In each series, the seventh sign signals the completion of the prophecies. The silence in Heaven during the seventh seal mirrors God's rest on the seventh day of the creation story. After God worked for six days to create the universe, what did he do on the seventh day? He rested.[e]

---

[e] **Genesis 2:2** And on the seventh day God ended his work which he had made; and he rested on the seventh day from all his work which he had made.

Chapter Synopsis

- Revelation 1:1 clearly states that the warning signs of Revelation would "shortly come to pass"
- Revelation's main signs are divided into seven seals, trumpets, and vials
- The first seal was fulfilled only a few years after John's visions occurred

The Seven Seals (Revelation 5:1-8:1)

- **First Seal:** The conquering Roman army under Trajan, 98-117 AD
- **Second Seal:** Roman civil wars begin, 193 AD
- **Third Seal:** Caracalla increases taxes, reducing food supply, 212 AD
- **Fourth Seal:** The Crisis of the Third Century, Plague of Cyprian, food scarcity, 235-284 AD
- **Fifth Seal:** The Diocletianic Persecution of Christians, 303-313 AD
- **Sixth Seal:** Constantine converts to "Christianity," 312 AD
  - After the sixth seal, John watched as angels "sealed the servants of our God in their foreheads"
  - Due to the deceptive nature of Catholicism, God's seal distinguishes between Christians and everyone else, including Catholics
- **Seventh Seal:** Theodosius I dies, 395 AD

REVELATION TIMELINE

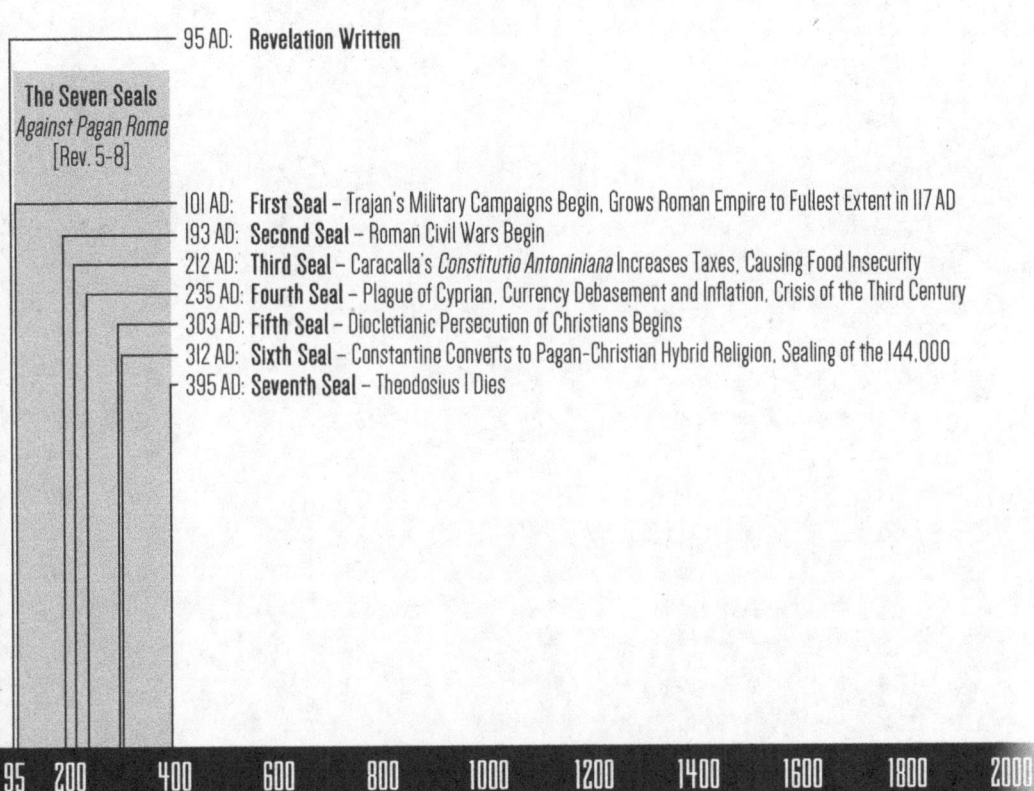

The Seven Seals
Against Pagan Rome
[Rev. 5-8]

- 95 AD: **Revelation Written**
- 101 AD: **First Seal** – Trajan's Military Campaigns Begin, Grows Roman Empire to Fullest Extent in 117 AD
- 193 AD: **Second Seal** – Roman Civil Wars Begin
- 212 AD: **Third Seal** – Caracalla's *Constitutio Antoniniana* Increases Taxes, Causing Food Insecurity
- 235 AD: **Fourth Seal** – Plague of Cyprian, Currency Debasement and Inflation, Crisis of the Third Century
- 303 AD: **Fifth Seal** – Diocletianic Persecution of Christians Begins
- 312 AD: **Sixth Seal** – Constantine Converts to Pagan-Christian Hybrid Religion, Sealing of the 144,000
- 395 AD: **Seventh Seal** – Theodosius I Dies

13

THE SEVEN TRUMPETS

After Constantine converted, his development of the pseudo-Christian religion we now call Roman Catholicism drove mainstream Christianity into the apostasy described in II Thessalonians 2:3. His conversion, and the *Edict of Milan* that followed, removed the pagan emperors as the "restrainer" of the Antichrist and allowed the bishop of Rome to operate the church free from the constraints and persecutions of the secular Roman government.

The bishop of Rome did not receive temporal power from Constantine, nor was he made the head of Catholicism in the fourth century. However, in 313 AD, the adversarial relationship between Rome's emperors and bishop suddenly transformed into a partnership. The idolatry of Babylon and Rome became known as the "veneration of saints" and "religious iconography" in the new apostate church. While it took time for Constantine's adaptation of Christianity to fully corrupt the true faith, his conversion set Paul's apostasy in motion.

In his next vision, John saw seven angels carrying trumpets. As with the seals, a new judgment was released each time an angel sounded their horn. Like the first four seals, the first four trumpets shared several similarities. In particular, the first three seals were especially integrated—all were on fire and either mixed with blood or causing death. The fulfillments of the first four trumpets in the physical world were also incredibly similar, each involving a military threat to the declining Western Roman Empire.

The First Trumpet

> **Revelation 8:7**
> 7 The first angel sounded, and there followed hail and fire mingled with blood, and they were cast upon the earth: and the third part of trees was burnt up, and all green grass was burnt up.

Emperor Theodosius' death left the Roman Empire in the hands of his young and ineffectual sons, and its territory was divided between Arcadius in the East and Honorius in the West. Gothic king Alaric I sensed this weakness and saw an opportunity. Upon learning of Theodosius' death, Alaric quickly mobilized his soldiers, revolted against the Romans, and marched toward the Eastern capital of Constantinople. The Goths were blocked from reaching the city by the Eastern Roman army, so the invaders turned their attention to less well-defended cities in Greece. Over the next two years, Alaric and his men sacked the harbor city of Piraeus in the port of Athens and plundered Corinth, Megara, Argos, and Sparta.[1] The Gothic conquest of Roman Greece was not the end of Alaric's ambitions. Emboldened by his successes against Arcadius, the barbarian king's ambition pulled his eyes towards Rome.

Honorius was only eight years old when he became co-emperor with his father and brother in 393 AD. After Theodosius' death, he was the sole ruler on the Western throne under the regency of the general Stilicho. In the spring of 402 AD, Alaric invaded Italy and faced off against Stilicho in two battles.[2] The first encounter was at Pollentia in northwestern Italy. Alaric's army was decisively defeated by the Romans, who recovered most of the treasure the Goths had amassed during their plundering of Greece and captured Alaric's wife and children. Stilicho offered truce terms to Alaric, which he declined. The second battle was fought in Verona in June. Again, Alaric was defeated, and again, Stilicho offered a truce. This time, however, Alaric wisely accepted and withdrew his forces from the Italian peninsula.[3]

In 406, the Western Empire was facing a soldiers' revolt in Britain and an invasion in Gaul from the combined militaries of the Vandals, Suevi, and Alans. Alaric saw this as another opportunity and prepared to invade Italy again the following year. The other crises strained Rome's military capacity, and Stilicho was forced to pay Alaric four thousand pounds of gold to leave.[4]

Meanwhile, in the imperial court, a minister named Olympius persuaded Honorius that Stilicho was secretly conspiring to overthrow him. The young, submissive emperor arrested the general and ordered his execution. After the assassination, Olympius went on a purge, killing Stilicho's family and any of the officials believed to have been loyal to him. Even the wives and children of Stilicho's foederati—the foreign auxiliary forces under Rome's control—did not escape the massacre. Infuriated by this betrayal, the foederati defected en masse to Alaric.[5] Olympius' miscalculation left Rome without a standing army to defend the Italian peninsula for the remainder of its empire.[6]

Once the foederati changed their allegiance to the Goths, an emboldened Alaric invaded Italy again. The empire's capital had moved to Ravenna by this time, but Rome remained its greatest prize. In September 408, the Goths laid siege to the former capital to starve its residents into surrendering. The desperate Romans paid Alaric five thousand pounds of gold, thirty thousand pounds of silver, and several thousand silks and animal hides in exchange for peace.[7] Honorius also promised to appoint Alaric as the head of the Roman army, but when the emperor reneged on this appointment, the Gothic king laid siege to Rome again in 409.[8]

When Alaric lifted this siege, he appointed a figurehead emperor in Rome and began discussions with Honorius in Ravenna. With talks ongoing, Sarus, an ally of the emperor, attacked Alaric and his men. Alaric viewed this attack as having been ordered by Honorius and immediately ended the negotiations. After this final betrayal, Alaric turned back to Rome.

Historians do not know how Alaric entered the city through its Salarian Gate, but the likeliest answer is that he was simply let in by the Gothic slaves who resided there.[9] Upon breaching the city on August 24, 410, the Goths sacked Rome for three days—the first time Rome had been pillaged in eight hundred years.[10]

In his poem *The Gothic War*, the contemporary Roman writer Claudian described Alaric's 402-403 AD Gothic invasion as being "like a storm of hail or a pestilence."[11] The eighteenth and nineteenth century theologians did not miss this analogy written by a poet alive during the first of Alaric's invasions. Charles Daubuz,[12] W. Boyd Carpenter,[13] and Joseph Benson[14] all referred to Claudian's poem in their commentaries on John's Revelation—each seeing the fulfillment of the first trumpet's blood-filled hailstorm in Alaric.

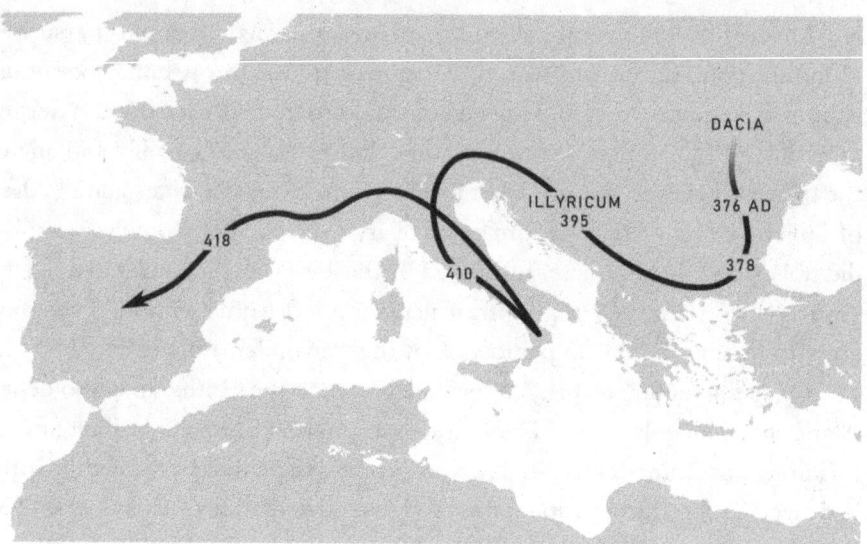

Figure 30: Migration of the Goths from Dacia to Illyricum, eventually settling in Spain in 418 AD.

"The Third Part"

John's descriptions of five of the first six trumpets include the phrase "the third part." Edward Bishop Elliott dedicated an entire section of *Horae Apocalypticae* to the question of what this phrase might represent. His analysis examined several possibilities, eventually settling on a peculiar interpretation of the division of the Roman Empire.

In 395 AD, the Roman Empire was divided between East and West for the final time. However, that would be only two parts, not three. The empire was also subdivided into four Praetorian Prefectures—Gaul and Italy in the Western Empire, Oriens in the East, and Illyricum, which bridged the border between the Eastern and Western Empires. However, this would similarly be an empire split into four parts, not three.

The Goths controlled much of Illyricum at the time of the final imperial division. Alaric and his soldiers launched their attacks on Greece and Italy from Illyricum, and when they needed a respite from campaigning, the Goths withdrew to safety there. Elliott views "the third part" as a tripartite split of Roman territory between the Western Empire, Eastern Empire, and Goth-controlled Illyricum.[15]

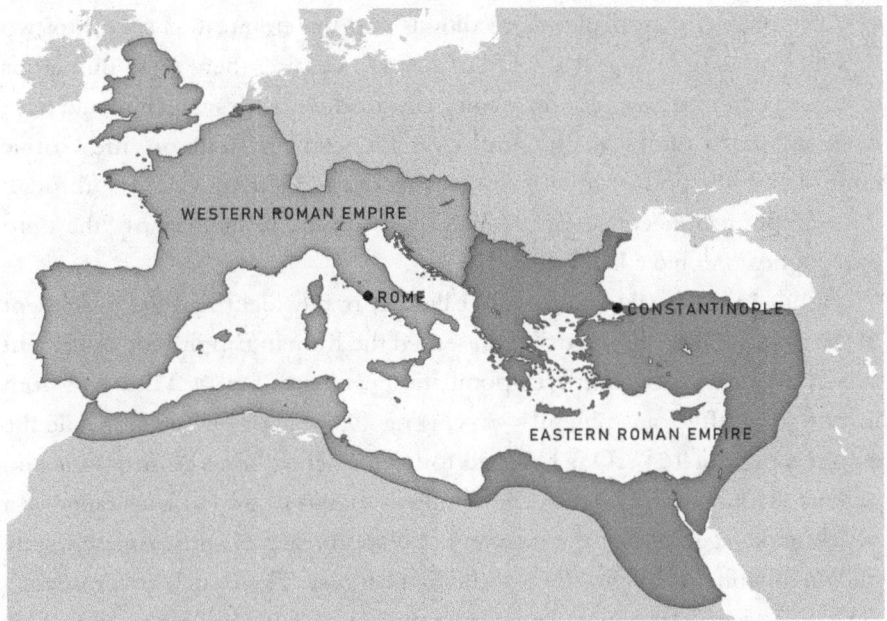

Figure 31: Final division of the Roman Empire after the death of Theodosius I, 395 AD.

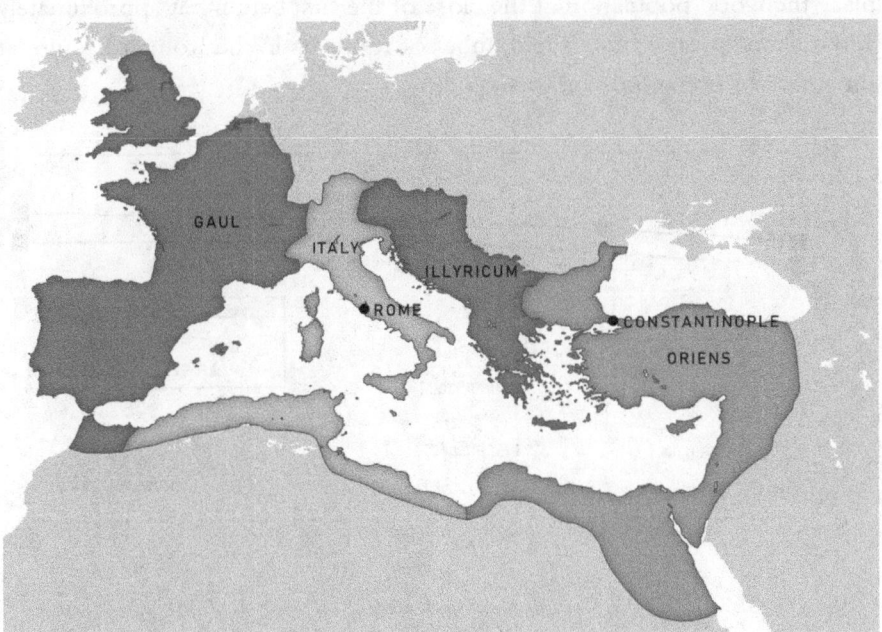

Figure 32: The four Praetorian Prefectures of the Roman Empire under Theodosius I, 395 AD.

The problem with Elliott's reading is that the empire was split into two or four parts. Throughout the life of Rome's empire, there were numerous incursions on territory, bloody revolts, and frontier battles which would have been similar to the Goths' control over Illyricum. In addition, the Gothic control over the prefecture was not permanent and did not even last through the trumpet prophecies. Elliott's hypothesis on the fulfillment of "the third part" appears to have been forced.

While his rationale was flawed, Elliott correctly identified the fulfillment of the phrase. "The third part" represented the Roman Empire for a different reason: its population. Imperial population estimates for 14 AD range from forty-five to fifty-four million[16]—averaging 49.5 million subjects—while the empire's peak in 164 AD is believed to have reached between fifty-nine and seventy-six million.[17] Using the 67.5 million midpoint of that later range as a benchmark suggests that the Roman population reached approximately sixty million inhabitants by the close of the first century. The Dutch government's HYDE Project 3.1 estimated a global population of 195 million in 100 AD,[18] and Colin McEvedy and Richard Jones proposed a slightly more conservative trajectory, from 170 million in 1 AD to 190 million in 200 AD. These figures place the world population at the close of the first century at approximately 180 million—nearly triple the number of residents in the Roman Empire at the time of Revelation's authorship.[19]

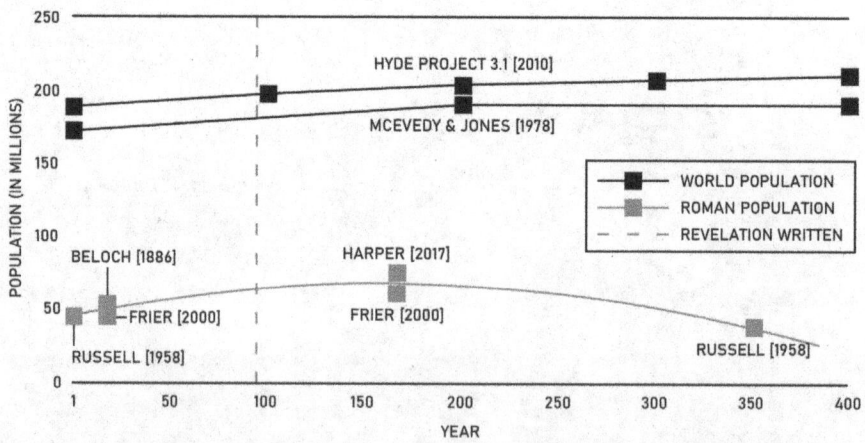

Figure 33: Global and Roman Empire population estimates, 1 AD-400 AD.[20] *When Revelation was written in 95 AD (dashed vertical line), the Roman Empire's population was approximately 60 million, or one-third of Colin McEvedy and Richard Jones' global population estimate of 180 million.*

The Second Trumpet

> **Revelation 8:8-9**
> 8 And the second angel sounded, and as it were a great mountain burning with fire was cast into the sea: and the third part of the sea became blood;
> 9 And the third part of the creatures which were in the sea, and had life, died; and the third part of the ships were destroyed.

The central detail revealed in the verses covering the second trumpet is the presence of the sea. Just as the bloody, burning hailstorm was "cast upon the earth," this trumpet's burning mountain was "cast into the sea," turning it into blood. Alaric's Gothic army attacked the Romans on land, spreading bloodshed wherever the hail of war fell. In contrast, the military threat in the second trumpet was nautical.

The Vandals were a Germanic people who had gradually migrated from eastern Europe to Spain. In 429 AD, they crossed the Strait of Gibraltar into present-day Morocco. From there, the Vandal army pushed eastward through North Africa, defeating the Romans in every engagement.

The Vandals' military victories forced the Romans to negotiate a peace treaty in 435, resulting in the cession of Rome's North African territories of Mauretania and western Numidia. The fragile treaty lasted four years until the Vandal king Genseric successfully invaded the Roman province of Africa Proconsularis and took the port city of Carthage on October 19, 439.[21]

Carthage offered the Vandals a valuable strategic port and the ability to launch naval attacks against Roman coastal cities across the Mediterranean.[22] In 441 AD, the Vandals utilized their new navy to invade Sicily. Valentinian agreed to another peace in 442,[23] relinquishing more territory in North Africa to the Vandals[24] and officially recognizing them as a sovereign, independent kingdom. The 442 treaty marked the first time a barbarian tribe received this status in the history of the Roman Empire.[25]

The Vandal Kingdom quickly became the dominant naval power in the Mediterranean Sea. Its fleet was so active in looting the coastal cities of the Roman Empire that the Old English name for the Mediterranean Sea was *Wendelsæ*, which translates to *Vandal Sea*.[26]

As a condition of the 442 treaty, Valentinian agreed to marry his daughter Eudocia to Genseric's son Huneric, but the wedding was postponed due to

Eudocia's young age. In 455, Valentinian was assassinated, and the affluent senator Petronius Maximus ascended to the throne by bribing the Praetorian Guards for their support. To legitimize himself, Maximus married Eudocia to his own son, Palladius.

King Genseric—whose son had been promised Eudocia's betrothal as a condition of the 442 AD peace agreement—used this marriage as an excuse to sail to Rome. With the Vandal navy fast approaching, Maximus' support evaporated, and he prepared to flee the city. As the frightened emperor rode through the city's gates without his guards, he was spotted by an angry mob that stoned him to death. Three days later, on June 2, 455, the Vandal army entered Rome and plundered the city.[27]

The English word "vandalism" comes from the Vandals' fourteen-day sack of Rome. However, most modern scholars disagree with the ancient historians who claimed the Vandals engaged in the willful and indiscriminate destruction of the city. It is more likely that the Catholic chroniclers of the day embellished the widespread devastation of Rome. Genseric and Huneric were followers of Arius' Christian teachings, which contradicted the Nicene Creed adopted by Catholicism. There was a major schism between Nicene Catholicism and Arian Christianity at the time, and the Catholic writers may have resented Genseric, as the Vandal king insisted that all his religious and political advisors adopt Arianism.[28] The Nicene Catholic bishop of Carthage, Quodvultdeus, refused to adopt Arianism and was exiled to Naples shortly after the Vandal conquest of his city. In Naples, the bishop's sermons painted a dark picture of the Vandal army as violent plunderers, contributing to their barbaric reputation.[29]

Nicene Catholicism, as adopted by the Vatican, posits the Trinity—God the Father, Jesus Christ, and the Holy Spirit—as three co-equal Gods in one. This interpretation of the Trinity as equal and uncreated Gods was not taught by Jesus or his apostles. A doctrine interpreted as polytheistic would have struggled to appeal to the devoutly monotheistic Jews. Notably, the belief in three equal divinities in the Trinity parallels the triune gods found in ancient pagan religions, including Babylonian mythology.[30]

The original Nicene Creed denounced the Arians' views on Jesus, stating, "But those who say: 'There was a time when he was not;' and 'He was not before he was made;' and 'He was made out of nothing,' or 'He is of another substance' or 'essence,' or 'The Son of God is created,' or 'changeable,' or 'alterable'—they are condemned by the holy Catholic and apostolic Church." The Catholic Church adopted this philosophy as official doctrine at the First Council of Nicaea in 325 AD.[31]

Contrarily, Arianism taught that God the Father was a supreme deity—God Almighty—and Jesus was his only begotten son. The Arians theorized that God the Father made Jesus sometime before the creation story in the book of Genesis, and was superior to him. Jesus himself said there were things that God the Father knew, but he did not. In Mark 13:32, Jesus tells his disciples that only God knows the day he will return to earth. The first verse of Revelation calls the book "The Revelation of Jesus Christ, which *God gave unto him*." The Arians believed the only sensible explanation was that Jesus was subservient to God the Father. The Trinity is only one example of a doctrinal deviation pitting Arians like Genseric against Nicene Catholics.

The metaphor of a burning mountain thrown into the sea alludes to the mountainous region where the Vandals lived when Revelation was written, as they are believed to have resided around the Carpathian Mountains in the late first century. The symbolism of fire and blood in these verses predicted how these invading soldiers would bring war, violence, and death from the mountains to the sea.

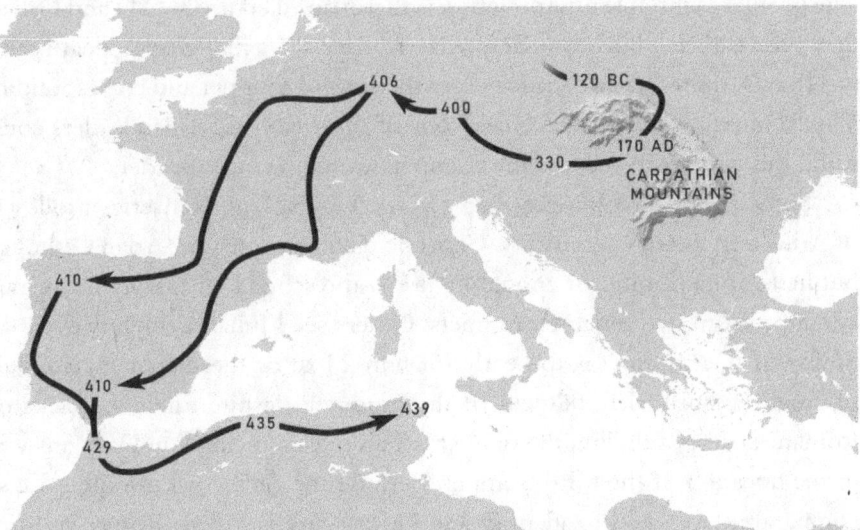

Figure 34: Vandal migration from the Carpathian Mountains to Spain, then to Carthage in 439 AD.

The Third Trumpet

> **Revelation 8:10-11**
> **10** And the third angel sounded, and there fell a great star from heaven, burning as it were a lamp, and it fell upon the third part of the rivers, and upon the fountains of waters;
> **11** And the name of the star is called Wormwood: and the third part of the waters became wormwood; and many men died of the waters, because they were made bitter.

John saw the third trumpet as a burning star that fell on "the third part" of rivers and fountains. The star, whose name was Wormwood, poisoned the water, turning it bitter and causing death. The Futurists theorize that a literal meteorite will speed toward the earth and somehow poison one-third of the world's rivers. We already know that Futurism is inaccurate, but how could one meteorite poison one-third of all the rivers on earth as they suggest?

Several candidates have been proposed for the burning star of the third trumpet. Some Catholic commentators have suggested early Christian writers such as Arius, Origen, or Pelagius—whose opinions were often considered unorthodox by Rome—as any views contradicting the Catholic interpretation of the Bible would be defined by the Vatican as poisoning the spiritual waters. The problem with this interpretation is that Arius died in 336 AD and Origen died even earlier—both long before the trumpets began. Pelagius' death came in 418 AD, more than a decade before the second trumpet and corresponding Vandal invasion of North Africa. None of these early Christian leaders could fulfill this prophecy because the trumpets would be out of order.

Some believe the burning star was the Vandal king Genseric, a follower of Arius' version of Christianity. Genseric did persecute non-Arian Catholics, but he is not a significant enough figure in the scheme of history to warrant attention from two separate trumpets. Others see Muhammad, however, the timing of this trumpet is too early for him. Most of these characters would represent a spiritual fulfillment of this trumpet, despite military attacks on Roman territory fulfilling the first two. This makes them all unlikely answers to the question of the third trumpet. Because the first three trumpets are so comparable, we need to identify another military threat to Rome, and one that occurred after the start of the second trumpet in 429 AD.

In 451 AD, Attila and the Huns began their now-infamous invasion of Roman Gaul. Marching westward along the Danube, Attila's army sacked and plundered cities throughout modern France, enriching himself and his men at the expense of the local civilians before ultimately facing off against the Roman army and their allies in the Battle of the Catalaunian Plains.

The Roman defense was led by the decorated general Flavius Aëtius. His forces were joined by the Alans, Visigoths, and several small tribes, each with a vested interest in stopping the Huns' advance. The Visigoth faction of the alliance was commanded by their king, Theodoric I. For their part, the Huns had allied with the Ostrogoths, Franks, Burgundians, and others.

At the start of the battle, Attila attacked the center of the Roman line where Aëtius had positioned the Alanian infantrymen. After several hours of combat, the Huns had methodically eliminated most of the Alanian force, but the Roman line held firm in its position. Believing his side to be on the verge of victory, Theodoric sent his Visigoth forces to attack the Huns' left flank. In the chaos of the attack, Theodoric was thrown from his horse and trampled to death by his own cavalry. The loss of their king energized the Visigoth soldiers, who pushed the opposing Ostrogothic line backward.

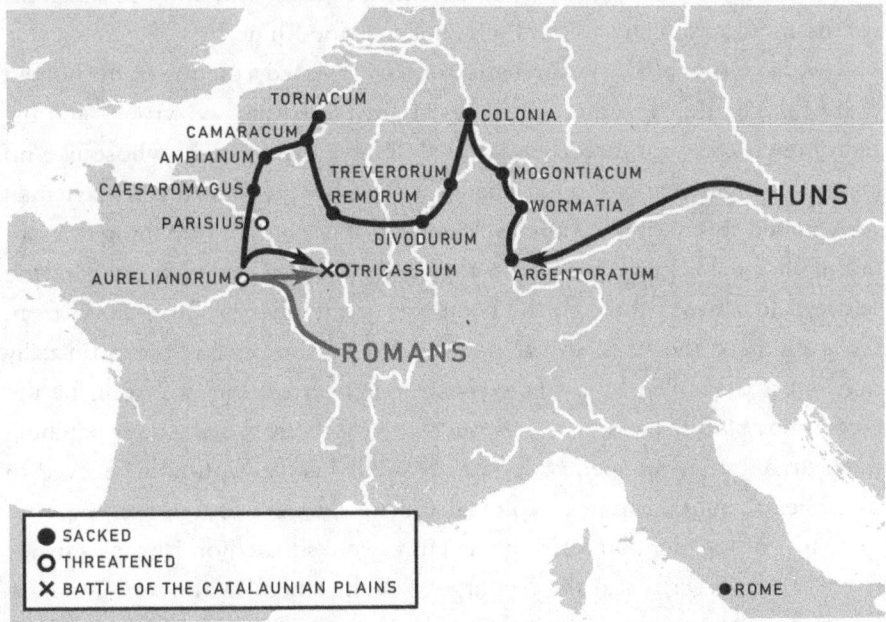

Figure 35: Approximate path of the 451 AD Gallic military campaign of Attila and the Huns.

The armies fought to a draw so costly and exhausting that after surveying the plains the next morning, neither commander was interested in continuing the fight. Sixth-century historian Cassiodorus, who spoke to many veterans of the battle, reported it was "a conflict fierce, various, obstinate, and bloody; such as could not be paralleled either in the present or in past ages."[32] So many men were killed on the Catalaunian Plains that the unknown author of the *Chronica Gallica Anno 511* (*The Gallic Chronicle of 511*) wrote "cadavera vero innumera," meaning "the corpses were innumerable."[33]

Later that morning, the body of King Theodoric was found under a mass of dead soldiers. His death left the Visigoth army under the command of his son, Thorismund. The prince had performed well in battle, but he had several brothers who threatened his claim to the throne.

The alliance between the Romans and Visigoths was fragile, as they were two enemies united by a common threat. After two days of posturing and a brief siege of Attila's camp, the armies still had not resumed fighting. Aëtius, concerned that the much larger force of the Visigoths would turn on his army once Attila had been dispelled, encouraged Thorismund to return home and stake his claim to the Visigothic Kingdom. Attila, believing the departure of the Visigoths to be a feigned retreat intended to draw him into battle, led his remaining forces in an eastward retreat across the Rhine.[34]

Jordanes—a famously unreliable source—painted a picture of the human cost of the battle. "Hand to hand they clashed in battle," he wrote, "and the fight grew fierce, confused, monstrous, unrelenting—a fight whose like no ancient time has ever recorded. There such deeds were done that a brave man who missed this marvelous spectacle could not hope to see anything so wonderful all his life long. For, if we may believe our elders, a brook flowing between low banks through the plain was greatly increased by blood from the wounds of the slain. It was not flooded by showers, as brooks usually rise, but was swollen by a strange stream and turned into a torrent by the increase of blood. Those whose wounds drove them to slake their parching thirst drank water mingled with gore."[35] While his description is believed to be embellished, it illustrates a colossal and considerable loss of life.

Most of the cities targeted by the Huns were situated on Europe's major rivers. Attila, described as the "scourge of all the lands" by the contemporary Greek diplomat and historian Priscus, slaughtered an incalculable number of

Roman civilians along the banks of these rivers on his Gallic campaign. The blood and rotting corpses he left scattered in Europe's rivers would easily poison the waters with disease, making it toxic to those downstream.[36]

In this prophecy, we find another celestial object—a "great star"—falling from Heaven. The star represents a powerful leader, comparable to the sun, moon, and stars of both Isaiah's and Ezekiel's prophecies[37] and the sixth seal of Revelation.[38] Like a shooting star, Attila appeared almost out of nowhere and disappeared just as suddenly. Attila's invasions of the Western Empire only lasted a little more than a year. After he attacked Roman Gaul in 451, Attila briefly reentered northern Italy the next year until he realized there was not enough food available on the peninsula to feed his troops due to a famine and returned home.

Aëtius, who would be given the title "Last of the True Romans" by sixth-century historian Procopius, was the final great general of Western Rome.[39] For thirty years, Valentinian had viewed him as a political threat. After the children of Aëtius and Valentinian married in 453 AD, the emperor suspected his general was plotting to place his son Gaudentius on the throne.

That same year, Attila suddenly died while celebrating his own wedding, which Valentinian believed removed the Huns as the primary military threat to the Romans. On September 21, 454 AD, while Aëtius was attending court in Ravenna, Valentinian leaped from his chair and declared that he would no longer allow himself to be the victim of the general's drunkenness, nor permit him to steal his empire. Unsheathing his sword, the emperor struck Aëtius on the head, killing him instantly.[40]

The assassination was promptly seen as foolish and unnecessary. When Valentinian boasted of the murder to the advisors in his court, one counselor proclaimed, "I am ignorant, sir, of your motives or provocations; I only know that you have acted like a man who cuts off his right hand with his left."[41]

Fire symbolizes war or cleansing in prophecy. The fiery hail, mountain, and star of John's vision were metaphors for military conquests against Rome as punishment for the empire's persecution and corruption of Christianity. The prophetic star fell upon rivers, as the cities sacked by Attila were located along the major rivers of Gaul. The wormwood plant's bitter taste and aquatic habitat allude to the corpses Attila left in the rivers, which poisoned the water and caused the deaths of many who drank it downstream.

The Fourth Trumpet

The first three trumpets—hail, a mountain, and a falling star—all caused extensive damage to the Roman Empire and its people through invasions. Olympius' murder of the families of Stilicho's men left the Romans with no standing army in Italy. Petronius Maximus' betrayal of Genseric's peace treaty directly led to the Vandals' sack of Rome. Attila's campaign caused extensive bloodshed and further drained Rome of resources. Valentinian's treacherous murder of General Aëtius left Rome without its last great military mind. Each of these events created the ideal conditions for the ultimate collapse of the already diminished empire.

> **Revelation 8:12-13**
> 12 And the fourth angel sounded, and the third part of the sun was smitten, and the third part of the moon, and the third part of the stars; so as the third part of them was darkened, and the day shone not for a third part of it, and the night likewise.
> 13 And I beheld, and heard an angel flying through the midst of heaven, saying with a loud voice, Woe, woe, woe, to the inhabiters of the earth by reason of the other voices of the trumpet of the three angels, which are yet to sound!

John saw the first three trumpets as earthly events—a burning hailstorm, a volcano thrown into the sea, and a great meteorite crashing to earth. The fourth trumpet was different. He wrote a depiction of celestial events similar to the sixth seal—the darkening of a third part of the sun, moon, and stars. With this prophecy, there is no earthquake, so we know it does not imply a religious event. However, the fourth trumpet signifies an event so substantial that it set human civilization into the Dark Ages for one thousand years—the collapse of the Western Roman Empire.

The final Roman emperor, Romulus Augustulus, took the throne at age nine in 475, though the juvenile emperor was little more than a figurehead. His father, Orestes, was the Magister Militum—the highest military officer in the empire—and Romulus' regent. Orestes ousted the penultimate emperor, Julius Nepos, and declared his son the new emperor. Nepos fled to his home province of Dalmatia, where he continued to be recognized as the rightful Western Roman emperor by the Eastern emperor Zeno.[42]

The Roman Empire had been deteriorating for over a century. Caracalla's *Constitutio Antoniniana*, currency debasement, inflation, and the Crisis of the Third Century were among the many factors that contributed to its decline. The fifth century's barbarian incursions only hastened the once-formidable empire's downfall. To this point, Rome had survived, but the constant state of war drained the aging empire of men and treasure.

In 476, the commander of the Germanic foederati in Italy, Odoacer, led a coalition force of various tribes into Italy. Not much is known about the army he compiled, though historians believe that it was comprised of many of Attila's former allies, primarily the Heruli and Sciri. The foederati stationed in Italy, desperate for autonomy, appealed to Orestes for a land grant on the peninsula. When the de facto emperor refused their petition, the foederati responded by defecting to Odoacer. Fearing for his life, Orestes fled Ravenna for Pavia, where he was captured and executed by Odoacer loyalists.

From Pavia, the rebel army advanced on Ravenna with little resistance. With no forces remaining under his command, Romulus was powerless to defend his capital, and the five-hundred-year-old Western Roman Empire had finally reached its anti-climactic end.[43]

Emperor de jure Romulus Augustulus was spared from execution due to his youth. The victorious Odoacer declared himself nominally subordinate to the Eastern emperor Zeno, though both the Italian peninsula and the Illyrian territories of Dalmatia and Pannonia were firmly under his control. With the young emperor deposed, the foederati bestowed upon Odoacer the new title "King of Italy." The short-lived reign of the Kings of Italy followed the sixth king of Revelation 17:10, the Roman emperors, and preceded the eighth king, the papal Antichrist.

Revelation 8:12 projects the empire's power structure onto the third part of the sun, moon, and stars. Orestes was the strongest authority in Rome's empire, just as the sun is the strongest light in the sky. Romulus Augustulus' ascension occurred solely because Orestes bestowed imperial authority upon him, just as the moon reflects its light from the sun. The faint light radiating from distant stars suggests a group of less powerful politicians. The Senate, which consisted of several thousand members by the fifth century, survived the empire's fall, though with negligible significance at best. After 476, the Senate was reduced to operating as the town council of Rome.[44]

The Fifth Trumpet: The First Woe

Before the fifth trumpet sounded, John saw another angel who warned, "Woe, woe, woe, to the inhabiters of the earth by reason of the other voices of the trumpet of the three angels, which are yet to sound!" The final three trumpets, or "woes," are the last three warnings for Roman Catholicism. If the church did not change its ways, God would bring his judgment upon it.

Eighty-one years elapsed from Alaric's 395 AD Gothic revolt against the Romans until the collapse of the Western Empire in 476. The King James Bible only dedicated 252 English words to define the sights and sounds of the first four trumpets in Revelation. Comparatively, it required 331 words to meticulously describe the fifth trumpet and 1,020 for the sixth. The reason for the longer passages may be that God meant to emphasize the significance of the three woes in relation to the four earlier trumpets, as the last three trumpets represent major transformations that have had profound political and religious ramifications throughout history.

The Military Leader

> **Revelation 9:1-2**
> 1 And the fifth angel sounded, and I saw a star fall from heaven unto the earth: and to him was given the key of the bottomless pit.
> 2 And he opened the bottomless pit; and there arose a smoke out of the pit, as the smoke of a great furnace; and the sun and the air were darkened by reason of the smoke of the pit.

Like Attila two trumpets prior, the fifth trumpet opens with a falling star. This initial clue suggests a leader who believed himself to be divine, as his fall from Heaven mirrors Satan's fall. This man receives a key, which he uses to open the pit of Hell. When he opens it, so much smoke is released that the sun is shielded, making it difficult for John to see. We can surmise from this imagery that the smokescreen created by this agent of Satan is symbolic of spiritual chaos, as he would shade many from the light of God. Unlike the leaders represented by the four earlier trumpets, this man had a dual role—military commander and spiritual leader.

God's Commands to the Army of Locusts

> **Revelation 9:3-6**
> 3 And there came out of the smoke locusts upon the earth: and unto them was given power, as the scorpions of the earth have power.
> 4 And it was commanded them that they should not hurt the grass of the earth, neither any green thing, neither any tree; but only those men which have not the seal of God in their foreheads.
> 5 And to them it was given that they should not kill them, but that they should be tormented five months: and their torment was as the torment of a scorpion, when he striketh a man.
> 6 And in those days shall men seek death, and shall not find it; and shall desire to die, and death shall flee from them.

Limitations are placed on the army of locusts in verses four and five. The extent of their damage is restricted to those who do not have God's seal on their foreheads. The word "hurt" in this context means a spiritual damnation, as there are several examples of the same word usage throughout Revelation. The church in Smyrna was promised they would not be "hurt of the second death" if they overcame their challenges. After Constantine's conversion in the sixth seal of Revelation 7:2-3, four angels were given the power to "hurt the earth and the sea," but only after God had protected the true Christians. Just as the spiritual damage those four angels caused did not affect faithful Christians, the military that the locust army represented was important, not for the physical death it caused, but for the spiritual death.

In this trumpet, God explicitly protects the grass, "any green thing," and the trees, just as he protected the earth, sea, and trees while his angel sealed Christians in Revelation 7. The green color of vigorous plants symbolizes life and growth. This suggestion is the same for Christians—those of us who are spiritually alive and growing will be protected, but those who are not alive in Christ will be spiritually damned.

Verse five provides the length of the conflicts, as the army is limited to tormenting men for five prophetic months—or one hundred fifty years—before it settles down. During this period, the third part of men would "seek death, and shall not find it." The inaccessibility of death in this trumpet tells us the locust army might kill individuals, but it would not conquer the final piece of Rome's empire—the Byzantine Empire.

Description of the Locusts

> **Revelation 9:7-10**
> 7 And the shapes of the locusts were like unto horses prepared unto battle; and on their heads were as it were crowns like gold, and their faces were as the faces of men.
> 8 And they had hair as the hair of women, and their teeth were as the teeth of lions.
> 9 And they had breastplates, as it were breastplates of iron; and the sound of their wings was as the sound of chariots of many horses running to battle.
> 10 And they had tails like unto scorpions, and there were stings in their tails: and their power was to hurt men five months.

The locusts and scorpions are evidence of the army's location of origin. The locusts were "like unto horses prepared unto battle," implying an army relying on cavalry. This inference is reinforced in verse nine, which says, "The sound of their wings was as the sound of chariots of many horses running to battle." Locusts and scorpions signify a desert-based army, particularly one from Arabia. Interestingly, in Exodus 10:13, the eighth plague brought upon Egypt was an east wind that carried locusts from Arabia.[a]

Figure 36: The east wind of Exodus 10:13 brought locusts from Arabia to Egypt.

---

[a] **Exodus 10:13** And Moses stretched forth his rod over the land of Egypt, and the Lord brought an east wind upon the land all that day, and all that night; and when it was morning, the east wind brought the locusts.

The French orientalist Count Volney described the swarms of Arabian locusts in his *Travels Through Syria and Egypt*, writing, "The inhabitants of Syria have remarked that locusts are always bred by too mild winters, and that they constantly come from the desert of Arabia."[45] The sixteenth-century Moorish diplomat and author Leo Africanus and the eighteenth-century Dutch author Cornelis de Bruijn confirmed similar experiences with locusts when writing of their travels to the region.[46] Recently, massive swarms of locusts plagued the peninsula for three years following high levels of rainfall in 2018.[47]

The symbol of a scorpion also draws comparisons to the Arabian Desert. In a passionate monologue recorded in Deuteronomy 8, Moses advised the Israelites not to forget all God had done for them. In his speech, he detailed how God brought them out of the Arabian Desert when they escaped Egypt. Moses named some of the hardships they had faced while wandering there—a list that included scorpions.[b]

In John's vision, the locusts wore "crowns like gold" on their heads. He used the same Greek word for crown as he used in the first seal: στέφανοι, or *stefanoi*, which means "wreath, chaplet, especially the conqueror's wreath or a crown of victory." Another definition is "that which encircles, surrounds."[48] This Arabian army often wore turbans adorned with chains and gold-inlaid or gilded helmets—crowns *like* gold, not crowns *of* gold.[49] These locusts also wore iron breastplates, which was typical for medieval armies.

The warriors not only wore distinctive clothes—they were also physically unique. Revelation 9:9 explains they had the "faces of men" and the "hair of women," suggesting bearded men with long hair. Pliny the Elder, the Roman author and military commander and a contemporary of John, wrote about the hairstyles of Arabian men in *Natural History*, "The Arabs either wear the mitra, or else go with their hair unshorn, while the beard is shaved, except upon the upper lip; some tribes, however, leave even the unshaven beard."[50]

Both locusts and scorpions are inherently Arabian, but even the mention of horses is also a cursory reference to one of the oldest equine species, the Arabian horse.[51] "The teeth of lions" in verse eight also alludes to the Arabian habitat of the lion during the Middle Ages and the fifth trumpet.[52]

---

[b] **Deuteronomy 8:15** Who led thee through that great and terrible wilderness, wherein were fiery serpents, and scorpions, and drought, where there was no water; who brought thee forth water out of the rock of flint;

The Destroyer

> **Revelation 9:11-12**
> **11** And they had a king over them, which is the angel of the bottomless pit, whose name in the Hebrew tongue is Abaddon, but in the Greek tongue hath his name Apollyon.
> **12** One woe is past; and, behold, there come two woes more hereafter.

According to Revelation 9:11, the name of the demonically-inspired great star who led this army is *Abaddon* in Hebrew and *Apollyon* in Greek, both of which mean "destroyer."[53] Similar to the name of Mystery Babylon, Abaddon is not the man's literal name but a figurative one, as providing the leader's actual name would be uncharacteristic of a prophecy.

Historical Fulfillment

Only one Arabian of the correct period—closely following the fourth trumpet and the fall of Rome—fits this description: Muhammad, the founder of Islam. In 609 AD, Muhammad told his family he was visited by the angel Gabriel in a cave near Mecca in modern-day Saudi Arabia. Three years later, in 612, he began to preach publicly, proclaiming, "There is only one god, and Muhammad is his prophet."[54] As soon as Muhammad started preaching in Mecca, he was persecuted by the city's polytheistic inhabitants for preaching monotheism. This persecution would intensify until he and his followers fled to the nearby city of Medina.

While residing in Medina, Muhammad united the city's tribes under his command. In 629, he gathered ten thousand Muslim converts, marched on Mecca, and took the city with little fighting. By the time of his death in 632, Muhammad's forces controlled most of the Arabian Peninsula. Although his military career was short-lived, his religious beliefs inspired a succession of other Islamic military conquerors.

Following Muhammad's death, the first two caliphates expanded Islam's reach through conquest. By 661 AD, the Rashidun Caliphate had seized the rest of Arabia, Syria, Persia, and Egypt. After the first caliphate's fall, the Umayyad Caliphate extended as far as the Atlantic coast of North Africa and the Iberian Peninsula in the west and modern Pakistan in the east.[55]

Today, Islam and the Qur'an *spiritually blind* one-quarter of the world's population, keeping them from seeing the true God—just as the smoke from the pit of Hell shaded the sun in Revelation 9:2. However, for Muhammad to be the correct fulfillment of the fifth trumpet, a corresponding event one hundred fifty years after 612 AD would need to be found in the year 762.

In 750 AD, the second Islamic caliphate, the Umayyads, collapsed during the Abbasid Revolution. Several years after the Abbasids took power, they began scouting locations to build a new capital. In 762, the caliph al-Mansur commissioned the city along a bend in the Tigris River in modern Iraq near the Euphrates. The name he chose was *Madinat al-Salam*, which means "City of Peace." After campaigning for one hundred fifty years, the locust soldiers who had swarmed from the Arabian Desert under Mohammad and created one of the largest empires in history finally settled down *at peace* in the city known today as Baghdad.[56]

These early Muslim conquests ate away at the territory of the Byzantine Empire as the provinces in Africa, Egypt, Judea, and Syria fell into the hands of the Islamic armies. The first woe had substantially damaged what remained of the once-great Roman Empire. The Byzantine Empire was "hurt" for five prophetic months but was not killed.

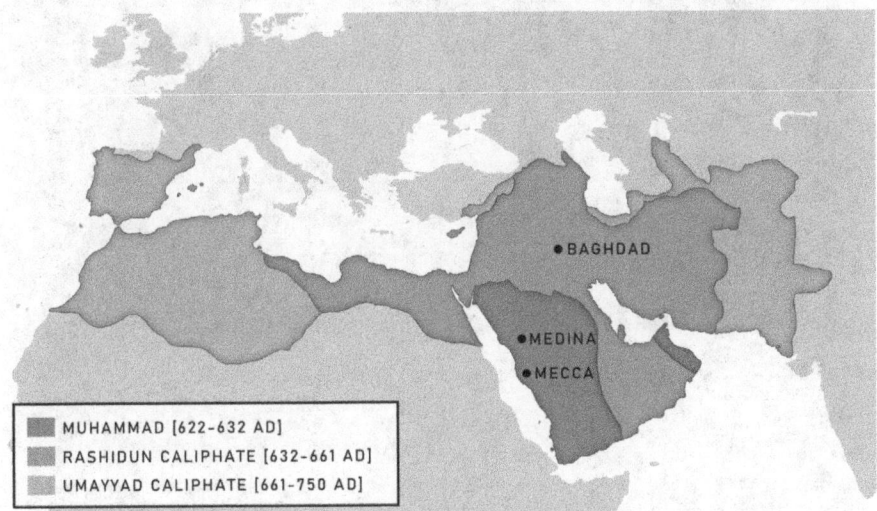

Figure 37: Muslim military expansion under the early caliphates, 622-750 AD.

Figure 38: Muhammad's army at the 625 AD Battle of Uhud, from the Siyer-i Nebi, 1595. The bearded Islamic horsemen were depicted with gold-colored helmets and steel breastplates.

Figure 39: A caravan of Muslim cavalry led by Abd Allah ibn Jahsh, brother-in-law of Muhammad, from the Siyer-i Nebi, 1595. The Islamic soldiers' helmets were painted in metallic gold.

The Sixth Trumpet: The Second Woe

Time Frame and Location

> **Revelation 9:13-15**
> 13 And the sixth angel sounded, and I heard a voice from the four horns of the golden altar which is before God,
> 14 Saying to the sixth angel which had the trumpet, Loose the four angels which are bound in the great river Euphrates.
> 15 And the four angels were loosed, which were prepared for an hour, and a day, and a month, and a year, for to slay the third part of men.

Revelation 9:13-21 describes the prophecy of the sixth trumpet. In the passage's first verse, John hears a voice coming from the horns of the golden altar in Heaven. The altar imagery mirrors the fourth chapter of Leviticus, which describes a purification ceremony the Israelite priests would perform when either they or the Israelites sinned.[c] First, the priest would slaughter a young bull at the door of the Tabernacle as an offering to God. The animal's blood was then collected and sprinkled upon the altar's horns. According to Leviticus 16:18, the same ceremonial sacrifice occurred annually on the Day of Atonement.[d] These ritual sacrifices were a penance for sin and allude to the intent of the sixth trumpet: the Roman Empire had sinned against God by persecuting Christians and still had not repented.

The fulfillment of the sixth trumpet would take even longer than the fifth. Verse fifteen says four angels were prepared for "an hour, and a day, and a month, and a year" to slay the third part of men. Under the day-year principle, one prophetic day, month, and year would indicate a fulfillment lasting 391 years. The prophetic hour—or one twenty-fourth of the Hebrew year—would add just fifteen days. After the 391 years and fifteen days had ended, what remained of the Roman Empire would finally die.

---

[c] **Leviticus 4:25** And the priest shall take of the blood of the sin offering with his finger, and put it upon the horns of the altar of burnt offering, and shall pour out his blood at the bottom of the altar of burnt offering.

[d] **Leviticus 16:18** And he shall go out unto the altar that is before the Lord, and make an atonement for it; and shall take of the blood of the bullock, and of the blood of the goat, and put it upon the horns of the altar round about.

This is a clear escalation from the prior trumpet, when the locust army hurt the Byzantines but was ordered not to kill. The fifth trumpet said death would be out of reach, even for those who wanted to die.[e] Although God shifted the focus of his judgments from Rome to Constantinople with the fifth trumpet, the Islamic army only tormented the Byzantine Empire. The sixth trumpet would go beyond the confines of the fifth, ultimately "slaying" the last vestige of Rome's fabled empire.

To find the correct fulfillment of the sixth trumpet, we need to subtract 391 years from the fall of the Byzantine Empire in 1453 AD, which brings us to 1062. Next, we must locate the conquerors of the Byzantine Empire, the Ottoman Turks, and their relation to that year.[57] We also learn from the first several verses where the sixth trumpet would begin. Verse fourteen states the four angels were "bound in the great river Euphrates," so the river should be the geographical focus of our search.

The one regional power at the start of the eleventh century that would have been a formidable threat to the Byzantines was the Ghaznavid Empire under Mahmud of Ghazni. However, Mahmud was far more interested in a conquest of the Indian lands to his east, so the threat his army posed to the Byzantines far to the west was minimal. Upon Mahmud's death in 1028, his sons fought over the empire, eventually losing much of the Ghaznavid lands to the Seljuk Dynasty in the Battle of Dandanaqan in 1040.[58] This battle was before 1062 and east of the Euphrates, so it would not satisfy the fulfillment of the prophecy.[59]

At this point in Middle Eastern history, Mesopotamia was controlled by the Buyid Dynasty, whose land extended across both sides of the Euphrates. Once the Ghaznavids lost at Dandanaqan, the Buyids shared their eastern border with the Seljuks, who retained strong military ambitions.

These ambitions would be achieved within fifteen years. In December 1055, the Seljuk sultan Tughril deposed the Buyid emir al-Malik al-Rahim, effectively taking Baghdad. The Buyids still controlled some land as a Seljuk vassal state under the final emir, Abu Mansur Fulad Sutun, whose reign ended when he died in battle against the Shabankara tribe. Shortly after his death, the Seljuks took the rest of the Buyid lands in early to mid-1062 AD.[60]

---

[e] **Revelation 9:6** And in those days shall men seek death, and shall not find it; and shall desire to die, and death shall flee from them.

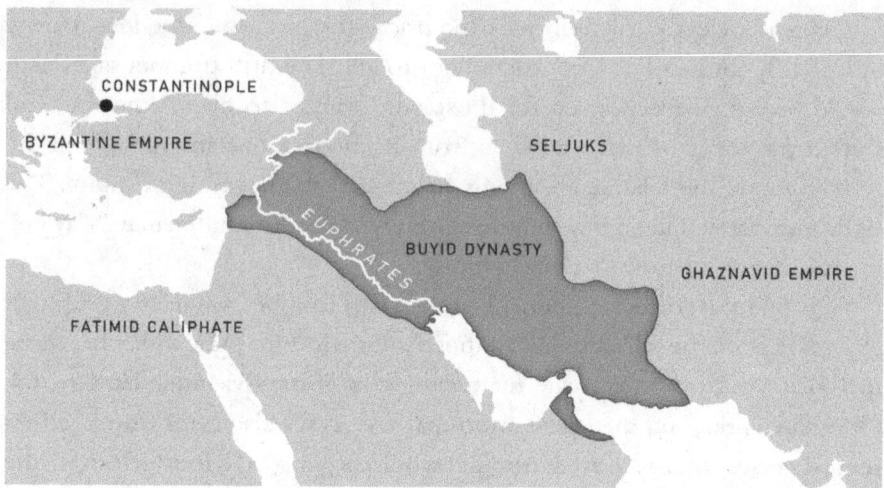

Figure 40: Buyid Dynasty, which controlled the land around the Euphrates River, 1055 AD.

The Seljuks were an ethnically Turkish people who originated southeast of the Caspian Sea. In the decades following the fall of the Buyids, the Seljuk armies advanced into Anatolia and fought a series of conflicts known as the Byzantine-Seljuk Wars. As a result of the first war, the Seljuks established the Sultanate of Rûm—their first infringement on Byzantine territory.

The next several centuries would bring chaos and instability as various regional powers fought over territory and the Seljuks became a target of the earliest Catholic crusaders from Europe. The Seljuks ultimately collapsed in 1194 AD at the hands of the Khwarazmians, leaving the Sultanate of Rûm as the last remnant of their empire.[61] When Rûm was later defeated, it created an opportunity for new regional powers to arise.

The Ottoman Turks were the people nearest Constantinople in the early fourteenth century. Situated in Anatolia on the opposite side of the Bosporus Strait, the Ottoman army laid siege to a diminished Constantinople at least five times before ultimately conquering the city in 1453 AD. For the 391 years after the Seljuk Turks conquered the Buyid Dynasty in 1062 AD, ethnically Turkish armies assaulted the Byzantine Empire and its capital. The "hour, and a day, and a month, and a year" culminated in 1453 when the final siege of Constantinople resulted in the city's collapse. This decisive defeat marked the end of the Byzantine Empire, also known as the Eastern Roman Empire, the last remaining fragment of the "third part of men."[62]

THE SEVEN TRUMPETS

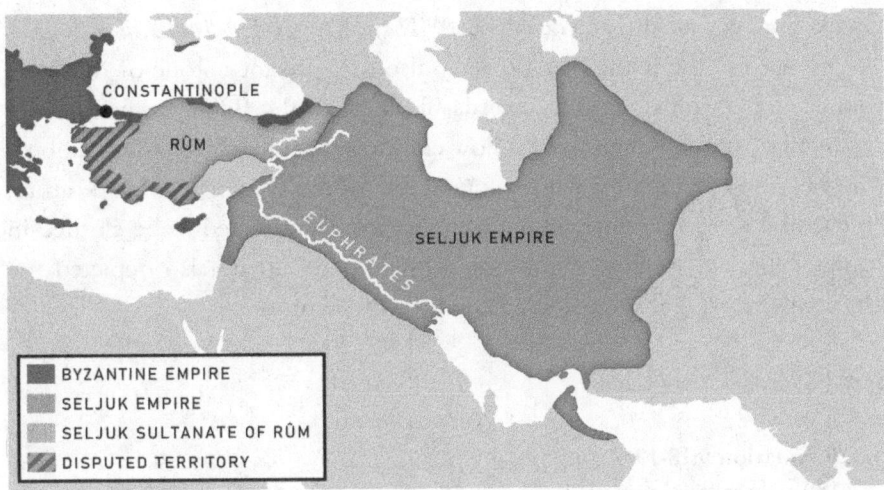

Figure 41: *The Seljuk Empire in the late eleventh century. The Seljuks conquered the Buyids in 1062 AD.*

Description of the Army

> **Revelation 9:16-17**
> **16** And the number of the army of the horsemen were two hundred thousand thousand: and I heard the number of them.
> **17** And thus I saw the horses in the vision, and them that sat on them, having breastplates of fire, and of jacinth, and brimstone: and the heads of the horses were as the heads of lions; and out of their mouths issued fire and smoke and brimstone.

Like the locust army, these conquerors are again described as a cavalry. The King James Bible incorrectly renders the number of horsemen from the Greek as "two hundred thousand thousand," meaning two hundred million. However, based on the original Greek in the *Textus Receptus*, "δύο μυριάδες μυριάδων,"[63] this may have been a misinterpretation. The Greek phrase "δύο μυριάδες μυριάδων" could translate to "two myriads of myriads." The Old Turkish word for myriad is *tümän*, which was a standard unit of measurement that translates to "ten thousand."[64] However, δύο μυριάδες μυριάδων could also be rendered as "two ten thousands," which would mean an army that consisted of twenty thousand horsemen.[65]

John saw the horsemen wearing "breastplates of fire, and of jacinth, and brimstone." Biblical scholars believe these descriptors are metaphors for the colors worn by the soldiers. Fire suggests a red color in the Bible. The Koine

Greek word for jacinth is ὑακίνθινους.⁶⁶ *Thayer's Greek-English Lexicon* defines ὑακίνθινους as "the name of a flower...also of a precious stone of the same color, i.e., dark-blue verging towards black."⁶⁷ In the Bible, brimstone is a synonym of sulfur, which has a yellow coloring. Theologian Charles Daubuz, who saw these comparisons to colors, wrote of the Ottoman soldiers' attire, "the Ottomans from their first appearance having affected to be clothed in scarlet, blue, and yellow."⁶⁸ Several contemporary artists also depicted the Ottomans wearing these colors in the fifteenth century.

Their Power Is in Their Mouth

> **Revelation 9:18-19**
> **18** By these three was the third part of men killed, by the fire, and by the smoke, and by the brimstone, which issued out of their mouths.
> **19** For their power is in their mouth, and in their tails: for their tails were like unto serpents, and had heads, and with them they do hurt.

Revelation 9:18 explains that the third part of men would be killed using the fire, smoke, and brimstone coming from the mouths of the Ottoman invaders. Before the mid-fifteenth century, the European and Middle Eastern weaponry used in battle was primarily limited to swords and spears in close combat and medium-range projectile weapons such as trebuchets or archers. By no later than the Ottoman-Hungarian Wars of 1443-1444, the Ottoman infantrymen regularly carried arquebuses, an early long-barreled gun similar to a musket, making the Ottomans among the first militaries to use firearms in Europe.⁶⁹

When a soldier fires a long gun, he rests his weapon against his cheek to better aim his weapon. Gunpowder contains brimstone, as it is made from sulfur, charcoal, and potassium nitrate. In the first century, well before the advent of firearms, it would be conceivable for John to define a long gun as fire, smoke, and brimstone that "issued out of their mouths."

Verse nineteen says the army's power was not only in their mouths but also in their tails. Edward Bishop Elliott interpreted the word "tails" as a reference to the standards of the Ottoman army, called pashas, which were long poles with horse tails hanging from the top. The more powerful a man was, the more tails his pasha would have. Provincial governors and generals would have one or two, depending on their rank or position within the army and government. Only the Ottoman grand vizier would have three tails on his pasha. To Elliott, the horse tails displayed the power of rank, while the fire, smoke, and brimstone coming out of the soldiers' mouths represented the power of military force.[70]

However, a closer investigation of the original Koine Greek is required. Constantin Tischendorf's *Greek New Testament* uses οὐραῖσ and οὐραί for the two words the King James Version translates as "tails" in Revelation 9:19.[71] Although the Greek root word οὐρά, or *ourá*, can mean the tail of an animal, the second definition; "of an army marching, the rear-guard, rear," is more relevant to this verse.[72] This would suggest John saw the Ottoman soldiers' military power fired not only from the mid-range arquebuses resting against the mouths of infantry, but also from the rear guard. The Ottomans had as many as seventy cannons,[73] the largest of which could fire projectiles from over a mile away.[74] For the first time, armies in Europe had the advantage of long-range weaponry.

Idolatry and Sorcery

> **Revelation 9:20-21**
> **20** And the rest of the men which were not killed by these plagues yet repented not of the works of their hands, that they should not worship devils, and idols of gold, and silver, and brass, and stone, and of wood: which neither can see, nor hear, nor walk:
> **21** Neither repented they of their murders, nor of their sorceries, nor of their fornication, nor of their thefts.

After the Byzantine Empire fell, the Catholic Church did not change its behavior. Church doctrine continued to encourage Catholics to practice idol worship through graven images, exactly as verse twenty prophesied. Paul's apostasy accelerated between the falls of the Western and Eastern Roman Empires. The medieval Roman Catholic Church fell deeper into superstition, false doctrine, sorcery, and idolatry. It committed mass murder against the Christians who refused to participate in Catholic paganism. As the Anglican priest John Woodhouse wrote, "It was in a corrupt period of the Church, when the altar of Religion called for vengeance; when idolatry in particular was a reigning vice...Yet the progress of this evil was slow and gradual; and it was a long time before it could justly be said to have amounted to that general prevalence described in the twentieth and twenty-first verses. This character is not fairly and generally applicable to the Christian Church, before the sixth century. But toward the end of the sixth and the beginning of the seventh century, the measure of this iniquity became full."[75]

The designation of the final three trumpets as woes evokes Isaiah 5:20, which reads, "Woe unto them that call evil good, and good evil."[f] The Roman Catholic Church's distortion of good and evil is obvious to avid Bible readers. The rituals, iconography, and saint veneration within Catholicism are easily recognizable through their pagan roots as sorcery, idolatry, and polytheism. Constantine's apostasy had distorted Christianity so absolutely that Catholics today perform rituals akin to witchcraft, pray to graven images, and venerate saints as if they were minor deities.

After the 391-year prophecy, the sixth trumpet continues. John had a series of three distinct visions that set the stage for the final trumpet. He first sees a vision of an angel holding a little book. Next, John is told to measure the temple of God and its altar, but exclude its courtyard. After he finishes measuring, John sees two witnesses who testify on God's behalf until their deaths. Only after these three visions are fulfilled will the seventh trumpet be allowed to sound.

The Little Book

> **Revelation 10:1-2**
> 1 And I saw another mighty angel come down from heaven, clothed with a cloud: and a rainbow was upon his head, and his face was as it were the sun, and his feet as pillars of fire:
> 2 And he had in his hand a little book open: and he set his right foot upon the sea, and his left foot on the earth,

The first vision begins when an angel descends from Heaven with a little book in his hand at the start of Revelation 10. Later in the passage, the angel swears by God that time is running out for Catholics, stating, "There should

---

[f] **Isaiah 5:20** Woe unto them that call evil good, and good evil; that put darkness for light, and light for darkness; that put bitter for sweet, and sweet for bitter!

be time no longer." Next, a voice from Heaven declares that when this time runs out, the seventh trumpet will end the "mystery of God." When it finally sounds, all the superstitions, sorcery, rituals, and false doctrine of the Roman Catholic *religion* will be peeled away from the Christian *faith*, leaving a purer form of true Christianity for believers.

> **Revelation 10:5-7**
> 5 And the angel which I saw stand upon the sea and upon the earth lifted up his hand to heaven,
> 6 And sware by him that liveth for ever and ever, who created heaven, and the things that therein are, and the earth, and the things that therein are, and the sea, and the things which are therein, that there should be time no longer:
> 7 But in the days of the voice of the seventh angel, when he shall begin to sound, the mystery of God should be finished, as he hath declared to his servants the prophets.

The association between the phrase "the mystery of God" and the false church of Mystery Babylon is unmistakable. If John's description of Mystery Babylon did not make her representation of Catholicism clear, the use of the word "mystery" to define the cryptic deceptions of Catholic dogma provides more evidence. The seventh trumpet would finally expose its duplicity.

> **Revelation 10:8-10**
> 8 And the voice which I heard from heaven spake unto me again, and said, Go and take the little book which is open in the hand of the angel which standeth upon the sea and upon the earth.
> 9 And I went unto the angel, and said unto him, Give me the little book. And he said unto me, Take it, and eat it up; and it shall make thy belly bitter, but it shall be in thy mouth sweet as honey.
> 10 And I took the little book out of the angel's hand, and ate it up; and it was in my mouth sweet as honey: and as soon as I had eaten it, my belly was bitter.

In the rest of the chapter, John takes the book, which represents the Bible, and eats it, making his stomach bitter. By ingesting the Bible, John was symbolically receiving it on behalf of the Christian people and preserving it for the rest of time.

This vision's placement following the "hour, and a day, and a month, and a year" is extraordinary. Shortly before the fall of Constantinople, Johannes

Gutenberg invented the printing press. The first complete book he printed was the Latin Vulgate Bible, and the first copies were sold less than two years after the fall of Constantinople in 1453.

On March 12, 1455, Enea Silvio Piccolomini—who would become Pope Pius II—wrote to Cardinal Juan de Carvajal after visiting Frankfurt. "It seems what I had been told was true," he wrote, "I have not seen entire Bibles, but I have seen signatures of five folded sheets." Piccolomini called Gutenberg an "amazing man" and told Cardinal Carvajal, "I shall try to buy a volume for you but I fear this will not be possible, not only because of the distance, but because copies are sold even before they are completed."[76]

At this moment, less than two years after Constantinople's fall, the first printed Bibles began to make scripture more easily accessible. While these Bibles were still prohibitively expensive, Gutenberg's movable type printing press would be refined, progressively making the scriptures more available to the masses.

John's stomachache likely represents the deep angst felt by the leaders of the Protestant Reformation. Once these men were able to read and analyze the Bible for themselves, they realized Catholics had been deceived by their own church. The words of scripture were uncomfortable to read, as the Bible disagreed with Catholic teaching.

Measuring the Temple

With the Bible now secured, John resumes prophesying. In a short scene at the beginning of Revelation 11, he is commanded to measure the temple of God in Heaven and its altar, but ignore its courtyard. In the process, John is also directed to measure those worshipping inside the temple.

> **Revelation 11:1-2**
> 1 And there was given me a reed like unto a rod: and the angel stood, saying, Rise, and measure the temple of God, and the altar, and them that worship therein.
> 2 But the court which is without the temple leave out, and measure it not; for it is given unto the Gentiles: and the holy city shall they tread under foot forty and two months.

Measuring is an act of evaluation. The angel charges John with analyzing God's temple to determine the standard for salvation. He then measures the worshippers inside the temple to ensure they satisfy God's expectations. As Jesus said in Matthew 7, "Not every one that saith unto me, Lord, Lord, shall enter into the kingdom of heaven; but he that doeth the will of my Father which is in heaven...And then will I profess unto them, I never knew you: depart from me, ye that work iniquity."[77]

Some Historicists believe John is measuring the Roman Catholic Church, but that interpretation is backward. He is unmistakably scrutinizing *the temple of God*, not a false church. John was measuring God's temple to determine the criteria for being worthy of worshipping God for eternity.

Notably, John is told to leave the courtyard out so it can be "given unto the Gentiles." The angel predicts these Gentiles will tread on the holy city for forty-two prophetic months, another reference to the Great Tribulation. If the courtyard was left to those who would tread on the holy city during the Tribulation, these were not typical Gentiles, as the conventional definition of a Gentile is any non-Jew. However, because the Gentiles described here were the driving force behind the Tribulation, this indicates the people relegated to the courtyard are not the non-Jews but the non-Christians, specifically, the Roman Catholics.

A reasonable inference can be made that the courtyard is left unmeasured because those attempting to worship God who do not meet his standard will find themselves trapped there when they are prohibited from entering the temple of Heaven. The temple walls draw a distinction, separating those God regards as true Christians from those he does not. Sadly, Catholics will find themselves confined outside the temple walls.

In the timeline of Revelation, the measuring of the temple aligns with the years before the Protestant Reformation. Martin Luther was ordained as a priest in April 1507. Over the next decade, he studied the Bible in-depth, eventually learning of the many ways the Catholic Church had fulfilled the prophecy of Mystery Babylon. He would spend the rest of his life writing about how far the Catholic Church had fallen away from the pure, organic faith at the heart of Christianity. When Luther and the other leaders of the Protestant Reformation measured the temple of God, they found Catholics were unworthy of eternal life.

The Two Witnesses

> **Revelation 11:3-6**
> **3** And I will give power unto my two witnesses, and they shall prophesy a thousand two hundred and threescore days, clothed in sackcloth.
> **4** These are the two olive trees, and the two candlesticks standing before the God of the earth.
> **5** And if any man will hurt them, fire proceedeth out of their mouth, and devoureth their enemies: and if any man will hurt them, he must in this manner be killed.
> **6** These have power to shut heaven, that it rain not in the days of their prophecy: and have power over waters to turn them to blood, and to smite the earth with all plagues, as often as they will.

Next, the angel—who was likely Jesus—tells John he would send his two witnesses to prophesy for 1,260 days. There is much debate on what or who the witnesses represent. Many Futurists see the witnesses as a reappearance of the prophets Enoch and Elijah, neither of whom saw death according to the Bible. Others say Moses and Elijah, who appeared alongside Jesus at his transfiguration. If Futurism is correct, the witnesses would arrive at the start of the Tribulation. But God would not warn us that Jesus' return was nearing through the return of prophets. According to *The Pulpit Commentary*, "It is inconceivable that Moses and Elias, or any other of the saints of God, should return from Paradise to suffer as these two witnesses."[78]

Most Historicists agree that the number of witnesses is at least partially a reference to Hebrew law. Both Deuteronomy 17:6 and 19:15 regulate the reliability of witnesses' claims against a defendant. In these verses, Moses stated that testimony from a second, corroborating witness was required for a legal claim to be credible.[g] The New Testament book of Hebrews also refers to this aspect of ancient Mosaic law.[h]

---

[g] **Deuteronomy 17:6** At the mouth of two witnesses, or three witnesses, shall he that is worthy of death be put to death; but at the mouth of one witness he shall not be put to death.

Deuteronomy 19:15 One witness shall not rise up against a man for any iniquity, or for any sin, in any sin that he sinneth: at the mouth of two witnesses, or at the mouth of three witnesses, shall the matter be established.

[h] **Hebrews 10:28** He that despised Moses' law died without mercy under two or three witnesses:

Generally, Historicists see the two witnesses as at least an allusion to the law. This interpretation suggests God is commanding us to be witnesses for the gospel beyond the unreliability that exists from a single witness. Several times in Biblical history, God commissioned witnesses as pairs. Moses and Aaron, Elijah and Elisha, Joshua and Caleb, Paul and Barnabas, and Paul and Silas all appeared together as witnesses for God.

While some Historicists believe the two witnesses are only a reference to Moses' Deuteronomic Code, others believe this reference is foundational but interpret the witnesses as the Old and New Testaments. During the 1,260 years of the Great Tribulation, the Bible was largely inaccessible, but it never reached a point of extinction. Whenever the privileged few who could read the Bible studied it, the Old and New Testaments testified on God's behalf.

There is a valid reference point in the Old Testament book of Zechariah that supports this interpretation. In Zechariah 4, Zerubbabel had a vision of a candlestick flanked by two olive trees. The trees emptied their oil into the candlestick to fuel its flames. An angel interpreted the trees in the vision for him, stating, "These are the two anointed ones, that stand by the Lord of the whole earth."[i] There is also support for the Israelites' use of olive oil as lamp fuel in Exodus 27:20, where they were commanded to use it in the Tabernacle to "cause the lamp to burn always."[j]

In Zechariah 4, there is only one candlestick. In Revelation 11, there are two. Supporters of the theory that the witnesses represent the Old and New Testaments point to this as additional evidence for their interpretation. Zerubbabel, an Old Testament prophet, saw only one candlestick because he lived before the New Testament was written. Two olive trees were there to provide oil, but at the time, only one candlestick's flame needed fuel.

Another possible solution is that the two witnesses represent lineages of believers. Two individual witnesses would not be physically able to testify for

---

[i] **Zechariah 4:11-14** 11 Then answered I, and said unto him, What are these two olive trees upon the right side of the candlestick and upon the left side thereof? 12 And I answered again, and said unto him, What be these two olive branches which through the two golden pipes empty the golden oil out of themselves? 13 And he answered me and said, Knowest thou not what these be? And I said, No, my lord. 14 Then said he, These are the two anointed ones, that stand by the Lord of the whole earth.

[j] **Exodus 27:20** And thou shalt command the children of Israel, that they bring thee pure oil olive beaten for the light, to cause the lamp to burn always.

1,260 years, but a group could. John wrote in Revelation 1:20 that the seven candlesticks in Jesus' presence in Heaven represented the seven churches to whom Revelation was written.[k] The Christian churches have kept the flame of the gospel alive for millennia, just as the light of the candlestick in the Tabernacle was never to be extinguished.

The actual fulfillment of this passage may be an amalgamation of these interpretations. The true Christian church kept the light of the gospel shining throughout some of the darkest times for the faith—the Roman persecutions and Tribulation. The members of the church—the olives from the trees—provide oil to fuel the candlesticks—the church. The angel says the witnesses, the Old and New Testaments, represent the olive trees and the candlesticks. In Matthew 5, Jesus compared the testimony and faith of his disciples to a light when he commanded his followers not to hide their faith under a bushel, but to put it on a candlestick to share their light with others.[l]

> **Revelation 11:7-10**
> 7 And when they shall have finished their testimony, the beast that ascendeth out of the bottomless pit shall make war against them, and shall overcome them, and kill them.
> 8 And their dead bodies shall lie in the street of the great city, which spiritually is called Sodom and Egypt, where also our Lord was crucified.
> 9 And they of the people and kindreds and tongues and nations shall see their dead bodies three days and an half, and shall not suffer their dead bodies to be put in graves.
> 10 And they that dwell upon the earth shall rejoice over them, and make merry, and shall send gifts one to another; because these two prophets tormented them that dwelt on the earth.

Revelation 11:7 says that after the witnesses finish their testimony, they will be killed, and their lifeless bodies will lie in the street for three and a half

---

[k] **Revelation 1:20** The mystery of the seven stars which thou sawest in my right hand, and the seven golden candlesticks. The seven stars are the angels of the seven churches: and the seven candlesticks which thou sawest are the seven churches.

[l] **Matthew 5:14-16** 14 Ye are the light of the world. A city that is set on an hill cannot be hid. 15 Neither do men light a candle, and put it under a bushel, but on a candlestick; and it giveth light unto all that are in the house. 16 Let your light so shine before men, that they may see your good works, and glorify your Father which is in heaven.

days. About a century before the Reformation, two leading theologians, Jan Hus and Jerome of Prague, called for changes to the Catholic Church. Jerome was inspired by the writings of John Wycliffe, which he brought to Hus. Hus then wrote extensively about his own ideas based on Wycliffe's concepts. In 1414, Hus was called to appear at the Council of Constance to explain his beliefs. King Sigismund, a Catholic, granted safe passage to Hus, and Jerome joined him to provide support. Upon arrival, they were immediately arrested by Pope John XXIII and later burned at the stake for heresy. For a thorough understanding of the nauseating behavior that took place at Constance, this was the same council that ordered John Wycliffe's bones to be exhumed and burned at the stake.

At the Fifth Lateran Council, no one spoke against the Catholic Church's proclamations, as advocates for church reforms remembered the wickedness and betrayal of the Catholic leaders at Constance a century earlier. In their nineteenth-century work, *The Commentary Critical and Explanatory on the Whole Bible*, expositors David Brown, Andrew Robert Fausset, and Robert Jamieson described this event. "It is a curious historical coincidence," they explained, "that, at the fifth Lateran Council, May 5, 1514, no witness (not even the Moravians who were summoned) testified for the truth, as Hus and Jerome did at Constance; an orator ascended the tribunal before the representatives of Papal Christendom, and said, 'There is no reclaimant, no opponent.'"[79] The Catholic Church's martyrdom of Hus and Jerome remained fresh in the minds of the pre-Reformation Protestants. No one felt emboldened enough to testify on behalf of scripture in front of all of Catholicism, and God's two witnesses were killed.

> **Revelation 11:11-13**
> **11** And after three days and an half the spirit of life from God entered into them, and they stood upon their feet; and great fear fell upon them which saw them.
> **12** And they heard a great voice from heaven saying unto them, Come up hither. And they ascended up to heaven in a cloud; and their enemies beheld them.
> **13** And the same hour was there a great earthquake, and the tenth part of the city fell, and in the earthquake were slain of men seven thousand: and the remnant were affrighted, and gave glory to the God of heaven.

Next, the angel explains that the two witnesses will lie dead in the street for three and a half prophetic days before being resurrected. Three and a half years after the Fifth Lateran Council, the great earthquake of Revelation 11:13 occurred. As the story goes, on October 31, 1517, Martin Luther nailed the *Ninety-Five Theses* to the door of All Saints' Church in Wittenberg, Germany, sparking the Protestant Reformation. Martin Luther was the first significant theologian to publicly stand up for scripture against Catholicism since the deaths of Jan Hus and Jerome. By publishing his *Theses*, Luther testified as a witness for scripture. This event resurrected the two witnesses, caused the earthquake, and ended the sixth trumpet. After the trumpet ends, we are told, "Behold, the third woe cometh quickly."

> **Revelation 11:14**
> 14 The second woe is past; and, behold, the third woe cometh quickly.

The Seventh Trumpet: The Third Woe

The woes were God's last three warnings to the Roman Catholic Church to change its ways. By October 1517, two of the three woes had been fulfilled, and the Catholic Church failed to heed God's warnings. With the third woe, God would no longer target the governments of Rome and Constantinople. Because the Catholic Church had not repented for its sacrilegious practices, God would begin to focus all his vengeance on the Vatican itself.

> **Revelation 11:15-17**
> 15 And the seventh angel sounded; and there were great voices in heaven, saying, The kingdoms of this world are become the kingdoms of our Lord, and of his Christ; and he shall reign for ever and ever.
> 16 And the four and twenty elders, which sat before God on their seats, fell upon their faces, and worshipped God,
> 17 Saying, We give thee thanks, O Lord God Almighty, which art, and wast, and art to come; because thou hast taken to thee thy great power, and hast reigned.

After their October 31, 1517, publication, it took little time for the ideas of Luther's *Ninety-Five Theses* to spread. The German theologian Friedrich Myconius, a close friend of Luther's, wrote, "Hardly fourteen days had passed when these propositions were known throughout Germany and within four weeks almost all of Christendom was familiar with them." By no later than December, printed copies of the *Theses* in pamphlet and broadsheet form had appeared in the German cities of Leipzig, Nuremberg, and Basel.

Even Martin Luther was surprised by how quickly his words spread. In a March 1518 letter to one of his Nuremberg publishers, he wrote of the *Theses*, "They are printed and circulated far beyond my expectation."[80] The Protestant Reformation had "come quickly" after the publication of Luther's *Ninety-Five Theses* brought a conclusion to the sixth trumpet.

The Reformation called into question the dogma of Catholicism. Finally, more than twelve hundred years after Constantine's apostasy, men measured the virtues of the church and found it to be anti-Christian. The Reformers quickly unraveled the fraudulence of the Catholic Church and exposed it as a pagan institution. Revelation 11:15-17 illustrates Heaven's reaction to the Reformation, where the temple is opened and the twenty-four elders sitting around the throne celebrate and praise God.

> **Revelation 11:18-19**
> 18 And the nations were angry, and thy wrath is come, and the time of the dead, that they should be judged, and that thou shouldest give reward unto thy servants the prophets, and to the saints, and them that fear thy name, small and great; and shouldest destroy them which destroy the earth.
> 19 And the temple of God was opened in heaven, and there was seen in his temple the ark of his testament: and there were lightnings, and voices, and thunderings, and an earthquake, and great hail.

As illustrated in verses eighteen and nineteen, the Catholic world reacted far differently to the Protestant Reformation than Heaven did. During the Counter-Reformation, Catholic religious and political leaders responded with astonishing violence, persecuting Christians wherever Protestantism spread.

Chapter Synopsis

The Seven Trumpets (Revelation 8:2-11:19)
- **First Trumpet:** Alaric's Goths revolt against the Romans, invade Italy, and sack Rome, 395-410 AD
- **Second Trumpet:** Genseric's Vandals attack Roman seaports and sack Rome, 429-455 AD
- **Third Trumpet:** Attila and the Huns invade Gaul and Italy, 451-452 AD
- **Fourth Trumpet:** Odoacer conquers the Roman Empire, 476 AD
- **Fifth Trumpet:** Founding and expansion of Islam, 612-762 AD
  - Lasted five prophetic months, or 150 calendar years
  - Start of 150 years: Muhammad first preaches Islam publicly, 612 AD
  - End of 150 years: Abbasids settle in Baghdad, 762 AD
- **Sixth Trumpet:** Defeat of Buyids until *Ninety-Five Theses*, 1062-1517 AD

Turks Attack the Byzantine Empire (Revelation 9:13-21)
  - "An hour, and a day, and a month, and a year," or about 391 years
  - Start of 391 years: Seljuk Turks conquer Buyids, 1062 AD
  - End of 391 years: Ottoman Turks conquer the Byzantines, 1453 AD

The Little Book (Revelation 10:1-11)
  - An angel gives John a little book, which represents the Bible
  - Represents the printing press making the Bible accessible, 1455 AD

Measuring the Temple (Revelation 11:1-2)
  - The Reformers begin to see how Catholicism does not measure up to God's Word in the late fifteenth and early sixteenth centuries

The Two Witnesses (Revelation 11:3-14)
  - Metaphor for the Old and New Testaments
  - The two witnesses were "killed" when no one testified for the Bible at the Fifth Lateran Council, May 5, 1514 AD
  - Three and a half years later, the two witnesses were resurrected when Martin Luther published his *Ninety-Five Theses*, October 31, 1517 AD
- **Seventh Trumpet:** After Martin Luther published the *Theses*, his ideas quickly spread, causing the Protestant Reformation, November 1517 AD

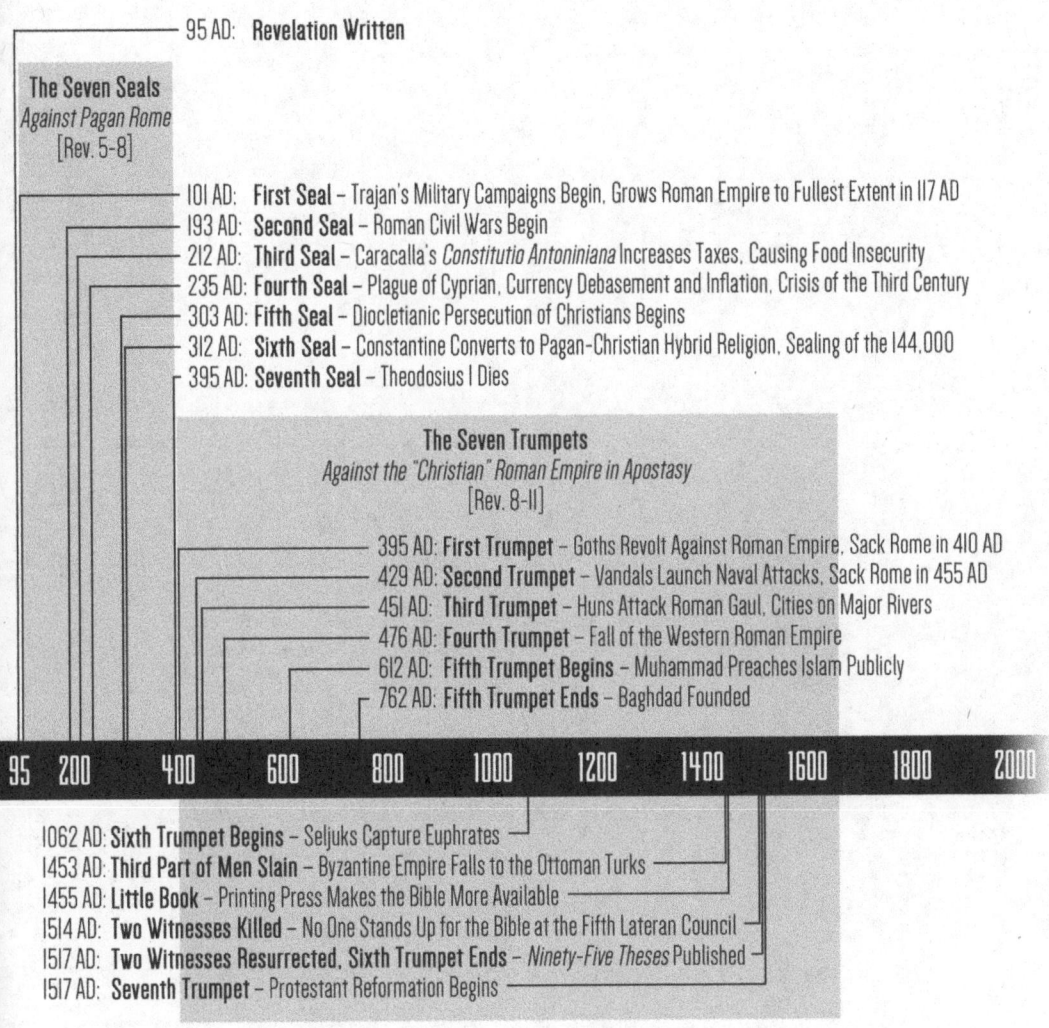

14

THE INTERLUDE

After the seven trumpets sounded, John experienced several visions that expanded on the adversarial relationship between Satan and Christianity. For simplicity, we will call this the "interlude" of Revelation. The visions found in Revelation 12-14 were placed here because they detail the centuries-long religious conflicts between good and evil, God and Satan, and Christianity and Catholicism. Most of these topics are not tied to a specific event or point in history, so they cannot be placed in chronological order. Instead, Christ revealed them to John as a part of the seventh trumpet because the Protestant Reformation ended the "mystery of God." After these visions clarify what is and is not the true Christian faith, the final seven judgments begin.

The Dragon and the Woman

> **Revelation 12:1-2**
> 1 And there appeared a great wonder in heaven; a woman clothed with the sun, and the moon under her feet, and upon her head a crown of twelve stars:
> 2 And she being with child cried, travailing in birth, and pained to be delivered.

In his first vision after the seventh trumpet sounded, John saw a dragon and a woman in labor. As we identified with Mystery Babylon, a woman in prophecy represents the church. While Mystery Babylon—a false church—was a prostitute, this woman has no defined sexual exploits, so she represents followers of God. In the ancient past, before the death and resurrection of Jesus Christ, God's chosen people were the Jews. Today, she represents the faithful followers of Christ—the Christian church. This woman personifies a continuum of God's people throughout time. She was seen with a crown of twelve stars representing the twelve tribes of Israel and the twelve original disciples of Jesus—the foundations on which the Jewish and Christian faiths were built.

The early Christian faith went through incredible pain. The woman in labor is travailing, representing the many saints who were martyred, tortured, and persecuted. This woman's representation of the church will be reinforced in the last verse of the chapter, where we learn that Satan attacks the remnant of the woman's seed following the death of Christ. The original disciples of Jesus and later believers spread the gospel and created new Christians—the seed of the woman.

> **Revelation 12:3-5**
> **3** And there appeared another wonder in heaven; and behold a great red dragon, having seven heads and ten horns, and seven crowns upon his heads.
> **4** And his tail drew the third part of the stars of heaven, and did cast them to the earth: and the dragon stood before the woman which was ready to be delivered, for to devour her child as soon as it was born.
> **5** And she brought forth a man child, who was to rule all nations with a rod of iron: and her child was caught up unto God, and to his throne.

However, this woman is not alone. Next, we are introduced to Satan as a great red dragon. In verse four, he throws one-third of the stars in Heaven down to earth to try to kill the woman's son once she gives birth. Many of the metaphors in Revelation 12 have dual meanings. The first interpretation of the chapter is a retelling of the story of the life of Jesus. Satan's attempt to devour the infant child refers to Herod's effort to kill Jesus by slaughtering Bethlehem's male infants, an incident commonly called the "Massacre of the Innocents."[a] In the figurative second reading, the woman represents God's

---

[a] **Matthew 2:16** Then Herod, when he saw that he was mocked of the wise men, was exceeding wroth, and sent forth, and slew all the children that were in Bethlehem, and in all the coasts thereof, from two years old and under, according to the time which he had diligently inquired of the wise men.

followers, first the Jews and then the Christians. The infant is again Jesus, who was born to a woman in the lineage of faithful Jews, while the "remnant of the woman's seed" represents the Christians who would follow him.

The dragon's seven heads and ten horns allude to the role Rome played in Satan's efforts to destroy both the infant Jesus and, later, the early church. The iron rod Jesus will use to rule the nations is a reference to scripture, just as Paul compared God's Word to a sword in Ephesians 6:17.[b]

> **Revelation 12:6**
> 6 And the woman fled into the wilderness, where she hath a place prepared of God, that they should feed her there a thousand two hundred and threescore days.

In the first interpretation, the parallels between the woman and Mary continue. Just as God helped Mary, Joseph, and Jesus flee to Egypt to avoid Herod's decree, the woman flees the dragon by escaping to the wilderness.[c] This flight to Egypt—a pagan *spiritual wilderness*—protects the Christian faith by saving the infant Jesus. The second, figurative meaning centers around the Tribulation. The allusion to 1,260 days suggests the Christian faith would find refuge and survive the persecution and turmoil that had yet to come.

> **Revelation 12:7-9**
> 7 And there was war in heaven: Michael and his angels fought against the dragon; and the dragon fought and his angels,
> 8 And prevailed not; neither was their place found any more in heaven.
> 9 And the great dragon was cast out, that old serpent, called the Devil, and Satan, which deceiveth the whole world: he was cast out into the earth, and his angels were cast out with him.

However, God was not going to permit Satan's attempt to kill his church to succeed. In verse seven, the archangel Michael commands a force of angels

---

[b] **Ephesians 6:17** And take the helmet of salvation, and the sword of the Spirit, which is the word of God:

[c] **Matthew 2:13** And when they were departed, behold, the angel of the Lord appeareth to Joseph in a dream, saying, Arise, and take the young child and his mother, and flee into Egypt, and be thou there until I bring thee word: for Herod will seek the young child to destroy him.

into battle against Satan and his angels. Satan loses the war, resulting in his expulsion from Heaven. He is forced down to earth, where he "deceiveth the whole world." This is another indication that Satan would establish a false religion disguised as Christianity to fool those who follow it.

> **Revelation 12:10-12**
> **10** And I heard a loud voice saying in heaven, Now is come salvation, and strength, and the kingdom of our God, and the power of his Christ: for the accuser of our brethren is cast down, which accused them before our God day and night.
> **11** And they overcame him by the blood of the Lamb, and by the word of their testimony; and they loved not their lives unto the death.
> **12** Therefore rejoice, ye heavens, and ye that dwell in them. Woe to the inhabiters of the earth and of the sea! for the devil is come down unto you, having great wrath, because he knoweth that he hath but a short time.

After Satan is cast down to earth, John hears a loud voice from Heaven summarizing what has taken place in this classic battle between good and evil. This voice celebrates after seeing that Satan has been defeated in the battle. Verses nine and twelve tell us that Satan and his angels were not expelled to Hell directly. While the imagery of Satan inhabiting Hell while simultaneously tormenting those of us on earth has been romanticized, this chapter calls that depiction into question. In actuality, the Bible does not say Satan is exiled to Hell until much later, in Revelation 20:10. Until then, Satan resides on earth, wreaking havoc from among us.

Revelation 12:11 is a reference to Jesus' crucifixion. It identifies his death as the deciding factor in the struggle between Michael and Satan. After giving Jesus' sacrifice credit for the resiliency and strength of Christianity, the voice tells Heaven to celebrate their hard-won spiritual victory over Satan, while warning the inhabitants of earth that things were about to get much worse.

> **Revelation 12:13-14**
> **13** And when the dragon saw that he was cast unto the earth, he persecuted the woman which brought forth the man child.
> **14** And to the woman were given two wings of a great eagle, that she might fly into the wilderness, into her place, where she is nourished for a time, and times, and half a time, from the face of the serpent.

When Satan realizes he is on earth, he immediately starts persecuting the Christian community. However, the woman receives two wings to fly to the wilderness and escape this persecution. The phrase "time, and times, and half a time" is interpreted in the same way as in Daniel 7:25, as three and a half prophetic years, or 1,260 calendar years. The reference to 1,260 years is not a reference to the length of this suffering, as Satan did not limit Christian persecution to the years 538-1798 AD. The reference is an acknowledgment of the continued perseverance of Christianity through the worst persecution it would face, and an indication that it would survive the Great Tribulation.

The persecution of the early Christians by the Romans and Jewish leaders was so great that it forced many of the early believers to abandon Judea and evangelize elsewhere. Even during this early period of persecution, God fed and nurtured the Christian church through a time of great danger, preserving it for the future.

> **Revelation 12:15-16**
> **15** And the serpent cast out of his mouth water as a flood after the woman, that he might cause her to be carried away of the flood.
> **16** And the earth helped the woman, and the earth opened her mouth, and swallowed up the flood which the dragon cast out of his mouth.

Satan's assault on Christianity accelerates like a flood in verse fifteen. The flood metaphor alludes to an overwhelming persecution. Before Christianity could be submerged and drowned, the earth opens its mouth and swallows the flood, rescuing the woman. The swallowing of the flood echoes Jesus' Olivet Discourse when he predicted the days of the Great Tribulation would be "shortened."[d] When General Berthier deposed Pope Pius VI in 1798 and ended papal temporal power, the flood of the Tribulation vanished.

> **Revelation 12:17**
> **17** And the dragon was wroth with the woman, and went to make war with the remnant of her seed, which keep the commandments of God, and have the testimony of Jesus Christ.

---

[d] **Matthew 24:22** And except those days should be shortened, there should no flesh be saved: but for the elect's sake those days shall be shortened.

Satan did not abandon his war against Christianity after the end of the Tribulation. When the papacy lost temporal power, it also lost the ability to use force against Christians. The Catholic Church needed to change its tactics if it was going to destroy Christianity successfully. One strategy was to use the Jesuits, who fought Satan's war on Christianity covertly. Another was to utilize the temptations of secular pleasures until the believers' faith became lukewarm.[e] After the Reformation, the Philadelphian church era was on fire for God, spreading the gospel worldwide. Satan was losing his battle against the Christian faith, and he knew it. He became desperate in Revelation 12:17, which indicates Satan went to war with the "remnant of the woman's seed"—the rest of the true Christian church. The church age after Philadelphia was today's Laodicean church, about which Jesus had nothing positive to say. He warned our faith would be unenthusiastic, which seems to be evidence of the effectiveness of Satan's clandestine war.

Before Revelation was written, Peter and Paul each wrote similar things about the last days, and both were remarkably accurate in their descriptions of the twenty-first-century church. In II Peter 3, Peter wrote that the last days would bring a society fixated on personal pleasure and lust—selfish people who want to do what is best for them without thinking of others.[f]

Peter also warned that many who professed to be Christian would lose faith in Jesus' return to earth, asking, "Where is the promise of his coming?" Peter seems to foreshadow Futurism, as many alive today believe we have not experienced any of the signs of Revelation. The Christians who do not recognize the fulfillment of Revelation's prophecies could easily lose hope that Jesus will ever return. However, Historicists see the events that fulfilled these prophecies as "the promise of his coming" that the Futurists still seek.

In II Timothy 3, Paul wrote his own end-times prophecy. Calling the last days "perilous times," he warned that we would be "lovers of pleasures more than lovers of God." His words seem to describe our era, as we certainly live

---

[e] **Revelation 3:15-16** 15 I know thy works, that thou art neither cold nor hot: I would thou wert cold or hot. 16 So then because thou art lukewarm, and neither cold nor hot, I will spue thee out of my mouth.

[f] **II Peter 3:3-4** 3 Knowing this first, that there shall come in the last days scoffers, walking after their own lusts, 4 And saying, Where is the promise of his coming? for since the fathers fell asleep, all things continue as they were from the beginning of the creation.

in perilous times for Christianity, and Paul's portrayal of lukewarm Christians mirrors the same type of selfishness described by Peter. People today may attend church and profess to be Christian, but do their actions match their words? Do they share God's Word with others? Do they help those in need?[g]

By examining the behaviors of today's Christians, a reasonable inference can be made that Satan was finally successful in his war against Christianity. The self-centered, "live your best life" attitudes of today's Christians suggest they have lost focus on saving non-believers. Christians have forgotten Jesus' commandment in Matthew 6 to focus on accumulating spiritual treasures in Heaven rather than living the materialistic life that II Timothy 3:1-5, II Peter 3:3-4, and Revelation 3:16-17 all warn against.[h]

> **Matthew 6:19-21**
> **19** Lay not up for yourselves treasures upon earth, where moth and rust doth corrupt, and where thieves break through and steal:
> **20** But lay up for yourselves treasures in heaven, where neither moth nor rust doth corrupt, and where thieves do not break through nor steal:
> **21** For where your treasure is, there will your heart be also.

The Two Beasts

After the vision of the dragon and the woman, John wrote about the beasts of the sea and the land—the Antichrist and the False Prophet. God's decision to place the vision of these two evil figures here in Revelation 13 is not accidental. Once the Reformers opened the eyes of the world to the truth about Catholicism, Christians were finally able to identify the Antichrist and False Prophet, which is why their descriptions occur here. As Revelation 10:7 predicted, the mystery of God had ended.

---

[g] **II Timothy 3:1-5** 1 This know also, that in the last days perilous times shall come. 2 For men shall be lovers of their own selves, covetous, boasters, proud, blasphemers, disobedient to parents, unthankful, unholy, 3 Without natural affection, trucebreakers, false accusers, incontinent, fierce, despisers of those that are good, 4 Traitors, heady, highminded, lovers of pleasures more than lovers of God; 5 Having a form of godliness, but denying the power thereof: from such turn away.

[h] **Revelation 3:16-17** 16 So then because thou art lukewarm, and neither cold nor hot, I will spue thee out of my mouth. 17 Because thou sayest, I am rich, and increased with goods, and have need of nothing; and knowest not that thou art wretched, and miserable, and poor, and blind, and naked:

The Antichrist's papal identity became more evident after the Protestant Reformation. At this point, the False Prophet was born when the Jesuits and the Jesuit superior general were founded. Just as God sealed Christians when Constantine distorted Christianity, Catholics received the mark of the beast when they continued practicing their religion even after the Reformers solved the "mystery of God." This vision fits perfectly after the seventh trumpet in the chronological continuum of Revelation.

The Lamb and the 144,000 First Fruits

While chapter twelve presents the battle between Satan and Christianity and chapter thirteen introduces Satan's human collaborators, Revelation 14 provides a different view. In these visions, God revealed his promises to save the Christians who follow his commandments and remain faithful to him.

> **Revelation 14:1-5**
> **1** And I looked, and, lo, a Lamb stood on the mount Sion, and with him an hundred forty and four thousand, having his Father's name written in their foreheads.
> **2** And I heard a voice from heaven, as the voice of many waters, and as the voice of a great thunder: and I heard the voice of harpers harping with their harps:
> **3** And they sung as it were a new song before the throne, and before the four beasts, and the elders: and no man could learn that song but the hundred and forty and four thousand, which were redeemed from the earth.
> **4** These are they which were not defiled with women; for they are virgins. These are they which follow the Lamb whithersoever he goeth. These were redeemed from among men, being the firstfruits unto God and to the Lamb.
> **5** And in their mouth was found no guile: for they are without fault before the throne of God.

The initial 144,000 souls "redeemed from the earth" are labeled *first fruits*. They are virgins who follow Jesus wherever he goes, have no dishonest words in their mouths, and are found to be without fault by God. The first fruits are presumably the same 144,000 whom God sealed in Revelation 7:4.[i]

---

[i] **Revelation 7:4** And I heard the number of them which were sealed: and there were sealed an hundred forty and four thousand of all the tribes of the children of Israel.

While the bar for first fruits is almost unreachable, the good news for the rest of us is these are the *first* souls, but not the *only* souls, harvested by God. After the 144,000 were sealed in Revelation 7:4, John wrote about a much larger group—an innumerable "great multitude" standing in Heaven in white robes.[j] If we do not meet the rigorous criteria to be a first fruit, we still have hope for eternal life. Fortunately for us, God does not require Christians to be celibate and without fault for their entire lives to meet the criteria to spend eternity in Heaven, as we will see later in this chapter.

The Three Angels' Messages

Once the first fruits are collected, three angels pass on vital messages to the rest of us. Their advice encapsulates God's warnings for Christians after the Protestant Reformation. The first angel commands Christians to serve God. The second makes a declaration about the status of Mystery Babylon. Finally, the third angel has a stern warning for those who continue to follow Catholicism after the Reformation.

> **Revelation 14:6-7**
> 6 And I saw another angel fly in the midst of heaven, having the everlasting gospel to preach unto them that dwell on the earth, and to every nation, and kindred, and tongue, and people,
> 7 Saying with a loud voice, Fear God, and give glory to him; for the hour of his judgment is come: and worship him that made heaven, and earth, and the sea, and the fountains of waters.

The first angel holds the scriptures and preaches the gospel to the world in every language. In his sermon, he instructs Christians to do three things: fear God, give him glory, and worship him. According to the twenty-four elders in Heaven, God created us for his pleasure.[k] This first angel instructs us to serve God by fearing, glorifying, and praising him.

---

[j] **Revelation 7:9** After this I beheld, and, lo, a great multitude, which no man could number, of all nations, and kindreds, and people, and tongues, stood before the throne, and before the Lamb, clothed with white robes, and palms in their hands;

[k] **Revelation 4:11** Thou art worthy, O Lord, to receive glory and honour and power: for thou hast created all things, and for thy pleasure they are and were created.

> **Revelation 14:8**
> 8 And there followed another angel, saying, Babylon is fallen, is fallen, that great city, because she made all nations drink of the wine of the wrath of her fornication.

The second angel announces the fall of Mystery Babylon to the world. This is not Babylon's permanent destruction. The Roman Catholic Church lost credibility during the Reformation, as its pseudo-Christian disguise had fallen. The Reformers removed the façade that had deceived many, allowing Christians to see the truth about the pope and his church.

> **Revelation 14:9-11**
> 9 And the third angel followed them, saying with a loud voice, If any man worship the beast and his image, and receive his mark in his forehead, or in his hand,
> 10 The same shall drink of the wine of the wrath of God, which is poured out without mixture into the cup of his indignation; and he shall be tormented with fire and brimstone in the presence of the holy angels, and in the presence of the Lamb:
> 11 And the smoke of their torment ascendeth up for ever and ever: and they have no rest day nor night, who worship the beast and his image, and whosoever receiveth the mark of his name.

The message from the third angel warns against taking the Antichrist's mark. It is evident from this passage that the church of Mystery Babylon remained active after the seventh trumpet, as it was still capable of branding the followers of the papacy with the Antichrist's mark. To this day, Roman Catholicism continues to mislead would-be Christians with false doctrine. Unfortunately, Catholics conflate adhering to what their church teaches them with following God's Word. In following Vatican dogma, they are unwittingly allowing themselves to be spiritually marked by the Antichrist beast. Until the ultimate destruction of Babylon, which does not occur until Revelation 18, Catholics will continue to fall victim to the Antichrist's deceit.

Verse ten cautions anyone who worships the beast that they "shall be tormented with fire and brimstone." The third angel's message aligns with Jesus' words in Matthew 7:21-23.[1] Catholics believe they are following the

---

[1] **Matthew 7:21-23** 21 Not every one that saith unto me, Lord, Lord, shall enter into the kingdom of heaven; but he that doeth the will of my Father which is in

Christian faith by adhering to Catholic doctrine. They believe in Jesus Christ and display their faith outwardly. Unfortunately, Catholics—and lukewarm Christians along with them —will be devastated when they reach Heaven and Jesus rejects them with the words, "I never knew you: depart from me."

> **Revelation 14:12-13**
> **12** Here is the patience of the saints: here are they that keep the commandments of God, and the faith of Jesus.
> **13** And I heard a voice from heaven saying unto me, Write, Blessed are the dead which die in the Lord from henceforth: Yea, saith the Spirit, that they may rest from their labours; and their works do follow them.

Next, the faithful Christians who recognize and overcome the papal ruse receive a different promise from the third angel. According to him, those of us who have faith in Jesus and live by his commandments will be considered blessed by God. After death, true Christians will be given a respite from our earthly persecutions—our "labors"—if we die as faithful followers of Christ.

The phrase "their works do follow them" in verse thirteen has significant implications. Many Protestant pastors and denominations preach that we only need to believe in Jesus to earn eternal life. This would mean faith was a license to sin without suffering the consequences of eternal damnation.

Revelation 14:13 disagrees with this principle. Belief in Jesus Christ is a *prerequisite* to making it to Heaven, but not the only requirement. Christians who receive eternal life also do so because "their works do follow them." This does not mean our works alone could get us into Heaven. Instead, in addition to our faith in Jesus, we will be judged based on our actions during our time on earth. As James wrote, "Faith without works is dead."[m]

The book of James is an excellent epistle to read in its entirety. It was intended to guide Christians outside of Israel on how to live a godly life. All Christians should make the time to read this short book and work diligently to live by it.

---

heaven. 22 Many will say to me in that day, Lord, Lord, have we not prophesied in thy name? and in thy name have cast out devils? and in thy name done many wonderful works? 23 And then will I profess unto them, I never knew you: depart from me, ye that work iniquity.

[m] **James 2:20** But wilt thou know, O vain man, that faith without works is dead?

Harvesting the Earth

The First Harvest

> **Revelation 14:14-16**
> **14** And I looked, and behold a white cloud, and upon the cloud one sat like unto the Son of man, having on his head a golden crown, and in his hand a sharp sickle.
> **15** And another angel came out of the temple, crying with a loud voice to him that sat on the cloud, Thrust in thy sickle, and reap: for the time is come for thee to reap; for the harvest of the earth is ripe.
> **16** And he that sat on the cloud thrust in his sickle on the earth; and the earth was reaped.

After the three angels communicate their messages, John's vision shifts to the Christians who do not meet the standard of first fruits. These believers still successfully follow the instructions the three angels provided and live a life that would make Jesus proud, but they are not entirely without fault like the 144,000 first fruits.

John's vision of this harvest began with a visitation from a supernatural being who reminded him of Jesus. The description of this individual, whom John refers to as "like unto the Son of man," elicits the same impression of the angel in Revelation 10. This character is seated upon a cloud, wearing a golden crown, and holding a sickle. John's account implies authority as if the Christ-like figure were a sitting judge preparing to issue his verdict.

Next, John sees another angel coming from the temple in Heaven with a message for Jesus. This second angel says, "Thrust in thy sickle, and reap: for the time is come for thee to reap; for the harvest of the earth is ripe." The angel who looks like Jesus then judges the earth, deciding who deserves to be harvested based on their faith and actions. The representation of a Jesus-like angel reaping the earth suggests this harvest is of the true Christians who had faithfully served God. These believers are collected to be brought with Jesus to their eternal reward in Heaven, where they receive "rest from their labors."

In this passage, two pairs of angels reap the earth. In each pair, one angel carrying a sickle harvests the earth at the command of the second. The angel who told Jesus to reap originated from the temple of God, the same temple measured by John in Revelation 11:1-2. The temple implies piety, as the first souls reaped were good Christians who had faithfully worshipped God.

The Second Harvest and the Winepress

> **Revelation 14:17-18**
> 17 And another angel came out of the temple which is in heaven, he also having a sharp sickle.
> 18 And another angel came out from the altar, which had power over fire; and cried with a loud cry to him that had the sharp sickle, saying, Thrust in thy sharp sickle, and gather the clusters of the vine of the earth; for her grapes are fully ripe.

The metaphor of two harvests would be familiar to first-century Jews. In ancient times, Israel had two distinct harvests. The seven-week-long Jewish harvest season began with the reaping of barley just before the celebration of Passover, and it ended with the harvesting of wheat during Shavuot.[1]

Just as the harvest comes when crops are ripe, the earth was not prepared to be harvested until the Protestant Reformation allowed Christians to see Catholicism for what it was. Once the Bible could be read and the Reformers wrote extensively on the topic of the Catholic Church's anti-Christian dogma and deception, there was no excuse for ignorance. The Catholics were given the mark of the papal beast, making them ripe for judgment.

The second sickle-brandishing angel received his command to reap from an angel who came from the altar in Heaven. As we learned from the sixth trumpet, the altar alludes to the need for repentance based on the atonement ceremonies in Leviticus 16. This second harvest is not one of Christians but of sinners. This is made more apparent when we find the angel who gives the second command to reap has the "power over fire"—an allusion to Hell.

> **Revelation 14:19-20**
> 19 And the angel thrust in his sickle into the earth, and gathered the vine of the earth, and cast it into the great winepress of the wrath of God.
> 20 And the winepress was trodden without the city, and blood came out of the winepress, even unto the horse bridles, by the space of a thousand and six hundred furlongs.

The souls of this second harvest are cast into "the winepress of the wrath of God." After the harvested sinners are thrown into this winepress, John describes it as "trodden" or flattened underfoot. This depiction is the same method that first-century winemakers would use to press grapes. In ancient times, vineyards and winepresses were traditionally located outside of the city, as the winepress in John's vision is. We know the city in verse twenty is Rome because it is the same city as in verse eight, where it is named as "Babylon."[n] By writing, "the winepress was trodden without the city," John was leveraging the historical location of the winepress to imply the city itself will be left out of God's judgment, for now.

In the ancient world, when a winepress was trodden, the juice from the grapes spilled out. John departs from the metaphor of grapes in verse twenty; the product of the spiritual winepress is not described as the juice of grapes but the blood of the sinners cast into the press, which represents a spiritual death after God's judgment. So much blood was spilled in this judgment that John describes it as reaching the horse bridles, or around five feet high. The blood from the press was not only high but wide, covering sixteen hundred furlongs. A furlong, or one-eighth of a mile, was an English measurement used by the King James Version's translators to make the nomenclature more familiar to contemporary seventeenth-century readers. The Greek word used in the original text was σταδιων, or *stadia*. A single stadion equals 630 feet, so sixteen hundred stadia would be a length of nearly 191 miles.[2] The amount of blood spilled, five feet high across 191 miles, does not have an apparent literal fulfillment. However, the implication is that the judgment of sinners would be vast, an almost immeasurable amount of spiritual death.

John used the term "great city" ten times in the book of Revelation. The first nine all refer to Babylon, meaning Rome. The tenth is New Jerusalem—God's pure replacement for the evils of Rome. Similarly to the third angel's message, which declared Rome had made the nations "drink of the wine of the wrath of her fornication," the followers of Catholicism and all other non-Christians are cast into the winepress of the wrath of God's judgment as a punishment for their sins.

---

[n] **Revelation 14:8** And there followed another angel, saying, Babylon is fallen, is fallen, that great city, because she made all nations drink of the wine of the wrath of her fornication.

Chapter Synopsis

- The Protestant Reformers identified the truth about Catholicism, which is why these visions occurred with the seventh trumpet

The Dragon and the Woman (Revelation 12:1-17)
- The dragon represents Satan
- The woman represents God's followers, first Jews, then Christians
- The dragon attempts to kill the infant Jesus, which would have also killed Christianity in its infancy
- God protects the woman in the wilderness, just as he protected Mary, Joseph, and Jesus in Egypt and Christianity during the Tribulation
- After losing the spiritual battle in Heaven, Satan is cast down to earth, where he persecutes Christians
- Christians overcome Satan by the blood of Christ
- After the end of the Tribulation, Satan makes war with the remnant of the woman's seed—the remaining Christians

Beasts of the Sea (Revelation 13:1-10) and Earth (Revelation 13:11-18)
- The beast of the sea is the Antichrist, the papacy
- The beast of the earth is the False Prophet, the Jesuit superior general

The Lamb and the First Fruits (Revelation 14:1-5)
- 144,000 Christians with the seal of God "were redeemed from the earth"

The Three Angels' Messages (Revelation 14:6-13)
- **First Angel:** "Fear God, and give glory to him; for the hour of his judgment is come: and worship him."
- **Second Angel:** "Babylon is fallen, is fallen, that great city, because she made all nations drink of the wine of the wrath of her fornication."
- **Third Angel:** "If any man worship the beast and his image, and receive his mark in his forehead, or in his hand, The same shall drink of the wine of the wrath of God."

Harvesting the Earth and the Winepress (Revelation 14:14-20)
- An angel with the appearance of Jesus harvests Christians who remained faithful, worshipped God, and did not take the Antichrist's mark
- He is told to harvest by an angel who comes from God's temple
- Another angel reaps those who remain and casts them into a winepress as punishment for their sins

15

GOD'S WRATH IS POURED OUT

The Seven Vial Judgments

Revelation's chronological order helps us correctly identify the historical events corresponding to the book's end-times prophecies. John saw the first warning signs as a scroll with seven seals. Historicists believe the first six seals targeted ancient Rome at its height, from the end of the first century until the legalization of Christianity in the Roman Empire. The seventh seal brought about the next series of seven signs, defined in Revelation as seven trumpets. The first six trumpets occurred from 395 AD until the fall of the Byzantine Empire in 1453. After the first six trumpets, Revelation 10's prophecy of the little book represents the first printed Bible in 1455. In Revelation 11, early Protestants measured God's temple and found Catholicism did not meet God's standards. The two witnesses—the Old and New Testaments—were killed at the Fifth Lateran Council and resurrected with the *Ninety-Five Theses*. When the seventh trumpet sounded, it brought the Protestant Reformation.

The Vatican convened the Council of Trent across twenty-five sessions from 1545 to 1563 to devise the Catholic Church's response to the Protestant Reformation. While a few minor internal reforms were made to address some of the Reformers' grievances, Catholic leadership turned to persecution and violence—including a dramatic escalation in the Inquisitions—to force the Protestants to submit to the Vatican's self-perceived religious authority. The

Counter-Reformation officially continued until the end of the Great Turkish War in 1699, although some elements, including the notorious Jesuit Order, are still active today.[1]

While the seal and trumpet signs impacted Rome's political empire, the seven vials would instead target Rome's religious authority, as the idolatrous Catholic Church continued to sin. The seventh trumpet triggered the power shift between Catholicism and Christianity as described in the message to the Philadelphian church and Revelation 11-14. In the next two chapters, John describes seeing seven angels holding vials containing the last seven plagues. An analysis of the sequence of Revelation's prophecies and the events that fulfilled them proves that the final seven plagues must follow the beginning of the Protestant Reformation on October 31, 1517.

The command given to these seven angels comes from the same temple in Heaven that was opened during the seventh trumpet,[a] indicating the voice belongs to God. The Catholic Church had failed to heed the warnings of the seals and trumpets and repent of its sins. Its doctrine continued to corrupt Christianity, leading many to idol worship and polytheism. The seven vials shift the target of God's wrath away from the Roman and Byzantine Empires and onto the Roman Catholic Church and its interests.

Most Historicists support the belief that the first three vials represent a series of events leading up to and including the French Revolution. Many respected nineteenth-century Biblical expositors—including Edward Bishop Elliott, Albert Barnes, George Stanley Faber, and William Cunningham—took this view in their respective commentaries.[2]

The First Vial

> **Revelation 16:1-2**
> 1 And I heard a great voice out of the temple saying to the seven angels, Go your ways, and pour out the vials of the wrath of God upon the earth.
> 2 And the first went, and poured out his vial upon the earth; and there fell a noisome and grievous sore upon the men which had the mark of the beast, and upon them which worshipped his image.

---

[a] **Revelation 11:19** And the temple of God was opened in heaven, and there was seen in his temple the ark of his testament: and there were lightnings, and voices, and thunderings, and an earthquake, and great hail.

In *Horae Apocalypticae*, Edward Bishop Elliott adopted this interpretation for the first vial. To Elliott, the "noisome and grievous sore upon the men which had the mark of the beast" was an indication of atheism's spread across France in the years preceding the French Revolution. Historians traditionally date the beginning of the Enlightenment to the death of King Louis XIV in 1715. Also known as the Age of Reason, the Enlightenment elevated science and reason over faith. This inverted the paradigm from what Catholic France had previously known and allowed atheism to spread swiftly throughout the country. By the 1780s, the adoption of atheism had escalated dramatically, culminating in the French Revolution. In the early 1790s, the Revolutionaries systematically attacked religion on all fronts and even seized all property that belonged to the Catholic Church.

Elliott detailed an event on November 7, 1793, when the bishop of Paris, Jean-Baptiste-Joseph Gobet, and other clergymen from his diocese attended the National Convention held by the French Revolutionaries. He agreed to openly declare that no religion was necessary other than "liberty, equality, and morality." Afterward, the "Goddess of Reason," played by the provocatively-dressed wife of politician Antoine-François Momoro, was paraded to the Notre-Dame de Paris by members of the National Convention, clergy, and others, where she was set upon an altar and worshipped. The Revolutionaries renamed the Notre-Dame the "Temple of Reason" and held the "Festival of Reason" in the cathedral on November 10. The radicals then burned Bibles and crucifixes, participated in orgies, abolished all religious emblems, masses, ceremonies, and worship, and had a donkey drink sacramental wine from a Catholic Eucharist chalice.[3]

The spread of atheism in France, the nation dubbed the "oldest daughter of the church," allowed the rage of the French Revolutionaries to be poured out upon Catholicism.[4] The atheists harassed and persecuted the "men which had the mark of the beast" and "worshipped his image," and France's greatest Catholic monument, the Notre-Dame, was desecrated.

The Second Vial

> **Revelation 16:3**
> 3 And the second angel poured out his vial upon the sea; and it became as the blood of a dead man: and every living soul died in the sea.

The second vial's prophecy closely parallels the second trumpet. When the second trumpet sounded in Revelation 8:8, "a great mountain burning with fire was cast into the sea: and the third part of the sea became blood." Comparatively, the second vial also targets the sea and turns it into blood.

Edward Bishop Elliott began his analysis of the second, third, and fourth vials by writing, "Here is described the outspreading of the evil, and of the mortality and destruction consequent thereon, to different parts of Anti-Christendom. And first, under the second vial, to its sea."[5] In his view, these early vial judgments were also levied against France. Elliott interpreted the fulfillment of the second vial as a series of naval battles that caused France a vast loss of life and territory.

In 1791, the wealthiest and most important of France's colonies, Saint-Domingue, was ravaged by a widespread slave revolt. The British and Spanish militaries entered the conflict in support of the Haitian slaves after France declared war against them in 1793.

The rebellion quickly intensified into a full-scale war for independence. In 1803, the British again aided the slaves, this time with a naval blockade that prevented the arrival of supplies and reinforcements for the French. By 1804, the Empire of Haiti had gained its independence.[6]

While the Haitian Revolution took place overseas from mainland France, the fulfillment of the second vial also included a succession of major naval battles fought during the French Revolution and Napoleonic Wars. The Siege of Toulon in 1793 left roughly half of the French navy in ruins. The 1794 invasion of Corsica and the Fourth Battle of Ushant caused further losses, as the West Indian islands of Dominica, Saint Lucia, and Tobago were ceded to Britain along with other overseas French possessions. In June of 1795, Lord Bridport and the British won another naval victory at the expense of the French in the Battle of Groix.

France's allies also suffered naval defeats with comparable losses of life and territory. The British captured the Cape of Good Hope from the Dutch during the Battle of Muizenberg in September 1795. Spain, now an ally of the French, lost the Battle of Cape St. Vincent in 1797. The same year, the Dutch navy was routed by the British in the Battle of Camperdown. The British also defeated the French navy in the Battle of the Nile and the Battle of Trafalgar. In total, France lost approximately two hundred ships of the line, between three and four hundred frigates, and countless smaller vessels during these naval battles.[7]

The Third Vial

> **Revelation 16:4**
> 4 And the third angel poured out his vial upon the rivers and fountains of waters; and they became blood.

When the third trumpet sounded, a great star from Heaven representing Attila the Hun "fell upon the third part of the rivers, and upon the fountains of waters."[b] Similarly, the third vial also targets the "rivers and fountains of waters." Once again, the third vial echoes the corresponding third trumpet—a trend that will continue through the remaining vials. The second trumpet, third trumpet, and second vial were all fulfilled through the earth's physical seas, rivers, and fountains of waters, so a reasonable assumption can be made that the third vial should also be taken to represent tangible waters.

Elliott interpreted Revelation 16:4 as an expansion of the battles between the French Revolutionaries and the First Coalition armies into the rural areas of Europe, as the Rhine, Meuse, Danube, and Po River valleys all saw conflict and bloodshed.

While there is sufficient evidence that the expansion of the Revolution battles represented the fulfillment of the vial, there is another, more specific event that adds additional credibility to this view. Between November 16, 1793, and February 27, 1794, several mass executions occurred in Nantes, France. On the orders of the French Revolutionary Jean-Baptiste Carrier, thousands of French men, women, and children suspected of supporting the Catholic monarchy were executed by forced drowning in the Loire River.[8] Not only had the Revolution's battles expanded to the rural areas of France, but its assaults on the Catholic religion had also.

---

[b] **Revelation 8:10-11** 10 And the third angel sounded, and there fell a great star from heaven, burning as it were a lamp, and it fell upon the third part of the rivers, and upon the fountains of waters; 11 And the name of the star is called Wormwood: and the third part of the waters became wormwood; and many men died of the waters, because they were made bitter.

The larger Vendée region of northwest France suffered around 175,000 executions for the perceived failure of its residents to support the Revolution. The principal targets of these executions were not only the Vendéean priests and nuns but also the Catholic laity who elevated faithfulness to their church above allegiance to the Revolution.[9]

> **Revelation 16:5-7**
> 5 And I heard the angel of the waters say, Thou art righteous, O Lord, which art, and wast, and shalt be, because thou hast judged thus.
> 6 For they have shed the blood of saints and prophets, and thou hast given them blood to drink; for they are worthy.
> 7 And I heard another out of the altar say, Even so, Lord God Almighty, true and righteous are thy judgments.

In verses five through seven, after the third vial is poured out, an angel delivers a short commentary declaring that God is justified in judging the Catholics—those who "have shed the blood of saints and prophets." When all the other vials simply document what John experienced in his vision, the placement of this monologue between the third and fourth vials seems to indicate that the fourth vial would bring a change in target.

France's Catholic laity and low-level clergy felt the pain of the first three vial judgments. The first vial spread atheism amongst the people. The second caused the deaths of many seamen in the French navy. The third vial brought the execution of many rural French clergymen and parishioners. The fourth vial would directly target the Papal States in Italy, shifting the wrath of God from individual Catholics in France to the church itself.

The Fourth Vial

> **Revelation 16:8-9**
> 8 And the fourth angel poured out his vial upon the sun; and power was given unto him to scorch men with fire.
> 9 And men were scorched with great heat, and blasphemed the name of God, which hath power over these plagues: and they repented not to give him glory.

When the fourth angel pours out the contents of his vial on the sun, it scorches men with fire. The second and fourth vials are the only two in which

John uses pronouns to refer to the targets of God's judgments. While John sees both vials poured out on things—the sea and the sun—his pronoun choices differ. The pronoun used for the sea in the second vial was *it*, which suggests it would involve a thing rather than a person. However, in the fourth vial, the pronoun chosen for the sun was *him*. The scriptural text indicates that the sun in the fourth vial was only a metaphor and would be fulfilled by a man. Since this vial gives power to the sun, the prophecy's fulfillment would occur when this individual is empowered.

The third vial prophecy was fulfilled after the French Revolution spread to the rural valleys of France. When King Frederick William II of Prussia and Holy Roman Emperor Leopold II declared support for France's deposed King Louis XVI and Queen Marie Antoinette, the Revolution expanded into the War of the First Coalition.[10] Near the conclusion of this war, a rising star general was awarded command of France's Army of Italy in 1796. Famous for his victorious strategy in the Siege of Toulon, a young General Napoleon Bonaparte used his newly awarded power to attack the Kingdom of Sardinia. His Montenotte campaign against the Sardinian and Habsburg armies would result in a military victory so conclusive that the Sardinians entirely withdrew from the war after only two weeks.[11]

The significance of the combatant armies is that the French military was atheist, while both the Sardinians and Habsburgs were Catholic. Most of the countries of the Coalition—the Spanish Empire, Holy Roman Empire, Papal States, Kingdom of Portugal, and Kingdom of Naples, among others—were either Catholic or partially Catholic. God used the atheist French Republic to punish the Catholic armies of the Coalition through this vial, symbolically scorching them with the fire of war for their "fornication" with the Roman Catholic Church.[12]

Napoleon Bonaparte's rise to the command of the French Army of Italy satisfied the prophecy of the sun's empowerment in Revelation 16:8. The general, who once said, "If I had to choose a religion, the sun as the universal giver of life would be my god," scorched the European continent with fire through his military conquests, much like Alaric, Genseric, and Attila during the three burning trumpets.

The Fifth Vial

The fifth vial is incredibly clear in its prophecy predicting the darkening of the seat of the Antichrist. In fact, in his 1701 work *Apocalyptical Key*, the Scottish Presbyterian minister Robert Fleming accurately predicted this vial would lead to the loss of papal temporal power sometime between 1794 and 1848, nearly a century before the prophecy was fulfilled.[13]

> **Revelation 16:10-11**
> 10 And the fifth angel poured out his vial upon the seat of the beast; and his kingdom was full of darkness; and they gnawed their tongues for pain,
> 11 And blasphemed the God of heaven because of their pains and their sores, and repented not of their deeds.

Napoleon's ascension to the rank of general directly led to the fifth vial. Here, again, a vial imitates a trumpet. In Revelation 9, a star from Heaven fell to earth and commanded an army of locusts, which tormented those who did not have God's seal for 150 years. God used the Muslim armies to weaken the Catholic Byzantine Empire. Similarly, God used the atheist French armies to diminish the Catholic Church at its heart, in papal Rome itself.

John's description of the fifth vial illustrates how God would exercise his wrath against the seat of the Antichrist. The judgment on the beast's seat of power is so significant that it plunges into darkness, causing the people there to feel severe pain. Even still, the followers of the Antichrist papacy remain defiantly unrepentant.

This vial is the last concerning the conflict between Revolutionary France and the Catholic Church. Edward Bishop Elliott interpreted the fulfillment of the fifth vial as the 1797 Peace of Tolentino between Revolutionary France and the Papal States.[14] However, while the pope ceded several territories to Napoleon and France, the seat of the papacy was unimpacted. Therefore, the Peace of Tolentino was likely an incorrect interpretation of this prophecy.

The Archbasilica of Saint John Lateran in Rome has historically served as the official administrative seat of the papacy. In the late eighteenth century, popes no longer resided in the basilica's adjoining palace, choosing to live in Rome's Quirinal Palace instead. However, whenever the city was threatened with invasion, popes would retreat behind the formidable defensive walls of the Vatican. The consequential fifth vial would transpire during an invasion such as this, as God's wrath would finally reach the seat of the Antichrist in Rome itself.

The fifth vial represents the removal of the papacy's temporal power by French general Louis-Alexandre Berthier in 1798. The significance of this event in the timeline of Revelation cannot be understated—it marked the end of papal supremacy, brought a close to the tyranny of the Great Tribulation, and removed the papacy's ability to persecute Christians. After Pope Pius VI was deposed, he was exiled to France, where he would die in captivity.[15] The moment Rome lost its pope, it also lost its status as a papal seat. When the pope was deposed and exiled, the beast's seat was thrust into darkness, and the fifth vial was fulfilled.

Chapter Synopsis

- God levied the seven vial judgments against the Catholic Church and its interests

The First Five Vials (Revelation 15:1-16:11)

- **First Vial:** Spread of atheism through France during the Enlightenment, beginning in 1715 AD
- **Second Vial:** Haitian Revolution and the devastation of the French navy during a series of naval battles, beginning in 1791 AD
- **Third Vial:** Rural battles during the French Revolution and drownings at Nantes in the Loire River, beginning in 1793 AD
- **Fourth Vial:** Napoleon takes command of the French Army of Italy in 1796 AD
- **Fifth Vial:** The French general Louis-Alexandre Berthier invades Rome, deposes Pope Pius VI, and removes papal temporal power in 1798 AD
  - This event also marked the end of the 1,260-year Great Tribulation

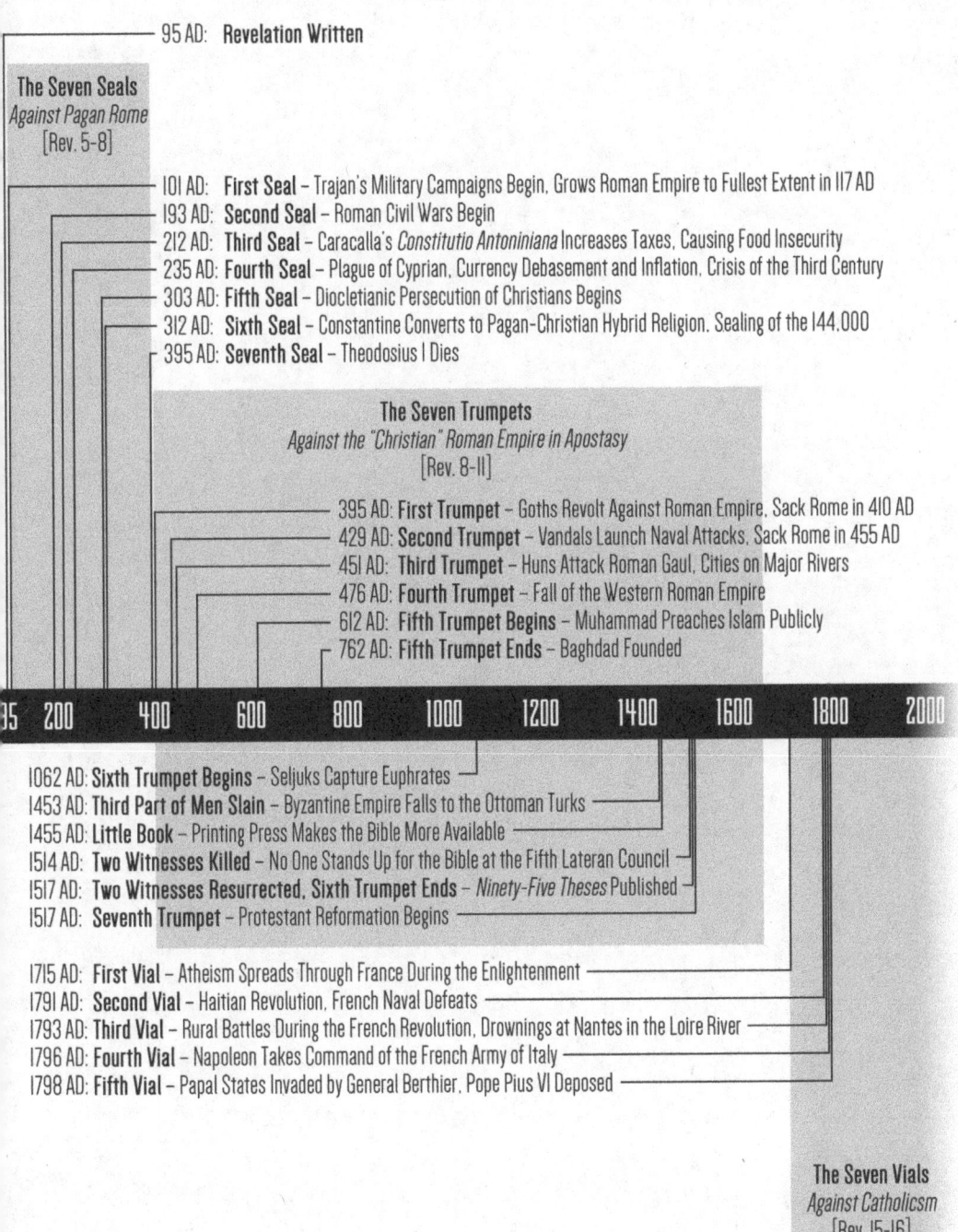

V

TODAY

16

THE SIXTH AND SEVENTH VIALS

The Sixth Vial

The sixth vial is conceivably the most well-known of all the prophecies in the book of Revelation, possibly the entire Bible. It is primarily known for the Battle of Armageddon prophecy, but several interconnected prophecies occur when the sixth angel's vial is emptied. Although this vial has not yet been fully realized, its fulfillment began over a century ago.

> **Revelation 16:12-16**
> **12** And the sixth angel poured out his vial upon the great river Euphrates; and the water thereof was dried up, that the way of the kings of the east might be prepared.
> **13** And I saw three unclean spirits like frogs come out of the mouth of the dragon, and out of the mouth of the beast, and out of the mouth of the false prophet.
> **14** For they are the spirits of devils, working miracles, which go forth unto the kings of the earth and of the whole world, to gather them to the battle of that great day of God Almighty.
> **15** Behold, I come as a thief. Blessed is he that watcheth, and keepeth his garments, lest he walk naked, and they see his shame.
> **16** And he gathered them together into a place called in the Hebrew tongue Armageddon.

At the opening of the passage, the sixth angel pours out his vial upon the Euphrates. The Euphrates is a significant river in the Bible. It was one of the four rivers that flowed from the Garden of Eden in Genesis[a] and marked one of the borders of the territory God promised to give to Abraham and his descendants.[b] The King James Bible mentions it by name twenty-one times, demonstrating the river's importance.

As John watches, the sixth angel's vial causes the Euphrates to run dry. According to verse twelve, the drying up of the river allows "the way of the kings of the East" to "be prepared." Next, three "unclean spirits like frogs" leave the mouths of the dragon, Antichrist, and False Prophet. These three evil spirits influence political leaders around the world and incite global wars on an unprecedented scale. The third and final component of the sixth vial—the element that makes this one of the most well-known prophecies in the Bible—is the infamous Battle of Armageddon.

Three Unclean Spirits Like Frogs

The fulfillment of the sixth vial begins with the start of World War I in 1914. Despite the common misconception, World War I was not limited in scope to participants from Europe and North America. The era of European imperialism had consolidated most of the world under the control of only a few countries. The territories and colonies of the British, French, German, Italian, and Russian empires were pulled into the war alongside their parent nations. This dramatically expanded the conflict until it involved most of the globe. The first of the three frog-like spirits was fulfilled when World War I began because that meant "the kings of the earth and of the whole world" had been gathered in battle.

---

[a] **Genesis 2:10-14** 10 And a river went out of Eden to water the garden; and from thence it was parted, and became into four heads. 11 The name of the first is Pison: that is it which compasseth the whole land of Havilah, where there is gold; 12 And the gold of that land is good: there is bdellium and the onyx stone. 13 And the name of the second river is Gihon: the same is it that compasseth the whole land of Ethiopia. 14 And the name of the third river is Hiddekel: that is it which goeth toward the east of Assyria. And the fourth river is Euphrates.

[b] **Genesis 15:18** In the same day the Lord made a covenant with Abram, saying, Unto thy seed have I given this land, from the river of Egypt unto the great river, the river Euphrates:

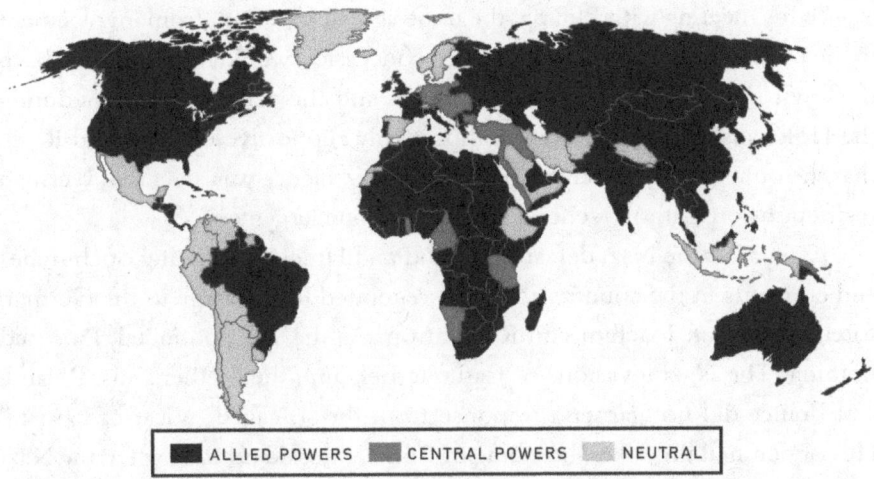

Figure 42: The alliances of World War I. European colonization brought most of the world into the war.

The popes and Jesuits played a significant role in instigating the crises that led to World Wars I and II. Their influence explains why these three evil spirits come from the mouths of the dragon, Antichrist, and False Prophet. World War I did not immediately begin after the shocking assassination of Archduke Franz Ferdinand, the heir presumptive to the Austro-Hungarian throne, on June 28, 1914. Pope Pius X and Cardinal Secretary of State Rafael Merry del Val helped to push the European continent into a war. On July 26, 1914, Baron Freiherr von Ritter, Bavaria's diplomatic representative to the Vatican, wrote to his government. "The Pope approves of Austria's harsh treatment of Serbia," Ritter reported. "He has no great opinion of the armies of Russia and France in the event of a war against Germany. The Cardinal Secretary of State does not see when Austria could make war if she does not decide to do so now."[1]

A similar story unfolded at the dawn of World War II. Weeks before the Nazi invasion of Poland, a secret meeting was held between Pope Pius XII and Hitler's envoy, Philipp, Landgrave of Hesse. According to the Vatican's own transcript of the meeting, Pius was especially encouraging of Germany's objectives. "No one here is anti-German," the pope said. "We love Germany. We are pleased if Germany is great and powerful. And we do not oppose any particular form of government, if only the Catholics can live in accordance with their religion."

In his meeting with Philipp, the pope agreed to refrain from involvement in the political affairs of the Nazis. This concession would have included both the environment of German antisemitism and the genocide of Jews during the Holocaust. Pope Pius was so thoroughly supportive of the Third Reich that the only thing he received in return for his silence was an end to German restrictions on Catholic schools and attacks on clergymen.

Even after the Nazi defeat of Poland and Hitler's shuttering of churches and convents in the country, the pope reiterated his message to the German foreign minister, Joachim von Ribbentrop. As the war continued, Pius said nothing. The Nazi invasions of Catholic Belgium, the Netherlands, Poland, and France did not garner a response from the so-called "Vicar of Christ." He condemned the Allies' bombing of Rome, but said nothing when the Nazi Gestapo rounded up the Jews of the city for extermination. He even refrained from excommunicating Hitler, Benito Mussolini, and Heinrich Himmler, all of whom remained Catholic to their deaths.[2]

Pius knew of the Nazi extermination program by 1942, but he remained silent. German priest Lothar Koenig sent a letter to Robert Leiber, the pope's personal secretary, notifying him that up to six thousand Jews and Poles were being sent to the gas chambers in Poland every day. Yet, publicly, the Vatican maintained reports of the extermination camps were unsubstantiated.[3]

At the close of the war, Pius' clergymen also established and facilitated escape routes, called Vatican ratlines, which helped many Nazi war criminals evade the Allies. While serving as the rector of the German-speaking Collegio Teutonico seminary in Rome, Austrian bishop and Nazi sympathizer Alois Hudal organized a ratline that abetted the escape of exceptionally heinous Nazis. Franz Stangl, Gustav Wagner, and Alois Brunner—the commanding officers of concentration camps—all fled Europe with his help, as did Adolf Eichmann, the architect of the Holocaust.[4] In his autobiography, *Römische Tagebücher*, Bishop Hudal wrote, "I thank God that He [allowed me] to visit and comfort many victims in their prisons and concentration camps and to help them escape with false identity papers."[5] The "victims" Hudal helped were not the innocent Jews held in Nazi concentration camps, they were the Nazi war criminals held by the Allies. Later, even more sophisticated ratlines would be established through the San Girolamo degli Illirici Seminary College in Rome by the Bosnian Croat Catholic priest Krunoslav Draganović.[6]

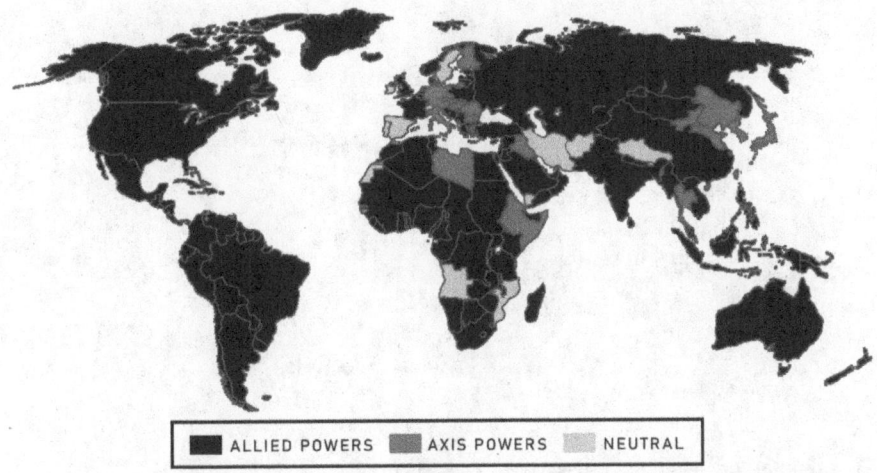

Figure 43: The alliances of World War II impacted even more territory than World War I.

The Euphrates Runs Dry

The Vatican's involvement in both World Wars lends credibility to its anti-Christian status and the fulfillment of the prophecy of the three frog-like spirits, but how could World War I mark the beginning of the fulfillment of the sixth vial prophecy if the Euphrates has never run dry? The answer is simple. Like most prophecies in Revelation, the "drying up" of the Euphrates is a metaphorical description of a literal event.

The exact language used in the King James Bible says that the Euphrates dries up so that "the way of the kings of the East might be prepared." When attempting to understand the symbolism of this verse, it is critical to recall the meaning of "kings" in Biblical prophecy. As was the case in Daniel 7 and Revelation 17, these kings are not individuals—they are leadership positions.

Once again, the fulfillment of the sixth vial reverberates with semblances to its corresponding trumpet. The parallels are the Euphrates, the fall of an empire headquartered in Constantinople, and the involvement of the Turks. The Seljuk Turks' overthrow of the Buyid Dynasty in 1062 and the Ottoman Turks' defeat of the Byzantine Empire at Constantinople in 1453 marked the beginning and ending of the sixth trumpet's 391-year prophecy. The same Ottoman Empire whose rise occurred during the sixth trumpet would play a significant role in fulfilling the sixth vial through its own collapse.

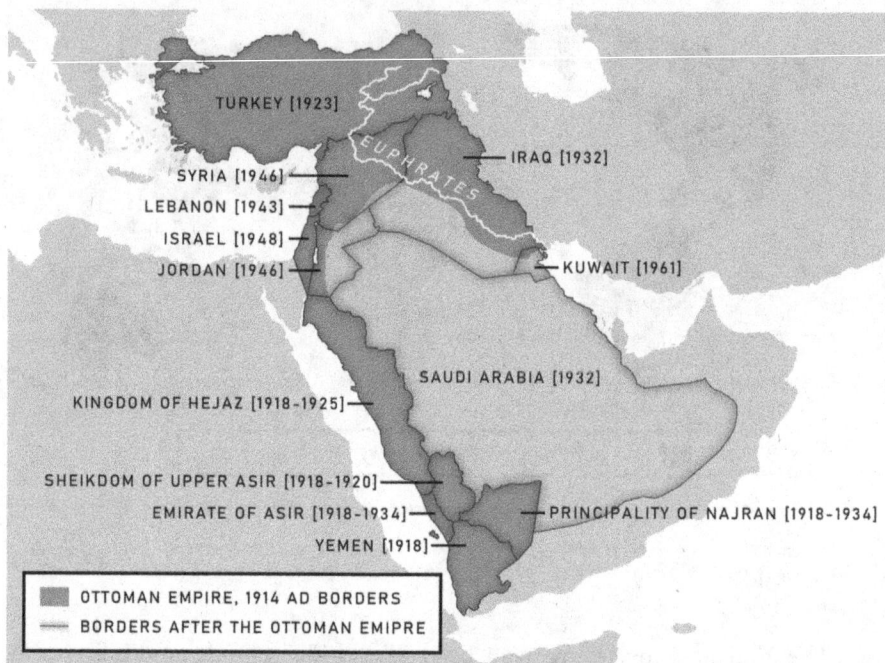

Figure 44: The Middle East before and after World War I. The Ottoman Empire's collapse prepared "the way of the kings of the East"—new states that eventually arose from former Ottoman territory.

Before World War I, the Ottoman Empire controlled the entire length of the Euphrates. The Turks had held this area since 1555 AD, during the reign of Suleiman the Magnificent. As World War I began, the empire allied with the Central Powers—Germany, Austria-Hungary, and Bulgaria.

After the Central Powers lost the war, the Ottoman Empire soon faded from history, and its territory was eventually divided into several new states. The "drying up" of the Euphrates was a metaphor for the empire's forfeiture of territory around the river. The land the Ottomans relinquished following the conflict ultimately formed all or part of Turkey, Yemen, Lebanon, Iraq, Jordan, Syria, Saudi Arabia, Kuwait, and Israel—the new "kings of the East."[7]

Battle of Armageddon

One critical element of the sixth vial prophecy has yet to be clarified: the infamous Battle of Armageddon. As World War I neared its conclusion in September 1918, the Ottoman army was in full retreat from the British forces. General Edmund Allenby, commander of the British Egyptian Expeditionary

Force, directed his army's advance northward from Sinai and into Palestine. Starting on September 19, a series of fierce engagements unfolded against the Ottomans in the region north of Jerusalem near Tabsor, Nablus, Tulkarm, and Arara in the Judean Hills. As the British maintained their relentless push, further fighting erupted near Nazareth, Afulah, Beisan, Jenin, and Samakh. The success of this week-long offensive pressed the demoralized Ottoman forces into Syria.

History is written by the victors, so General Allenby selected the name of the overarching battle. He chose the "Battle of Megiddo" specifically for its religious significance, as clashes occurred in the area surrounding the site of Megiddo where the Biblical Battle of Armageddon takes place.[8]

Futurists and Preterists claim this was a forced fulfillment of prophecy by Allenby. While he indeed chose the battle's name because of its religious undertones, that in no way invalidates the battle from fulfilling the Battle of Armageddon. The Battle of Megiddo, World Wars I and II, and the collapse of the Ottoman Empire each align perfectly with the sixth vial.

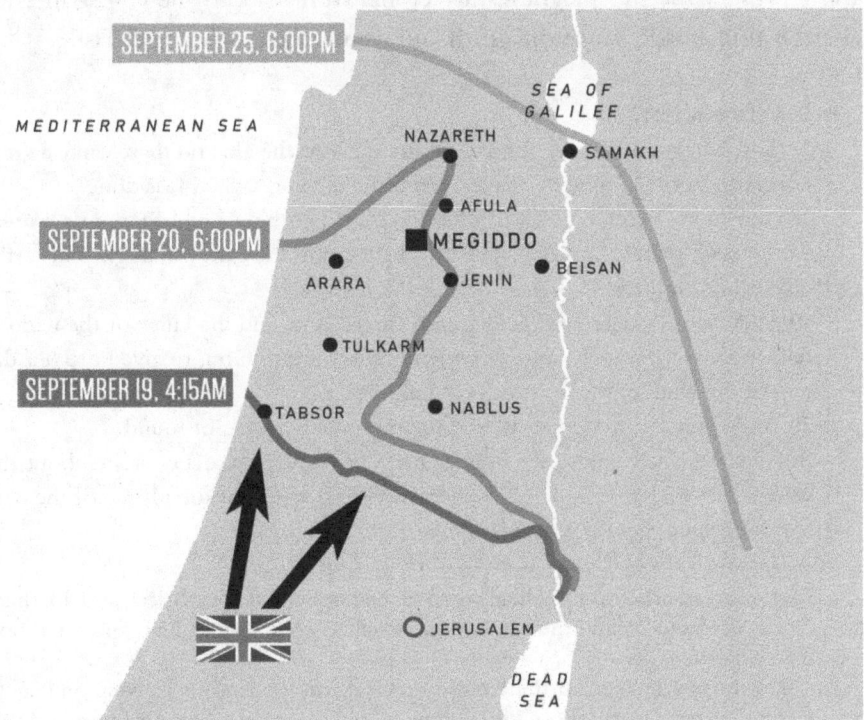

Figure 45: Locations of the military engagements and battle lines of the Battle of Megiddo, September 1918.

Tragically, one part of the sixth vial remains unfulfilled. If we view the frog spirits as individual wars, rather than merely a collective influence behind the first World War, a third global conflict becomes inevitable. The beginning of World War III will close the sixth vial, as the third unclean frog-like spirit will be fulfilled once the whole world is gathered for battle one last time. Chronologically, we have finally arrived at the intersection of Revelation's prophecies and our current historical moment.

The Seventh Vial

God's seventh and final vial judgment on earth is extremely cataclysmic. It is described in the Biblical text as a "great earthquake, such as was not since men were upon the earth, so mighty an earthquake, and so great." This final prophetic earthquake is more severe than those of Constantine's conversion[c] and the Protestant Reformation.[d] This religious upheaval is characterized as an unparalleled paradigm shift in history. The outpouring of the seventh vial will represent the most significant tectonic shift in both the Christian faith and the global order since the death and resurrection of Jesus Christ.

> **Revelation 16:17-21**
> **17** And the seventh angel poured out his vial into the air; and there came a great voice out of the temple of heaven, from the throne, saying, It is done.
> **18** And there were voices, and thunders, and lightnings; and there was a great earthquake, such as was not since men were upon the earth, so mighty an earthquake, and so great.
> **19** And the great city was divided into three parts, and the cities of the nations fell: and great Babylon came in remembrance before God, to give unto her the cup of the wine of the fierceness of his wrath.
> **20** And every island fled away, and the mountains were not found.
> **21** And there fell upon men a great hail out of heaven, every stone about the weight of a talent: and men blasphemed God because of the plague of the hail; for the plague thereof was exceeding great.

---

[c] **Revelation 6:12** And I beheld when he had opened the sixth seal, and, lo, there was a great earthquake; and the sun became black as sackcloth of hair, and the moon became as blood;

[d] **Revelation 11:19** And the temple of God was opened in heaven, and there was seen in his temple the ark of his testament: and there were lightnings, and voices, and thunderings, and an earthquake, and great hail.

Considering the first-century authorship of Revelation and the context of the book, the "great city" divided into three parts in Revelation 16:19 is irrefutably Rome. The commentator W. Boyd Carpenter wrote in Charles Ellicott's *A Bible Commentary for English Readers* that he believed the great city splitting into three parts indicates Rome will "lose its power of cohesion."[9] However, this separation may mean several things: a figurative division of Rome, a literal division of the city into three parts, a rift between three distinct factions of the Roman Catholic Church, three distinct types of destruction, or even the complete devastation of Rome and Vatican City.

After the seven vials conclude, Revelation 17 describes Mystery Babylon so Christians can see exactly what this final vial would destroy. The second verse of Revelation 18 not only indicates that the Catholic Church will be destroyed, but also that it will "become the habitation of devils, and the hold of every foul spirit."[e] Although the Catholic Church's vindictive campaign of persecution and slaughter against medieval Christians and Reformation-era Protestants was not sufficient for everyone to see the demonic inspiration behind Roman Catholicism, in W. Boyd Carpenter's opinion, the seventh vial will eliminate any remaining doubt.

However, the rest of Revelation 18 supports the interpretation that the tripartite division will include physical destruction. Verses eight and eighteen describe Rome as "burning." Verses ten, seventeen, and nineteen predict she will be made "desolate" in only one hour, providing more evidence of rapid physical destruction. Under the day-year principle, one prophetic hour—or one twenty-fourth of a 360-day Hebrew year—is fifteen days.

The burning described in chapter eighteen is not symbolic. During John's first three trumpet visions, the allegorical hailstorm, mountain, and great star were the objects on fire. This suggests that their burning was also a metaphor, signifying military conflicts. The reference to burning found in Revelation 18 is not merely symbolic, as it specifically names Mystery Babylon as the target. This would indicate that Rome's burning in the seventh vial is tangible, not metaphorical, as verse twenty-one predicts the city will be violently thrown down until she "shall be found no more at all."

---

[e] **Revelation 18:2** And he cried mightily with a strong voice, saying, Babylon the great is fallen, is fallen, and is become the habitation of devils, and the hold of every foul spirit, and a cage of every unclean and hateful bird.

> **Revelation 18:8-10, 18-21**
>
> **8** Therefore shall her plagues come in one day, death, and mourning, and famine; and she shall be utterly burned with fire: for strong is the Lord God who judgeth her.
> **9** And the kings of the earth, who have committed fornication and lived deliciously with her, shall bewail her, and lament for her, when they shall see the smoke of her burning,
> **10** Standing afar off for the fear of her torment, saying, Alas, alas that great city Babylon, that mighty city! for in one hour is thy judgment come.
> **18** And cried when they saw the smoke of her burning, saying, What city is like unto this great city!
> **19** And they cast dust on their heads, and cried, weeping and wailing, saying, Alas, alas that great city, wherein were made rich all that had ships in the sea by reason of her costliness! for in one hour is she made desolate.
> **20** Rejoice over her, thou heaven, and ye holy apostles and prophets; for God hath avenged you on her.
> **21** And a mighty angel took up a stone like a great millstone, and cast it into the sea, saying, Thus with violence shall that great city Babylon be thrown down, and shall be found no more at all.

When the seventh vial destroys Rome, other "cities of the nations" also fall. As with Rome, the indications point to a destruction in the natural world. Since the Bible predicts this will be the most substantial earthquake in human history because of its devastation of the Vatican and multiple "cities of the nations," it is difficult to imagine a scenario where the seventh vial could be limited to spiritual destruction. After all, how could the populations of entire cities spiritually fall away from God in only fifteen days?

Unfortunately, the simplest fulfillment for modern readers to visualize, which would also be supported by a literal reading of the scriptural text, is a nuclear war. There has never been a major armed conflict between nuclear powers. While nuclear-armed nations have fought against each other in proxy wars, any direct confrontation between two nuclear powers would render conventional weapon systems meaningless. Adversaries would fight until one nation began to lose, at which point nuclear weapons would be threatened or deployed. This theory might also explain why the seventh vial judgment of Revelation 16 is poured out "into the air." Nuclear weapons explode before they reach the ground to increase their effectiveness, and John also may have written this description after seeing the mushroom clouds of nuclear bombs.

However, since the day-year principle suggests a fifteen-day fulfillment, the war may begin with conventional weapons until the nuclear destruction of Rome occurs on day fifteen. World War III, which would fulfill the third frog-like spirit in the sixth vial, could also fulfill the seventh vial by destroying Rome and other cities. As uncomfortable as it may be to consider, a third World War could easily check all remaining boxes of the vial prophecies.

It is also easy to envision a scenario where another large-scale war would impact Rome. Article V of the North Atlantic Treaty Organization (NATO) charter requires its thirty-one member nations to defend any NATO member that is attacked by a non-NATO nation.[10] If a NATO country is attacked, the treaty requires Italy to support their NATO allies. This chain of events would mean any war involving a NATO nation would put a target on Rome and the cities of the other NATO member nations who respond. The multinational alliance created to prevent World War III may be the catalyst that causes it.

In Revelation 18:8, a famine follows Mystery Babylon's destruction. Any war involving the United States or Europe would cause a dramatic disruption in the world's food supply chain and cause substantial shortages. However, this famine could also theoretically be the result of a nuclear winter. The soot injected into the atmosphere would block the sun for several years, causing widespread crop failure and famine. This is not a prediction, only an analysis of the geopolitical environment in the nuclear weapons age that could fulfill all elements of the seventh vial.

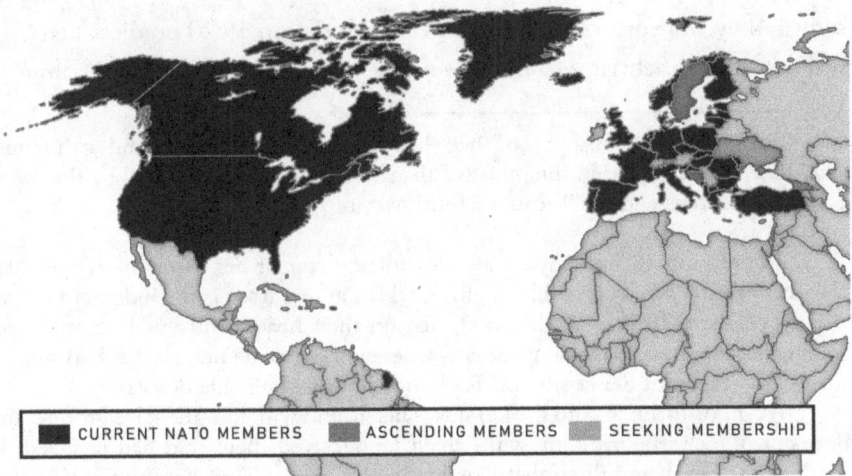

Figure 46: Member nations of the North Atlantic Treaty Organization, 2024.

We know that the vials emulate their trumpets. After the sixth trumpet, John is told the seventh trumpet will "cometh quickly." This may also imply that the seventh vial will closely follow the sixth. The start of World War III will close the sixth vial, and the destruction of Rome will fulfill the seventh.

A literal demolition of Vatican City may not fulfill the split of Rome into thirds. When Rome is destroyed, the cardinals located elsewhere may cause a schism. For example, the politically left-leaning churches in Europe and the United States may want to continue taking the Catholic Church down the road of activist causes. The more conservative African, South American, and Asian churches may wish to revert to traditional Catholicism, but in different ways. These fragments may want unique doctrine, pulling Catholicism apart.

However, the likely interpretation is a reference to a prophecy by Ezekiel. In Ezekiel 5, the prophet foreshadowed the 597 BC Babylonian conquest of Jerusalem by shaving all his hair and dividing it into three parts. Ezekiel was commanded to burn one third, strike another with a sword, and scatter the final third into the wind—representing God's punishment through famine, war, and exile.[f] Revelation 16:19 mirrors Jerusalem's tripartite destruction and may be a prophecy of nuclear explosion, radiation poisoning, and starvation.

The inclusion of a famine in Revelation 18:8 after Rome's destruction will require enough time for the food supply to be exhausted. Unfortunately, there is no Biblical indication of the amount of time that will elapse between the annihilation of Rome and the second coming of Jesus Christ.[g]

It is important to note that whoever the pope is at the time of Christ's return, they will survive the seventh vial. Revelation 19:20 predicts that God will cast the Antichrist into the lake of fire *alive* after Jesus' second coming.[h]

---

[f] **Ezekiel 5:12** A third part of thee shall die with the pestilence, and with famine shall they be consumed in the midst of thee: and a third part shall fall by the sword round about thee; and I will scatter a third part into all the winds, and I will draw out a sword after them.

[g] **Revelation 18:10** Standing afar off for the fear of her torment, saying, Alas, alas that great city Babylon, that mighty city! for in one hour is thy judgment come.
Revelation 18:19 And they cast dust on their heads, and cried, weeping and wailing, saying, Alas, alas that great city, wherein were made rich all that had ships in the sea by reason of her costliness! for in one hour is she made desolate.

[h] **Revelation 19:20** And the beast was taken, and with him the false prophet that wrought miracles before him, with which he deceived them that had received the mark of the beast, and them that worshipped his image. These both were cast alive into a lake of fire burning with brimstone.

The Vatican has faced a number of significant controversies during Pope Francis' pontificate. Upon his papal election in 2012, Francis was tasked with fixing the Vatican's finances, which were the focus of a €4 billion tax evasion scandal.[11] One of the most revealing issues exposed by another controversy for the Catholic Church, dubbed the Vati-Leaks scandal, was the significant internal criticism Pope Francis received for his hesitancy to condemn child rapists amongst his clergy. The pope demonstrably supported the American cardinal Theodore McCarrick,[12] Chilean bishop Juan Barros,[13] Argentinian priest Julio César Grassi,[14] and others while privately working to cover up their crimes until mounting evidence made the sexual assaults more damaging to deny than to acknowledge.

Francis' approval of *Fiducia Supplicans*, a declaration on Catholic doctrine allowing priests to bless same-sex couples, has caused a remarkable backlash within the church. In response, the Catholic episcopal conferences of Poland, Hungary, and the entire continent of Africa have barred their priests from blessing homosexual relationships.[15] The bishops of Ukraine said the *Fiducia Supplicans* was "perceived as permission to sin." German Cardinal Gerhard Ludwig Müller called the decree "a sacrilegious and blasphemous act against the Creator's plan." Archbishop Tomasz Peta of Kazakhstan said Francis had "seriously abused the Holy Name of God," labeling *Fiducia Supplicans* a "great deception and evil" that disregarded the "truth of the gospel."[16] Cardinal Robert Sarah called it "a heresy that seriously undermines the Church."[17]

At the Vatican's first World Children's Day, on May 25, 2024, transsexual activist Carmine De Rosa danced in drag at Rome's Olympic Stadium while young children sat in a circle around him. Later that day, Pope Francis met with those children at the same venue. After the predictable backlash from the Catholics who found the behavior of their church reprehensible, De Rosa claimed, "I was wanted at this event for the type of show I carry on stage."[18]

The pontificate of Francis has been tremendously controversial within church circles. When given the choice, the pope has favored immoral activist causes over Biblical teaching, often causing many to question his judgment and motives. While it may be baffling to some to see a supposedly Christian leader support such perverted ideology, this behavior is exactly what should be expected from an anti-Christian leader like the Antichrist.

Corroborating Evidence for the Seventh Vial Elsewhere in the Bible

Revelation is not the only place where the events of the seventh vial are depicted. The Bible describes an environment of tremendous anguish and despair immediately preceding Christ's second coming in several passages, including many in the Old Testament.

Isaiah 59:10 describes a scene where people alive just before the second coming cannot see during the daytime.[i] Isaiah 62 is a chapter about God's promise to restore Jerusalem's glory during the millennium reign after Jesus returns. Verse four indicates God will restore the city's land from desolation.[j]

Although Israel's climate is primarily dry and arid, the country is home to an active and innovative agricultural industry. Israel is a world leader in the production of fruit such as pomegranates, nectarines, plums, dates, pomelit, strawberries, and avocados.[19] Isaiah 62 suggests that a catastrophe will occur which causes Israel to become a wasteland shortly before the second coming.

Jeremiah 31 is another Old Testament chapter commonly interpreted as a reference to the millennium reign. The prophet illustrated a distressed Israel stricken with grief and sorrow before Jesus returns to end the Jews' suffering. In Jeremiah 31:13, God promises the Jews he will "turn their mourning into joy" and "make them rejoice from their sorrow."

> **Jeremiah 31:13**
> **13** Then shall the virgin rejoice in the dance, both young men and old together: for I will turn their mourning into joy, and will comfort them, and make them rejoice from their sorrow.

Much of the tenor of Isaiah's and Jeremiah's prophecies are reflected by Zephaniah, but in greater detail. Zephaniah 1:15 describes the day of the Lord as a time of wrath, trouble, and distress. The verse gets worse, depicting a day of wasteness, desolation, darkness, gloominess, clouds, and thick darkness.

---

[i] **Isaiah 59:10** We grope for the wall like the blind, and we grope as if we had no eyes: we stumble at noon day as in the night; we are in desolate places as dead men.

[j] **Isaiah 62:4** Thou shalt no more be termed Forsaken; neither shall thy land any more be termed Desolate: but thou shalt be called Hephzibah, and thy land Beulah: for the Lord delighteth in thee, and thy land shall be married.

> **Zephaniah 1:14-16**
> 14 The great day of the Lord is near, it is near, and hasteth greatly, even the voice of the day of the Lord: the mighty man shall cry there bitterly.
> 15 That day is a day of wrath, a day of trouble and distress, a day of wasteness and desolation, a day of darkness and gloominess, a day of clouds and thick darkness,
> 16 A day of the trumpet and alarm against the fenced cities, and against the high towers.

This is the part of Zephaniah's account that suggests that a nuclear war could be coming. After a nuclear war, the Earth's atmosphere would be filled with soot from the fires caused by the blasts. This soot would block out a significant percentage of the sun's light, leaving a dark, gloomy, cloudy planet.

Zephaniah then goes further, prophesying about the impact on humans in verse seventeen. God will "bring distress upon men" so that they walk the earth as if they are blind. This would make sense if the world is shrouded in darkness. The prophet also predicts that people's "blood shall be poured out as dust, and their flesh as the dung." This part of the prophecy evokes the impact the heat from nuclear blasts would have on those nearest to ground zero as their bodies are essentially vaporized.[20]

> **Zephaniah 1:17-18**
> 17 And I will bring distress upon men, that they shall walk like blind men, because they have sinned against the Lord: and their blood shall be poured out as dust, and their flesh as the dung.
> 18 Neither their silver nor their gold shall be able to deliver them in the day of the Lord's wrath; but the whole land shall be devoured by the fire of his jealousy: for he shall make even a speedy riddance of all them that dwell in the land.

The gloominess of the days before the second coming is also prophesied in Zechariah 14:6, which states, "the light shall not be clear, nor dark." This indicates daytime will appear like dusk, as the soot in the stratosphere after a nuclear war would filter out most sunlight.

> **Zechariah 14:6**
> 6 And it shall come to pass in that day, that the light shall not be clear, nor dark:

However, the clearest description of the events of the seventh vial found outside of Revelation comes from II Peter 3:10-12. Peter's words read as if he were watching a nuclear explosion as it happened. He describes the skies "passing away" with a loud noise, the "elements" melting under the pressure of extreme heat, and the earth and the things in it burning up and dissolving. Verse twelve even goes as far as to say the heavens will be on fire.

> **II Peter 3:10-12**
> **10** But the day of the Lord will come as a thief in the night; in the which the heavens shall pass away with a great noise, and the elements shall melt with fervent heat, the earth also and the works that are therein shall be burned up.
> **11** Seeing then that all these things shall be dissolved, what manner of persons ought ye to be in all holy conversation and godliness,
> **12** Looking for and hasting unto the coming of the day of God, wherein the heavens being on fire shall be dissolved, and the elements shall melt with fervent heat?

This prophecy of the days just before Christ's return delivers the clearest support for the nuclear war theory. A nuclear fireball would not only appear as if the heavens were on fire, but the force and power of the explosion would easily dissolve even the most heat-resistant materials with temperatures four thousand degrees Fahrenheit hotter than the surface of the sun.

Zechariah 13 predicts that two-thirds of the people in "all the land" will die shortly before Christ's second coming, and the one-third who survive will suffer through unprecedentedly trying times. This widespread death can be easily attributed to the nuclear war of the seventh vial.

> **Zechariah 13:7-9**
> **7** Awake, O sword, against my shepherd, and against the man that is my fellow, saith the Lord of hosts: smite the shepherd, and the sheep shall be scattered: and I will turn mine hand upon the little ones.
> **8** And it shall come to pass, that in all the land, saith the Lord, two parts therein shall be cut off and die; but the third shall be left therein.
> **9** And I will bring the third part through the fire, and will refine them as silver is refined, and will try them as gold is tried: they shall call on my name, and I will hear them: I will say, It is my people: and they shall say, The Lord is my God.

The prophecies in this passage have two unique interpretations. First, after the shepherd—or Jesus—is executed, the sheep—his disciples—will be scattered. Second, this chapter refers to the experiences of Jesus' followers immediately before the second coming, which is foretold in the next chapter.

This prophecy does not describe the desolation of Israel during the First Jewish-Roman War. If we assume this prophecy was only intended to refer to the first-century Jews of Judea, only one-third of the Jews living there died during the conflict—a considerably lower number than the two-thirds that Zechariah's prophecy predicts will die. Bible commentators are also unsure of the meaning of "all the land." Zechariah 12-14 refers to an invasion of Israel before Christ's return, but this phrase may also imply a global calamity. Zechariah 12:11 predicts the mourning in Israel will equal the death of King Josiah, who was killed in Hadadrimmon by the Egyptian pharaoh Necho II.[k]

The Jews Return to God

The catastrophe of the seventh vial will cause unimaginable suffering in the world. Human nature causes us to turn to God during times of tragedy, as those who are normally skeptical of him look for comfort and answers in a "higher power" who is bigger than ourselves.

The Bible tells us that the Jewish people will also respond similarly to the trauma of the seventh vial. Because there was no term for "Christians" until after the life of Christ, it is unclear if the word "Jews" in these prophecies predicts that only the Jews will return to God, or if the prophecy implies that the lukewarm Laodicean Christians of today will follow God more faithfully as well. Prophecies predicting the Jews will return to God before the second coming are found in several places in the Old Testament, including Hosea 5:15 and Zechariah 12:10.[l]

---

[k] **Zechariah 12:11** In that day shall there be a great mourning in Jerusalem, as the mourning of Hadadrimmon in the valley of Megiddon.

[l] **Hosea 5:15** I will go and return to my place, till they acknowledge their offence, and seek my face: in their affliction they will seek me early.

Zechariah 12:10 And I will pour upon the house of David, and upon the inhabitants of Jerusalem, the spirit of grace and of supplications: and they shall look upon me whom they have pierced, and they shall mourn for him, as one mourneth for his only son, and shall be in bitterness for him, as one that is in bitterness for his firstborn.

Chapter Synopsis

The Sixth Vial (Revelation 16:12-16)
- Began to be fulfilled in 1914 AD with the start of World War I
- **Three Unclean Spirits Like Frogs:** Three World Wars encouraged by Satan, the papacy, and the Jesuit superior general, beginning in 1914 AD
- **Drying Up of the Euphrates:** Fall of the Ottoman Empire, 1918 AD
  - The Ottoman Empire's collapse prepared the way for the "kings of the East"—the modern Middle Eastern nations
- **The Battle of Armageddon:** The Battle of Megiddo, 1918 AD
- The last part of the sixth vial to be fulfilled is the third frog-like spirit—World War III

The Seventh Vial (Revelation 16:17-21)
- Vial is poured out into the air
- Rome will be destroyed
  - Other cities will also be destroyed
- The greatest spiritual earthquake in history divides Babylon into thirds
- Brings Mystery Babylon "into remembrance before God"

Destruction of Mystery Babylon (Revelation 18:1-24)
- Mystery Babylon's ruin will occur in one prophetic hour—fifteen days
- Mystery Babylon "shall be utterly burned with fire" and plagued with death, mourning, and famine
- World leaders will stand afar off and mourn the destruction when they see the smoke of her burning
- Jesus Christ's second coming will not immediately follow the destruction of Rome
- The Jews, and possibly the lukewarm Christians, will return to God

REVELATION TIMELINE

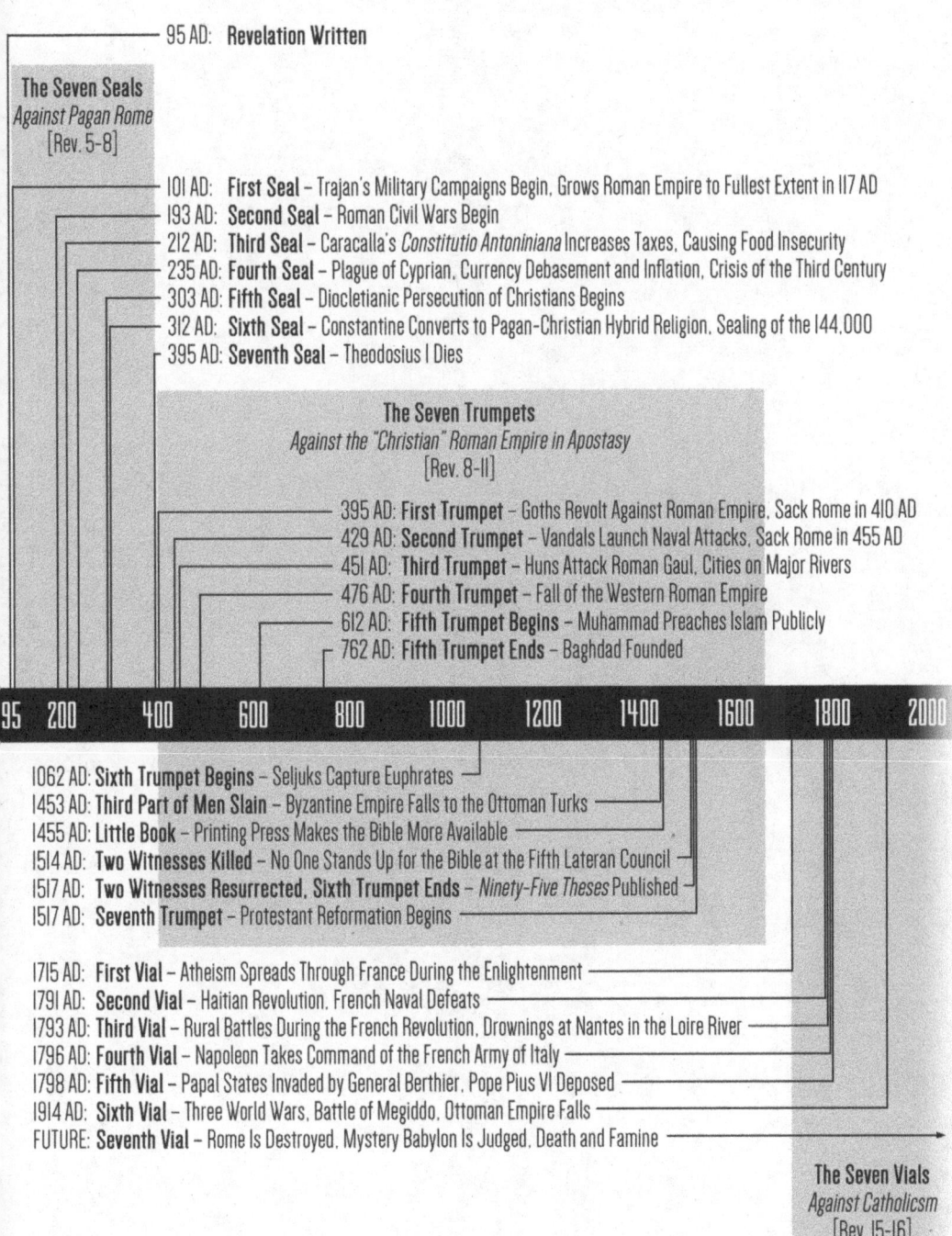

17

THE SECOND COMING

The Return of Jesus Christ

The Christians' return to faithfulness during the seventh vial catastrophe appears to be the catalyst that will cause God to shorten humanity's suffering and initiate Jesus' second coming. God promises he will "turn their mourning into joy, and will comfort them, and make them rejoice from their sorrow," indicating that he will relieve the pain and suffering caused by the event that compelled the halfhearted Christians to return to God in desperation.[a]

Surprisingly, there is little information about Christ's second coming in Revelation. John describes seeing Heaven open to reveal Jesus sitting upon a white horse with an army behind him. He illustrates Jesus' appearance and the appearance of his soldiers. Then John hears an angel calling birds of prey to prepare themselves to eat the flesh of God's enemies, who had gathered to fight against Jerusalem.[b]

---

[a] **Jeremiah 31:13** Then shall the virgin rejoice in the dance, both young men and old together: for I will turn their mourning into joy, and will comfort them, and make them rejoice from their sorrow.

[b] **Revelation 19:11-18** 11 And I saw heaven opened, and behold a white horse; and he that sat upon him was called Faithful and True, and in righteousness he doth judge and make war. 12 His eyes were as a flame of fire, and on his head were many crowns; and he had a name written, that no man knew, but he himself. 13 And he was clothed with a vesture dipped in blood: and his name is called The Word of God.

> **Revelation 19:19**
> 19 And I saw the beast, and the kings of the earth, and their armies, gathered together to make war against him that sat on the horse, and against his army.

Next, Jesus leads his army down to earth to fight the Antichrist and the armies of the "kings of the earth," fulfilling a prophecy made centuries earlier by the Old Testament prophet Zechariah.[1] After prophesying that two-thirds of the people in all the land would die before the second coming, he detailed the danger that Israel will face at that time.

> **Zechariah 14:1-2**
> 1 Behold, the day of the Lord cometh, and thy spoil shall be divided in the midst of thee.
> 2 For I will gather all nations against Jerusalem to battle; and the city shall be taken, and the houses rifled, and the women ravished; and half of the city shall go forth into captivity, and the residue of the people shall not be cut off from the city.

The First Battle

This battle over Jerusalem appears to differ from Revelation's sixth and seventh vial prophecies about World War III. Revelation 19 does not contain much information about this battle before Jesus arrives to rescue Jerusalem, but Old Testament prophets indicate these wars may be related. The timing of these prophecies—immediately before Christ's return—suggests that the battle over Jerusalem occurs shortly after the seventh vial and World War III. A nuclear war would preoccupy the West, providing a distraction that allows the Arab countries to attack Israel. An Israeli attack on Iran or a retaliation

---

14 And the armies which were in heaven followed him upon white horses, clothed in fine linen, white and clean. 15 And out of his mouth goeth a sharp sword, that with it he should smite the nations: and he shall rule them with a rod of iron: and he treadeth the winepress of the fierceness and wrath of Almighty God. 16 And he hath on his vesture and on his thigh a name written, King Of Kings, And Lord Of Lords. 17 And I saw an angel standing in the sun; and he cried with a loud voice, saying to all the fowls that fly in the midst of heaven, Come and gather yourselves together unto the supper of the great God; 18 That ye may eat the flesh of kings, and the flesh of captains, and the flesh of mighty men, and the flesh of horses, and of them that sit on them, and the flesh of all men, both free and bond, both small and great.

against Islamic terror groups may lead Muslim countries to ally against Israel. Whatever the scenario, Jerusalem will face a major crisis.

However, God promises he will not allow Israel to be defeated. We have learned that the Battle of Armageddon prophecy was fulfilled in 1918 during World War I. This is a different battle, one of two led by Jesus himself after his return. After the nations gather to fight against Jerusalem in verse two, he will descend to the location of his ascension, the Mount of Olives. Verse four explains that his feet will touch the ground with such force that the mountain will split in two, shifting one half to the north and the other to the south.

> **Zechariah 14:3-5**
> 3 Then shall the Lord go forth, and fight against those nations, as when he fought in the day of battle.
> 4 And his feet shall stand in that day upon the mount of Olives, which is before Jerusalem on the east, and the mount of Olives shall cleave in the midst thereof toward the east and toward the west, and there shall be a very great valley; and half of the mountain shall remove toward the north, and half of it toward the south.
> 5 And ye shall flee to the valley of the mountains; for the valley of the mountains shall reach unto Azal: yea, ye shall flee, like as ye fled from before the earthquake in the days of Uzziah king of Judah: and the Lord my God shall come, and all the saints with thee.

Isaiah also prophesied about the location of Christ's return, writing that he would "come down to fight for Mount Zion," an alternate name for the city of Jerusalem.

> **Isaiah 31:4-5**
> 4 For thus hath the Lord spoken unto me, Like as the lion and the young lion roaring on his prey, when a multitude of shepherds is called forth against him, he will not be afraid of their voice, nor abase himself for the noise of them: so shall the Lord of hosts come down to fight for mount Zion, and for the hill thereof.
> 5 As birds flying, so will the Lord of hosts defend Jerusalem; defending also he will deliver it; and passing over he will preserve it.

The Antichrist and False Prophet Are Thrown Into Hell

> **Revelation 19:20-21**
> **20** And the beast was taken, and with him the false prophet that wrought miracles before him, with which he deceived them that had received the mark of the beast, and them that worshipped his image. These both were cast alive into a lake of fire burning with brimstone.
> **21** And the remnant were slain with the sword of him that sat upon the horse, which sword proceeded out of his mouth: and all the fowls were filled with their flesh.

During the battle, the Antichrist and False Prophet are cast alive into the Lake of Fire. Jesus kills all the remaining soldiers in the multinational alliance that threatened Jerusalem. As you might presume, Jesus will slaughter these soldiers with little effort. Zechariah 14:12 reaffirms how Christ's supernatural power will eradicate all the soldiers who took up arms against Jerusalem. This passage does not appear to describe the seventh vial, as the annihilation of Jerusalem's enemies in Revelation 19:21 occurs after the destruction of Rome in Revelation 16 and Jesus' second coming in Revelation 19:11-18.

> **Zechariah 14:12**
> **12** And this shall be the plague wherewith the Lord will smite all the people that have fought against Jerusalem; Their flesh shall consume away while they stand upon their feet, and their eyes shall consume away in their holes, and their tongue shall consume away in their mouth

Christ's Millennium Reign and the First Resurrection

> **Revelation 20:1-3**
> **1** And I saw an angel come down from heaven, having the key of the bottomless pit and a great chain in his hand.
> **2** And he laid hold on the dragon, that old serpent, which is the Devil, and Satan, and bound him a thousand years,
> **3** And cast him into the bottomless pit, and shut him up, and set a seal upon him, that he should deceive the nations no more, till the thousand years should be fulfilled: and after that he must be loosed a little season.

After the battle, Satan is captured and imprisoned in the bottomless pit. His confinement will last a thousand years, ushering in a period of peace and tranquility known as Jesus' millennium reign. While Satan is bound in the pit, he will be unable to influence the world. With Satan conquered, Jesus' first official act after the battle will be to bring the Christian martyrs back to life to reign with him as a reward for remaining faithful despite their suffering. This event is described in Revelation as the "first resurrection."

The Christians who died of causes other than religious persecution will not be raised from the dead during the first resurrection. Instead, they will remain in their graves until the start of judgment day. The Christians revived after the millennium will still qualify for eternal life, but will not receive the honor of reigning on earth with Jesus.

> **Revelation 20:4-6**
> **4** And I saw thrones, and they sat upon them, and judgment was given unto them: and I saw the souls of them that were beheaded for the witness of Jesus, and for the word of God, and which had not worshipped the beast, neither his image, neither had received his mark upon their foreheads, or in their hands; and they lived and reigned with Christ a thousand years.
> **5** But the rest of the dead lived not again until the thousand years were finished. This is the first resurrection.
> **6** Blessed and holy is he that hath part in the first resurrection: on such the second death hath no power, but they shall be priests of God and of Christ, and shall reign with him a thousand years.

God Makes a New Covenant with Israel

In Jeremiah 31, God promises to "make a new covenant with the house of Israel." When Jeremiah was alive, the Jews were God's people under the Mosaic covenant. Centuries later, they abandoned him when they rejected his Messiah. This prophecy refers to a future covenant that God will make after the Jews return to him. God's promise to establish a new covenant with his followers after they return to him is also prophesied in Jeremiah 32:38-40, Ezekiel 11:19-20, Ezekiel 16:60-62, and Romans 11:25-27.[c] After this new

---

[c] **Jeremiah 32:38-40** 38 And they shall be my people, and I will be their God: 39 And I will give them one heart, and one way, that they may fear me for ever, for the good of them, and of their children after them: 40 And I will make an everlasting

covenant is made, God will gather the Christians from all nations in Israel, where they will live in peace.[d]

> **Jeremiah 31:31-34**
> 31 Behold, the days come, saith the Lord, that I will make a new covenant with the house of Israel, and with the house of Judah:
> 32 Not according to the covenant that I made with their fathers in the day that I took them by the hand to bring them out of the land of Egypt; which my covenant they brake, although I was an husband unto them, saith the Lord:
> 33 But this shall be the covenant that I will make with the house of Israel; After those days, saith the Lord, I will put my law in their inward parts, and write it in their hearts; and will be their God, and they shall be my people.
> 34 And they shall teach no more every man his neighbour, and every man his brother, saying, Know the Lord: for they shall all know me, from the least of them unto the greatest of them, saith the Lord: for I will forgive their iniquity, and I will remember their sin no more.

---

covenant with them, that I will not turn away from them, to do them good; but I will put my fear in their hearts, that they shall not depart from me.
    Ezekiel 11:19-20 19 And I will give them one heart, and I will put a new spirit within you; and I will take the stony heart out of their flesh, and will give them an heart of flesh: 20 That they may walk in my statutes, and keep mine ordinances, and do them: and they shall be my people, and I will be their God.
    Ezekiel 16:60-62 60 Nevertheless I will remember my covenant with thee in the days of thy youth, and I will establish unto thee an everlasting covenant. 61 Then thou shalt remember thy ways, and be ashamed, when thou shalt receive thy sisters, thine elder and thy younger: and I will give them unto thee for daughters, but not by thy covenant. 62 And I will establish my covenant with thee; and thou shalt know that I am the Lord:
    Romans 11:25-27 25 For I would not, brethren, that ye should be ignorant of this mystery, lest ye should be wise in your own conceits; that blindness in part is happened to Israel, until the fulness of the Gentiles be come in. 26 And so all Israel shall be saved: as it is written, There shall come out of Sion the Deliverer, and shall turn away ungodliness from Jacob: 27 For this is my covenant unto them, when I shall take away their sins.

  [d] **Jeremiah 32:37** Behold, I will gather them out of all countries, whither I have driven them in mine anger, and in my fury, and in great wrath; and I will bring them again unto this place, and I will cause them to dwell safely:
    Ezekiel 28:26 And they shall dwell safely therein, and shall build houses, and plant vineyards; yea, they shall dwell with confidence, when I have executed judgments upon all those that despise them round about them; and they shall know that I am the Lord their God.

It is important to recognize that the 1948 creation of a Jewish state did not fulfill these prophecies. Today, Israel is surrounded by enemies and exists in a constant state of conflict. It is hard to imagine God describing the Jews living in Israel today as "dwelling safely," and he certainly has not "executed judgments upon all those that despise them round about them." Instead, this prophecy portrays a future amassing of all the Christians from every country at the start of the millennium.

Peace in Israel

The Christians and Messianic Jews in Israel will experience immense joy and blessings during the millennium. Zechariah 2:10 tells these followers of Jesus to "sing and rejoice" in anticipation of Christ's return.[e] Isaiah 2:2-4 says that people from "all nations shall flow unto" the Lord's house, meaning Christians will migrate to Jerusalem to learn from Christ. During this period, nations will no longer go to war.[f] Isaiah expressed a similar view to Zechariah when he predicted these pilgrims would travel "with songs and everlasting joy upon their heads" and that their "sorrow and sighing shall flee away."[g] God's blessings on the Christians traveling to Jerusalem will be so prominent that it will compel ten men to grasp onto their clothing and insist on joining their pilgrimage, having heard that God is with them.[h]

---

[e] **Zechariah 2:10** Sing and rejoice, O daughter of Zion: for, lo, I come, and I will dwell in the midst of thee, saith the Lord.

[f] **Isaiah 2:2-4** 2 And it shall come to pass in the last days, that the mountain of the Lord's house shall be established in the top of the mountains, and shall be exalted above the hills; and all nations shall flow unto it. 3 And many people shall go and say, Come ye, and let us go up to the mountain of the Lord, to the house of the God of Jacob; and he will teach us of his ways, and we will walk in his paths: for out of Zion shall go forth the law, and the word of the Lord from Jerusalem. 4 And he shall judge among the nations, and shall rebuke many people: and they shall beat their swords into plowshares, and their spears into pruninghooks: nation shall not lift up sword against nation, neither shall they learn war any more.

Isaiah 66:18 For I know their works and their thoughts: it shall come, that I will gather all nations and tongues; and they shall come, and see my glory.

[g] **Isaiah 35:10** And the ransomed of the Lord shall return, and come to Zion with songs and everlasting joy upon their heads: they shall obtain joy and gladness, and sorrow and sighing shall flee away.

[h] **Zechariah 8:23** Thus saith the Lord of hosts; In those days it shall come to pass, that ten men shall take hold out of all languages of the nations, even shall take

Isaiah wrote extensively about the perfection of Jesus' millennium reign. Isaiah 4:2-4 predicts that he will cleanse the "filth" of Israel and Jerusalem, leaving only holy people who are deserving of his presence.[i] The final eleven chapters of the book of Isaiah are teeming with incredible prophecies about Christ's millennium reign. Isaiah 40:3-5,[j] Isaiah 52:13-15,[k] and Isaiah 61:3[l] all predict that the holiness and glory of the Lord will be manifested. According to Isaiah 65:22, lifespans during the millennium will grow to "the lifetime of a tree."[m] Isaiah 65:20 even tells us that lives will be so long that centenarians will be considered in their youth.[n]

---

hold of the skirt of him that is a Jew, saying, We will go with you: for we have heard that God is with you.

[i] **Isaiah 4:2-4** 2 In that day shall the branch of the Lord be beautiful and glorious, and the fruit of the earth shall be excellent and comely for them that are escaped of Israel. 3 And it shall come to pass, that he that is left in Zion, and he that remaineth in Jerusalem, shall be called holy, even every one that is written among the living in Jerusalem: 4 When the Lord shall have washed away the filth of the daughters of Zion, and shall have purged the blood of Jerusalem from the midst thereof by the spirit of judgment, and by the spirit of burning.

[j] **Isaiah 40:3-5** 3 The voice of him that crieth in the wilderness, Prepare ye the way of the Lord, make straight in the desert a highway for our God. 4 Every valley shall be exalted, and every mountain and hill shall be made low: and the crooked shall be made straight, and the rough places plain: 5 And the glory of the Lord shall be revealed, and all flesh shall see it together: for the mouth of the Lord hath spoken it.

[k] **Isaiah 52:13-15** 13 Behold, my servant shall deal prudently, he shall be exalted and extolled, and be very high. 14 As many were astonied at thee; his visage was so marred more than any man, and his form more than the sons of men: 15 So shall he sprinkle many nations; the kings shall shut their mouths at him: for that which had not been told them shall they see; and that which they had not heard shall they consider.

[l] **Isaiah 61:3** To appoint unto them that mourn in Zion, to give unto them beauty for ashes, the oil of joy for mourning, the garment of praise for the spirit of heaviness; that they might be called trees of righteousness, the planting of the Lord, that he might be glorified.

[m] **Isaiah 65:22** They shall not build, and another inhabit; they shall not plant, and another eat: for as the days of a tree are the days of my people, and mine elect shall long enjoy the work of their hands.

[n] **Isaiah 65:20** There shall be no more thence an infant of days, nor an old man that hath not filled his days: for the child shall die an hundred years old; but the sinner being an hundred years old shall be accursed.

The Final Battle with Satan

At the end of the millennium reign, Satan will be freed from his "prison" of the bottomless pit. In a vengeful rage, he will manipulate world leaders, deceiving them into believing that they can somehow defeat Jesus in battle. Like the battle at the start of the millennium when Jesus returned to earth to save Jerusalem, God will again save the city with amazing supernatural power. In this last battle, God will send fire from heaven to devour the enemies of the Christians living with Jesus in Jerusalem, defeating Satan and his allies for the final time.

> **Revelation 20:7-10**
> 7 And when the thousand years are expired, Satan shall be loosed out of his prison,
> 8 And shall go out to deceive the nations which are in the four quarters of the earth, Gog, and Magog, to gather them together to battle: the number of whom is as the sand of the sea.
> 9 And they went up on the breadth of the earth, and compassed the camp of the saints about, and the beloved city: and fire came down from God out of heaven, and devoured them.
> 10 And the devil that deceived them was cast into the lake of fire and brimstone, where the beast and the false prophet are, and shall be tormented day and night for ever and ever.

The Second Resurrection and Judgment Day

After Satan's defeat, he will be cast into Hell to spend eternity with the papal Antichrist, the False Prophet, and anyone else who is not found worthy of eternal life. Then, with no evil influences remaining, God will resurrect the dead who were excluded from the first resurrection. According to Revelation 20:12, people from all levels of society will stand before God as equals while they are judged according to their actions. This description of judgment day provides conclusive evidence that the theory of sola fide—salvation through faith alone—is incorrect. If believing that Jesus is the Son of God is enough to gain entrance into Heaven, there would be no reason for God to judge the works of all mankind.

> **Revelation 20:11-13**
> **11** And I saw a great white throne, and him that sat on it, from whose face the earth and the heaven fled away; and there was found no place for them.
> **12** And I saw the dead, small and great, stand before God; and the books were opened: and another book was opened, which is the book of life: and the dead were judged out of those things which were written in the books, according to their works.
> **13** And the sea gave up the dead which were in it; and death and hell delivered up the dead which were in them: and they were judged every man according to their works.

After the final judgment concludes, those who fail to attain salvation will be cast into the lake of fire. The term "second death" is found four times in Revelation, including in Jesus' reward to the church in Smyrna,[o] and after the judgment day in Revelation 20:14. The phrase refers to the eternal, spiritual death awaiting sinners after their natural deaths.

> **Revelation 20:14-15**
> **14** And death and hell were cast into the lake of fire. This is the second death.
> **15** And whosoever was not found written in the book of life was cast into the lake of fire.

A New Heaven, New Earth, and New Jerusalem

The faithful Christians God finds worthy of salvation will not fall victim to the horrors of the second death. After his final victory, God creates a new Heaven and Earth, symbolizing the new era of renewal and regeneration that Isaiah foretold centuries before John's Revelation.[p] Peter wrote a prophecy in which Jesus promised his followers that a new Heaven and Earth will be created.[q] Ezekiel also prophesied of a grand new Temple.[2] This continuity of prophecy between the Old and New Testaments is astonishing.

---

[o] **Revelation 2:11** He that hath an ear, let him hear what the Spirit saith unto the churches; He that overcometh shall not be hurt of the second death.

[p] **Isaiah 65:17** For, behold, I create new heavens and a new earth: and the former shall not be remembered, nor come into mind.

[q] **II Peter 3:13** Nevertheless we, according to his promise, look for new heavens and a new earth, wherein dwelleth righteousness.

> **Revelation 21:1-2**
> **1** And I saw a new heaven and a new earth: for the first heaven and the first earth were passed away; and there was no more sea.
> **2** And I John saw the holy city, new Jerusalem, coming down from God out of heaven, prepared as a bride adorned for her husband.

The words John uses to describe the majesty of God's presence in this era are exceptionally inspirational. If you ever find yourself struggling to share God's Word with others or ashamed to tell people that you are a Christian, read Revelation 21:3-8 and remember what awaits those who faithfully follow him without hesitation or shame.

> **Revelation 21:3-8**
> **3** And I heard a great voice out of heaven saying, Behold, the tabernacle of God is with men, and he will dwell with them, and they shall be his people, and God himself shall be with them, and be their God.
> **4** And God shall wipe away all tears from their eyes; and there shall be no more death, neither sorrow, nor crying, neither shall there be any more pain: for the former things are passed away.
> **5** And he that sat upon the throne said, Behold, I make all things new. And he said unto me, Write: for these words are true and faithful.
> **6** And he said unto me, It is done. I am Alpha and Omega, the beginning and the end. I will give unto him that is athirst of the fountain of the water of life freely.
> **7** He that overcometh shall inherit all things; and I will be his God, and he shall be my son.
> **8** But the fearful, and unbelieving, and the abominable, and murderers, and whoremongers, and sorcerers, and idolaters, and all liars, shall have their part in the lake which burneth with fire and brimstone: which is the second death.

Hosea's Three Days Prophecy and the Second Coming

The Old Testament book of Hosea contains a fascinating prophecy on the timing of Christ's second coming. The prophet wrote that after Jesus' time on earth, he would return to Heaven for two days. Then, after the two days are complete, he will resurrect his followers who will "live in his sight" for the third day.

> **Hosea 5:14-6:2**
>
> **14** For I will be unto Ephraim as a lion, and as a young lion to the house of Judah: I, even I, will tear and go away; I will take away, and none shall rescue him.
>
> **15** I will go and return to my place, till they acknowledge their offence, and seek my face: in their affliction they will seek me early.
>
> **6:1** Come, and let us return unto the Lord: for he hath torn, and he will heal us; he hath smitten, and he will bind us up.
>
> **2** After two days will he revive us: in the third day he will raise us up, and we shall live in his sight.

The resurrection described by Hosea is the same one described by John in Revelation 20:4-6. Once the Christian martyrs are resurrected after Jesus' second coming, they will live on earth with him during his millennium reign. This suggests the third "day" in Hosea's prophecy will be fulfilled by the one thousand years of the millennium. If each "day" in Hosea's prophecy equals *exactly* one thousand years, the first two days would begin at Jesus' ascension in 30 AD and end in 2030. Although Jesus said, "ye know neither the day nor the hour" of his second coming, Hosea *may* have told us the year.[r]

Identifying the Antichrist and Mystery Babylon is of significantly greater scriptural importance than determining the timing of Jesus' second coming. Rather than inciting fear through apocalyptic imagery, the book of Revelation serves a practical dual purpose: warning the early Christians of an impending false religion and equipping future believers with the tools to recognize it.

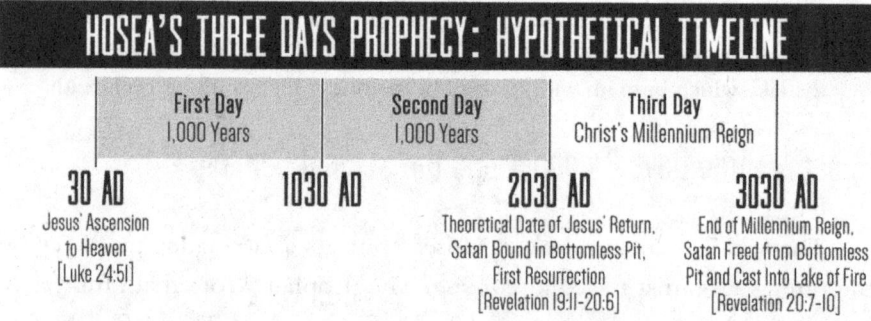

Figure 47: Hosea's Three Days prophecy, which may predict the approximate year of Jesus' second coming.

---

[r] **Matthew 25:13** Watch therefore, for ye know neither the day nor the hour wherein the Son of man cometh.

Chapter Synopsis

The Return of Jesus Christ (Revelation 19:11-21)
- The Antichrist and world leaders will gather armies to fight against Jesus
- Jesus will return to the Mount of Olives (Zechariah 14:1-9)
- After their defeat, the Antichrist and False Prophet are thrown into Hell

Millennium Reign and Final Battle with Satan (Revelation 20:4-15)
- After the second coming, Jesus will bind Satan in the bottomless pit for a thousand years and raise the Christian martyrs in the first resurrection
- Satan will be released from the bottomless pit after the millennium
- He will deceive the nations and gather them to battle against Jesus
- Satan will be defeated and thrown into Hell
- After Christ's victory, he will resurrect the rest of the dead in the second resurrection so God can judge our works, casting the sinners into Hell

A New Heaven, New Earth, and New Jerusalem (Revelation 21:1-22:5)
- After Satan is finally defeated and thrown into Hell, God creates a new Heaven, a new Earth, and a new Jerusalem

Hosea's Three Days Prophecy (Hosea 5:14-6:2)
- Jesus will "return to his place" for two days until the Jews "acknowledge their offence, and seek my face"
  - This probably means that both the Jews and the lukewarm Christians will return to God
- After the Jews return to God, he will raise his followers from the dead, and they will live "in his sight" for the third day
  - Revelation tells us that the "first resurrection" will occur when Jesus raises the Christian martyrs from the dead when he returns
  - The martyrs will reign with Christ during the millennium
  - The third day in Hosea's prophecy represents the millennium reign, as the prophet says, "after two days will he revive us: in the third day he will raise us up, and we shall live in his sight"
  - Therefore, the first two days would represent a two-thousand-year period between Jesus' ascension in 30 AD and his second coming

18

THE END

The Bible's indictment against Roman Catholicism is as conclusive as it is damning. Mystery Babylon is a prostitute, which represents a false church in prophecy. This false church is in Rome, the "city of seven hills," but has a worldwide influence—encompassing many peoples, multitudes, nations, and tongues—just as John wrote it would in Revelation 17:15. When Constantine fused pure Christianity with Roman paganism, the apostasy foreshadowed by Paul in II Thessalonians 2 pulled would-be Christians away from Jesus and into the pagan religion of Catholicism. Roman Catholicism's founding dates to the Babylonian sun cult, which eventually found a home in ancient Rome, giving Mystery Babylon her name. The sun cult origin is evident in traditional Catholic symbology, including halos, the monstrance, church décor, and the Jesuits' logo. There is no other rational interpretation for Mystery Babylon.

The prophet Daniel predicted the Roman origin of the Antichrist. Three of the ten kingdoms that surfaced after the fall of the Roman Empire were defeated before the bishop of Rome received his full power from Justinian as "the head of all the Holy Churches." After the third kingdom was defeated, "power was given him over all kindreds, and tongues, and nations," precisely as Revelation 13:7 predicted.[a]

---

[a] **Revelation 13:7** And it was given unto him to make war with the saints, and to overcome them: and power was given him over all kindreds, and tongues, and nations.

Throughout the Middle Ages and Reformation, the Vatican persecuted and martyred a significant number of Christians. This fulfilled the prophecies of Daniel 7:21 and Revelation 13:7, which predicted that the Antichrist would "make war with the saints"—a charge the many Christian victims of papal persecution would certainly agree applies. Historically, the popes have made unbelievably grandiose and heretical statements. These egotistical narcissists often spoke "great things" and equated themselves to Jesus by assuming the title "Vicar of Christ," which means "substitute Christ."

However, the Antichrist does not operate alone. The second beast of Revelation 13, referred to three times in Revelation as the "False Prophet," aids the Antichrist pope's deceitfulness. The False Prophet, who represents the corrupt clergy, particularly the Jesuit superior general, breathed life back into the Antichrist beast when the papacy faced its greatest threat. After the early Protestant Reformers exposed Catholicism as a false Christian church, the Jesuit Order was founded with a supposed mission of reconciliation—not a reconciliation of man with God, but of Protestants with the Catholic Church. Jesuit priests created the dishonest interpretations of Preterism and Futurism to mislead Christians and discredit the Protestant Reformers, who accurately associated the Antichrist and Mystery Babylon with the papacy and Roman Catholicism. The cunning Jesuits then infiltrated Protestantism to change its doctrine from the inside. Today, most Protestant denominations teach the inaccurate Futurist interpretation, and most Protestants believe the Catholic Church is Christian.

Daniel's Seventy Weeks Prophecy revealed the prophetic timeline known as the "day-year principle" to Christian theologians. This blueprint advocates for a Great Tribulation of 1,260 years rather than 1,260 days. The bishop of Rome received temporal authority in Rome after the Ostrogothic occupation of the city ended in March 538 AD. This gave the pope new temporal power to govern Christendom however he saw fit. Papal power rapidly expanded until the Roman pontiff became the greatest opponent to the Christian faith. Over the next 1,260 years, popes persecuted Christians by branding them as heretics, ostracizing them from society, and even executing many of the more prominent true Christians. Throughout history, an untold number of martyrs have died at the hands of the popes and false prophets.

Catholic doctrine is far from Biblical. Scripture declares Jesus is the only mediator between God and man. Yet, Catholicism gives this role to Mary and venerates her as a minor deity. Neither Mary nor any other venerated saint can hear our prayers and mediate on our behalf. In Catholicism, the pope is considered the head of the earthly church—a position the Bible reserves for Jesus Christ alone. The graven images in cathedrals and churches throughout the Catholic world are prayed to like the idols of the ancient pagans. The Catholic Church proclaims itself the gatekeeper of salvation, a ridiculous and sacrilegious claim. Catholic doctrine aligns not only with idolatry but with witchcraft and sorcery. Teaching salvation is obtained through performing the seven sacraments is no different from advocating for witchcraft, the belief that taking specific actions will generate a supernatural outcome. Repeating a certain number of Rosary prayers to be absolved from sin is akin to reciting a spell. Jesus advised us against impulsively reciting prayers in Matthew 6:7, when he said, "But when ye pray, use not vain repetitions, as the heathen do: for they think that they shall be heard for their much speaking."

The Vatican leaders know all of this. They understand their fulfillments of Mystery Babylon and the Antichrist, and this knowledge compelled them to prohibit Bible possession for more than a millennium in a desperate move of self-preservation. Medieval popes martyred the translators and publishers of scripture to control access to the Bible. In the nineteenth century, church leaders made every attempt to stifle and shutter Bible Societies. They claim that only the Catholic Church can interpret scripture so they can hide their fraudulence. The Vatican even conducted masses in Latin until the 1960s to further conceal God's Word from the laity.

> **Mark 13:22**
> 22 For false Christs and false prophets shall rise, and shall shew signs and wonders, to seduce, if it were possible, even the elect.

If you are Catholic, the realization that your own religion has deceived you must be emotionally devastating. The good news is that there is still time. Scrutinize your beliefs and determine what is more important to you: the Christian faith or the Catholic religion? Would you rather follow God's Word or adhere to a series of religious rituals and ceremonies created by men, even though most have little or no basis in the teachings of Jesus Christ? Are your religious views shaped by what you learned from reading the Bible or what you were told to believe by priests and pastors? When was the last time you read the Bible for yourself?

You can place your faith in God and his Word, or you can follow the Catechism of the Catholic Church, but not both. This is a decision that only you can make. The pagan rituals and doctrine of Catholicism are everything the Bible warns us against. Thankfully, God placed these prophecies in the Bible to help us avoid the deception of Mystery Babylon and her Antichrist. Included in those warnings was a message explicitly intended for Catholics: Revelation 18:4-5.

> **Revelation 18:4-5**
> 4 And I heard another voice from heaven, saying, Come out of her, my people, that ye be not partakers of her sins, and that ye receive not of her plagues.
> 5 For her sins have reached unto heaven, and God hath remembered her iniquities.

Jesus did not come to earth to establish a new religion. He came to save us and ignite our faith in God. Similarly, God never intended a religion to be the way to Heaven. Religious rituals, idolatry, ceremonies, and the repetition of prayers to be absolved of sin all align more closely with paganism than Christianity. Faith should be organic—something we believe that guides our behavior and that we openly share with others—not structured rituals.

Mystery Babylon the Great was not the only false church prophesied in Revelation 17. Verse five describes the name on her forehead, which includes the title "Mother of Harlots." Catholicism gave birth to other false churches, as many Protestant denominations followed Catholicism's lead and became comparably ritualistic, establishing their own religious traditions, symbolism, and ceremonies. Due to Catholicism's influence on Christianity, Protestants often accept the Nicene interpretation of the Trinity as Biblical truth, display graven images in many of their churches, repeat some prayers mindlessly, and rarely practice adult baptism.

This does not necessarily mean you should leave your church. Read your Bible frequently—especially the New Testament. Examine and analyze your church's beliefs and teachings to see how they adhere to God's Word—and question everything. What does your pastor believe about Revelation?

Do not abandon other believers in Christ, especially the Catholics whom Rome has deceived. Reach out to other believers and tell them what you have learned about Revelation's prophecies. Start new Bible studies and support groups with other Christians to read God's Word and apply it to your lives together, outside the influence and futile rituals of some organized religions.

The Bible is not opposed to structured Christian gatherings. Jesus said, "Where two or three are gathered together in my name, there am I in the midst of them."[b] It was this assembly of believers that the Bible repeatedly refers to as "the church." The Bible does not prohibit church gatherings, it encourages them. Although scripture promotes the practices of baptism[c] and communion,[d] it warns against performing empty rituals,[e] vain repetitions of prayers,[f] sorcery, and idolatry.[g]

---

[b] **Matthew 18:20** For where two or three are gathered together in my name, there am I in the midst of them.

[c] **Matthew 28:19** Go ye therefore, and teach all nations, baptizing them in the name of the Father, and of the Son, and of the Holy Ghost:

[d] **Luke 22:19** And he took bread, and gave thanks, and brake it, and gave unto them, saying, This is my body which is given for you: this do in remembrance of me.

[e] **Mark 7:13** Making the word of God of none effect through your tradition, which ye have delivered: and many such like things do ye.

[f] **Matthew 6:7** But when ye pray, use not vain repetitions, as the heathen do: for they think that they shall be heard for their much speaking.

II Timothy 2:16 But shun profane and vain babblings: for they will increase unto more ungodliness.

[g] **I Corinthians 6:9-10** 9 Know ye not that the unrighteous shall not inherit the kingdom of God? Be not deceived: neither fornicators, nor idolaters, nor adulterers, nor effeminate, nor abusers of themselves with mankind, 10 Nor thieves, nor covetous, nor drunkards, nor revilers, nor extortioners, shall inherit the kingdom of God.

Galatians 5:19-21 19 Now the works of the flesh are manifest, which are these; Adultery, fornication, uncleanness, lasciviousness, 20 Idolatry, witchcraft, hatred, variance, emulations, wrath, strife, seditions, heresies, 21 Envyings, murders, drunkenness, revellings, and such like: of the which I tell you before, as I have also told you in time past, that they which do such things shall not inherit the kingdom of God.

Revelation 21:8 But the fearful, and unbelieving, and the abominable, and murderers, and whoremongers, and sorcerers, and idolaters, and all liars, shall have their part in the lake which burneth with fire and brimstone: which is the second death.

A Warning About Futurism

In this era of the sixth vial of Revelation, we are nearing the end of God's judgments on Catholicism and the world. While we anxiously wait for the third frog-like spirit to close this vial when it gathers the world together for World War III, the world is becoming more dangerous. Today's society faces numerous threats, many of which come to us from the elitists in government and business. To the detriment of the rest of us, the hubris and greed of the powerful have often led to many of the world's evils, including wars, financial collapses, and harmful public policies. In recent years, the Futurists have seized on a frightening emerging technology to claim that their eschatological interpretation is correct: central bank digital currencies (CBDCs).

Like cryptocurrencies, central bank digital currencies are digital tokens built upon blockchain technology. While cryptocurrency is decentralized, or not directly controlled by a government, CBDCs are issued by a country or supranational group such as the European Union. These digital coins can be used to exchange goods and services the way paper money is today.

Soon, your money will be stored in the form of CBDC in a digital wallet and tied to a profile called a Digital ID. Every person will have one of these profiles containing all of their personal information: taxes, financial reports and statements, credit scores, medical and prescription records, employment information, travel documents such as passports and driver's licenses, vehicle registration, property registration, business registration, gun permits, voting records, and more.[1] Australia is already utilizing Digital ID for everything from transferring money, applying for a rental property, registering children in sports, enrolling in childcare, accessing government services, and signing up for a new cell phone plan.[2] Europe is currently launching the same system, and other nations will follow. In her 2020 State of the Union address, Ursula von der Leyen, President of the European Commission, said Digital ID will be a profile "that any citizen can use anywhere in Europe to do anything from paying your taxes to renting a bicycle. A technology where we can control ourselves what data is used and how."[3]

The result of Digital ID will be a punitive program for non-compliance, mirroring the Social Credit System already used in China to control citizens.[4] Under this tyrannical scheme, anyone the government deems non-compliant will be unable to access the CBDC in their own bank accounts or verify their identity online. They will then be blocked from the internet and monetary system until they are back in compliance. They will be unable to buy food or water, pay their mortgage, or purchase electricity or gas to heat their home and power their vehicles. As George Orwell said, "Real power is achieved when the ruling class controls the material essentials of life, granting and withholding them from the masses as if they were privileges."

Eventually, Digital IDs and CBDCs will replace the fiat currencies used today. In January 2022, the United States Federal Reserve Board released a report that noted, "a CBDC could fundamentally change the structure of the U.S. financial system."[5] Less than two months later, on March 9, 2022, Joe Biden signed Executive Order 14067, entitled "Executive Order on Ensuring Responsible Development of Digital Assets." This order directed the United States government to develop a CBDC dollar.[6] The International Monetary Fund (IMF) is currently working on a centralized foreign exchange platform for CBDCs to facilitate transactions between countries.[7]

The Bank for International Settlements (BIS), which operates as the bank for central banks, recently revealed the depth of the globalists' plans. In their 2023 Annual Report, the BIS detailed a system in which every asset we own is assigned a digital token in a blockchain. A central ledger would record all assets over a certain value. Real estate, vehicles, bullion, furniture, collectibles, bicycles—the globalists will record everything owned by anyone in the world, and any assets you do not declare will be seized. According to the BIS, there will even be strict rules for using your own possessions.[8]

Today, the CBDCs that have already launched are optional. However, participation in the globalists' scheme will soon be mandatory. As Worldcoin CEO Alex Blania recently said, "Something like World ID will eventually exist, meaning that you will need to verify on the internet, whether you like it or not."[9] At the 2023 World Government Summit in Dubai, the Chairman of the World Economic Forum, Klaus Schwab, proclaimed, "Who masters those technologies will, in some way, be the masters of the world."[10] This is not conjecture or a conspiracy theory—these are their words. With CBDCs and Digital ID, the government will restrict how and where you spend your money. Digital currencies will be an instrument of control—the ultimate tool of enslavement.

Like the World Economic Forum, the United Nations and other globalist organizations are claiming that "climate change" and "sustainability" are the basis for these oppressive, fundamental changes. The U.N.'s plan, which is disingenuously titled Agenda 2030 for Sustainable Development, confirms participation in this new system will be compulsory, as it can only succeed if everyone joins. According to the U.N., "Leave no one behind is the central, transformative promise of the 2030 Agenda for Sustainable Development and its Sustainable Development Goals."[11]

This disturbing innovation would allow the government to record and control all our transactions. The globalists will have the power to unilaterally turn off your ability to buy and sell without due process if you do not comply with their demands. If you violate government restrictions, post anything online the globalists deem "disinformation," buy too much meat, do not take a vaccine, or travel too far from home, your transactions will be declined.

The infrastructure to freeze our financial assets is already in place. In 2021, Canadian Prime Minister Justin Trudeau required Covid-19 vaccination for any commercial truckers to cross the United States-Canada border. Many of the truckers who were unwilling to take an experimental vaccine met at several places throughout Canada and formed what became known as the Freedom Convoy. The truckers converged on Ottawa and blockaded the city as a form of protest against the mandates. On February 20, 2022, Trudeau's government responded by freezing the financial accounts of any individuals and businesses involved with the protest.[12] Once the globalists realized the Canadian government had exposed its ability to freeze its citizens' financial accounts, Trudeau's government reversed its position the following day and released the truckers' assets.[13]

If the globalists cannot be stopped, life will soon get extremely difficult for us. Christians will be targeted and persecuted especially harshly. Tyrants hate religion more than anything else because Christians choose to obey God rather than them.

To truly understand the depths of the lust for power and control of the evil men and women who consider themselves our betters, you must suspend your own morality. You must not allow yourself to think, "They would never do that; that's too evil." The people who reach the highest levels of business and government have uncontrollable ambition and greed. The elite stop at nothing to get what they want and do not care about you—they are perfect vessels for Satan's darkest aspirations. As Ronald Reagan said, "Government is not the solution to the problem. Government is the problem."

Comprehending this new authoritarian financial revolution will help you refute the uninformed Futurists' false claims about Revelation. Although the scriptural evidence shows that Historicism is the only accurate interpretation of the end times, Futurists will point to the government's ability to restrict buying and selling as evidence supporting their misguided opinions. Even if you are forced to accept a mark to turn your bank accounts back on, this is still not evidence of Futurism's accuracy. Do not allow yourself or those you care about to fall victim to the Futurist ruse.

Historicism Today

When the Protestant Reformers identified the Roman Catholic Church as Mystery Babylon and the papacy as the Antichrist, the Vatican responded by inventing the verifiably inaccurate theories of Preterism and Futurism. The Jesuits manipulated scripture by placing a gap between the sixty-ninth and seventieth weeks of Daniel's prophecy and applying its final two verses to the Antichrist rather than Jesus. These false interpretations allegorize most of the prophecies in Revelation whenever any missing fulfillments cannot be found. Preterism takes "The Revelation of Jesus Christ" and applies it to the Jews rather than Christians. Also, Futurism disregards Revelation 1:1, which states that the prophecies in Revelation "must shortly come to pass."[h]

The Jesuits have been so successful in their campaign against the ideas of the Reformers that Historicism is often discredited as no more than anti-Catholic propaganda by supporters of the Vatican, including many Protestant leaders and seminary schools. The Catholic Church dismisses Historicism without ever challenging the merits of its Biblically-accurate interpretation—a debate they know they would lose.

---

[h] **Revelation 1:1-3** 1 The Revelation of Jesus Christ, which God gave unto him, to shew unto his servants things which must shortly come to pass; and he sent and signified it by his angel unto his servant John: 2 Who bare record of the word of God, and of the testimony of Jesus Christ, and of all things that he saw. 3 Blessed is he that readeth, and they that hear the words of this prophecy, and keep those things which are written therein: for the time is at hand.

Today, most pastors who preach about John's prophecies teach Futurism without questioning it. Likewise, many Christians in today's lukewarm church age do not bother to study the book of Revelation. Far too often, Christians blindly trust what their priests and pastors teach instead of studying the Bible for themselves.

Many Christians have allowed the theory of sola fide and Edward Irving's concept of the rapture to cloud their judgment. They think those who believe in Jesus will be taken to Heaven before the prophecies of Revelation begin, so they do not attempt to understand the book's signs and symbols.

One day, Jesus will return, and we will each have to give an account of how we lived our lives. Claiming you were misled by your pastor or priest on topics such as sola fide when you could have read the Bible for yourself will not be a sufficient excuse for why your faith was lukewarm. This is why Jesus warned the Laodiceans, "I will spue thee out of my mouth."

You do not need to spend years studying scripture to peel away the layers of false teaching. If you read your Bible regularly, any false teaching will be exposed. Embrace the true gospel that remains—let it guide your actions so that God will judge your works favorably. Focus on how you live your life, help others, share your faith, and represent Jesus Christ well during your time on earth. Follow Jesus' advice to the seven churches, emphasizing Smyrna and Philadelphia, and remember that your works will be judged.

We all have the free will to live our lives however we choose. You can live a Christian life founded on scripture, no matter how difficult the future becomes, or you can ignore God's commandments. You can share your faith with others or keep it secret. The 1.3 billion Catholics in the world desperately need to understand Revelation—how will you help them?

REVELATION TIMELINE

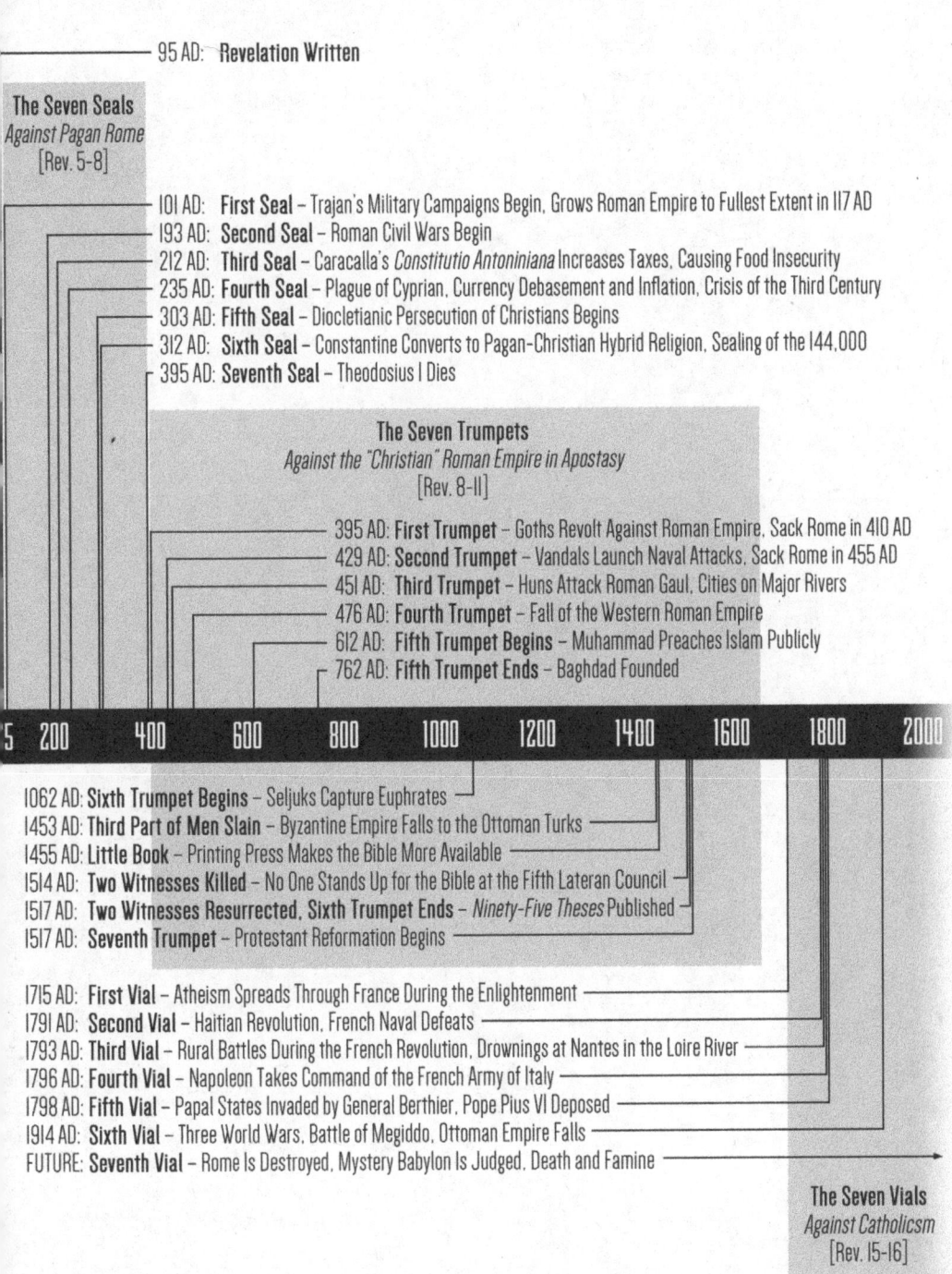

95 AD: Revelation Written

The Seven Seals
Against Pagan Rome
[Rev. 5-8]

- 101 AD: **First Seal** – Trajan's Military Campaigns Begin, Grows Roman Empire to Fullest Extent in 117 AD
- 193 AD: **Second Seal** – Roman Civil Wars Begin
- 212 AD: **Third Seal** – Caracalla's *Constitutio Antoniniana* Increases Taxes, Causing Food Insecurity
- 235 AD: **Fourth Seal** – Plague of Cyprian, Currency Debasement and Inflation, Crisis of the Third Century
- 303 AD: **Fifth Seal** – Diocletianic Persecution of Christians Begins
- 312 AD: **Sixth Seal** – Constantine Converts to Pagan-Christian Hybrid Religion, Sealing of the 144,000
- 395 AD: **Seventh Seal** – Theodosius I Dies

The Seven Trumpets
Against the "Christian" Roman Empire in Apostasy
[Rev. 8-11]

- 395 AD: **First Trumpet** – Goths Revolt Against Roman Empire, Sack Rome in 410 AD
- 429 AD: **Second Trumpet** – Vandals Launch Naval Attacks, Sack Rome in 455 AD
- 451 AD: **Third Trumpet** – Huns Attack Roman Gaul, Cities on Major Rivers
- 476 AD: **Fourth Trumpet** – Fall of the Western Roman Empire
- 612 AD: **Fifth Trumpet Begins** – Muhammad Preaches Islam Publicly
- 762 AD: **Fifth Trumpet Ends** – Baghdad Founded
- 1062 AD: **Sixth Trumpet Begins** – Seljuks Capture Euphrates
- 1453 AD: **Third Part of Men Slain** – Byzantine Empire Falls to the Ottoman Turks
- 1455 AD: **Little Book** – Printing Press Makes the Bible More Available
- 1514 AD: **Two Witnesses Killed** – No One Stands Up for the Bible at the Fifth Lateran Council
- 1517 AD: **Two Witnesses Resurrected, Sixth Trumpet Ends** – *Ninety-Five Theses* Published
- 1517 AD: **Seventh Trumpet** – Protestant Reformation Begins

- 1715 AD: **First Vial** – Atheism Spreads Through France During the Enlightenment
- 1791 AD: **Second Vial** – Haitian Revolution, French Naval Defeats
- 1793 AD: **Third Vial** – Rural Battles During the French Revolution, Drownings at Nantes in the Loire River
- 1796 AD: **Fourth Vial** – Napoleon Takes Command of the French Army of Italy
- 1798 AD: **Fifth Vial** – Papal States Invaded by General Berthier, Pope Pius VI Deposed
- 1914 AD: **Sixth Vial** – Three World Wars, Battle of Megiddo, Ottoman Empire Falls
- FUTURE: **Seventh Vial** – Rome Is Destroyed, Mystery Babylon Is Judged, Death and Famine

The Seven Vials
Against Catholicsm
[Rev. 15-16]

FUTURE: **Jews Return to God, Jerusalem is Invaded, Second Coming of Jesus Christ, Millennium Reign**

VI

APPENDIX

Time Frames and Fulfillments in the Books of Daniel and Revelation

The Ten Kingdoms of Daniel 7 and Their Dates of Collapse

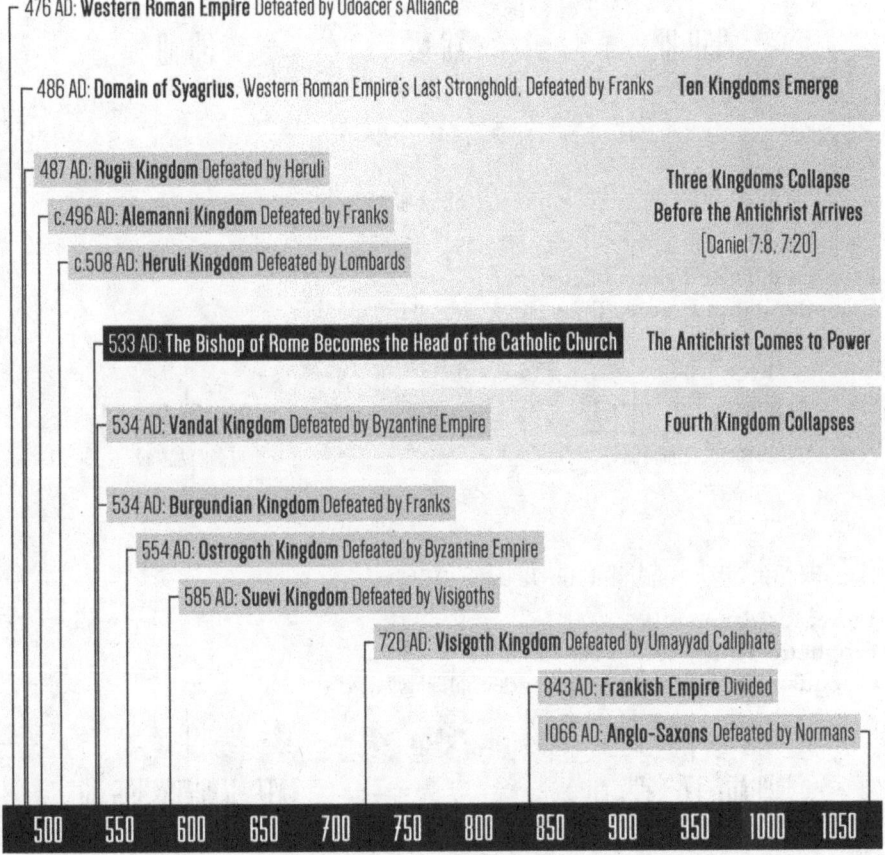

Figure 48: Illustration of the dates the ten kingdoms of Daniel 7 collapsed. Justinian I elevated the bishop of Rome to the "head of all the Holy Churches" in 533. This occurred after exactly three of the ten kingdoms had fallen, but before the fourth kingdom—the Vandals—collapsed in March of 534 AD. The Vandals, Ostrogoths, and Anglo-Saxons were the three kingdoms defeated with assistance from the papacy.

Daniel's Seventy Weeks Prophecy: The Coming of the Messiah

Verses: Daniel 9:20-27
Prophetic Time Frame: Seventy weeks
Calendar Time Frame: 490 years

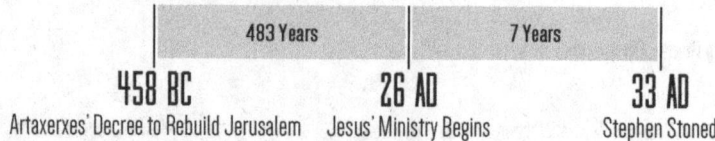

483 Years	7 Years
458 BC	**26 AD**	**33 AD**
Artaxerxes' Decree to Rebuild Jerusalem	Jesus' Ministry Begins	Stephen Stoned

The Smyrna Church Age: Diocletian's Great Persecution

Verse: Revelation 2:10
Prophetic Time Frame: Ten days
Calendar Time Frame: Ten years

10 Years

FEBRUARY 23, 303 AD — Feast of Terminalia
FEBRUARY 313 AD — Edict of Milan

The Seventh Seal: The Death of Theodosius I

Verse: Revelation 8:1
Prophetic Time Frame: Half an hour
Calendar Time Frame: Seven and a half days

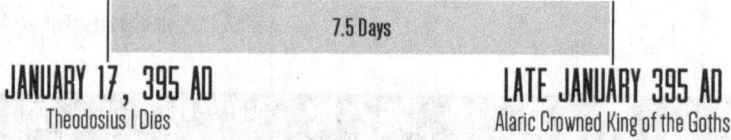

7.5 Days

JANUARY 17, 395 AD — Theodosius I Dies
LATE JANUARY 395 AD — Alaric Crowned King of the Goths

The Fifth Trumpet: Muhammad and Islam

Verses: Revelation 9:5, 9:10
Prophetic Time Frame: Five months
Calendar Time Frame: 150 years

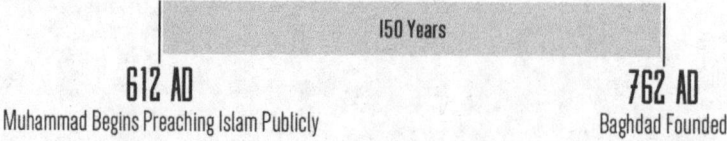

150 Years

612 AD — Muhammad Begins Preaching Islam Publicly
762 AD — Baghdad Founded

The Sixth Trumpet: The Fall of Constantinople

Verse: Revelation 9:15
Prophetic Time Frame: An hour, and a day, and a month, and a year
Calendar Time Frame: 391 years and fifteen days

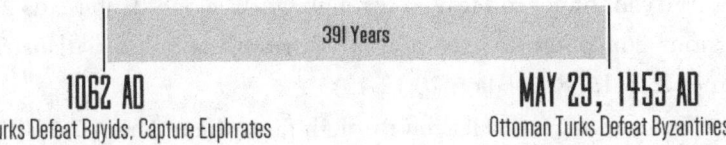

1062 AD — Seljuk Turks Defeat Buyids, Capture Euphrates
MAY 29, 1453 AD — Ottoman Turks Defeat Byzantines
391 Years

The Two Witnesses: The Fifth Lateran Council and *Ninety-Five Theses*

Verse: Revelation 11:9
Prophetic Time Frame: Three and a half days
Calendar Time Frame: Three and a half years

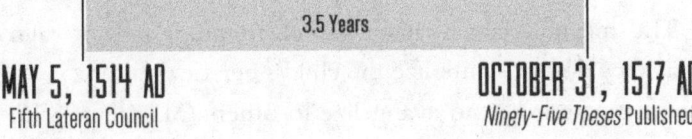

MAY 5, 1514 AD — Fifth Lateran Council
OCTOBER 31, 1517 AD — *Ninety-Five Theses* Published
3.5 Years

The Great Tribulation: Papal Temporal Power and Persecution

Verses: Daniel 7:25, 12:7, Revelation 11:2-3, 12:6, 12:14, 13:5
Prophetic Time Frame: Three and a half years, forty-two months, or 1,260 days
Calendar Time Frame: 1,260 years

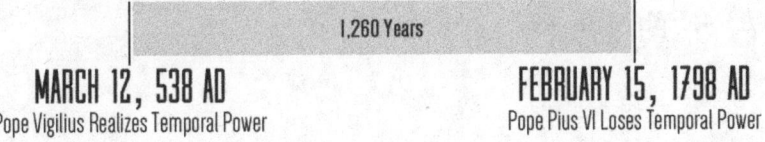

MARCH 12, 538 AD — Pope Vigilius Realizes Temporal Power
FEBRUARY 15, 1798 AD — Pope Pius VI Loses Temporal Power
1,260 Years

The Seventh Vial: Rome Destroyed and Judged by God

Verses: Revelation 18:10, 17, 19
Prophetic Time Frame: One hour
Calendar Time Frame: Fifteen days

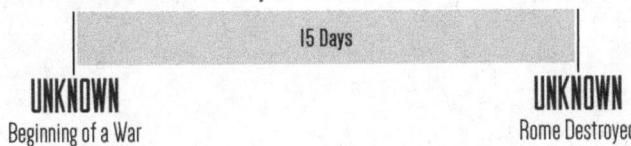

UNKNOWN — Beginning of a War
UNKNOWN — Rome Destroyed
15 Days

The Path to Salvation According to Scripture

- Belief in Jesus Christ is a requirement for salvation (Acts 16:31)
  - We cannot get to Heaven through works alone (Ephesians 2:8-9)
- Actions contribute to salvation (II Corinthians 9:7, Galatians 5:22-24, James 2:15-16, Revelation 20:12-13)
  - We cannot get to Heaven through faith alone (James 2:14-26)
- Words contribute to salvation (Romans 10:9-10, Matthew 12:36-37)
- Actions can prevent salvation (Proverbs 6:16-19, I Corinthians 6:9-10, Galatians 5:16-21, II Timothy 2:19, 3:1-5, Revelation 21:7-8)
- Baptism is a requirement for salvation (John 3:5, Mark 16:16, Acts 2:38)
  - Christians who were baptized in the Bible first believed in Jesus, then they confessed their sins and were baptized
  - This means infant baptism and christenings are not valid baptisms as they do not symbolize the child's personal faith
- Jesus commanded us to evangelize to others (Matthew 28:19, Acts 1:8, Romans 10:15)
- Regularly confess your sins to other believers (Matthew 3:2, Acts 19:18, James 5:16)
- Repent to God and ask him to forgive you from your sins (Psalms 32:5, 51:1-14, Acts 2:38, I John 1:9)
- Forgive those who wrong you (Matthew 6:14-15, 18:21-22, Luke 6:37, 17:3-4, Ephesians 4:32, Colossians 3:13)

NOTES

Chapter 1: Interpretations

1. Henry George Liddell and Robert Scott, *An Intermediate Greek-English Lexicon* (New York: American Book Company, 1882), s.v. "ἔσχατος," 319.
2. Liddell and Scott, *Intermediate Greek-English Lexicon*, s.v. "λόγος," 476–77.
3. Cornelius Tacitus, *Annals*, trans. John Jackson, vol. 4 (London: William Heinemann; Cambridge, MA: Harvard University Press, 1937), 283 (15.44).
4. Gaius Suetonius Tranquillus, "Nero," in *The Twelve Caesars*, trans. Robert Graves (London: The Folio Society, 1964), 237–42.

Chapter 2: Daniel's Dreams

1. Joshua J. Mark, "Nebuchadnezzar II," *World History Encyclopedia*, last modified November 7, 2018, accessed February 21, 2023, https://www.worldhistory.org/Nebuchadnezzar_II/.
2. Henry W. F. Saggs, "Nebuchadnezzar II," *Encyclopaedia Britannica Online*, last modified January 16, 2023, accessed January 21, 2023, https://www.britannica.com/biography/Nebuchadnezzar-II.
3. E. J. Bickerman, "Nebuchadnezzar and Jerusalem," in *Studies in Jewish and Christian History* (Leiden: Brill, 2007), 961–74.
4. *Encyclopaedia Britannica Online*, s.v. "Babylonian Captivity," by the Editors of Encyclopaedia Britannica, last modified January 6, 2023, accessed February 21, 2023, https://www.britannica.com/event/Babylonian-Captivity.
5. Jer. 52:24–28 (KJV).
6. Dan. 2:1–5 (KJV).
7. Dan. 2:5–13 (KJV).
8. Dan. 2:14–19 (KJV).
9. W. Sibley Towner, "Daniel," in *Interpretation: A Bible Commentary for Teaching and Preaching* (Westminster: John Knox Press, 1984), 36.
10. Joseph S. Exell and H. D. M. Spence-Jones, *The Pulpit Commentary*, vol. 13, *Daniel, Hosea & Joel* (Peabody, MA: Hendrickson Publishers, 1950), 71.

11. Julian Bennett, "Trajan," in *The Cambridge Ancient History*, vol. 11, *The High Empire, A.D. 70–192*, eds. Alan K. Bowman, Peter Garnsey, and Dominic Rathbone, 2nd ed. (Cambridge: Cambridge University Press, 2000), 96–131.
12. Paul-Alain Beaulieu, "The Sojourn in Arabia," in *The Reign of Nabonidus, King of Babylon 556–539 B.C.* (New Haven, CT: Yale University Press, 1989), 165.
13. Rainer Albertz, *Israel in Exile: The History and Literature of the Sixth Century B.C.E.* (Society of Biblical Literature, 2003), 69–70.
14. Beaulieu, "Sojourn in Arabia," 168–69.
15. Pierre Briant, *From Cyrus to Alexander: A History of the Persian Empire* (University Park, PA: Pennsylvania State University Press, 2002), 31.
16. Herodotus, *The Histories*, trans. A. D. Godley, rev. ed., vol. 1 (1920; repr., Cambridge, MA: Harvard University Press, 1975), 167–77 (1.127–1.135).
17. Partha Bose, *Alexander the Great's Art of Strategy* (New York: Gotham Books, 2003), 93–96.
18. Ulrich Wilcken, *Alexander the Great* (New York: W.W. Norton & Company, 1967), 146.
19. Werner Eck and Sarolta A. Takács, *The Age of Augustus*, trans. Deborah Lucas Schneider (Oxford: Blackwell Publishing, 2003), 50.
20. Cassius Dio, *Roman History*, trans. Earnest Cary, Loeb Classical Library, vol. 6 (Cambridge, MA: Harvard University Press, 1955), 313–15 (54.12.1–5).
21. Ronald Syme, "Imperator Caesar: A Study in Nomenclature," *Historia: Zeitschrift für Alte Geschichte* 7, no. 2 (1958): 172–88.
22. Edward Bishop Elliott, *Horae Apocalypticae*, 3rd ed., vol. 3 (London: Seeley, Burnside, and Seeley, 1846), 116–18 ("The Ten Horns of the Beast").
23. Paul the Deacon, *History of the Lombards*, trans. William Dudley Foulke (Philadelphia: University of Pennsylvania Press, 1974), 31–33 (1.19).
24. Gregory of Tours, *History of the Franks*, trans. Ernest Brehaut (New York: Columbia University Press, 1916), 39–41 (2.30–31).
25. Alexander Sarantis, "The Justinianic Herules: From Allied Barbarians to Roman Provincials," in *Neglected Barbarians*, ed. Florin Curta (Turnhout: Brepols Publishers, 2010), 361–402.
26. *Britannica Online*, s.v. "Vandal."
27. Edward Bishop Elliott, *Horae Apocalypticae*, 5th ed., vol. 3 (London: Seeley, Jackson, and Halliday, 1862), 120–42 ("The Ten Horns of the Beast").

Chapter 3: Daniel's Seventy Weeks

1. Jer. 25:11–12, 29:10 (KJV).
2. Dan. 9:20–23 (KJV).
3. 2 Chron. 36:22–23 (KJV).
4. Rick Lanser, "Scriptural Support for the Decree of Daniel 9:25," Bible Archaeology Report, last modified November 15, 2019, accessed February 26, 2023, https://biblearchaeology.org/abr-projects-main/the-daniel-9-24-27-project-2/4589-the-going-forth-of-artaxerxes-decree-part1.
5. Ezra 7:7–9 (KJV).
6. Luke 3:1–3 (KJV).

7 Michael P. Speidel, "Tiberius," in *Riding for Caesar: The Roman Emperor's Horseguard* (London: Batsford, 1994), 8.
8 Suetonius, "Tiberius," in *The Twelve Caesars*, trans. Robert Graves (London: The Folio Society, 1964), 121–22.
9 Matt. 3:13–17; Mark 1:9–11; Luke 3:21–23 (KJV).
10 Fred Espenak, "Phases of the Moon: 0001 to 0100," AstroPixels, last modified December 21, 2014, accessed February 4, 2024, http://astropixels.com/ephemeris/phasescat/phases0001.html.
11 Heb. 10:1–18 (KJV).
12 *Britannica Online*, s.v. "Herod."
13 *Britannica Online*, s.v. "Jerusalem."
14 *Britannica Online*, s.v. "Herod."
15 Flavius Josephus, *The Jewish War*, in *The Works of Flavius Josephus*, trans. William Whiston, vol. 1 (Philadelphia: Lippincott, Grambo & Co., 1850), 262 (2.14.4).
16 Josephus, *The Jewish War*, 262–63 (2.14.5).
17 Josephus, *The Jewish War*, 272–73 (2.17.2).
18 Josephus, *The Jewish War*, 263 (2.14.6).
19 Josephus, *The Jewish War*, 263–64 (2.14.9).
20 Josephus, *The Jewish War*, 293 (3.1.1–3).
21 Josephus, *The Jewish War*, 365 (4.10.4).
22 Josephus, *The Jewish War*, 402 (5.11.1).
23 Josephus, *The Jewish War*, 426 (6.4.1).
24 Josephus, *The Jewish War*, 428–29 (6.4.7).
25 Moshe David Herr, "The History of Eretz Israel," in *The History of Eretz Israel: The Roman-Byzantine Period*, ed. Menahem Stern (Jerusalem: Yad Izhak Ben-Zvi, 1984), 288.
26 Matt. 15:22–24 (KJV).
27 Acts 6:8 (KJV).
28 Acts 6:11–15 (KJV).
29 Acts 15:7–9 (KJV).
30 2 Sam. 6:17 (KJV).
31 Isa. 9:6–7; Matt. 1:1; Luke 1:32; John 7:42 (KJV).
32 Anathea E. Portier-Young, "Languages of Identity and Obligation: Daniel as Bilingual Book," *Vetus Testamentum* 60, no. 1 (2010): 98–115, https://sci-hub.ru/10.1163/004249310X12585232748109.
33 Bruce M. Metzger, *The Early Versions of the New Testament: Their Origin, Transmission and Limitations* (Oxford: Oxford University Press, 1977), 347.
34 Samuel Rolles Driver, "Daniel," in *An Introduction to the Literature of the Old Testament* (New York: Meridian Books, 1956), 458–83.
35 Franz Rosenthal, *Die Aramaistische Forschung* (Leiden: Brill, 1964), 60–71.
36 Kenneth A. Kitchen, "The Aramaic of Daniel," in *Notes on Some Problems in the Book of Daniel*, by Donald John Wiseman et al. (London: The Tyndale Press, 1965), 43–44.
37 Gleason L. Archer Jr., "Daniel," in *The Expositor's Bible Commentary*, vol. 7, *Daniel and the Minor Prophets*, eds. Frank E. Gaebelein et al. (Grand Rapids, MI: Zondervan, 1985), 4.

38. Martin Hengel, *Judaism and Hellenism: Studies in Their Encounter in Palestine During the Early Hellenistic Period*, vol. 1 (London: SCM Press, 1974), 267–309.
39. *Encyclopaedia Britannica*, 11th ed., vol. 22 (Cambridge: Cambridge University Press, 1911), s.v. "Porphyry," 104.
40. Archer, "Daniel," 7:13.
41. Erich S. Gruen, *The Hellenistic World and the Coming of Rome* (Berkeley: University of California Press, 1984), 431–36.
42. Jona Lendering, "Livy, *Periochae* 56-60 [58.4]," *Livius.org*, last modified July 11, 2020, accessed February 28, 2024, https://www.livius.org/sources/content/livy/livy-periochae-56-60/.
43. John Leach, *Pompey the Great* (London: Croom Helm, 1978), 93–96.
44. Duane W. Roller, *Cleopatra: A Biography* (Oxford: Oxford University Press, 2010), 150–51.
45. David Malick, "An Introduction to the Book of Daniel," Bible.org, last modified June 14, 2004, accessed February 28, 2023, https://bible.org/article/introduction-book-daniel.
46. Bruce K. Waltke, "The Date of the Book of Daniel," *Bibliotheca Sacra* 133, no. 532 (October 1976): 321–22.
47. Flavius Josephus, *Antiquities of the Jews*, in *The Works of Flavius Josephus*, trans. William Whiston, vol. 1 (Philadelphia: Lippincott, Grambo & Co., 1850), 388 (11.8.5).
48. Rabbi Adin Even-Israel Steinsaltz, "Megilla 16b," in *Koren Talmud Bavli*, Noé ed., vol. 12, *Ta'anit-Megilla* (Jerusalem: Koren Publishers, 2020), 297.

Chapter 4: The Apostasy

1. Shana Zaia, "Going Native: Šamaš-šuma-ukīn, Assyrian King of Babylon," *Iraq* 81 (2019): 247–68.
2. Jona Lendering, "Bêl-šimânni and Šamaš-eriba," *Livius.org*, last modified September 14, 2020, accessed December 7, 2023, https://www.livius.org/articles/person/bel-simanni-and-samas-eriba/.
3. J. Hampton Keathley III, *Studies in Revelation: Christ's Victory Over the Forces of Darkness* (Richardson: Biblical Studies Press, 1999), 63–72.
4. Lendering, "Livy, Periochae 56–60."
5. Jonathan Bardill, "The Symbol from the Sun, the Standard, and the Sarcophagus," in *Constantine, Divine Emperor of the Christian Golden Age* (Cambridge: Cambridge University Press, 2012), 159–70.
6. Eusebius, *The Life of the Blessed Emperor Constantine* (London: Samuel Bagster and Sons, 1845), 27 (1.29).
7. Bardill, "Symbol from the Sun," 159–70.
8. John Wesley, "Sermons, III, 71-114," in *The Works of John Wesley*, vol. 3 (Nashville: Abingdon Press, 1986), 263–64.
9. Thomas Jefferson, "To Timothy Pickering, Esq.," in *The Writings of Thomas Jefferson*, vol. 7, ed. H. A. Washington (New York: J. C. Riker, 1861), 210–11.
10. Jefferson, "To Doctor Waterhouse," in *Writings of Thomas Jefferson*, 7:257–58.
11. René Ostberg, "Holy See," *Encyclopaedia Britannica Online*, last modified July 19, 2022, accessed September 4, 2023, https://www.britannica.com/topic/Holy-See.

12 1 Cor. 3:17; 1 Cor. 6:19; Eph. 2:20-22 (KJV).
13 Joseph S. Exell and H. D. M. Spence-Jones, eds., *The Pulpit Commentary*, vol. 21, *I & II Thess., Timothy, Titus, Philemon, Hebrews, James* (Peabody, MA: Hendrickson Publishers, 1980), 24.
14 John Gill, *An Exposition of the New Testament*, vol. 3 (London: Mathews and Leigh, 1809), 256–57; Matthew Poole, *Annotations Upon the Holy Bible*, vol. 2 (London: Thomas Parkhurst, 1852), 760–61 (2 Thess. 2:4).
15 2 Thess. 2:6 (NKJV, NASB).

Chapter 5: Mystery Babylon

1 Rev. 12:3–9 (KJV).
2 "The Seven Hills of Rome," *Italy Magazine*, accessed April 11, 2023, https://www.italymagazine.com/dual-language/seven-hills-rome.
3 Poole, *Annotations Upon the Holy Bible*, 3:995 (Rev. 17).

Chapter 6: Mystery Solved

1 Theodore Alois Buckley, "The Bull of our Holy Lord, the Lord Pius, by Divine Providence Fourth Pope: Touching the Form of the Oath of the Profession of Faith," in *The Canons and Decrees of the Council of Trent* (London: George Routledge and Co., 1851), 279–80.
2 Carol Glatz, "Vatican Statistics Show Continued Growth in Number of Catholics Worldwide," *National Catholic Reporter*, March 26, 2021, accessed August 5, 2023, https://www.ncronline.org/vatican/vatican-statistics-show-continued-growth-number-catholics-worldwide.
3 William J. King, "Colors Worn By Cardinals and Bishops," Simply Catholic, accessed March 2, 2023, https://www.simplycatholic.com/colors-worn-by-cardinals-and-bishops/.
4 *Britannica Online*, s.v. "Seven Hills of Rome."
5 Gosciwit Malinowski, "Septimontium (Seven Hills) as conditio sine qua non for a City to Pretend to be a Capital," *Horizons* 8, no. 1 (2017): 3–26.
6 Matthew Henry, "Revelation XVII. Ver. 7–14," in *A Commentary on the Holy Bible*, vol. 6, *Romans to Revelation* (London: The Religious Tract Society, 1835), 635–36.
7 Dan. 2:40–43 (KJV).
8 Dan. 7:24 (KJV).
9 Elliott, *Horae Apocalypticae* (3rd ed.), 3:117 ("The Ten Horns of the Beast").
10 David A. Plaisted, "Estimates of the Number Killed by the Papacy in the Middle Ages and Later," Archive.org, March 20, 2022, accessed June 29, 2024, https://archive.org/details/estimates-of-the-number-killed-by-the-papacy-in-the-middle-ages-and-later.
11 *Britannica Online*, s.v. "Counter-Reformation."
12 Ferrell Jenkins, "English Bible Translations Through 1611 A.D.," *Truth Magazine* 4, no. 6 (March 1960): 2–5.
13 Pope Innocent III, "CXLI. Universis Christi Fidelibus Tam In Urbe Metensi Quam Ejus Dioecesi Constitutis," Patrologia Latina Database, accessed May 21, 2024, https://artflsrv04.uchicago.edu/philologic4.7/PLD/navigate/6007/2/3/143.

14. Various Authors, "The Woman Drunken with the Blood of the Saints," in *Illustrations of Popery* (New York: J. P. Callender, 1838), 387.
15. Edward Peters, ed., "Council of Toulouse, 1229," in *Heresy and Authority in Medieval Europe* (Philadelphia: University of Pennsylvania Press, 1980), 194–95.
16. Daniel Lortsch, *Historie de la Bible en France* (Paris: Agence de la Société Biblique Britanique et Etrangère, 1910), 14.
17. "Council of Constance 1414-18," Papal Encyclicals Online, February 20, 2020, accessed March 30, 2023, https://www.papalencyclicals.net/councils/ecum16.htm.
18. "John Wycliffe," *Christianity Today*, March 25, 2023, accessed March 30, 2023, https://www.christianitytoday.com/history/people/moversandshakers/john-wycliffe.html.
19. *Britannica Online*, s.v. "William Tyndale."
20. Buckley, "Concerning Prohibited Books," 284–85.
21. Buckley, "Concerning Prohibited Books," 285–86.
22. William McGavin, "The Protestant No. XXX," in *The Protestant: A Series of Essays on the Principal Points of Controversy Between the Church of Rome and the Reformed*, 10th ed., vol. 1 (Glasgow: Blackie & Son, 1837), 234.
23. Richard Frederick Littledale, "Discouragement of the Bible," in *Plain Reasons Against Joining the Church of Rome* (London: Society for Promoting Christian Knowledge, 1912), 91.
24. D. B. Ray, "Against the Bible," in *The Papal Controversy Involving the Claim of the Roman Catholic Church to be the Church of God* (St. Louis: National Baptist Publishing Company, 1892), 479.
25. James M. Gillis, "Bible Societies," in *The Catholic Encyclopedia* (1907), s.v. "Bible Societies."
26. Charles Elliott, "Scripture," in *Delineation of Roman Catholicism: Drawn from the Authentic and Acknowledged Standards of the Church of Rome*, vol. 1 (New York: G. Lane & P. P. Sanford, 1842), 63–64.
27. Pope Leo XII, *The Encyclical Letter of Pope Leo the XII: To His Venerable Brethern... with an English Translation of the Same* (Dublin: Richard Coyne, 1824), 16–17.
28. Richard P. Blakeney, *Popery in Its Social Aspect: Being a Complete Exposure of the Immorality and Intolerance of Romanism* (Toronto: The Gospel Witness, 1875), 136–37.
29. Pope Gregory XVI, "Inter Praecipuas," May 8, 1844, Papal Encyclicals Online, accessed April 10, 2023, https://www.papalencyclicals.net/greg16/g16inter.htm.
30. Pope Pius XII, "Divino Afflante Spiritu" (encyclical, September 30, 1943), The Vatican, accessed March 30, 2023, https://www.vatican.va/content/pius-xii/en/encyclicals/documents/hf_p-xii_enc_30091943_divino-afflante-spiritu.html.
31. "USCCB Approved Translations of the Sacred Scriptures for Private Use and Study by Catholics," United States Conference of Catholic Bishops, last modified July 18, 2023, accessed August 7, 2023, https://www.usccb.org/offices/new-american-bible/approved-translations-bible.
32. David Daniell, *The Bible in English: Its History and Influence* (New Haven, CT: Yale University Press, 2003), 439.

33 Second Vatican Council, "Decree on Ecumenism: Unitatis Redintegratio" (November 21, 1964), sec. 3, The Vatican, accessed August 26, 2023, https://www.vatican.va/archive/hist_councils/ii_vatican_council/documents/vat-ii_decree_19641121_unitatis-redintegratio_en.html.

34 Richard McBrien, *Lives of the Popes: The Pontiffs from St. Peter to John Paul II* (San Francisco: HarperCollins, 1997), 25.

35 Pope Paul VI, "Apostolic Constitution Indulgentiarum Doctrina" (January 1, 1967), sec. 7, The Vatican, accessed August 26, 2023, https://www.vatican.va/content/paul-vi/en/apost_constitutions/documents/hf_p-vi_apc_01011967_indulgentiarum-doctrina.html.

36 Tom Nash, "How to Get to Heaven," Catholic Answers, January 14, 2021, accessed August 8, 2023, https://www.catholic.com/qa/how-to-get-to-heaven; "Sacraments and Sacramentals," United States Conference of Catholic Bishops, last modified July 18, 2023, accessed August 8, 2023, https://www.usccb.org/prayer-and-worship/sacraments-and-sacramentals.

37 Jas. 2:14–26 (KJV).

38 *Catechism of the Catholic Church*, 2nd ed. (Vatican City: Libreria Editrice Vaticana, 1997), no. 1131, accessed November 4, 2023, https://www.vatican.va/archive/ENG0015/_INDEX.HTM.

39 Dan. 8:25 (KJV).

40 Johann Peter Kirsch, "Pius I," in *The Catholic Encyclopedia*, vol. 12 (New York: Robert Appleton Company, 1911), s.v. "Pius I."

41 McBrien, *Lives of the Popes*, 25.

42 *Compendium of the Catechism of the Catholic Church* (Vatican City: Libreria Editrice Vaticana, 2005), accessed April 13, 2023, https://www.vatican.va/archive/compendium_ccc/documents/archive_2005_compendium-ccc_en.html.

43 *Catechism of the Catholic Church*, no. 969.

44 *Catechism of the Catholic Church*, "The First Commandment."

45 Exo. 20:2–4 (NRSVCE).

46 *Catechism of the Catholic Church*, no. 2132.

47 James Butler, "Lesson XIV: On the Ten Commandments," in *The Most Rev. Dr. James Butler's Catechism* (Dublin: Richard Grace & Sons, 1846), 36–37.

48 "General Council of Trent: Twenty-Fifth Session," Papal Encyclicals Online, February 20, 2020, accessed August 27, 2023, https://www.papalencyclicals.net/councils/trent/twenty-fifth-session.htm.

49 "The Fourth Lateran Council: 1215 A.D.," Papal Encyclicals Online, February 20, 2020, accessed August 27, 2023, https://www.papalencyclicals.net/councils/ecum12-2.htm.

50 Bruce W. Frier, ed., *The Codex of Justinian: A New Annotated Translation with Parallel Latin and Greek Text*, trans. Fred H. Blume, vol. 1 (Cambridge: Cambridge University Press, 2016), 223 (1.6.1–3).

51 Second Vatican Council, "Constitution on the Sacred Liturgy: Sacrosanctum Concilium" (December 4, 1963), The Vatican, accessed March 4, 2023, https://www.vatican.va/archive/hist_councils/ii_vatican_council/documents/vat-ii_const_19631204_sacrosanctum-concilium_en.html.

52 Buckley, "Concerning Prohibited Books," 284–86; *Compendium of the CCC*; Innocent III, "CXLI. Universis Christi Fidelibus."

Chapter 7: The Antichrist in Prophecy
1. Albert Barnes, *Notes on the Epistles to the Thessalonians, to Timothy, Titus, and Philemon* (Edinburgh: Gall & Inglis, 1840), 103–05 (2 Thess. 2).
2. Dan. 7:8, 7:20, 7:25; 2 Thess. 2:4 (KJV).

Chapter 8: The Antichrist Revealed
1. Frier, *The Codex of Justinian*, 1:33–35 (1.1.8.11).
2. *Britannica Online*, s.v. "Papacy."
3. Tertullian, "On Prescription Against Heretics," in *The Ante-Nicene Fathers*, eds. Alexander Roberts and James Donaldson, vol. 3 (New York: Charles Scribner's Sons, 1926), 243–63 (chap. 36).
4. Pope Innocent III, *Decretalium D. Gregorii Papae IX*, bk. 1, tit. 7, chap. 3, The Latin Library, accessed August 30, 2023, https://www.thelatinlibrary.com/gregdecretals1.html.
5. Pope Boniface VIII, "Unam Sanctam" (papal bull, November 18, 1302), Papal Encyclicals Online, accessed August 29, 2023, https://www.papalencyclicals.net/bon08/b8unam.htm.
6. Henry Grattan Guinness, "The Daniel Foreview of Romanism," in *Romanism and the Reformation* (London: Hodder and Stoughton, 1887), 25–26.
7. Guilielmi Barclaii, "Depotestate Papae in Principes Cristianos," in *De Potestate Papae: An & Quatenus in Reges & Principes Seculares ius & Imperium Habeat* (Franciscum Du Bois & Iacobum Garnich, 1609), 218–19; "Lying for the Glory of God," *The Protestant Magazine* 3, no. 1 (1911): 13.
8. Pope Leo XIII, "Praeclara Gratulationis Publicae" (apostolic letter, June 20, 1894), Papal Encyclicals Online, accessed August 29, 2023, https://www.papalencyclicals.net/leo13/l13praec.htm.
9. "Foreign Intelligence," *Evangelical Christendom*, January 1, 1895, 15.
10. E. Michaud, "Une Nouvelle Transubstantiation Papiste," *Le Catholique National*, no. 18 (July 13, 1895): 74–75.
11. Sydney F. Smith, "Does the Pope Claim to be God?," in *Publications of the Catholic Truth Society*, vol. 29 (London: Catholic Truth Society, 1896), 11.
12. Hieronymo Dal-Gal, *Saint Pius X: The New Italian Life of the Saint*, trans. Thomas F. Murray (Dublin: M. H. Gill and Son Ltd., 1954), 104–07.
13. *Le catholique national: organe des catholiques-chrétiennes de la Suisse romande*, Swisscovery Universität und PH Bern, accessed December 21, 2023, https://slsp-ube.primo.exlibrisgroup.com/permalink/41SLSP_UBE/17e6d97/alma99116695770805511.
14. Smith, "Does the Pope Claim to be God?," 10.
15. Michaud, "Une Nouvelle Transubstantiation Papiste," 74–75.
16. Don A. Schanche, "No Forgiveness 'Directly from God,' Pope Says," *Los Angeles Times*, December 12, 1984, 11.

17 Pope John Paul II, "Post-Synodal Apostolic Exhortation Reconciliatio et Paenitentia" (December 2, 1984), The Vatican, accessed August 30, 2023, https://www.vatican.va/content/john-paul-ii/en/apost_exhortations/documents/hf_jp-ii_exh_02121984_reconciliatio-et-paenitentia.html.
18 Herwig Wolfram, *History of the Goths*, trans. Thomas J. Dunlap (Berkeley: University of California Press, 1988), 278.
19 Peter Heather, *The Goths* (Oxford: Blackwell Publishers, 1996), 154.
20 Thomas S. Burns, *A History of the Ostrogoths* (Bloomington: Indiana University Press, 1984), 71.
21 Wolfram, *History of the Goths*, 279.
22 Walter Goffart, *The Narrators of Barbarian History (A.D. 550-800): Jordanes, Gregory of Tours, Bede, and Paul the Deacon* (Princeton: Princeton University Press, 1988), 68.
23 Heather, *The Goths*, 155.
24 Burns, *History of the Ostrogoths*, 72.
25 Gregory of Tours, *History of the Franks*, 39–41 (2.30–31).
26 Guy Halsall, *Barbarian Migrations and the Roman West, 376–568* (Cambridge: Cambridge University Press, 2007), 287.
27 Sarantis, "The Justinianic Herules," 361–402.
28 Edward Gibbon, *The History of the Decline and Fall of the Roman Empire*, vol. 3 (London: Strahan & Cadell, 1781), 440–42.
29 Peter Heather, *The Fall of the Roman Empire: A New History of Rome and the Barbarians* (Oxford: Oxford University Press, 2005), 396–98.
30 John Moorhead, *Justinian* (London: Longman, 1994), 68.
31 J. A. S. Evans, *The Age of Justinian: The Circumstances of Imperial Power* (London: Routledge, 1996), 125.
32 Chris Wickham, *The Inheritance of Rome: Illuminating the Dark Ages, 400–1000* (New York: Viking, 2009), 87.
33 Procopius, *Procopius in Seven Volumes*, trans. H. B. Dewing, vol. 2 (London: William Heinemann, 1961), 219–71 (4.2-7); David A. Warner, "Renovatio Imperii Romanorum," in *Medieval Germany: An Encyclopedia*, ed. John M. Jeep (New York: Garland, 2001), 469–70.
34 Klemens Löffler, "Ostrogoths," in *The Catholic Encyclopedia* (1913), s.v. "Ostrogoths."
35 Edward James, *Europe's Barbarians, AD 200–600* (London: Routledge, 2014), 83–87.
36 Procopius, *Procopius in Seven Volumes*, trans. H. B. Dewing, vol. 3 (London: William Heinemann, 1961), 143 (5.14.4–6).
37 Heather, *Fall of the Roman Empire*, 402.
38 J. Walton Barker, "Belisarius," *Encyclopaedia Britannica Online*, last modified February 25, 2023, https://www.britannica.com/biography/Belisarius; Richard Ernest Dupuy and Trevor Nevitt Dupuy, "The Opening of the Middle Ages: 400–600," in *The Harper Encyclopedia of Military History: From 3500 BC to the Present* (New York: HarperCollins, 1993), 203.
39 Eamon Duffy, *Saints and Sinners: A History of the Popes* (New Haven, CT: Yale University Press, 1997), 27.

40 Evans, *The Age of Justinian*, 189.
41 Procopius, *Procopius in Seven Volumes*, trans. H. B. Dewing, vol. 5 (London: William Heinemann, 1962), 407–19 (8.35).
42 Frank Barlow, *The English Church, 1066–1154: A History of the Anglo-Norman Church* (London: Longman, 1979), 61.
43 Ian W. Walker, *Harold: The Last Anglo-Saxon King* (Sutton: Stroud, 1997), 112.
44 N. J. Higham, *The Death of Anglo-Saxon England* (Stroud: Sutton Publishing, 1997), 134.
45 Duffy, *Saints and Sinners*, 121.
46 H. E. J. Cowdrey, *Pope Gregory VII, 1073–1085* (Oxford: Clarendon Press, 1998), 461.
47 David C. Douglas, *William the Conqueror: The Norman Impact Upon England* (Berkeley: University of California Press, 1964), 189.
48 Barlow, *The English Church*, 61.
49 Frier, *The Codex of Justinian*, 1:33–35 (1.1.8.11).
50 Elliott, *Horae Apocalypticae* (5th ed.), 3:167–72 ("Uprooting of Three Horns, Out of the Ten, Before the Beast").
51 Acts 13:14, 13:27, 13:42–44, 15:21, 16:13, 17:2, 18:4 (KJV).
52 Philip Schaff, *History of the Christian Church*, vol. 2, *History of Medieval Christianity* (New York: Charles Scribner & Co., 1867), 378–86.
53 Carl Joseph Hefele, *A History of the Councils of the Church*, trans. Henry Nutcombe Oxenham, vol. 2 (Edinburgh: T. & T. Clark, 1896), 316.
54 James Gibbons, *The Christian Sabbath* (Baltimore: The Catholic Mirror, 1893), 29.
55 "The Unexpected Origins of Popular Christmas Traditions," CBS News, December 25, 2018, accessed September 8, 2023, https://www.cbsnews.com/news/the-unexpected-pagan-origins-of-popular-christmas-traditions/.
56 Heather McDougall, "The Pagan Roots of Easter," *The Guardian*, April 3, 2010, accessed September 8, 2023, https://www.theguardian.com/commentisfree/belief/2010/apr/03/easter-pagan-symbolism.
57 Patrick J. Kiger, "How the Early Catholic Church Christianized Halloween," History, September 6, 2023, accessed September 8, 2023, https://www.history.com/news/halloween-samhain-celts-catholic-church.
58 Arnie Seipel, "The Dark Origins of Valentine's Day," NPR, February 13, 2011 (updated February 14, 2022), accessed September 8, 2023, https://www.npr.org/2011/02/14/133693152/the-dark-origins-of-valentines-day.
59 Bede, *The Ecclesiastical History of the English Nation*, trans. L. Gidley (London: James Parker, 1870), 87–90 (1.30).
60 R. A. Markus, "Gregory the Great and a Papal Missionary Strategy," in *Studies in Church History*, vol. 6, *The Mission of the Church and the Propagation of the Faith* (Cambridge: Cambridge University Press, 1970), 29–38.
61 *Britannica Online*, s.v. "Gregorian calendar."
62 *Code of Canon Law*, can. 331, accessed September 7, 2023, https://www.vatican.va/archive/cod-iuris-canonici/eng/documents/cic_lib2-cann330-367_en.html#SECTION_I.

⁶³ Henry Chadwick, "The Early Christian Community," in *The Oxford Illustrated History of Christianity*, ed. John McManners (Oxford: Oxford University Press, 1990), 56; Duffy, *Saints and Sinners*, 27.

Chapter 9: The Great Tribulation

1. Jonathan Ben-Dov, "A 360-Day Administrative Year in Ancient Israel: Judahite Portable Calendars and the Flood Account," *Harvard Theological Review* 114, no. 4 (2021): 431–50, https://www.cambridge.org/core/journals/harvard-theological-review/article/360day-administrative-year-in-ancient-israel-judahite-portable-calendars-and-the-flood-account/8F5696178CD94A096EA16DC811FC787D.
2. Elon Gilad, "The Hebrew Calendar: A Marvel of Ancient Astronomy and Math," *Haaretz*, September 25, 2014, accessed January 23, 2023, https://www.haaretz.com/jewish/2014-09-25/ty-article/.premium/the-secrets-of-the-hebrew-calendar/0000017f-db3f-df62-a9ff-dfff86dd0000.
3. Keum Young Ahn et al., "538 A.D. and the Transition from Pagan Roman Empire to Holy Roman Empire: Justinian's Metamorphosis from Chief of Staffs to Theologian," *International Journal of Humanities and Social Science* 7, no. 1 (2017): 44–85.
4. John McClintock and James Strong, "Pius VI," in *Cyclopaedia of Biblical, Theological, and Ecclesiastical Literature*, vol. 8 (New York: Harper & Brothers, 1894), 245–46.

Chapter 10: The Second Beast

1. Frier, *The Codex of Justinian*, 1:33–35 (1.1.8.11).
2. Joseph Henry Thayer, *A Greek-English Lexicon of the New Testament* (New York: American Book Company, 1889), s.v. "προσκυνέω," 548.
3. John de Marchi, *The Immaculate Heart: The True Story of Fatima* (New York: Farrar, Straus and Young, 1952), 130–39.
4. Jeffrey S. Bennett, *When the Sun Danced: Myth, Miracles, and Modernity in Early Twentieth-Century Portugal* (Charlottesville: University of Virginia Press, 2012), 69–123.
5. de Marchi, *Immaculate Heart*, 150.
6. de Marchi, *Immaculate Heart*, 62.
7. de Marchi, *Immaculate Heart*, 182–219.
8. Edward D. Andrews, "Papyrus 115 (P. Oxy. 4499, P115) Is a Fragmented Manuscript of the New Testament Containing Parts of the Book of Revelation," *Christian Publishing House Blog*, September 24, 2020, accessed October 8, 2023, https://christianpublishinghouse.co/2020/09/24/papyrus-115-p-oxy-4499-p115-is-a-fragmented-manuscript-of-the-new-testament-containing-parts-of-the-book-of-revelation/.
9. Irenaeus, *Five Books of S. Irenaeus Bishop of Lyons Against Heresies*, trans. John Keble (Oxford: James Parker and Co., 1872), 519 (5.30.1).
10. W. Boyd Carpenter, "The Revelation of St. John the Divine," in *A New Testament Commentary for English Readers*, ed. Charles John Ellicott, vol. 3 (London: Cassell and Company, 1897), 596–600 (Rev. 13).
11. Carpenter, "Revelation," 3:599–600 (Rev. 13).

12 Joseph Benson, *The New Testament of Our Lord and Saviour Jesus Christ: With Critical, Explanatory, and Practical Notes* (New York: Lane & Tippett, 1847), 760–62 (Rev. 13).

13 Benson, *The New Testament*, 762 (Rev. 13).

14 "Third Lateran Council – 1179 A.D.," Papal Encyclicals Online, last modified February 20, 2020, accessed October 10, 2023, https://www.papalencyclicals.net/councils/ecum11.htm.

15 Thomas A. Fudge, *The Crusade Against Heretics in Bohemia, 1418–1437: Sources and Documents for the Hussite Crusades* (Aldershot: Routledge, 2022), 49–52.

16 "The Jesuits," General Curia of the Society of Jesus, last modified August 7, 2023, accessed October 11, 2023, https://www.jesuits.global/about-us/the-jesuits/.

17 Richard Wilson, "The Pilot's Thumb: *Macbeth* and the Jesuits," in *The Lancashire Witches: Histories and Stories*, ed. Robert Poole (Manchester: Manchester University Press, 2002), 136.

18 Robert A. Maryks and Jonathan Wright, eds., *Jesuit Survival and Restoration: A Global History, 1773–1900* (Leiden: Brill, 2014).

19 Bertrand M. Roehner, "Jesuits and the State: A Comparative Study of Their Expulsions (1590–1990)," *Religion* 27, no. 2 (1997): 165–82.

20 *Funk & Wagnalls New Encyclopedia*, ed. Leon L. Bram (New York: Funk & Wagnalls, 1983), 15:36, s.v. "Jesuits."

21 J. E. C. Shepherd, *The Babington Plot: Jesuit Intrigue in Elizabethan England* (Springfield, OH: Wittenberg Publications, 1987), 12.

22 Roehner, "Jesuits and the State," 165–82.

23 Valerie Pirie, "Clement XIV," in *The Triple Crown: An Account of the Papal Conclaves from the Fifteenth Century to Modern Times* (London: Spring Books, 1965), 267–75.

24 F. L. Cross and E. A. Livingstone, eds., *The Oxford Dictionary of the Christian Church*, 3rd ed. rev. (Oxford: Oxford University Press, 2005), 366.

25 Malachi Martin, "Papal Objections," in *The Jesuits: The Society of Jesus and the Betrayal of the Roman Catholic Church* (New York: Simon & Schuster, 1987), 44.

26 Walter Schellenberg, *Hitler's Secret Service (The Labyrinth)*, trans. Louis Hagen (New York: Pyramid Books, 1958), 31–32.

27 David Brady, "The Contribution of British Writers Between 1560 and 1830 to the Interpretation of Revelation 13.16–18: (the Number of the Beast)," *Beiträge zur Geschichte der Biblischen Exegese* 27 (1983): 202.

28 Francisco Ribera, *Sacrum Beati Ioannis Apostoli, & Evangelistiae Apocalypsin Commentarij* (Antwerp: Martin Nutius, 1590).

29 Le Roy Edwin Froom, *The Prophetic Faith of Our Fathers*, vol. 3 (Washington, DC: Review and Herald Press, 1950), 303–24.

30 Washington Wilks, *Edward Irving: An Ecclesiastical and Literary Biography* (London: William Freeman, 1854), 273.

31 Froom, *Prophetic Faith of Our Fathers*, 3:257.

32 Edward Miller, *The History and Doctrines of Irvingism*, vol. 2 (London: C. Kegan Paul & Co., 1878), 8.

33 Thayer, *Greek-English Lexicon*, s.v. "γενεά," 112.

34 Drue Cressener, *The Judgments of God upon the Roman-Catholick Church from Its First Rigid Laws for Universal Conformity to It unto Its Last End* (London: Richard Chiswell, 1689), n.p. (Preface).
35 Irenaeus, *Against Heresies*, 521 (5.30.3).
36 Clement of Alexandria, "The Rich Man's Salvation," in *Clement of Alexandria*, trans. G. W. Butterworth (London: William Heinemann, 1919), 357.
37 Victorinus, "Commentary on the Apocalypse," in *The Ante-Nicene Fathers*, eds. Alexander Roberts and James Donaldson, vol. 7 (New York: Charles Scribner's Sons, 1926), 353.
38 Le Roy Edwin Froom, "V. Grotius—First Protestant to Adopt Alcazar's Preterism," in *The Prophetic Faith of Our Fathers*, vol. 2 (Washington, DC: Review and Herald Press, 1948), 521–24.
39 Moses Stuart, *A Commentary on the Apocalypse* (Andover, MA: Allen, Morrill and Wardwell, 1845), 464.
40 "Stèle," Musée du Louvre, last modified October 31, 2023, accessed April 8, 2024, https://collections.louvre.fr/en/ark:/53355/cl010174435.

Chapter II: The Seven Churches

1 Irenaeus, *Against Heresies*, 521 (5.30.3).
2 Justin Martyr, *Justin Martyr's Dialogue with Trypho the Jew*, trans. Henry Brown (Cambridge: Deightons, 1846), 181 (sec. 81).
3 Acts 26:14–18; Rom. 1:1 (KJV).
4 Cassius Dio, *Roman History*, trans. Earnest Cary, Loeb Classical Library, vol. 8 (Cambridge, MA: Harvard University Press, 1925), 349–51 (67.14.1–3).
5 Cassius Dio, *Roman History*, vol. 8 (1925), 361 (68.1.2).
6 Irenaeus, *Against Heresies*, 208–09 (3.3.4).
7 Thayer, *Greek-English Lexicon*, s.v. "ἀφίημι," 88–89.
8 Guillermo Altares, "Massacring Christians: A Stain on the Legacy of Marcus Aurelius as Rome's 'Enlightened Emperor'," *El País*, August 20, 2022, accessed September 27, 2023, https://english.elpais.com/culture/2022-08-20/massacring-christians-a-stain-on-the-legacy-of-marcus-aurelius-as-romes-enlightened-emperor.html.
9 Abel Mordechai Bibliowicz, *Jewish-Christian Relations: The First Centuries* (Jacksonville, FL: Movement Publishing, 2016), 42.
10 John Foxe, "Fourth Primitive Persecution," in *Foxe's Book of Martyrs* (London: Sherwood, Jones, and Co., 1824), 14.
11 James Rives, "The Decree of Decius and the Religion of Empire," *Journal of Roman Studies* 89 (1999): 135–54.
12 Alan K. Bowman, Peter Garnsey, and Averil Cameron, eds., *The Cambridge Ancient History*, vol. 12, *The Crisis of Empire, AD 193–337* (Cambridge: Cambridge University Press, 2005), 42–43.
13 Michael Gaddis, *There Is No Crime for Those Who Have Christ: Religious Violence in the Christian Roman Empire* (Berkeley: University of California Press, 2005), 29–67.
14 Num. 22–24 (KJV).
15 *Britannica Online*, s.v. "Roman Catholicism."
16 1 Kings 16:31–32, 18:4 (KJV).

17. *Britannica Online*, s.v. "Christianity."
18. "Where the Word 'Christian' Really Comes From," *Relevant Magazine*, June 5, 2023, accessed October 4, 2023, https://relevantmagazine.com/faith/where-christian-name-really-came/.
19. Gill, *Exposition of the New Testament*, 3:711.
20. Robert H. Mounce, *The Book of Revelation*, rev. ed., The New International Commentary on the New Testament (Grand Rapids: Wm. B. Eerdmans, 1997), 109.
21. Gordon D. Fee, *Revelation*, New Covenant Commentary Series (Eugene, OR: Cascade Books, 2011), 58.
22. G. K. Beale, *The Book of Revelation: A Commentary on the Greek Text*, The New International Greek Testament Commentary (Grand Rapids: Wm. B. Eerdmans, 1999), 303.

Chapter 12: The Seven Seals

1. Liddell and Scott, *Intermediate Greek-English Lexicon*, s.v. "στέφανοι," 745.
2. Carpenter, "Revelation," 3:559 (Rev. 6).
3. Bennett, "Trajan," 96–131.
4. *Britannica Online*, s.v. "Pax Romana."
5. Géza Alföldy, "The Crisis of the Third Century as Seen by Contemporaries," *Greek, Roman, and Byzantine Studies* 15, no. 1 (1974): 89–111.
6. Pliny the Elder, *The Natural History of Pliny*, trans. John Bostock and H. T. Riley, vol. 4 (London: Henry G. Bohn, 1856), 32–35 (18.20).
7. Edward Bishop Elliott, *Horae Apocalypticae*, 5th ed., vol. 1 (London: Seeley, Jackson, and Halliday, 1862), 164–65 ("The Third Seal").
8. Elliott, *Horae Apocalypticae* (5th ed.), 1:170 ("The Third Seal").
9. Olivier Hekster and Nicholas Zair, "Law and Citizenship," in *Rome and Its Empire, AD 193–284*, Debates and Documents in Ancient History (Edinburgh: Edinburgh University Press, 2008), 47–48.
10. Jeff Desjardins, "Currency and the Collapse of the Roman Empire," Visual Capitalist, February 19, 2016, accessed August 15, 2023, https://www.visualcapitalist.com/currency-and-the-collapse-of-the-roman-empire/.
11. *The Digest of Justinian*, ed. Alan Watson, vol. 1 (Philadelphia: University of Pennsylvania Press, 1985), 16 (1.5.17).
12. Cassius Dio, *Roman History*, trans. Earnest Cary, Loeb Classical Library, vol. 9 (Cambridge, MA: Harvard University Press, 1955), 297 (78.9.5).
13. Edward Gibbon, *The History of the Decline and Fall of the Roman Empire*, vol. 1 (London: Strahan & Cadell, 1781), 236.
14. Clifford Ando, *Imperial Ideology and Provincial Loyalty in the Roman Empire* (Berkeley: University of California Press, 2013).
15. Albert Barnes, *Notes, Explanatory and Practical, on the Book of Revelation* (New York: Harper & Brothers, 1860), 158–96 (Rev. 6).
16. "Severus Alexander," in *Scriptores Historiae Augustae*, trans. David Magie, vol. 2 (London: William Heinemann, 1924), 255 (39.3–4).

17. *The Digest of Justinian*, ed. Alan Watson, vol. 4 (Philadelphia: University of Pennsylvania Press, 1985), 433 (50.6.6.3).
18. "Aurelian," in *Scriptores Historiae Augustae*, trans. David Magie, vol. 3 (London: William Heinemann, 1932), 263 (35.1).
19. Barnes, *Notes, Explanatory and Practical, on the Book of Revelation*, 177–80 (Rev. 6).
20. Elliott, *Horae Apocalypticae* (5th ed.), 1:169–90 ("The Third Seal").
21. *Britannica Online*, s.v. "Vulgate."
22. Elliott, *Horae Apocalypticae* (5th ed.), 1:201–03 ("The Fourth Seal").
23. Udo Hartmann, "The Third-Century 'Crisis'," in *The Encyclopedia of Ancient Battles*, vol. 3, eds. Michael Whitby and Harry Sidebottom (Malden, MA: Wiley-Blackwell, 2017), 1047–67.
24. Desjardins, "Currency and the Collapse."
25. Desjardins, "Currency and the Collapse."
26. Rev. 6:8 (ESV, LSV, NRSV).
27. Rev. 6:8 (NIV, NASB, CSB).
28. Rev. 6:8 (GNT, NLT, CEV).
29. Thayer, *Greek-English Lexicon*, s.v. "θάνατος," 282–83.
30. Thayer, *Greek-English Lexicon*, s.v. "χλωρός," 669.
31. Sabine R. Huebner, "The 'Plague of Cyprian': A Revised View of the Origin and Spread of a 3rd-c. CE Pandemic," *Journal of Roman Archaeology* 34, no. 1 (2021): 151–74.
32. "The Two Gallieni," in *Scriptores Historiae Augustae*, trans. David Magie, vol. 3 (London: William Heinemann, 1932), 27 (5.5).
33. Kyle Harper, "Solving the Mystery of an Ancient Roman Plague," *The Atlantic*, November 1, 2017, accessed August 13, 2023, https://www.theatlantic.com/science/archive/2017/11/solving-the-mystery-of-an-ancient-roman-plague/543528/.
34. Barnes, *Notes, Explanatory and Practical, on the Book of Revelation*, 162–96 (Rev. 6).
35. Elliott, *Horae Apocalypticae* (5th ed.), 1:190–203 ("The Fourth Seal").
36. Norman Douglas, *Birds and Beasts of the Greek Anthology* (Florence: Tipografia Giuntina, 1927), 18.
37. N. B. Kinnear, "The Past and Present Distribution of the Lion in South Eastern Asia," *Journal of the Bombay Natural History Society* 27 (1886): 33–39.
38. V. G. Heptner and A. A. Sludskii, *Mammals of the Soviet Union*, trans. P. M. Rao, vol. 2, pt. 2 (New Delhi: Amerind Publishing Co., 1992), 83–95.
39. *Britannica Online*, s.v. "Domestic reforms of Diocletian."
40. Gaddis, *There Is No Crime for Those Who Have Christ*, 29–67.
41. Gibbon, *Decline and Fall*, 1:676–704.
42. Barnes, *Notes, Explanatory and Practical, on the Book of Revelation*, 162–96 (Rev. 6).
43. Benson, *The New Testament*, 728–29 (Rev. 6).
44. Rev. 2:11 (KJV).
45. *Britannica Online*, s.v. "Edict of Milan."
46. Elliott, *Horae Apocalypticae* (5th ed.), 1:321–26 ("The Half-Hour's Silence In Heaven").
47. Donald Senior et al., eds., *The Catholic Study Bible* (New York: Oxford University Press, 1990), 398–99.

Chapter 13: The Seven Trumpets

1. *Britannica Online*, s.v. "Alaric."
2. Michael Kulikowski, *The Tragedy of Empire: From Constantine to the Destruction of Roman Italy* (Cambridge, MA: The Belknap Press of Harvard University Press, 2019), 122.
3. Kulikowski, *Tragedy of Empire*, 135.
4. Thomas S. Burns, *Barbarians within the Gates of Rome: A Study of Roman Military Policy and the Barbarians, ca. 375–425 A.D.* (Bloomington: Indiana University Press, 1994), 215.
5. Burns, *Barbarians within the Gates of Rome*, 224–25.
6. Penny MacGeorge, *Late Roman Warlords* (Oxford: Oxford University Press, 2002), 171.
7. John Julius Norwich, *Byzantium: The Early Centuries* (London: Viking, 1988), 134.
8. A. D. Lee, *From Rome to Byzantium AD 363 to 565: The Transformation of Ancient Rome* (Edinburgh: Edinburgh University Press, 2013), 113.
9. Thomas Hodgkin, "Alaric," in *The Encyclopaedia Britannica*, 11th ed., vol. 1 (Cambridge: Cambridge University Press, 1911), 470–72.
10. James, *Europe's Barbarians*, 57.
11. Claudian, "The Gothic War," in *Claudian*, trans. Maurice Platnauer (London: William Heinemann, 1922), 139.
12. Charles Daubuz, *A Perpetual Commentary on the Revelation of St. John* (London: Charles Daubuz, 1730), 278–81 (Vision 2, pt. 3, trumpet 1).
13. Carpenter, "Revelation," 3:572 (Rev. 8).
14. Benson, *The New Testament*, 734–39 (Rev. 8).
15. Elliott, *Horae Apocalypticae* (5th ed.), 3:358–65 ("The Third Part").
16. Karl Julius Beloch, *Die Bevölkerung der griechisch-römischen Welt* (Leipzig: Duncker & Humblot, 1886), 507; Bruce W. Frier, "Demography," in *The Cambridge Ancient History*, vol. 11, *The High Empire, A.D. 70–192*, eds. Alan K. Bowman, Peter Garnsey, and Dominic Rathbone (Cambridge: Cambridge University Press, 2000), 827–54.
17. Walter Scheidel, "Demography," in *The Cambridge Economic History of the Greco-Roman World*, eds. Walter Scheidel, Ian Morris, and Richard Saller (Cambridge: Cambridge University Press, 2007), 38–86.
18. Kees Klein Goldewijk et al., "The HYDE 3.1 Spatially Explicit Database of Human Induced Land Use Change over the Past 12,000 Years," *Global Ecology and Biogeography* 20, no. 1 (2011): 73–86.
19. Colin McEvedy and Richard Jones, *Atlas of World Population History* (Harmondsworth: Penguin Books, 1978), 342.
20. Frier, "Demography," 827–54; Goldewijk et al., "HYDE 3.1 Spatially Explicit Database," 73–86; Kyle Harper, *The Fate of Rome: Climate, Disease, and the End of an Empire* (Princeton: Princeton University Press, 2017), 29–38; McEvedy and Jones, *Atlas of World Population History*, 342; J. C. Russell, "Late Ancient and Medieval Population," *Transactions of the American Philosophical Society* 48, pt. 3 (1958): 1–152; United States Census Bureau, "Historical Estimates of World Population," last modified December 5, 2022, accessed November 7, 2023,

https://www.census.gov/data/tables/time-series/demo/international-programs/historical-est-worldpop.html.
21. Roger Collins, "The Vandal Conquest and Vandal Rule, 429–534," in *The Cambridge Ancient History*, vol. 14, *Late Antiquity: Empire and Successors, A.D. 425–600*, eds. Averil Cameron, Bryan Ward-Perkins, and Michael Whitby (Cambridge: Cambridge University Press, 2000), 553.
22. Thomas Brown, "The Transformation of the Roman Mediterranean, 400–900," in *The Oxford History of Medieval Europe*, ed. George Holmes (Oxford: Oxford University Press, 1988), 3.
23. Collins, "Vandal Conquest and Vandal Rule," 553.
24. Averil Cameron, "The Vandal Conquest and Vandal Rule (A.D. 429–534)," in *The Cambridge Ancient History*, vol. 14, *Late Antiquity: Empire and Successors, A.D. 425–600*, eds. Averil Cameron, Bryan Ward-Perkins, and Michael Whitby (Cambridge: Cambridge University Press, 2000), 553–59.
25. J. Patout Burns and Robin M. Jensen, *Christianity in Roman Africa: The Development of Its Practices and Beliefs* (Grand Rapids, MI: Wm. B. Eerdmans Publishing, 2014), 64.
26. *Online Etymology Dictionary*, s.v. "Mediterranean," accessed October 21, 2023, https://www.etymonline.com/word/Mediterranean#etymonline_v_12521.
27. John Bagnell Bury, "Chapter II: Ricimer the Patrician," in *A History of the Later Roman Empire: From Arcadius to Irene (395 A.D. to 800 A.D.)* (London: Macmillan and Co., 1889), 234–35.
28. *Online Etymology Dictionary*, s.v. "Vandal."
29. Quodvultdeus of Carthage, *The Creedal Homilies*, trans. Thomas Macy Finn, Ancient Christian Writers 60 (New York: Newman Press, 2004).
30. Thomas Dennis Rock, "The Mystical Woman," in *The Mystical Woman and the Cities of the Nations* (London: William MacIntosh, 1867), 22–23.
31. Philip Schaff, "The Nicene Creed," in *The Creeds of Christendom, with a History and Critical Notes*, vol. 1 (New York: Harper & Brothers, 1877), 28–29.
32. Gibbon, *Decline and Fall*, 3:413–14.
33. R. Burgess, "The Gallic Chronicle of 511: A New Critical Edition with a Brief Introduction," in *Society and Culture in Late Antique Gaul: Revisiting the Sources*, eds. R. W. Mathisen and D. Shantzer (London: Routledge, 2017), 85–100.
34. Gibbon, *Decline and Fall*, 3:413–17.
35. Jordanes, *The Origin and Deeds of the Goths*, trans. Charles C. Mierow (Princeton, NJ: Princeton University Press, 1908), 64 (40).
36. Jordanes, *Origin and Deeds of the Goths*, 57 (35).
37. Isa. 13:1, 13:10; Isa. 34:4–5; Eze. 32:7–8 (KJV).
38. Rev. 6:12–14 (KJV).
39. E. Cobham Brewer, *Dictionary of Phrase and Fable* (Philadelphia: Henry Altemus Company, 1898), s.v. "Last of the Romans."
40. Priscus of Panium, *The Fragmentary History of Priscus: Attila, the Huns and the Roman Empire, AD 430–476*, trans. John Given (Merchantville, NJ: Arx Publishing, 2014), 125–27.
41. Gibbon, *Decline and Fall*, 3:429–31.
42. Gibbon, *Decline and Fall*, 3:490–92.
43. Gibbon, *Decline and Fall*, 3:492–94.

44 *Britannica Online*, s.v. "Senate: Roman History."
45 Constantine-François Volney, "Section V: Of the Locusts," in *Travels Through Syria and Egypt*, 2nd ed., vol. 1 (London: G. G. J. and J. Robinson, 1788), 306–07.
46 Elliott, *Horae Apocalypticae* (5th ed.), 1:433 ("The Local Origin of the First Woe").
47 Food and Agriculture Organization of the United Nations, "Desert Locust Upsurge (2019–2021)," accessed May 22, 2024, https://www.fao.org/ag/locusts/en/info/2094/index.html.
48 Liddell and Scott, *Intermediate Greek-English Lexicon*, s.v. "στέφανοι," 745.
49 Department of Arms and Armor, "Islamic Arms and Armor," *Heilbrunn Timeline of Art History*, Metropolitan Museum of Art, October 2004, http://www.metmuseum.org/toah/hd/isaa/hd_isaa.htm.
50 Pliny the Elder, *The Natural History of Pliny*, trans. John Bostock and H. T. Riley, vol. 2 (London: Henry G. Bohn, 1855), 91 (6.32).
51 Elliott, *Horae Apocalypticae* (5th ed.), 1:433 ("The Local Origin of the First Woe").
52 Kinnear, "Distribution of the Lion," 33–39.
53 Elliott, *Horae Apocalypticae* (5th ed.), 1:445 ("The Local Origin of the First Woe").
54 Edward Gibbon, *The History of the Decline and Fall of the Roman Empire*, vol. 5 (New York: AMS Press, 1974), 360.
55 Hugh Kennedy, *The Prophet and the Age of the Caliphates: The Islamic Near East from the Sixth to the Eleventh Century*, 3rd ed. (London: Routledge, 2016), 29–131.
56 Andrew Petersen, "Baghdad (Madinat al-Salam)," *Islamic Arts*, September 13, 2011, accessed November 1, 2023, https://web.archive.org/web/20160916131027/http://islamic-arts.org/2011/baghdad-madinat-al-salam/.
57 *Britannica Online*, s.v. "Fall of Constantinople."
58 B. Spuler, "Ghaznawids," in *The Encyclopaedia of Islam*, new ed., vol. 2, eds. B. Lewis, C. Pellat, and J. Schacht (Leiden: E. J. Brill; London: Luzac, 1991), 1051.
59 René Grousset, *The Empire of the Steppes: A History of Central Asia*, trans. Naomi Walford (New Brunswick, NJ: Rutgers University Press, 2002), 147.
60 C. E. Bosworth, "Iran under the Buyids," in *The Cambridge History of Iran*, vol. 4, *From the Arab Invasion to the Saljuqs*, ed. R. N. Frye (Cambridge: Cambridge University Press, 1975), 250–304; N. M. Lowick, "Seljuq Coins," *Numismatic Chronicle*, 7th ser., 10 (1970): 241–51.
61 Z. M. Buniyatov, *A History of the Khorezmian State under the Anushteginids, 1097–1231* (Samarkand: IICAS, 2015), 43.
62 *Britannica Online*, s.v. "Ottoman Empire."
63 Frederick Henry Ambrose Scrivener, ed., *The New Testament of Our Lord and Saviour Jesus Christ, Being the Authorised Version Set Forth in 1611, Arranged in Parallel Columns with the Revised Version of 1881 and with the Original Greek* (Cambridge: Cambridge University Press, 1882), 1042–43.
64 *The American Heritage Dictionary of the English Language*, 4th ed. (Boston: Houghton Mifflin, 2000), s.v. "toman."
65 Barnes, *Notes, Explanatory and Practical, on the Book of Revelation*, 258–65 (Rev. 9).
66 Scrivener, *The New Testament*, 1042–43.
67 Thayer, *Greek-English Lexicon*, s.v. "ὑακινθίνους," 633.
68 Daubuz, *A Perpetual Commentary*, 329 (Vision 2, pt. 3, trumpet 6, § 1).

69 Gábor Ágoston, "Firearms and Military Adaptation: The Ottomans and the European Military Revolution, 1450–1800," *Journal of World History* 25, no. 1 (2014): 85–124.
70 Brewer, *Dictionary of Phrase and Fable*, s.v. "Pasha of Three Tails."
71 Constantin von Tischendorf, "John's Apocalypse," in *Novum Testamentum Graece* (Leipzig: Bernhardi Tauchnitz, 1873), 417.
72 Liddell and Scott, *Intermediate Greek-English Lexicon*, s.v. "οὐρά," 577–78.
73 Michael Lee Lanning, *The Battle 100: The Stories Behind History's Most Influential Battles* (Naperville, IL: Sourcebooks, Inc., 2005), 139–40.
74 Paul Davis, "Constantinople (1453)," in *100 Decisive Battles* (Oxford: ABC-CLIO, 1999), 166.
75 John Chappel Woodhouse, *The Apocalypse, or, Revelation of Saint John, Translated; with Notes, Critical and Explanatory* (London: J. Brettell, 1805), 263–64.
76 Mary Wellesley, "Gutenberg's Printed Bible is a Landmark in European Culture," *Apollo Magazine*, September 8, 2018, accessed November 4, 2023, https://www.apollo-magazine.com/gutenbergs-printed-bible-landmark-european-culture/.
77 Matt. 7:21–23 (KJV).
78 Joseph S. Exell and H. D. M. Spence-Jones, eds., *The Pulpit Commentary*, vol. 22, *Epistles of Peter, John & Jude. The Revelation* (Peabody, MA: Hendrickson Publishers, 1980), 289–90.
79 Andrew Robert Fausset, "Revelation XI," in *A Commentary, Critical and Explanatory, on the Old and New Testaments*, vol. 1, by Robert Jamieson, Andrew Robert Fausset, and David Brown (New York: S. S. Scranton and Co., 1873), 577.
80 "How Luther Went Viral," *The Economist*, December 17, 2011, accessed November 5, 2023, https://www.economist.com/christmas-specials/2011/12/17/how-luther-went-viral.

Chapter 14: The Interlude
1 Daubuz, *A Perpetual Commentary*, 446–56 (Vision 2, pt. 3, trumpet 7, § 8).
2 Edward Gulbekian, "The Origin and Value of the Stadion Unit Used by Eratosthenes in the Third Century B.C.," *Archive for History of Exact Sciences* 37, no. 4 (December 1987): 359–63.

Chapter 15: God's Wrath Is Poured Out
1 Joshua J. Mark, "Counter-Reformation," *World History Encyclopedia*, last modified May 31, 2022, accessed March 5, 2023, https://www.worldhistory.org/Counter-Reformation/.
2 Barnes, *Notes, Explanatory and Practical, on the Book of Revelation*, 393–418 (Rev. 16).
3 Elliott, *Horae Apocalypticae* (3rd ed.), 3:306–26 ("The First Vial").
4 "Why is France Nicknamed the 'Eldest Daughter' of the Church?," Ensemble en France, accessed March 6, 2023, https://www.ensemble-en-france.org/en/why-is-france-nicknamed-the-eldest-daughter-of-the-church/.
5 Elliott, *Horae Apocalypticae* (5th ed.), 3:322 ("The Second, Third, and Fourth Vials").

6. *Britannica Online*, s.v. "Haitian Revolution."
7. Elliott, *Horae Apocalypticae* (5th ed.), 3:322–27 ("The Second, Third, and Fourth Vials").
8. Stanley Loomis, *Paris in the Terror* (Philadelphia: J.B. Lippincott Co., 1964), 289.
9. Henry Samuel, "Vendée French Call for Revolution Massacre to Be Termed 'Genocide'," *The Telegraph*, December 26, 2008, accessed September 18, 2023, https://www.telegraph.co.uk/news/worldnews/europe/france/3964724/Vende-French-call-for-revolution-massacre-to-be-termed-genocide.html.
10. Amy Tikkanen and Thinley Kalsang Bhutia, "Declaration of Pillnitz," *Encyclopaedia Britannica Online*, last modified August 20, 2023, accessed January 29, 2024, https://www.britannica.com/topic/Declaration-of-Pillnitz.
11. *Britannica Online*, s.v. "Napoleon I."
12. Rev. 9:21, 17:2, 18:3, 18:9, 19:2 (KJV).
13. Robert Fleming, *Apocalyptical Key: An Extraordinary Discourse on the Rise and Fall of Papacy* (Philadelphia: W. S. Young, 1848), 21; Henry Grattan Guinness, "Chapter VI," in *History Unveiling Prophecy* (New York: F.H. Revell, 1905), 343–50.
14. Elliott, *Horae Apocalypticae* (5th ed.), 3:395–410 ("The Fifth Vial").
15. *Britannica Online*, s.v. "Pius VI."

Chapter 16: The Sixth and Seventh Vials

1. Edmond Paris, *The Vatican Against Europe*, trans. A. Robson (London: P. R. Macmillan Limited, 1961), 14.
2. John Loughery, "The Pope Who Thought He Could Negotiate with Hitler," *Washington Post*, July 29, 2022, accessed January 30, 2024, https://www.washingtonpost.com/outlook/2022/07/29/pope-who-thought-he-could-negotiate-with-hitler/.
3. Nicole Winfield, "Letter Suggests Pope Pius XII Knew of Mass Gassings of Jews and Poles in 1942," *AP News*, September 16, 2023, accessed January 30, 2024, https://apnews.com/article/vatican-pius-holocaust-jews-pius-pope-poland-8c511a4b99345d98f54af69dda6d2a66.
4. Michael Phayer, *The Catholic Church and the Holocaust, 1930–1965* (Bloomington: Indiana University Press, 2000), 11.
5. Mark Aarons and John Loftus, "Bishop Hudal and the First Wave," in *Unholy Trinity: The Vatican, The Nazis, and the Swiss Bankers* (New York: St. Martin's Press, 1998), 37.
6. Aarons and Loftus, "Ratline," 88–119.
7. *Britannica Online*, s.v. "Ottoman Empire."
8. Alan Warwick Palmer, *Victory 1918* (New York: Grove Press, 1998), 238.
9. Carpenter, "Revelation," 3:610 (Rev. 16).
10. "Collective Defence and Article 5," North Atlantic Treaty Organization (NATO), last modified July 4, 2023, accessed July 25, 2023, https://www.nato.int/cps/en/natohq/topics_110496.htm.
11. Giuseppe Fonte and Alvise Armellini, "EU Orders Italy to Recover Unpaid Property Taxes by the Catholic Church," *Reuters*, March 3, 2023, accessed February 2, 2024, https://www.reuters.com/world/europe/eu-orders-italy-recover-unpaid-property-taxes-by-catholic-church-2023-03-03/.

12 "Archbishop Carlo Maria Viganò Gives First Extended Interview Since Calling on the Pope to Resign," *Washington Post*, June 10, 2019, accessed February 2, 2024, https://www.washingtonpost.com/world/europe/archbishop-carlo-maria-vigano-gives-his-first-extended-interview-since-calling-on-the-pope-to-resign/2019/06/10/00205748-8b79-11e9-b08e-cfd89bd36d4e_story.html.

13 Stephanie Kirchgaessner, "Vatican Supports Chilean Bishop Despite Allegations of Sex Abuse Cover-Up," *The Guardian*, March 31, 2015, accessed February 2, 2024, https://www.theguardian.com/world/2015/mar/31/vatican-juan-barros-chile-bishop-appointment-sex-abuse.

14 Luis Andres Henao and Nicole Winfield, "Pope Role in Study of Argentine Sex Abuse Case in Spotlight," *AP News*, September 18, 2018, accessed February 2, 2024, https://apnews.com/general-news-85cff83cc9e2448d802e15d80bae7765.

15 Tyler Arnold, "Pope Francis: Small Ideological Groups Oppose Same-Sex Blessings; Africa a 'Special Case'," *Catholic News Agency*, January 29, 2024, accessed February 2, 2024, https://www.catholicnewsagency.com/news/256671/pope-francis-small-ideological-groups-oppose-same-sex-blessings-africa-a-special-case.

16 Jonathan Luxmoore, "Episcopate Gives Rome a Rough Ride Over Fiducia Supplicans Declaration," *Church Times*, January 5, 2024, accessed February 2, 2024, https://www.churchtimes.co.uk/articles/2024/5-january/news/world/episcopate-gives-rome-a-rough-ride-over-fiducia-supplicans-declaration.

17 Kate Quiñones, "Cardinal Sarah Speaks Out Against Clergy Blessing Same-Sex Unions," *Catholic News Agency*, January 8, 2024, accessed February 2, 2024, https://www.ewtnnews.com/world/africa/cardinal-sarah-speaks-out-against-clergy-blessing-same-sex-unions?redirectedfrom=cna.

18 Michael Haynes, "Male Drag 'Artist' Dances for Kids at Vatican's World Children's Day," *LifeSiteNews*, May 27, 2024, accessed May 28, 2024, https://www.lifesitenews.com/news/male-drag-artist-dances-for-kids-at-vaticans-world-childrens-day/.

19 Danielle Abraham et al., "How Israel Became a World Leader in Agriculture and Water," Tony Blair Institute for Global Change, September 2, 2019, accessed August 9, 2024, https://institute.global/insights/economic-prosperity/how-israel-became-world-leader-agriculture-and-water.

20 Mark Lynas, "What the Science Says: Could Humans Survive a Nuclear War Between NATO and Russia?," *Alliance for Science*, March 10, 2022, accessed August 9, 2024, https://allianceforscience.org/blog/2022/03/what-the-science-says-could-humans-survive-a-nuclear-war-between-nato-and-russia/.

Chapter 17: The Second Coming
1 Zech. 13:8–14:21 (KJV).
2 Eze. 40:1–48:35 (KJV).

Chapter 18: The End
1 Joseph J. Atick et al., *Digital Identity Toolkit: A Guide for Stakeholders in Africa*, Working Paper (Washington, DC: World Bank Group, 2014), 12.

2. "Digital ID for Everyday Life," Australian Government, last modified February 1, 2024, accessed February 17, 2024, https://www.digitalidentity.gov.au/digital-identity-for-you/digital-id-for-everyday-life-0.
3. "Digital Identity for All Europeans," European Commission, last modified February 15, 2024, accessed February 17, 2024, https://commission.europa.eu/strategy-and-policy/priorities-2019-2024/europe-fit-digital-age/european-digital-identity_en.
4. Joanna England, "EU Consortium to Deliver Controversial Digital ID Wallets," *Fintech Magazine*, December 20, 2022, accessed February 17, 2024, https://fintechmagazine.com/digital-payments/eu-consortium-to-deliver-controversial-digital-id-wallets.
5. Board of Governors of the Federal Reserve System, *Money and Payments: The U.S. Dollar in the Age of Digital Transformation* (Washington, DC: Federal Reserve, 2022), https://www.federalreserve.gov/publications/files/money-and-payments-20220120.pdf.
6. Exec. Order No. 14067, 3 C.F.R. 14143 (2022).
7. Ahmed Eljechtimi, "IMF Working on Global Central Bank Digital Currency Platform," *Reuters*, June 19, 2023, accessed February 15, 2024, https://www.reuters.com/markets/imf-working-global-central-bank-digital-currency-platform-2023-06-19/.
8. Bank for International Settlements (BIS), "Blueprint for the Future Monetary System: Improving the Old, Enabling the New," in *Annual Economic Report 2023* (Basel: BIS, 2023), 85–105, https://www.bis.org/publ/arpdf/ar2023e3.htm.
9. Jeff Wilser, "An Orb, a Token and Money for Everyone: Worldcoin's CEO on Crypto's Most Daring Project," *CoinDesk*, July 10, 2023, accessed February 17, 2024, https://www.coindesk.com/consensus-magazine/2023/07/10/an-orb-a-token-and-money-for-everyone-worldcoins-ceo-on-cryptos-most-daring-project/.
10. Tim Newcombe, "Humans Might Not Survive the Fourth Industrial Revolution, Global Leader Says," *Popular Mechanics*, February 17, 2023, accessed February 15, 2024, https://www.popularmechanics.com/technology/a42955750/fourth-industrial-revolution-technologies/.
11. "Leave No One Behind," United Nations Sustainable Development Group, last modified February 8, 2024, accessed February 17, 2024, https://unsdg.un.org/2030-agenda/universal-values/leave-no-one-behind.
12. Aya Elamroussi, Holly Yan, and Amir Vera, "Canadian Authorities Freeze Financial Assets for Those Involved in Ongoing Protests in Ottawa," *CNN*, February 20, 2022, accessed February 17, 2024, https://www.cnn.com/2022/02/20/americas/canada-trucker-protest-covid-sunday/index.html.
13. Paul Vieira, "Canada Instructs Banks to Unfreeze Freedom-Convoy Accounts," *Wall Street Journal*, February 22, 2022, accessed February 17, 2024, https://www.wsj.com/articles/canada-instructs-banks-to-unfreeze-freedom-convoy-accounts-11645590500.

www.ingramcontent.com/pod-product-compliance
Lightning Source LLC
LaVergne TN
LVHW032156260326
834689LV00075B/187/J